Lecture Notes in Computer Science 6886

Commenced Publication in 1973
Founding and Former Series Editors:
Gerhard Goos, Juris Hartmanis, and Jan van Leeuwen

Claudio Sacchi   Boris Bellalta
Alexey Vinel   Christian Schlegel
Fabrizio Granelli   Yan Zhang (Eds.)

Multiple Access Communications

4th International Workshop, MACOM 2011
Trento, Italy, September 12-13, 2011
Proceedings

 Springer

Volume Editors

Claudio Sacchi
Fabrizio Granelli
University of Trento, 38050 Povo, Italy
E-mail: {sacchi, granelli}@disi.unitn.it

Boris Bellalta
Universitat Pompeu Fabra, 08018 Barcelona, Spain
E-mail: boris.bellalta@upf.edu

Alexey Vinel
Tampere University of Technology, 33101 Tampere, Finland
E-mail: alexey.vinel@tut.fi

Christian Schlegel
University of Alberta, Edmonton, AB, T6G 2V4, Canada
E-mail: schlegel@cs.ualberta.ca

Yan Zhang
Simula Research Laboratory, 1325 Lysaker, Norway
E-mail: yanzhang@simula.no

ISSN 0302-9743   e-ISSN 1611-3349
ISBN 978-3-642-23794-2   ISBN 978-3-642-23795-9 (eBook)
DOI 10.1007/978-3-642-23795-9
Springer Heidelberg Dordrecht London New York

Library of Congress Control Number: 2011935348

CR Subject Classification (1998): C.2, H.4, K.6.5, D.4.6, C.2.4, H.3, D.2

LNCS Sublibrary: SL 5 – Computer Communication Networks and Telecommunications

Typesetting: Camera-ready by author, data conversion by Scientific Publishing Services, Chennai, India

Printed on acid-free paper

Springer is part of Springer Science+Business Media (www.springer.com)

Preface

It is our great pleasure to present the proceedings of the 4th International Workshop on Multiple Access Communications (MACOM) that was held in Trento during September 12–13, 2011.

In 1961, Claude Shannon established the foundation for the discipline now known as "multi-user information theory" in his pioneering paper "Two-way Communication Channels", and later Norman Abramson published his paper "The Aloha System - Another Alternative for Computer Communications" in 1970, which introduced the concept of multiple access using a shared common channel.

During the ensuing 40 years of intensive study, numerous elegant theories and algorithms have been developed for multiple access communications. During the 1980s and 1990s the evolution of multiple-access techniques proceeded alongside the evolution of wireless networks. Novel multiple-access techniques like code-division multiple-access (CDMA) and orthogonal frequency-division multiple-access (OFDMA) provided increased spectral efficiency and flexibility in radio resource allocation as well as intrinsic anti-multipath and anti-interference properties. In this first decade of the twenty-first century, multiple-access techniques, derived from advanced wireless transmission methodologies and based on diversity concept, such as MC-CDMA, MIMO-OFDMA and SC-FDMA, have opened the doors to a resurgence of multiple-access. Modern multiple-access communications involve a host of challenges, not limited to physical layer design as in the past. Medium-access control (MAC) techniques play a crucial role in managing the radio resources. Recent developments in software and cognitive radios have led to notable advances in spectrum management. Old paradigms of multiple-access management based on "locked" and "exclusive" reservation policies of spectrum resources are being challenged by cognitive radios that allow activity sensing of the spectrum and to opportunistically occupy free parts of the spectrum.

Technical contributions to all these topics were presented and discussed at MACOM 2011 and are included in this volume. We received more than 40 submissions for the conference. After a thorough review process, 21 high-quality papers were accepted for presentation at the workshop. Submissions received at least three reviews from the members of the Technical Program Committee and/or external reviewers. Our gratitude goes to the members of the Technical Program Committee and external reviewers for their efforts. MACOM 2011 included five distinguished invited keynote speakers: Reuven Cohen, Christian Schlegel, Mike Devetsikiotis, Enrico Buracchini, and Andrea Buldorini.

Finally, we would like to take this opportunity to express our gratitude to our sponsors and supporters, together with the local organizers, who helped to make MACOM 2011 a very successful event. A special thank you is given to Dajana

Cassioli, of Radiolabs (Italy), head of the IEEE Italian Chapter VT06/COM19 for her support in obtaining local IEEE support, to Susanna Spinsante of the University of Ancona (Italy), Industrial Chair of MACOM 2011, to Christian Facchini of the University of Trento (Italy), MACOM 2011 Web and Publicity Chair, to Cristina Cano of the University Pompeu Fabra of Barcelona (Spain), MACOM 2011 Publication Chair and, last but not the least, to Martina Lorenzi of the Conference Office of the University of Trento for her support in the local organization.

September 2011   C. Sacchi
                                                            B. Bellalta
                                                             A. Vinel
                                                           C. Schlegel
                                                            F. Granelli
                                                             Y. Zhang

Organization

MACOM 2011 was organized by the DISI (Department of Information, Engineering and Computer Science) from the University of Trento, Italy, the NeTS/DTIC (Networking Technologies and Strategies Research Group—Department of Information and Communication Technologies) from UPF (Universitat Pompeu Fabra), Spain, and the TUT (Tampere University of Technology), Finland.

Executive Committee

General Chair

Claudio Sacchi   University of Trento, Italy

General Co-chairs

Boris Bellalta   Universitat Pompeu Fabra, Spain
Alexey Vinel   SPIIRAS, Russia

TPC Chairs

Christian Schlegel   University of Alberta, Canada
Fabrizio Granelli   University of Trento, Italy
Yan Zhang   Simula Research Lab, Norway

Publication Chair

Cristina Cano   Universitat Pompeu Fabra, Spain

Web and Publicity Chair

Christian Facchini   University of Trento, Italy

Ind. and Tech. Transfer Chair

Susanna Spinsante   Università Politecnica delle Marche, Italy

Steering Committee

Khalid Al-Begain   University of Glamorgan, Pontypridd, UK
Ernst Gabidulin   MIPT, Russia
Vitaly Gutin   ETU "LETI", Russia
Angel Lozano   Universitat Pompeu Fabra, Spain
Felix Taubin   SUAI, Russia

Victor Zyablov   IITP RAS, Russia
Vladmir Vishnevsky   IRE RAS, Russia
Bernhard Walke   RWTH Aachen University, Germany

Technical Program Committee

Sergey Andreev   Tampere University of Technology, Finland
Konstantin Avrachenkov   INRIA Sophia Antipolis, France
Florin Avram   Universite de Pau, France
Abdelmalik Bachir   Imperial College London, UK
Jaume Barcelo   Universidad Carlos III de Madrid, Spain
Boris Bellalta   Universitat Pompeu Fabra, Spain
Giuseppe Bianchi   University of Rome - Tor Vergata, Italy
Torsten Braun   University of Bern, Switzerland
Raffaele Bruno   IIT-CNR, Italy
Peter Buchholz   TU Dortmund, Germany
Cristina Cano   Universitat Pompeu Fabra, Spain
Andrea Cattoni   Aalborg University, Denmark
Eduardo Cerqueira   Federal University of Para, UFPA, Brazil
Matteo Cesana   Politecnico di Milano, Italy
Periklis Chatzimisios   Alexander TEI of Thessaloniki, Greece
Young-June Choi   Ajou University, Korea
Claudio Cicconetti   Intecs S.p.A., Italy
Roberto Corvaja   University of Padova, Italy
Tugrul Dayar   Bilkent University, Turkey
Alexandre de Baynast   European Microsoft Innovation Center,
                                    Germany
Javier Del Ser   Tecnalia Research and Innovation, Spain
Alexander Dudin   Belarusian State University, Belarus
Alexey Dudkov   NRPL Group, Finland
Azadeh Faridi   Universitat Pompeu Fabra, Spain
Lorenzo Favalli   University of Pavia, Italy
Stanislav Filin   NICT, Japan
Istvan Frigyes   Budapest University of Technologies, Hungary
Olga Galinina   Tampere University of Technology, Finland
Fabrizio Granelli   University of Trento, Italy
Gaoning He   Telecom ParisTech, France
Geert Heijenk   University of Twente, The Netherlands
Andras Horvath   University of Turin, Italy
Gang Uk Hwang   KAIST, Korea
Hazer Inaltekin   The University of Melbourne, Australia
Eduard Jorswieck   Dresden University of Technology, Germany
Markku Juntti   University of Oulu, Finland
Valentina Klimenok   Belarusian State University, Belarus
Vinay Kolar   Carnegie Mellon University, USA
Yevgeni Koucheryavy   Tampere University of Technology, Finland

David Malone	NUI Maynooth, Ireland
Michela Meo	Politecnico di Torino, Italy
Enzo Mingozzi	University of Pisa, Italy
Dmitri Moltchanov	Tampere University of Technology, Finland
Miquel Oliver	Universitat Pompeu Fabra, Spain
Dmitry Osipov	IITP RAS, Russia
Aleksi Penttinen	TKK Helsinki University of Technology, Finland
Vicent Pla	Universitat Politecnica de Valencia, Spain
Claudio Sacchi	University of Trento, Italy
Zsolt Saffer	Budapest University of Technology and Economics, Hungary
Alexander Safonov	Institute for Information Transmission Problems, Russian Academy of Science, Russia
Bruno Sericola	INRIA Rennes - Bretagne Atlantique, France
Pablo Serrano	Universidad Carlos III de Madrid, Spain
Susanna Spinsante	Università Politecnica delle Marche, Italy
Dirk Staehle	University of Würzburg, Germany
Andrea Tonello	University of Udine, Italy
Rob van der Mei	Centrum voor Wiskunde en Informatica, The Netherlands
Maria-Angeles Vazquez-Castro	Universidad Autonoma de Barcelona, Spain
Alexey Vinel	Saint Petersburg Institute for Informatics and Automation, Russia
Hongyi Wu	University of Louisiana at Lafayette, USA
Yunpeng Zang	RWTH Aachen, Germany
Brad Zarikoff	Simon Fraser University, Canada
Yan Zhang	Simula Research Laboratory and University of Oslo, Norway

Referees

Sergey Andreev	Marc Emmelmann	Dmitri Moltchanov
Abdelmalik Bachir	Christian Facchini	Dmitry Osipov
Jaume Barcelo	Lorenzo Favalli	Claudio Sacchi
Boris Bellalta	Istvan Frigyes	Christian Schlegel
Evgeny Belyaev	Olga Galinina	Susanna Spinsante
Giuseppe Bianchi	Majid Ghanbarinejad	Dirk Staehle
Raffaele Bruno	Fabrizio Granelli	Andrea Tonello
Cristina Cano	Marcel Jar	Alexey Vinel
Andrea Cattoni	Alexander Klein	Hongyi Wu
Periklis Chatzimisios	Yevgeni Koucheryavy	Yan Zhang
Claudio Cicconetti	Witold Krzymie	Olga Zlydareva
Roberto Corvaja	Ruizhi Liao	
Javier Del Ser	Michela Meo	

Sponsors

- IEEE ComSoc Technical Committee on Communications Systems Integration and Modeling (CSIM)
- IEEE Italy Chapter VT06/COM 19
- AEIT - Fed. Italiana di Elettrotecnica, Elettronica, Automazione, Inform. e Telecom
- Telecom Italia

Acknowledgements

- Wireless Networking for Moving Objects (WINEMO). IC0906 COST action
- Spanish Ministry of Science and Innovation (TEC2008-06055/TEC)
- Foundations and Methodologies for Future Communication and Sensor Networks (COMONSENS). CONSOLIDER-INGENIO 2010
- Research Council of Norway (project number 202524).

Table of Contents

Special Session on MAC Protocols for WSNs

System Analysis and Scheduling

Queuing Systems

A MAC Protocol for Cognitive Radio Wireless Ad Hoc Networks

Carla Passiatore and Pietro Camarda

Politecnico di Bari – Via Orabona, 4, 70125 Bari, Italy
{c.passiatore,p.camarda}@poliba.it

Abstract. Cognitive Radio (CR) technology allows an opportunistic use of the licensed spectrum by the CR users, avoiding harmful interference to primary users (PUs). The CR users must detect the spectrum holes left by PUs by performing sensing. CR Networks require MAC protocols with particular features compared to the classical MAC. We propose a MAC protocol for cognitive radio wireless ad-hoc networks, which has the advantages to be distributed, collision-free and of guaranteeing a fair channel assignment, also taking into account the requests of quality of service (QoS) of CR nodes. We proved, through statistical computations, that the protocol guarantees very high efficiency and channel utilization, assuring good global performance.

Keywords: Cognitive Radio, Ad-hoc Network.

1   Introduction

Cognitive Radio (CR) is a promising technology geared to solve the spectrum scarcity problem by opportunistically exploiting for transmission the vacant portions of the spectrum, ensuring that the licensed or primary users (PUs) of the spectrum are not affected [2], [6], [4]. In such a context it is necessary to learn about the spectrum occupancy by performing sensing operations in such a way to adapt to the dynamically changing of spectrum resources. CR networks make efficient use of bands such as television broadcast frequencies below 700 MHz, that have been recently marked for CR operation [10].

CR MAC protocols differ from classic protocols as they are adaptive to PU activity. They provide efficient channel sensing for determining its occupancy by PUs, and to share the available spectrum among CR users, called also secondary users (SU). The interference to PUs must be always kept to tolerable levels as PUs have a priority usage.

In literature, several CR MAC protocols have been proposed, which can be classified based on the structure and the channel access, [5]. In particular, based on the structure, they can be classified in centralized and distributed. Centralized MAC protocols need a central entity, such as a base station, that manages network activities, synchronizes and coordinates operations among nodes. The main defect is that the central entity is usually static.

C. Sacchi et al. (Eds.): MACOM 2011, LNCS 6886, pp. 1–12, 2011.

Distributed protocols do not have a central entity for the operation of the network but everything is based on a strong cooperation among CR nodes. The architecture is scalable, moreover it has flexible deployment and spectrum sensing is distributed. Factors which must be taken into account for the protocol design are the maintaining of time synchronization throughout the network and obtaining the information from surrounding nodes with minimum overhead.

In the following some of the promising MAC protocols for Cognitive Radio wireless ad hoc networks are briefly summarized. The DOSS MAC [8] is a random access protocol which exploits three radios assigned distinctly to the control, data and busy tone band, respectively. Whenever a node transmits or receives data on a given channel, it also emits a busy signal in the corresponding busy tone band. The limits of this protocol are the following. Two separate bands are necessary: one to manage busy tones and the other for data exchange on the common control channel (CCC). This is cause of a non efficient spectrum utilization. Additionally multiple transceivers are needed but two of them are not used for data communication.

The distributed channel assignment (DCA) MAC, [12], protocol is a simple extension of the IEEE 802.11 CSMA/CA protocol, [11]. It uses multiple transceivers, with a dedicated out-of-band CCC for signaling. The main drawback is the necessity of two transceivers for each user. Moreover, the protocol does not have as target to guarantee the quality of service (QoS) of the users.

In this paper, we propose a novel MAC protocol for cognitive radio wireless ad hoc networks. It is completely distributed and assures a fair channel assignment to CR users avoiding harmful interference to primary users, thanks to a periodic sensing action. Furthermore the resource distribution also takes into account the QoS requests by CR users by trying to approach the users needs.

The proposed protocol is slotted and collision free as an access window is provided in each slot, where the nodes exploit reserved minislots in order to try one at time to access the available channel.

We found, by implementing statistical calculations, that the protocol guarantees high efficiency and a good channel utilization.

The rest of the paper is organized as follows. In Sec. 2, our MAC protocol for Cognitive Radio Ad Hoc Networks is proposed. In Sec. 3 the mathematical model to evaluate the protocol is presented. In Sec. 4, the performance of the protocol are evaluated trough statistical computations. Finally, Sec. 5 draws the conclusions.

2   MAC Protocol for Cognitive Radio Ad Hoc Networks

In this section, the system architecture for the proposed multichannel MAC protocol will be described, in the context of a single hop wireless ad hoc network with N nodes and ch available channels. The proposed protocol has a periodic structure. We assume that the time axis is divided into cyclic periods consisting of sensing period, control time and time slots for transmission, as illustrated in Fig. 1. We assume that all nodes are synchronized; the synchronization can be obtained using a common control channel (CCC), ([3], [9]). During the sensing

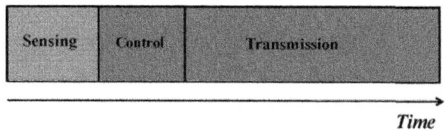

Fig. 1. Sequent of the activity periods in the network

period the nodes detect the channels which are not used by PUs and are available for cognitive transmission. After that, the control period starts where all the nodes are tuned to the common control channel. During this period, the nodes exchange information about the channels detected free during the sensing period. Furthermore, the control period is used to exchange announcements about nodes leaving or joining the network, so that each node can update accordingly its identifier (ID). IDs are used to plan the node access order to the network.

Each node is associated to a I_{QoS}. We quantified the QoS requirements with the help of a index proportional to the required bandwidth and in inverse proportion with the tolerated delay, as in [7]. The node, at the beginning of each period, computes and communicates the other users, its personal index, defined as follows:

$$I_{QoS} = \frac{B}{d},\tag{1}$$

where B is the minimum required bandwidth and d is the maximum tolerated delay. The secondary users are sorted in decreasing order, from the highest I_{QoS} to the smallest index. Then the $ID = 1$, namely $node\_1$, is given to the user which has the highest I_{QoS}. The proposed MAC protocol gives to the nodes with higher I_{QoS} the possibility to tempt the access first, in such a way to increase their probability to conquer the access to the channel.

In the following we explain the mechanism used for channel access. The transmission period is composed by multiple time slots. As illustrated in Fig. 2, the generic time slot is divided into two parts: the *Access Window* (AW), used for channel reservation, and the *Data Exchange window* (DEW), used for data exchange. All the nodes know which are the available channels, because these information is exchanged on the CCC. The available channels are sorted according to a common principle, as an example the channels are listed in decreasing order of band amplitude. At the beginning of the transmission period all the nodes are tuned on the same channel, namely $channel\_1$. When a node gains

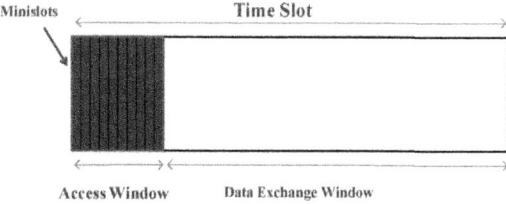

Fig. 2. Structure of a time slot

the access to the channel, it can begin the transmission, while the other nodes tune their interfaces on the second channel. The access mechanism goes on like this, until the duration of the access window is ended or the network channels are all busy. It is important to notice that the fist nodes which gain the medium access may occupy the channel with the greatest band. Consequently, the nodes with higher I_{QoS} may transmit more data with lower delay. Moreover they have the possibility to transmit more data because they accede to the channels with larger band and surely they have an access window shorter.

Specifically, the access window is divided in minislots, the maximum number of minislots is constrained by the length of the time slot and the access window. In a given time slot, nodes tune their interfaces on a channel, attempting the access, at the end of the AW over the previous channel, as shown in Fig. 3. During the first minislot $node\_1$ sends a request to send (RTS) packet to its intended receiver, which, being tuned on the same channel, replies with a clear to send (CTS) packet and the data exchange window starts. It is worth noticing that, in this specific case, $node\_1$ will certainly find the intended receiver tuned on the same channel. All the other nodes hear the CTS packet, which is the signaling that the channel is utilized for the communication, then they switch their radio interface to the $channel\_2$. The $node\_2$ tries the access sending, during the second minislot, an RTS packet to its intended receiver, if it is busy there will be no CTS. So in the next minislot, the $node\_3$ tries the access and so on until a node finds its intended receiver. The same procedure is performed on the following channels. The access mechanism is illustrated in Fig. 3. In Fig. 3 the AW on the first channel lasts a minislot. The total AW on the second channel is the union of the $AW1$ and the $AW2$, it consists of a total of three minislots; and so on for the following channels.

Let T_{ms} be the duration of a minislot and T_s of a time slot. To consider the worst case, the duration of the entire time slot T_s, can be expressed as the maximum duration of the access window plus the minimum duration of the data exchange window, namely Δ. Supposing that the maximum duration of the access window is equal to $h \cdot T_{ms}$, we have:

$$T_s = h \cdot T_{ms} + \Delta. \tag{2}$$

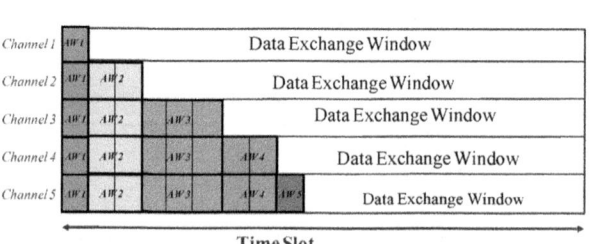

Fig. 3. Example of the access mechanism

Where in eq.(2) Δ is the time required to transmit an MSDU (MAC Service Data Unit). While T_{ms} is the time necessary for a RTS/CTS exchange. Note that, computed T_{ms} and Δ according to the network data rate and T_s, h is fixed. Moreover in the proposed approach the number of usable channels, namely ch, is related with h. In fact, even in the best case, where each node, which is attempting the channel access, finds its intended receiver, each AWi lasts a minislot, i.e. the total AW of the $channel\_j$ is long j minislots. If the maximum duration of the AW is composed by h minislots, the last channel on which it is possible the CTS/RTS exchange is the $channel\_h$. Other channels cannot be used because the maximum allowed AW duration is finished. This means that ch cannot be greatest than h, otherwise *(ch-h)* channels will be certainly unused.

3   Analytical Model

In this Section we present the mathematical model exploited for evaluating the performances of the proposed scheme.

To evaluate the performance of the medium access mechanism we realized a simulation tool, which computes the mean number of used channels, the time actually employed for the transmission and the efficiency of the network.

We use the theory of discrete time Markov chain to derive the needed performance indices. In the utilized Markov chain the state is defined by two variables (i, j); where i is the number of the channels already employed, and j is the number of exploited minislots. If the network is in the state (i, j) this means that, after the j-minislots the first i channels are busy, and that a user can attempt the access on the $channel\_(i+1)$. We studied the one step transition probability where the minislot is represented by the step. Starting from the generic state (i, j) at the end of a minislot, only two possibilities may occur: to transit in the state *(i,j+1)* if no transmission is happened, or in the opposite case to transit in the state *(i+1,j+1)*.

In Fig. 4 the state transition diagram of the Markov chain is shown, in the case where there are ch available channels, and an access window up to h minislots. The starting point is the state $(0, 0)$, where no channels and minislots have been engaged. The probability being in state *(i,j)*, to transit in the state *(i+1,j+1)* in one step, i.e. in a minislot, is called β_i, while the probability to transit in state *(i,j+1)* is called α_i. The two events are mutually exclusive, and:

$$\beta_i + \alpha_i = 1. \tag{3}$$

The probability α_i is the probability that the transmission does not happen in the minislot because the nodes which attempts the access does not find its intended receiver, so in the following minislot another node will try to transmit in the same channel. The probability that a node does not find the intended receiver, namely α_i, can be computed as the ratio between the number of busy nodes and the total number of nodes minus the one which is attempting the access. The probability α_i is the probability that a node, attempting the access,

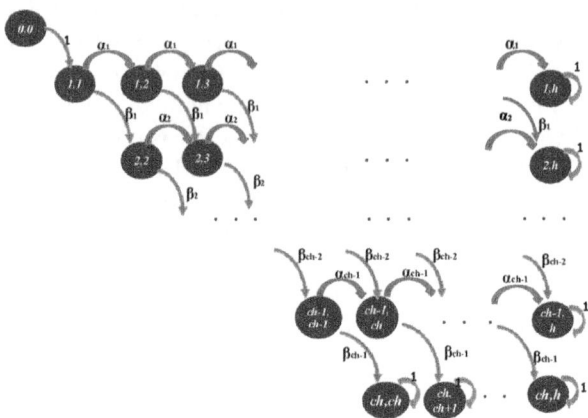

Fig. 4. State transition diagram with ch available channels, and an access windows of h minislots

choses a destination which is already reserved in another communication. It is equal to:

$$\alpha_i = \left(\frac{2 \cdot i}{N - 1} \right). \tag{4}$$

Instead, β_i, is computed with eq.(3).

Table 1 is the transition probability matrix associated to the Markov chain of Fig. 4, with $ch = 3$ and $h = 5$; the matrix is named Γ. For reasons of space and clarity in the table some states have been omitted . The (k, l) element of Γ, namely $\Gamma(k, l)$, is the probability to transit in one step from the state defined by the row k to the state of the column l. Note that the sum of the elements of a row is equal to 1. It is important to note that β_0, the probability to transit from the state$(0, 0)$ to the state $(1, 1)$, is 1: the first node which accesses to the medium surely finds the intended receiver, because in the proposed MAC protocol during the first minislot all nodes are tuned on the $channel\_1$. According to the eq.(3) α_0 is equal to 0. Moreover, in the rows associated to the states $(3, 3)$, $(3, 4)$, and $(3, 5)$ there is only an element not equal to 0. Generalizing in the rows related to the states (ch, x), with $ch \leq x \leq h$, only the element $\Gamma((ch, x), (ch, x))$ is equal to 1, all the other probabilities are null. If the network is in the state (ch, x), to keep busy another channel is not possible, as well as to transit in another state. Then the state (ch, x) is absorbent, if the network will be in this state it remain in the same state with probability 1. In Table 1 also the state $(1, 5)$, and $(2, 5)$ are absorbent because if the network in the last minislot has employed only one or two channels, the users will not have the opportunity to attempt again the access, because the access windows is ended. In general, the states (x, h), with $1 \leq x \leq ch$, are absorbent state.

According to Markov chain properties the transition matrix after h steps is equal to Γ^h. Since the access window minislots are h (see the eq.2), the matrix Γ^h contains the probabilities of channel using at the and of the time slot. In

Table 1. Transition matrix of the Markov chain.

	$0,0$	..	$1,1$	$1,2$	$1,3$	$1,4$	$1,5$	..	$2,2$	$2,3$	..	$3,3$	$3,4$	$3,5$
$0,0$	0	..	1	0	0	0	0	..	0	0	..	0	0	0
..	0	0	0	0	0	0	0	0	0	0	0	0	0	0
$1,1$	0	..	0	α_1	0	0	0	..	β_1	0	..	0	0	0
$1,2$	0	..	0	0	α_1	0	0	..	0	β_1	..	0	0	0
$1,3$	0	..	0	0	0	α_1	0	..	0	0	..	0	0	0
$1,4$	0	..	0	0	0	0	α_1	..	0	0	..	0	0	0
$1,5$	0	..	0	0	0	0	1	..	0	0	..	0	0	0
..	0	0	0	0	0	0	0	0	0	0	0	0	0	0
$2,2$	0	..	0	0	0	0	0	..	0	α_2	..	β_2	0	0
$2,3$	0	..	0	0	0	0	0	..	0	0	..	0	β_2	0
..	0	0	0	0	0	0	0	0	0	0	0	0	0	0
$3,3$	0	..	0	0	0	0	0	..	0	0	..	1	0	0
$3,4$	0	..	0	0	0	0	0	..	0	0	..	0	1	0
$3,5$	0	..	0	0	0	0	0	..	0	0	..	0	0	1

particular the sum of first $h+1$ elements of first row of the Γ^h is the probability that zero channels are busy at the end of the access window; the sum of the following $h+1$ elements is the probability that one channel is used, and so on. This probability, named $p_{ch}(i)$, is equal to:

$$p_{ch}(i) = \sum_{k=E}^{E+h} \Gamma^h(1,k),\qquad(5)$$

where in eq.(5) $E = (i \cdot (h+1)) + 1$.

The average number of utilized channels in the network, namely $\Omega(ch)$, can be calculated with the following equation:

$$\Omega(ch) = \sum_{i=0}^{ch} i \cdot p_{ch}(i).\qquad(6)$$

According to the eq.(6), $\Omega(ch)$ is the weighted average of the number of exploited channels, where the weights are the $p_{ch}(i)$, i.e. the probabilities that i channels are active.

4 Performance Evaluation

In this Section some indices to evaluate the performance of the proposed MAC protocol have been considered. In particular, the mean number of used channels and minislots in the network, the efficiency and throughput of the protocol have been derived.

In the simulations we suppose a network with secondary users which can attempt the access to the available channels. The duration of a time slot, T_s, is fixed to $1ms$. To compute the number of minislots which compose the access window we have to refer to the eq.(2). In particular assuming a data rate of 54

Mbps and a MSDU of 2304 bytes (i.e., the maximum length allowed in the IEEE 802.11 standard): the time to transmit a MSDU is equal to 342μs. Consequently, in the eq.(2) Δ assumes the value of the 342μs. While T_{ms} is equal to 21 μs, which are sufficient to allow one RTS/CTS exchange considering a short interframe space of 10 μs [1]. According to the eq.(2), h, the maximum number of allowed minislots, is 30. We referred to a data rate of 54 *Mbps*, but increasing the network data rate, h also grows. We computed the parameters supposing N, the number of nodes, increasing in the range [10:100], with steps of 10 units. Furthermore the number of available channels, ch, was changed in the range [3:12], with steps of 3 units. The parameters for the simulation are exposed in Table 2, with the related abbreviation.

Table 2. Simulation Parameters

Time slot	T_s	1ms
Minislot	T_{ms}	21μs
Access window	h	30 minislots
Number of nodes	N	[10:100]
Number of available channels	ch	[3:12]
Data Rate	DR	54 *Mbps*

Exploiting equations 5 and 6, the mean number of utilized channels is computed to test the performances of the introduced MAC protocol.

The results are shown in Fig. 5.

As shown in Fig. 5, when there are few nodes in the network, i.e. $N < 2 \cdot ch$, some channels are unused because they are more than is necessary. Instead the mean number of utilized channels approaches the number of available channels when the number of nodes N increases.

In the following we evaluate the efficiency, namely η_{ch}, defined as the ratio between the average value of the transmission time of useful data and the total duration of a time slot for each available channel. η_{ch} can be derived as follow:

$$\eta_{ch} = \frac{T_{us}}{T_s \cdot ch}, \tag{7}$$

where in eq.(7) T_{us} is the useful transmission time.

Aiming to compute T_{us} we have to evaluate the average number of minislots totally used in the network, namely ν. It is equal to sum of the minislots engaged on each channel of the network:

$$\nu = \sum_{k=1}^{ch} \o(k). \tag{8}$$

Where $\o(k)$ is the mean number of minislots engaged on the *channel_k*, that is:

$$\o(k) = \sum_{i=k}^{h} i \cdot \Gamma^{(i-1)}(1, A) \cdot \Gamma(A, A + H + 1). \tag{9}$$

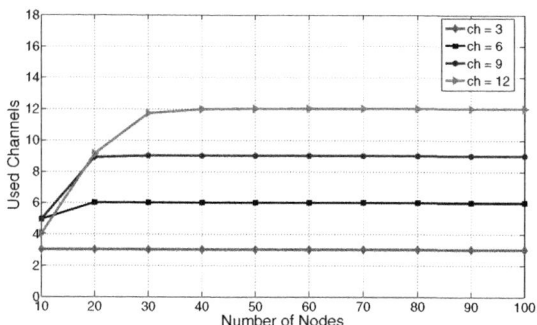

Fig. 5. Mean number of utilized channels

Where in eq.(9) $H=h+1$ and $A=H\cdot(k\text{-}1)+i$. Note that, computing $\o(1)$ according to the eq.(9), when $i=1$ and $k=1$, Γ^0 is a diagonal matrix, with the non null elements all equal to 1. Then, the contribution to the sum of $i=1$ is 1, while for $i \geq 2$ the result of $\Gamma^{(i-1)} \cdot \Gamma$ is always null. In consequence the mean number of minislots exploited on the $chennel\_1$ is equal to 1. This is an expected result, because on the first channel the DEW begins after a minislot, as explained in the last session.

$\o(k)$ is the weighted average of the minislots used on the $channel\_k$. The probability to exploit i minislots on the $channel\_k$ is composed by two parts: the probability to stay in the state $(k\text{-}1,i\text{-}1)$ and the probability to transit in the next minislot in the state (k,i). In eq.(9), the first part is expressed as: $\Gamma^{(i-1)}(1,A)$, which, according to the elemets of the transition matrix, is the probability to transit from the state $(0,0)$ to the state $(k,i\text{-}1)$ in $i-1$ minislots, i.e. the probability that at the $i-1$ minislot the users have occupied $k-1$ channels. In eq.(9) this probability is conditioned to the probabibility to transit from the the state $(k, i-1)$ to the state(k,i) in a step, it is expressed as $\Gamma(A, A+H+1)$.

By the eq.(8) is possible to compute the average number of minislots engaged on each used channel, namely $mean_{ms}$, as:

$$mean_{ms} = \frac{\nu}{\Omega(ch)}. \tag{10}$$

The values obtained by eq.(10) are the mean delay, expressed as number of minislots, to attend on each channel before to start the communication. The results are shown in Fig. 6.

The Fig. 6 shows as the waiting time grows with the increasing of the number of available channels. This is because increasing the number of channels, the number of users which have the possibility to communicate increases. This means that for a user which tempts the access on one of the last channels the probability to find the intender receiver is lower, because already many nodes are busy. As an example if the $node\_x$ tempts the access on the $channel\_6$, this means that the other 5 channels are used for communication, so 10 nodes are busy, among

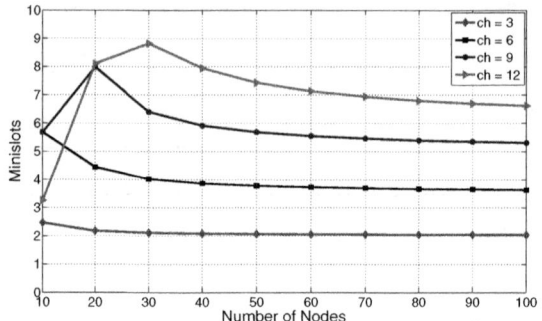

Fig. 6. Mean number of minislots utilized on each channels

these nodes may be the intended receiver of the $node\_x$: in this condition the value of α_6 grows. Then at the increasing of ch, the number of users which can transmit increases but also the mean waiting time does the same.

Finally we computed the useful transmission time, as:

$$T_{us} = \Omega(ch) \cdot [T_s - (mean_{ms} \cdot T_{ms})]. \tag{11}$$

Introducing eq.(11) in the initial eq.(7), the are all the elements to compute η_{ch}. In Fig. 7 the values of efficiency are shown varying the number of nodes and available channels in the network. The results are computed according to the parameters of Table 2 and the eq.(7).

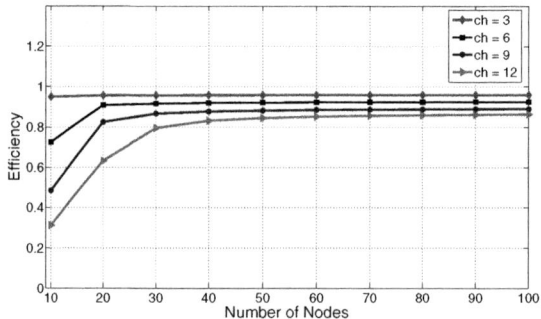

Fig. 7. The efficiency of the network

Fig. 7 shows that the efficiency increases with the increasing of the number of nodes. This is because increasing N the average number of used channels increases. Moreover the efficiency settles approximately in the range $[0.85, 0.95]$ in relation to the value of ch. This happens because increasing ch the number of employed minislots grows, and the efficiency is affected by this.

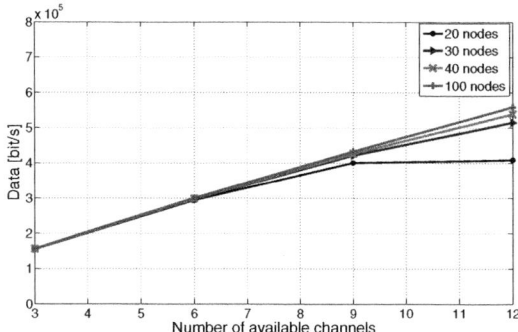

Fig. 8. The throughput of the network

According to the eq.(11) is possible to compute the total throughput of the network as:

$$throughput = T_{us} \cdot DR. \tag{12}$$

The results shown in Fig. 8, are computed according to the parameters of Table 2, varying the number of available channels.

Fig. 8 shows that the total throughput of the network grows with the increasing of the number of nodes and available channels.

5 Conclusions

In this paper a resource sharing algorithm was presented, which allows the optimized distribution of time slots among nodes in a single hop ad-Hoc network. The resource sharing method allows to implement a collision free MAC protocol. Furthermore, the method is able to optimize the resource assignment by taking into account the QoS requests of nodes, giving more bandwidth and granting less delays to nodes which have more performance requirements.

Performance evaluations proved that our method actually presents an efficient protocol and a very high channel utilization.

Acknowledgments. This work was partially funded by Apulia region, Italy, A.Q.P. Research Project "Modelli Innovativi per Sistemi Meccatronici," Del. CIPE 20/04, DM01 and Strategic Project PS_025.

References

1. IEEE standard for information technology telecommunications and information exchange between systems local and metropolitan area networks specific requirements. part 11: Wireless LAN medium access control (MAC) and physical layer (PHY) specifications (June 2007),
http://standards.ieee.org/getieee802/download/802.11-2007.pdf

2. Akyildiz, I.F., Lee, W.Y., Vuran, M.C., Mohanty, S.: NeXt generation dynamic spectrum access cognitive radio wireless networks: A survey. Computer Networks Journal 50(13), 2127–2159 (2006)
3. Akyildiz, I.F., Lee, W.Y., Chowdhury, K.R.: CRAHNs: Cognitive radio ad hoc networks. Ad Hoc Netw. 7, 810–836 (2009)
4. Challapali, K., Cordeiro, C., Birru, D.: Evolution of spectrum-agile cognitive radios: First wireless internet standard and beyond. In: Proc. of ACM International Wireless Internet Conference (August 2006)
5. Cormio, C., Chowdhury, K.R.: A survey on mac protocols in cognitive radio wireless networks. Ad Hoc Networks Journal 8(7), 1315–1329 (2009)
6. Haykin, S.: Cognitive radio: Brain-empowered wireless communications. IEEE Journal on Selected Areas in Communications 23(2), 201–220 (2005)
7. He, Q., Zhou, H.: Research on the routing algorithm based on qos requirement for cognitive radio networks. In: CSSE 2008: Proceedings of the 2008 International Conference on Computer Science and Software Engineering, pp. 1114–1117. IEEE Computer Society, Washington, D.C, USA (2008)
8. Ma, L., Han, X., Shen, C.: Dynamic open spectrum sharing for wireless ad hoc networks. In: Proc. of IEEE DySPAN (November 2005)
9. Ma, L., Han, X., Shen, C.: Dynamic open spectrum sharing mac protocol for wireless ad hoc network. In: Proc. of New Frontiers in Dynamic Spectrum Access Networks, p. 203 (November 2005)
10. Murroni, M., Popescu, V.: Cognitive radio HDTV multi-vision system in the 700 MHz UHF TV band. In: 2010 IEEE International Symposium on Broadband Multimedia Systems and Broadcasting, BMSB, Shanghai (March 2010)
11. Pawelczak, P., Venkatesha Prasad, R., L.Xia., Niemegeers, I.G.M.M.: Cognitive radio emergency networks - requirements and design. In: Proc. of IEEE DySPAN (November 2005)
12. Wu, S.L., Lin, C.Y., Tseng, Y.C., Sheu, J.P.: A new multi-channel mac protocol with on-demand channel assignment for multi-hop mobile ad hoc networks. In: Proceedings of the 2000 International Symposium on Parallel Architectures, Algorithms and Networks, ISPAN 2000. IEEE Computer Society, Los Alamitos (2000)

Design of a Robust Cognitive Control Channel for Cognitive Radio Networks Based on Ultra Wideband Pulse Shaped Signal

Gianmarco Baldini and Eduardo Cano Pons

Joint Research Centre – European Commission
Ispra, Italy
{gianmarco.baldini,eduardo.cano-pons}@jrc.ec.europa.eu

Abstract. In a collaborative Cognitive Radio Network (CRN), Cognitive Radio (CR) nodes exchange information to perform the cognitive radio functions. The exchange of information in collaborative CRNs is usually based on a Cognitive Control Channel (CCC). CCC can be classified as in-band channel or out-band channel. An Out-band CCC channel is a CCC, which uses a specific spectrum band. In this paper, the authors propose the design of an out-band CCC based on an Ultra Wideband pulse shaped signal. The proposed design is particularly resilient to external harmful interference and it is able to adapt its spectrum occupation to the primary wireless services present in the area. We define the requirements for the CCC and we provide simulation results to validate the design of the CCC against such requirements.

Keywords: Cognitive radio, ultra wideband, spectrum management.

1 Introduction

With the rapid evolution of microelectronics, wireless networking devices are becoming more versatile, powerful, and portable. This has enabled the development of software-defined radio (SDR) technology over the past 15 years, where the base-band digital processing is mostly performed in software. Because of its high degree of reconfigurability and easiness to program, SDR is a technology enabler for cognitive radio (CR). Cognitive radio is a radio or wireless communication that is able to change dynamically its transmission or reception parameters by using the information collected or sensed on the external environment [1]. Cognitive radio may enable the concept of Dynamic Spectrum Management (DSM), where radio frequency spectrum bands are dynamically assigned in function of time and space.

In collaborative cognitive radio networks (CRN), CR nodes exchange information to converge to a common allocation of spectrum bands or to improve the utilization of the spectrum. The exchange of information in collaborative CRN is usually based on a cognitive control channel (CCC) [2]. The CCC should be unique and known by all the CR nodes in the operational context, as it is used to initiate the execution of the CRN cognitive tasks like spectrum sensing, spectrum sharing and so on. CCC is usually classified as in-band channel or out-band channel. An Out-band channel is a CCC, which uses a specific spectrum band to exchange the cognitive control messages. This

C. Sacchi et al. (Eds.): MACOM 2011, LNCS 6886, pp. 13–23, 2011.
© Springer-Verlag Berlin Heidelberg 2011

paper describes the design of an out-band CCC based on an Ultra Wideband (UWB) pulse shaped signal which is particularly resilient to harmful interference and multipath fading effects. A similar approach has been suggested, but not developed in [3]. To the knowledge of the authors, this is the first paper, which describes a potential implementation of an UWB CCC.

The rest of the paper is organized as follows. In Section 2 we present the concepts of cognitive radio networks. Section 3 presents an overview of the UWB pulse technology and signal. Section 4 presents the CCC specifications and proposed cognitive radio architecture, which is validated by the simulations results in Section 5. Finally, section 6 provides the conclusions and future developments.

2 Cognitive Radio Networks

Cognitive Radio networks can be cooperative or non-cooperative. In cooperative networks, the cognitive radio nodes exchange information for each function described above to optimize the cognitive cycle processes. In non-cooperative networks, each node performs the above functions in isolation. Cooperative networks are usually more efficient than non-cooperative networks and they converge faster to an optimum solution ([4] and [5]). The focus of this paper is on cooperative cognitive radio networks.

Cooperative cognitive radio networks need the CCC to exchange the information for spectrum sensing, analysis and decision among the CR nodes.

Cognitive channels can be classified in two categories: in-band CCC and Out-band CCC. The in-band CCC implementation can be defined as the CCC implementation in which CCC information is being transmitted along with user data via the same radio interface (RI). A good example can be a cellular network (e.g., UMTS). In this case, CCC is a logical channel, which shares the resources with user data/voice transmission. The key disadvantage of this solution is the fact that the device is still required to conduct the scanning procedure in order to acquire knowledge about the RI where CCC is located. In order to implement the in-band CCC, a special mechanism, which would allow dissemination of CCC information through the related networks, must be developed. The out-band CCC can be defined as the CCC implementation in which one of the radio interfaces is exclusively used for dissemination of CCC information, where the cognitive channel use a spectrum band and channel definition specifically designed for the cognitive radio network.

The key advantage of the out-band approach is the easier implementation [6] as any CCC compliant terminal can retrieve the information of the CCC no matter what access technology it operates in. On the other hand, in order to implement out-band CCC each device needs to be employed with additional standardized radio interface allowing the reception of the CCC signal.

3 UltraWideBand

3.1 UltraWideBand (UWB) Impulse Channel

The Federal Communications Commission (FCC) in the United States approved the use of UWB technology for commercial applications under part 15 of its regulations in February 2002 [9]. The FCC report and order defined UWB as a signal with band-width to central frequency ratio greater than 20% or, alternatively, with a -10dB bandwidth exceeding 500 MHz in the frequency range of 3.1-10.6 GHz. The FCC permits UWB devices to operate on an unlicensed basis following restrictive power spectral masks for both indoor and outdoor environments. A maximum mean effec-tive isotropic radiated power (EIRP) spectral density of -41.3 dBm/MHz is estab-lished over all the 7.5 GHz operation bandwidth.

UWB signals can be generated in different manners. Mainly, two different UWB signal generation approaches have been established: the pulse-based UWB systems or single-band UWB systems and the multiband UWB system. The single-band ap-proach (i.e., Impulse Radio) is based on the continuous/discontinuous transmission of sub-nanosecond pulse based waveforms. Different types of pulse-based UWB sys-tems are commonly employed and they are differentiated from each other according to the associated multiple-access technique.

Considering an N_u-user environment, the general expression for the UWB Im-pulse Radio transmitted signal for the user k is expressed as:

$$s_{tx}^{(k)} = \frac{1}{\sqrt{N_s}} \sum_{j=-\infty}^{+\infty} b_{\lfloor j/N_s \rfloor}^{(k)} d_j^{(k)} w_{tx}\left(t - jT_f - c_j^{(k)}T_c - a_{\lfloor j/N_s \rfloor}^{(k)}\delta\right)$$
(1)

where N_s is the number of transmitted pulses in each symbol of duration T_s, T_f is the frame duration and T_c is the chip time. These time periods are related by: $T_s = N_s T_f = N_s N_h T_c$, where N_h is the total number of chip times per frame. The data information can be conveyed in the pulse polarity sequence $b^{(k)}$, and/or in the pulse position within the chip time, $a^{(k)}\delta$. The sequences $d^{(k)}$ and $c^{(k)}$ are the multiple-access Direct Sequence (DS) code and Time Hopping (TH) code respective-ly, which are unique per user. Both multiple-access code sequences are independent, periodic and orthogonal among all the N_u users. Finally, $\lfloor \cdot \rfloor$ represents the inferior integer part operator.

The signaling format used in this paper is based on a DS spreading code with $c_j^{(k)} = 0$ $\forall j, k$ in order to be compliant with the IEEE 802.15.4a standard.

Pulse polarity randomization codes, such as DS spreading codes, offer a higher spectral efficiency with respect to classical Impulse Radio systems that employ TH coding. The power spectral density (PSD) of a UWB with TH coding system presents non-removable discrete spectral lines, which cause severe reduction of power in order to fulfill the power spectral regulations represented in [11]. Conversely, the PSD of a pulse polarity randomization UWB signal shows a flat behavior when the number of pulses per symbol (i.e., the periodicity of the DS code sequence) is large [12]. Under these conditions, it is shown that the PSD of the transmitted signal is approximately the energy spectrum density of the individual pulse waveform, as expressed in (2). Therefore, the emitted power and the shape of the PSD of the transmitted signal can be fully controlled by the individual pulse waveforms,

$$Y_S \approx \left| W_{tx}(f) \right|^2 \qquad (2)$$

This spectral efficiency justifies the selection of DS spreading UWB systems in this paper.

3.2 Pulse Shaping: Linear Combination of Pulses

The UWB pulse waveform proposed in this paper is obtained by means of a linear combination of delayed replicas of a basic pulse [13] and [14]. This type of waveform is selected as one of the optional pulses to be employed in the IEEE 802.15.4a standard. The linear combination of pulses (LCP) waveform allows the full control and adaptation of the spectrum making it an ideal choice to be employed in cognitive radio platforms.

The general equation for the transmitted LCP waveform of duration T_w is given by

$$w_{tx}(t) = \sum_{m=1}^{N} A_m p(t - \tau_m) \qquad (3)$$

where $p(t)$ is the basic pulse shape of duration T_p, N is the total number of basic pulses, and A_i and τ_i are the amplitude and time delay of the i-th basic pulse respectively. To be compliant with the IEEE 802.15.4a standard, the maximum number of basic pulses is set to $N = 4$ and the time delays are chosen as $\tau_1 = 0$, $0 \leq \tau_m \leq 4$ ns for $m = 1,2,3$.

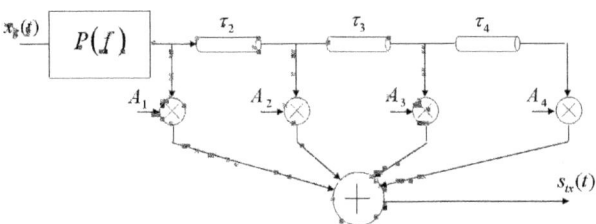

Fig. 1. LCP pulse block diagram

The high level block diagram of the LCP pulse shaper is shown in Figure 1. The input signal $x_\delta(t)$, expressed as:

$$x_\delta(t) = \frac{1}{\sqrt{N_s}} \sum_{j=-\infty}^{+\infty} b_{\lfloor j/N_s \rfloor}^{(k)} d_j^{(k)} \delta_D \left(t - jT_f - a_{\lfloor j/N_s \rfloor}^{(k)} \delta \right) \qquad (4)$$

with $\delta_D(t)$ denoting the Dirac delta function, sequentially passes through a basic pulse shape filter of frequency response $P(f)$ and a tapped delay line scheme.

An example of LCP construction, which illustrates the spectrum adaptation, is presented in Figure 2. Considering the presence of a Wi-Fi system operating at 5 GHz, a frequency notch can be placed in this band by choosing the LCP pulse (Pulse 1) with the following parameters: $A_1 = 1$, $A_2 = -1$, $A_3 = A_4 = 0$, $\tau_1 = \tau_3 = \tau_4 = 0$ and $\tau_2 = 0.2$ ns. The basic pulse waveform employed in this example is the 5th derivative of the Gaussian pulse [15].

Now considering the presence of a WiMAX signal, with bandwidth $B_w = 20$ MHz and center frequency $f_w = 3.5$ GHz, the PSD of the transmitted signal can be dynamically changed to protect the WiMAX service by placing the notch at f_w (Pulse 2). In this case, the tap delay is changed to $\tau_2 = 0.28$ ns. Therefore, spectrum adaptation can be obtained without changing the hardware structure of the pulse shaper.

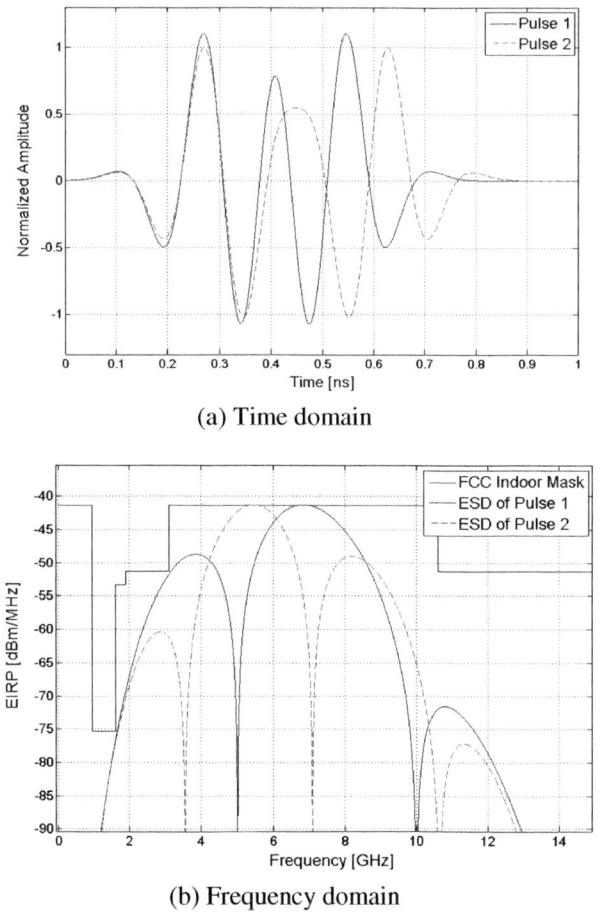

(a) Time domain

(b) Frequency domain

Fig. 2. Linear combination of pulses: Time and frequency domain and conformance to UWB spectrum regulations

3.3 Data Rate

The data rate of the UWB transmitted signal is given by the following expression:

$$R_b = \frac{1}{T_s} = \frac{1}{N_s T_f} \tag{5}$$

It is noticeable that the data rate decreases as the number of pulses per symbol increases. Since the CCC requires the information to be sent at low data rate and the pulse width of the LCP pulses is very short, as shown in Figure 2.(a), the number of pulses per transmitted symbol, N_s, is very large. This corresponds to a large processing gain value, which allows the information to be transmitted to long range receivers and to increase the system performance.

4 CRN Architecture and Specifications of the CCC

4.1 Cognitive Radio Network Architecture

The proposed solution is based on a collaborative CRN where a CCC is used to distribute the cognitive messages exchanged among the cognitive radio nodes.

Figure 3 provides a simplified description of the architecture of the cognitive radio network.

The main components of the cognitive radio network are:

- Cognitive base station, which includes the radio components (e.g., front-end) to provide wireless connectivity.
- Cognitive radio terminal. The cognitive radio terminals use the CCC to transmit cognitive control messages.

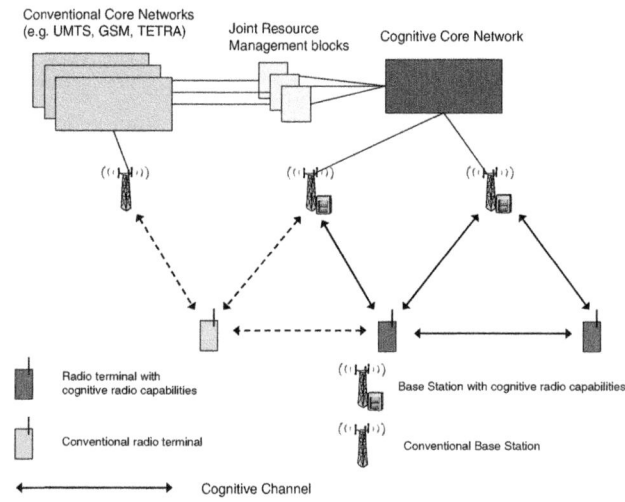

Fig. 3. Cognitive Radio Network architecture

- Conventional base station. This element is a base station of a conventional wireless network (e.g., UMTS, WiMAX).
- Conventional radio terminal. This element is a radio terminal based on conventional wireless network (e.g., UMTS, WiMAX, TETRA).
- Cognitive core network, which represents all the fixed elements of the cognitive radio network including the switching components, the authentication services and other functional blocks.
- Conventional core network, which represents all the fixed elements of the conventional radio networks.
- Joint resource management block. This element is used as a bridge between the cognitive radio network and the conventional core network. It is used to exchange information to optimize resource management.

The design of the cognitive radio network and CCC, which is proposed for this paper is based on the following concepts:

- The cognitive channel will be based on UWB pulse modulation and it will occupy a frequency band wider than 400 MHz. This frequency band can be located in a wide frequency range, which can span from 400 MHz to 12 GHz.
- Cognitive radio terminals entering the network may have not "a priori" knowledge of the range of frequencies used by the cognitive channel defined in the area apart from the knowledge that it is based on UWB pulse modulation. The cognitive radio network will define the spectrum bands used for the cognitive channel in a specific area. The assignment can depend on a number of factors: the first is the spectrum regulations in the area, then the type of environment (e.g., urban, rural) and the

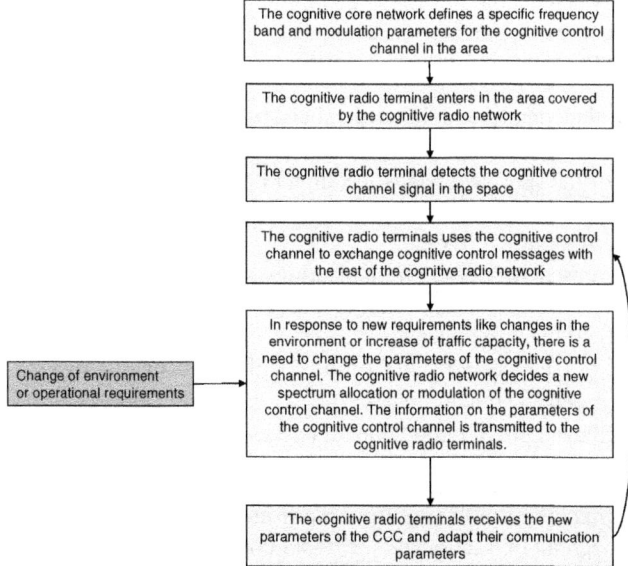

Fig. 4 Cognitive Radio workflow

number of parties involved. The core radio network will broadcast the cognitive channel in the specified frequency range and cognitive radio terminals entering in the area will scan the frequency range to identify the cognitive channel.

- Once a cognitive radio terminal has identified the CCC, it can use the CCC to exchange information. The cognitive radio terminal may transmit information on the sensed wireless communication systems in the area or other parameters like the received signal power. The CCC is also used to transmit information among the cognitive base stations and terminals on the allocated spectrum bands and the positions of primary services in the area.

Figure 4 summarizes the possible phases of the procedures executed by a cognitive radio terminal.

4.2 Cognitive Channel Requirements

An out-band CCC must validate the following requirements:

- Have enough capacity to transmit the cognitive control messages of a large network composed by hundreds of terminals.
- Minimize the interference with licensed wireless communication systems. Existing wireless networks or devices existing in the area should not be negatively impacted by the presence of a cognitive channel in the area.
- The cognitive channel should be designed for resilience against external interference of environment conditions (e.g., multipath fading), which could impact the quality of service.

The CCC deployment should minimize the impact on spectrum regulations and should be easily achievable in various geopolitical contexts.

A cognitive control message is estimated to be around 320 bytes in size, as it should contain the following information:

- Location of the cognitive radio terminal (12 bytes)
- Identifier of the cognitive radio terminal (2 bytes)
- Allocation of the spectrum bands. Using a bit mask to represent the spectrum to be allocated with a detail of 5 MHz, we can represent the spectrum range from 0 to 10 GHz with a mask of 250 Bytes.
- List of ten sensed wireless communications systems in the area and their powers levels. Using 2 bytes for the communication system identifier and 2 bytes for the power level, 40 bytes are needed.
- Power level of the received signal of the cognitive channel: 4 bytes.
- BER of the received signal: 4 bytes.
- Features of the cognitive radio node: 8 bytes.

Assuming a rate of transmission of the message every 30 seconds and considering a population of maximum 500 cognitive radio nodes in the area, we have an overall maximum throughput of 42666 Kbits, without considering security and integrity data.

$$((320 \times 8bits) \times 500nodes)/30 = 42666bits/\sec. \tag{6}$$

5 Simulations and Validations

In this section, we present the results of the simulations to verify that the proposed design of the CCC based UWB pulse shaped signal validates the requirements to:

- Minimize the interference with licensed wireless communication systems.
- provide the minimum data rate calculated in section 4.2

As described in the previous sections, it is possible to define the parameters and the notch of the UWB signal to avoid interference to licensed systems or to be conformant to existing spectrum regulations.

The licensed system used in the simulation is based on WiMAX 802.16d standard with a center frequency of 3.5 GHz and 20 MHz of band.

We used the following parameters to evaluate the impact of the UWB CCC on the WiMAX system:

- Bit Error Rate (BER), which is the number of bit errors divided by the total number of transferred bits during a specific time interval.
- Error Vector Magnitude (EVM), which expresses the difference between the expected complex voltage value of a demodulated symbol and the value of the actual received symbol.

The following parameters were defined for the simulation:

- average distance among the nodes equal to 200 meters, which translates to a free-space path loss of 89 dB.
- Sensitivity of the WiMAX receiver equal to -110 dBm.
- Bit data rate of the CCC of 43 Kbit/s.

Figure 5 describes the BER for the licensed WiMAX for two types of modulation: QPSK and 64-QAM in the presence or absence of the CCC.

As we can see from the Figure 5, the interference impact of the CCC based on UWB pulse shaped signal is negligible for the defined CCC bit data rate.

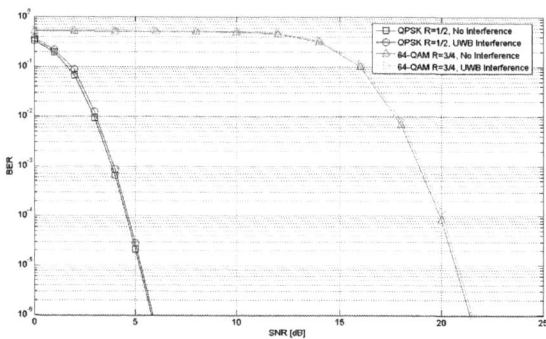

Fig. 5. BER of licensed WiMAX against SNR and CCC interference

Figure 6 describes the EVM for the licensed WiMAX for the QPSK modulation in presence and absence of the CCC.

Also, in this case, we can conclude that the interference impact of the CCC based on UWB pulse shaped signal is negligible for the defined CCC bit data rate.

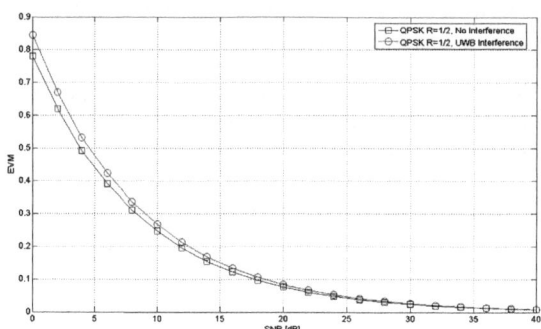

Fig. 6. EVM of licensed WiMAX against SNR and CCC interference

6 Conclusions and Future Developments

The paper presented the design of an out-band Cognitive Control channel based on UltraWideBand technology, which is particularly resilient against wireless interference and multi-path fading and which can adapt to the presence of primary licensed wireless services in the area. We demonstrated that the proposed CCC provides the required throughput and it does not affect primary users. The next steps are to design a complete MAC layer for the CRN based on the proposed CCC.

References

1. FCC ET Docket No. 03-108, Facilitating opportunities for flexible, efficient, and reliable spectrum use employing cognitive radio technologies, FCC Report and Order adopted (March 10, 2005)
2. Cordier, P., Houze, P., Jemaa, S.B., Simon, O., Bourse, D., Grandblaise, D., Moessner, K., Luo, J., Kloeck, C., Tsagkaris, K., Agusti, R., Olaziregi, N., Boufidis, Z., Buracchini, E., Goria, P., Trogolo, A.: E2r cognitive pilot channel concept. In: 15th IST Mobile and Wireless Communications Summit (2006)
3. Cabric, D., Mishra, S.M., Willkomm, D., Brodersen, R., Wolisz, A.: A cognitive radio approach for usage of virtual unlicensed spectrum. In: 14th IST Mobile and Wireless Communications Summit (2005)
4. Ganesan, G., Li, Y.: Agility improvement through cooperative diversity in cognitive radio. In: IEEE Global Telecommunications Conference, St. Louis, Missouri, USA, vol. 5, pp. 2505–2509 (November/December 2005)
5. Peng, C., Zheng, H., Zhao, B.Y.: Utilization and fairness in spectrum assignment for opportunistic spectrum access. In: ACM Mobile Networks and Applications, MONET (2006)

6. Han, C., Wang, J., Yang, Y., Li, S.: Addressing the control channel design problem: OFDM-based transform domain communication system in cognitive radio. Computer Networks, Cognitive Wireless Networks 52(4), 1286–1389 (2008)
7. Ma, L., Han, X., Shen, C.: Dynamic open spectrum sharing MAC protocol for wireless ad hoc network. In: DySPAN 2005, pp. 203–213 (November 2005)
8. Win, M.Z., Scholtz, R.A.: Ultra-wide bandwidth time-hopping spread-spectrum impulse radio for wireless multiple-access communications. IEEE Transactions Communications 48(4), 679–691 (2000)
9. Federal Communications Commission (FCC), Revision of Part 15 of the Commissions Rules Regarding Ultra-Wideband Transmission Systems. First Report and Order, ET Docket 98-153, FCC 02-48, pp. 1–118 (2002)
10. European Commission Decision 2007/131/EC, Allowing the Use of the Radio Spectrum for Equipment Using Ultra-Wideband Technology in a Harmonised Manner in the Community (June 2007)
11. Romme, J., Piazzo, L.: On the power spectral density of time-hopping impulse radio. In: IEEE Conference on Ultra-Wideband Systems and Technologies, Baltimore, MD, pp. 241–244 (2002)
12. Ye, Z., Madhukumar, A.S., Chin, F.: Power spectral density and in-band interference power of UWB signals at narrowband systems. In: IEEE International Conference on Communications (ICC 2004), Paris, vol. 6, pp. 3561–3565 (2004)
13. Di Benedetto, M.-G., De Nardis, L.: Tuning UWB signals by pulse shaping: towards context-aware wireless network. Eurasip Journal on Signal Processing, invited paper, Special Issue on Signal Processing in UWB Communications (2006)
14. Ameli, F., Piazzo, L.: Ultra-wide band spectrum shaping by means of a composite monocycle. Whyless.com Internal Report (2003)
15. Sheng, H., Orlik, P.V., Hiamovich, A., Cimini, L.J., Zhang, J.: On the spectral and power requirements for ultra-wideband transmission. In: Proceedings of the IEEE International Conference on Communications (ICC 2003), vol. 1, pp. 738–742 (2003)
16. Mcorkle, J.: Why such uproar over ultrawideband. Communications Design Magazine (2002)

An Urn Occupancy Approach for Cognitive Radio Networks in DTVB White Spaces

Leonardo Goratti, Gianmarco Baldini, and Alberto Rabbachin

Joint Research Center (JRC),
Via Enrico Fermi 2749, 21027 Ispra, Italy
{leonardo.goratti,gianmarco.baldini,alberto.rabbachin}@jrc.ec.europa.eu

Abstract. Cognitive Radio paradigm has recently received considerable interest to address the so called 'spectrum scarcity' problem. In the USA, the Federal Communications Commission recently issued the regulatory for the use of cognitive radio in the TV white space spectrum. The primary objective is the design of cognitive devices able to combine the use of spectrum sensing, GEO-location and cognitive control channel to manage the network. The recent standard ECMA-392 defines physical layer and medium access control protocols to manage the network in a fully distributed fashion.

In this work, we pursue the design of an efficient medium access control protocol for the cognitive control channel to flexibly and reliably exchange messages inside the cognitive radio network. Our main contributions are the following: 1) we propose a proprietary medium access control protocol based on the Standard ECMA-392; 2) we model the behavior of the cognitive radio network by means of a urn model approach and, 3) we investigate the ability of the cognitive devices to identify frequency holes (accounting for perfect and imperfect spectrum sensing) and in the end we study the network throughput.

Keywords: Cognitive Radio, medium access control, coupon collector's problem, TV white spaces.

1 Introduction

In the past decade, cognitive radio (CR) paradigm [1] has revolutionized our view of opportunities in wireless communications to a great extent. The key motivation is to optimize the use of underutilized radio resources. CR devices are intelligent radios that can learn from the environment and adapt their functionalities (data rate, modulation scheme, etc.). Standardization, regulation and certification activities are also being initiated in many parts of the world [2]. TV white spaces are one of the most promising applications for CR. ECMA-392 [3] [4] is a standard recently defined by the Cognitive Radio Alliance (CogNeA) [5] to manage the cognitive radio network (CRN) in a fully distributed fashion in TV white spaces.

Spectrum sensing and GEO-location are the two methods used to opportunistically access radio resources. Spectrum sensing relies on the capability of CR

C. Sacchi et al. (Eds.): MACOM 2011, LNCS 6886, pp. 24–38, 2011.

devices to sense signals as low as -114 dBm to find unused frequency holes. Sensing inefficiency yields harmful interference to the TV service. GEO-location relies on the use of a database (DB) that CR devices can query to know which frequencies are available in a certain geographical region. In the literature, the protection contour is defined as the distance beyond which a CR device is allowed to transmit.

In this work we focus on TV white spaces in the frequency region 470-790 MHz. We consider k CR devices able to combine both GEO-location and spectrum sensing capabilities. In fact, we assume that location aware (e.g., GPS equipped) CR devices have knowledge of the spectrum utilization in a certain geographical region after quering the DB. As time elapses, this initial knowledge may be incorrect if not properly updated by means of spectrum sensing. CR devices maintain connectivity and exchange general information (e.g., sensing information) by accessing the so called beacon period (BP) operating in the out-of-band cognitive control channel (CCC).

The frequency region for TV white spaces is divided in frequency channels of 6 MHz width (TV channel). We formulate the problem of CR devices sensing potentially available channels as a particular case of a more general set of problems known as *urn occupancy problems* [6]. In this work, CR devices follow the proprietary medium access control (MAC) protocol that we derive from ECMA-392. To the best knowledge of the authors, we provide a novel approach to analyze the capability of the CR devices to track the vacancy of the frequency channels by providing variations of the well known *coupon collector's problem*. We solve the urn occupancy problem by means of exponential generating functions (EGF) technique in the case of ideal sensing, but also including the events of false alarm and miss-detection.

The remainder of the paper is organized as follow. In Section 2 we briefly review the standard ECMA-392. In section 3 we formulate the problem we are aiming to solve. In section 4 we describe the system model and our proposed MAC protocol. In Section 5 we detail the proposed analytical method. In section 6 we show the results and in section 7 we draw the conclusions.

2   Standard ECMA-392

ECMA-392 standard [3] defines two basic network formation modes: master-slave network and peer-to-peer (P2P) network. In this work we rely on the P2P mode to form a distributed, ad-hoc, self-organizing, self-healing network. P2P network mode is based on the concept of the logical beacon group (BG), which is formed around each individual device.

The physical layer (PHY) is based on a 128-fft orthogonal frequency division multiplexing (OFDM). Each physical protocol data unit (PPDU) consists of a PLCP [1] preamble, header and payload. The preamble is mainly used for synchronization and channel estimation purposes. The header is encoded with

---

[1] Physical layer convergence protocol.

a outer encoder Reed-Solomon (RS) (23,15,4), with an inner convolutional encoder having rate 1/2 and modulated using quadrature phase shift key (QPSK). Payload is mapped either via QPSK, 16-QAM or 64-QAM and uses RS encoder, convolutional encoder, puncturing and interleaving.

2.1   MAC Layer

The devices scan the frequency channels to find out which ones are not occupied by the incumbent primary user (PU) or which could be occupied by a beaconing device. Time is discretized in superframes, whose structure is shown in Fig.1. The superframe consists of a BP, a data transfer period (DTP), a reservation based signaling window (RSW) (used only in master-slave mode) and a contention signaling window (CSW). Before CSW, a quite-period (QP) is scheduled. A newcomer device must scan for at least one superframe searching for beacons. If the newcomer does not sense any existing beacon, it can start its own BP. Otherwise, it must join the existing BG by accessing the BP.

The devices exchange general network information, maintain synchronization and connectivity by exchanging beacon frames during the BP. The BP is divided in beacon slots (BSs) and it commences with the beacon period start time (BPST). Devices transmit beacon frames in a unique collision-free BS and listen for beacons of neighbor devices in all the others. Newcomer devices attempt to join the BP by making access in a set of BSs referred to as mBPExtension [3], using S-Aloha access. The mBPExtension BSs are counted from the highest occupied busy slot (HOBS) at the current superframe. Devices include the beacon period occupancy information element (BPOIE) in their beacon frames to communicate their view of BSs occupation in the BP. To avoid an unnecessary long BP length, a device can contract BS occupation by shifting to the earliest available BS following the BPST.

During the QP all devices must be silent to enable reliable sensing of the channels. The QP period can be scheduled on regular basis and/or on-demand. The QP on regular basis can occur every mQPFrequency superframes [3] with a duration defined by the standard. On-demand QP can be scheduled when devices observe abnormal and/or unexpected behavior. After acquiring information on the incumbent, a device informs the other devices either with its beacon frame or during CSW.

The devices exchange data during the DTP, by means of channel reservation protocol (CRP) and prioritized contention access (PCA). The CRP constitutes the contention-free mechanism provided by the standard and resources can be negotiated either by means of the beacon frame (implicit mode) or by means of command frames (explicit mode). On the other hand, the PCA is very similar to the IEEE 802.11e enhanced distributed coordination function (EDCF) and it constitutes the contention-based transmission mechanism.

3   Problem Description

We define with 'White Space' a portion of the spectrum that is available for radio communications at a given time and space on a non-interfering basis to

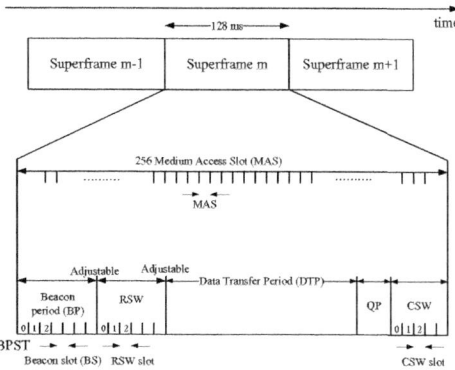

Fig. 1. ECMA-392 superframe structure [3]

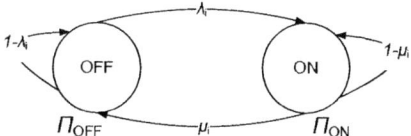

Fig. 2. Two-states model for a single frequency channel

licensed wireless services (e.g., digital TV). One of the most challenging tasks for a cognitive MAC protocol is to find out which frequency channels are idle (denoted by 0) or busy (denoted by 1) from PU's activity at a certain superframe. Performing correctly this task enables the cognitive devices to communicate between each other in unlicensed way, without causing harmful interference to the PU. We define the state of the system in correspondence of superframe t as: $\Theta(t) = \{\theta_1, \theta_2, ..., \theta_m\}$, where m denotes the total number of frequency channels and $\theta_i = \{0, 1\}$ denotes the state of the ith channel.

As in [7], we model a frequency channel with a two-states model, assuming all channels independent[2]. In general, a frequency channel can be in 'ON' state (busy) or in 'OFF' state (idle). Let λ_i be the switching rate from OFF to ON and μ_i the rate from ON to OFF. Solving the two-states model of Fig.2 we find that

$$\Pi_{\text{off}} = \frac{1}{1 + \rho_i} , \tag{1}$$

$$\Pi_{\text{on}} = 1 - \Pi_{\text{off}} = \frac{1}{1 + 1/\rho_i} ,$$

where Π_{off} and Π_{on} are the steady-state probabilities and $\rho_i = \lambda_i/\mu_i$ is the activity factor of the ith channel. In the remainder of this work we assume

---

[2] In a real system adjacent channels might be weakly correlated.

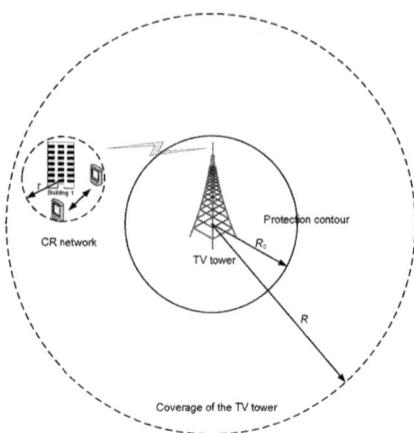

Fig. 3. Application scenario for CRN

$\rho_i = \rho$, $\forall i \in [1, m]$. The validity of the two-states model for modeling DTVB transmissions over error-channels have been widely studied and several models are available from the literature. Some of those models are reviewed in [10], [11] and [12]. Those works point out the limitations of the two-states model for the specific task of modeling digital video. Therefore, if one hand literature suggests the use of more accurate models, it cannot be considered the two-states model completely inaccurate, at least for the sake of estimating performance.

CR devices can asses the status of a frequency channel by means of sensing (or observation). Hereafter we assume the very general case in which parameters of the PU are totally unknown to the CR devices. Given that not all the channels might be observable, a number of studies in the literature focus on estimating the system state. For instance, this can be done by means of partially observable Markov decision processes (POMDP) [8] and inference techniques in general. A drawback of inference techniques is the high computational complexity. Depending on the type of the incumbent, estimate the system state might not always be necessary. In this work, we focus on the use of sensing information instead of applying techniques to predict the system state.

4   System Model

We study the CRN shown in Fig. 3. At the center of the coverage area is placed the TV tower, having transmission radius R and protection contour radius R_c. The CRN has a coverage radius $r << R$ and it is located beyond the protection contour of PU. Under this assumption we can assume that the signal of the PU is received almost in the same manner by the CR devices. In this scenario, cognition capabilities of the CR devices might be limited only by the environment surrounding the CRN, as obstructions or interferences (unintentional or intentional). Furthermore, we assume that the CR devices have downloaded information on frequency occupation from the DB (i.e., data base) at the beginning of their operations and rely on spectrum sensing for subsequent operations.

We assume m frequency channels of predefined bandwidth W that hereafter are interchangeably referred to as urns and k CR devices also referred to as balls. CR devices follow the MAC protocol described in the next section. At every superframe they perform sensing during the QP by choosing a frequency channel according to a random selection process. We model the random sensing problem as a set of balls thrown randomly and independently into a set of urns and we rely on [6] for the analysis.

Since the possibility of tracking the system state depends on the number of CR devices, two cases of interest arise: $k \leq m$ and $k > m$. Let T_c denote the amount of time that elapses before collecting at least one observation for all the channels. This is known in the literature as the coupon collector's problem (a special case of the urn occupancy problems). If the PU does not change frequency occupation within T_c, CR devices can observe the state of the system. We study the effectiveness of the random selection scheme, by exploiting sensing information for transmitting data.

4.1 Proposed MAC Protocol

We propose a variation of the MAC protocol summarized in Section 2.1 using an out-of-band CCC for spectrum management. The superframe structure of the proposed MAC protocol is showed in Fig. 4. The superframe commences with the BPST and we insert two signaling slots (SS) immediately after (as replacement of CSW). As in [3], we assume that newcomer devices join the network by accessing the BP. To allow continuous occupation of the BSs without BP contraction

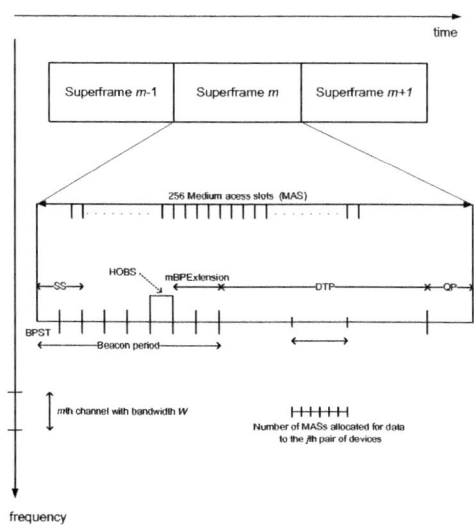

Fig. 4. Superframe structure of the proposed MAC protocol inspired by [3]

we assume that the devices access the mBPExtension slots using S-Aloha, but sending unicast beacon frames to the device occupying the HOBS. The device occupying the HOBS informs the newcomers whether they succeeded or not by reporting their MAC addresses in the corresponding BSs at the following superframe. Colliding devices must reattempt a new BS as defined in [3].

We assume that the devices sense frequency channels at every superframe during the QP and exchange sensing outcomes only throughout beacon frames. As a frequency channel is randomly selected, devices might sense the same frequency or not. In case the same frequency is sensed by more than one device, conflicting information yields the channel to be unavailable for data communication.

Data packets are exchanged during DTP, reserving available frequency channels by means of the implicit way defined by the CRP protocol [3]. In case a pair of devices gain access to a frequency channel by reserving MASs, they have exclusive use of the resources until do not advertise relinquishment or the PU does not occupy it. In this way data are exchanged in frequency division multiple access (FDMA) fashion. To minimize the possibility of causing harmful interference to the PU, the transmitter must do a clear channel assessment (CCA) prior transmitting.

5   System Analysis

From the literature, the convergence time for the coupon collector's problem is roughly estimated as: $T_c \approx O\big(m \cdot ln(m)\big)$. For urn occupancy problems, the case of labeled balls, denoted by z, thrown randomly into labeled urns, denoted by x, is solved by means of the EGF technique. EGF can be written as a formal power series [6]

$$F(x, z) = \sum_{i=0}^{\infty} \sum_{j=0}^{\infty} h_{i,j} x^i z^j \tag{2}$$

$$= \Big(g(z) + (x - 1)f(z)\Big)^m ,$$

where $h_{i,j}$ counts all possible allocations of interests, $g(z)$ is the generating function of all possible allocations and $f(z)$ is the generating function of the allocations of interest. In case a urn can receive any number of balls: $g(z) = e^z$. Vice versa, for a urn having finite storage capacity δ, we have $g(z) = (1 + z)^\delta$.

Using (2) we can derive all the moments of the random variable counting the allocations of interest. In particular, we compute the expected number of frequency channels that can be sensed with k devices as follows

$$E\{x\} = \frac{[z^k]\partial/\partial x F(x, z)}{[z^k]F(x, z)}\bigg|_{x=1} . \tag{3}$$

5.1   Computation of False Alarm and Detection Probabilities

We model CR devices sensing channels (seeking for the PU) with the simple energy detector (ED) receiver. The ED receiver squares and integrates the received signal and then it compares with a threshold γ. Let $r(t) = \sum_u \sqrt{E_s} s_u(t - uT_s) + n(t)$ be the received signal, where $s_u(t) = h(t) * p_u(t)$ is the convolution between the uth transmitted symbol of the PU $p_u(t)$ and the channel fading $h(t)$, E_s is the energy per symbol, T_s the symbol period, and $n(t)$ is the Additive White Gaussian Noise (AWGN) with two-sided power spectral density $N_0/2$. Furthermore, let $Y = \int_0^{T_s} |r(t)|^2 dt$ be the observed variable over the time τ_s based on which the decision busy/idle is taken. Considering the fading value h constant over τ_s and conditioning on h, Y is Chi-square (χ^2) distributed. We define false alarm the event in which a channel is assessed busy, though idle and miss-detection the event in which a channel is assessed idle, though busy. We denote the statistical hypothesis of false alarm and miss-detection with H_0 and H_1, respectively. Therefore, the probability of false alarm $p_{fa}(\gamma)$ and the probability of miss-detection $(p_{md}(\gamma) = 1 - p_d)$ can be written as

$$p_{fa}(\gamma) = \Pr\{Y \geq \gamma | H_0\} , \qquad (4)$$
$$p_{md}(\gamma) = \Pr\{Y < \gamma | H_1\} .$$

For the hypothesis H_0, Y follows a central χ^2 -distribution with $\kappa_{a1} = W \cdot T_s$ degrees of freedom. On the other hand, for hypothesis H_1, Y follows a non-central χ^2 distribution with non-centrality parameter $\Lambda_{a1} = WT_s(E_s/N_0)$ and $\kappa_{a2} = W \cdot T_s$ degrees of freedom. In order to include the effect of the channel fading on the detection of the PU signal, we proceed by defining the characteristic function (CF) of Y conditioned on h as

$$\Psi_{Y|h}(js) = \frac{1}{\sqrt{1 - js}} e^{\frac{-jsh E_s/N_0}{1 - js}} . \qquad (5)$$

By tacking the expectation over h, the CF of Y can be expressed as

$$\Psi_Y(js) = \frac{1}{\sqrt{1 - js}} \Psi_{h^2}\left(\frac{-jsE_s/N_0}{1 - js}\right) . \qquad (6)$$

By using the inversion theorem, the probability of detection can then by calculated as

$$P_d(\gamma) = \frac{1}{2} - \frac{1}{2\pi} \int_0^\infty \frac{\Psi_Y(-js)e^{js\gamma} - \Psi_Y(js)e^{-js\gamma}}{js} ds . \qquad (7)$$

Referring to the two-states model of Fig.2, the probability of sensing correctly a channel (p_c), without predicting the state of the system with inference techniques, is expressed as

$$p_c = \left((1 - \Pi_{off})p_d + \Pi_{off}(1 - p_{fa})\right) . \qquad (8)$$

5.2 Exponential Generating Functions Approach

Using (3) and the framework described in [6], we first solve the coupon collector's problem.

Proposition 1. *Let the random selection scheme of CR devices sensing frequency channels be characterized by the pair (m, k). Let also n denote the number of channels that a device can sense during the QP (depending on hardware limitations) and p_c be the correct sensing probability defined in (8). The average number of superframes T_c to collect at least one observation for all the channels is expressed by*

$$T_c = \left\{ min\ t \in \mathbb{N} : E_t\{x\} = m - 1 \right\}, \tag{9}$$

where $E_t\{\cdot\}$ is the expectation at superframe $t = 1, 2, ...$

Proof. We first write the EGF for the coupon collector's problem as follows

$$F(x, z) = \left(e^z + (x - 1)(e^z - 1) \right)^{m'}, \tag{10}$$

with $m' = m-1$ that is, after the first draw it is more difficult to sense a channel that was not probed already. Some of the n sensing information will be correct with probability p_c according to a Binomial distribution with average $n \cdot p_c$. As this holds for all the k devices, we can compute the following: $k' = (n \cdot p_c \cdot k) - 1$.

Applying (3) and assuming $\partial/\partial x F(x, z) = F'(x, z)$, we obtain

$$F(1, z) = e^{z \cdot m'} = \sum_{j=1}^{\infty} (m')^j \frac{z^j}{j!}, \tag{11}$$

$$F'(1, z) = m' \cdot \left(e^{z \cdot m'} - e^{z \cdot (m'-1)} \right).$$

Taking the coefficient of the term $[z^{j=k'}]$ we obtain:

$$E\{x\} = (m - 1) \cdot \left(1 - \left(1 - \frac{1}{m-1} \right)^{n p_c k - 1} \right). \tag{12}$$

As k devices sense the frequency channels at every superframe, we can rewrite (12) substituting $k(t) = t \cdot k$ and so obtain $E_t\{x\}$. We finally notice from (12) that for $n = 1$, $p_c = 1$ we have the classical coupon collector's problem.

As urn models are a very general framework, we produce a variation of the coupon collector's problem to compute the average number of idle channels sensed by the CR devices.

Corollary 1. *For the random selection scheme following the hypothesis of Proposition 1 and assuming false alarm probability p_{fa}, we compute the average number of frequency channels sensed idle during a superframe as follows*

$$E\{x\} = m_{off} = m \cdot \Pi_{off} \left(1 - \left(1 - \frac{1}{m} \right)^{n(1-p_{fa})k} \right). \tag{13}$$

Proof. We prove the thesis for $n = 1$. We first write the EGF conditioned on l occupied channels by the PU: $F(x, z|l) = \left(1 + x(e^z - 1)\right)^{m-l}$. We assume the distribution of l occupied channels Binomial with probability: $\binom{m}{l}(1 - \Pi_{\text{off}})^l \Pi_{\text{off}}^{m-l}$. Taking the expectation with respect to l, we obtain:

$$F(x, z) = \left(1 + x\Pi_{\text{off}}(e^z - 1)\right)^m.$$

We make the change of variable $y = x \cdot \Pi_{\text{off}}$ and we calculate (3) in $y = 1$. To complete the proof, when the devices seek for idle channels, only $(1 - p_{\text{fa}}) \cdot k$ will make a correct assessment.

6 Results

The CR devices are independently deployed in an anulus of radius $R_c < r \leq R$, as shown in Fig.3. Let R_s denote the symbol rate for both BP and DTP and d be the distance of the CRN from the TV tower. Computing the well known Friis expression using the parameters of Table 1 we derive that

$$
\begin{aligned}
(E_s/N_0)|_{dB} = &\\
= P_{\text{tx}} + G\text{tx} + G\text{rx} - &\zeta_0 - \zeta(\text{d}) -\\
- P_{\text{n}} - N_{\text{f}} - I - &10 \cdot log_{10}(R_s/W) ,
\end{aligned}
\tag{14}
$$

where ζ_0 is the loss at 1 m, $\zeta(\text{d})$ the loss at d meters and $G_{\text{tx}} = G_{\text{rx}} = 0$ dB are the antenna gains. As described in Section 4.1, CR devices negotiate resources

Table 1. System parameters [3] [4] [9]

Parameter	Comments	Value
P_{tx}	TV tower transmit power	25 KW
R_s	data rate	4.75 Mbps
W	TV channel bandwidth	6 MHz
R	TV tower coverage radius	80 Km
R_c	protection contour radius	30 Km
f_c	center frequency	630 MHz
α	path-loss exponent	2
I	total losses	-25 dB
N_f	noise figure	6 dB
τ_{SF}	superframe duration	128 ms
τ_{MIFS}	minimum interframe space	2 μs
SS	number of signaling slots	2 slots
τ_{BS}	beacon slot duration	1 ms
τ_{QP}	QP duration	5 ms
L_p	payload size	4095 bytes
L_{ack}	ACK frame size	10 bytes

by means of the CRP protocol to communicate in FDMA fashion. To minimize the possibility of causing harmful interference to the PU, a transmitter must sense the assigned channel before starting the communication. Hence, at regime, the CRN not only can rely on the sensing information obtained during the QP but also on the knowledge of the channels that carry useful data communication. Let G denote the intensity of the channel traffic generated by the overall CRN network normalized to the superframe duration. We define as transmission opportunity with probability $q = \Pi_{\text{off}}(1 - p_{\text{fa}})G/k$, the probability of the event that CR devices exploit idle channels. At regime, the average number of frequency channels occupied by data communication is

$$m_S = \sum_{i=0}^{min\{k,m-1\}} \binom{m}{i} i \cdot q^i (1 - q)^{m-i} \, , \tag{15}$$

where $m - 1$ denotes that at least one channel must be occupied by the PU and we assume up to k active CR links (in general is topology dependent). Each pair of devices transmits packets of maximum PHY service data unit (PSDU) size with duration $\tau_{\text{p}} = L_{\text{p}}/R_{\text{s}}$ (including the PLCP header). Between each packet transmission a minimum interframe space (MIFS) occurs. We also assume that transmission of packets follows the positive acknowledgment (ACK) scheme, with $\tau_{\text{ack}} = L_{\text{ack}}/R_{\text{s}}$. Hence, the overall DTP duration is $\tau_{\text{DTP}} = \tau_{\text{SF}} - \tau_{\text{BP}} - \tau_{\text{QP}}$, with $\tau_{\text{BP}} = \text{SS} + \tau_{\text{BS}} \cdot k$. The number of messages exchanged by the jth pair of devices can be written as

$$N_j = \frac{\tau_{\text{DTP}}}{\tau_{\text{p}}} \, , \tag{16}$$

$$\tau_{u,j} = \tau_{\text{DTP}} - N_j \cdot (\tau_{\text{MIFS}} + \tau_{\text{ack}}) \, ,$$

where $\tau_{u,j}$ is the duration of the useful period to exchange data. Therefore, we calculate the average throughput per superframe S, measured in number of bits, as follows

$$S = R_{\text{s}} \sum_{j=0}^{m_s-1} \tau_{u,j} \, . \tag{17}$$

Although the throughput calculation of (17) is over simplified, is used to estimate network performance. Since channels carrying data communication are sensed before transmitting data, CR devices can sense the remaining ones during the QP. In this case, after recomputing (13) for $m' = m - m_{\text{s}}$, the CRN improves its knowledge on the number of the idle channels up to

$$M = m'_{\text{off}} + m_{\text{s}} \geq m'_{\text{off}} \, . \tag{18}$$

6.1   Numerical Results

In Fig. 5 we show the probability of detection computed in Section 5.1 in case of Nakagami fading with severity index g_{f}. The term Ψ_{h^2} in (6) is the CF of the Gamma distribution.

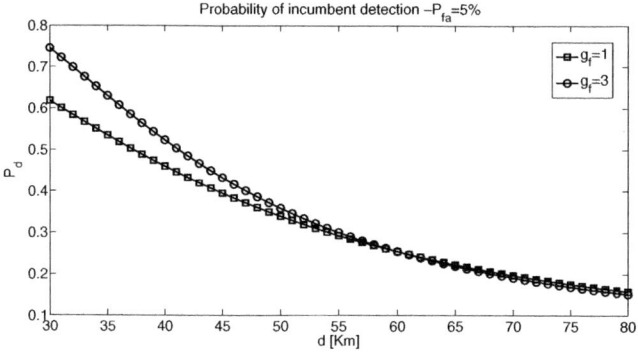

Fig. 5. Probability of detection in Nakami fading with different values of the severity index g_f

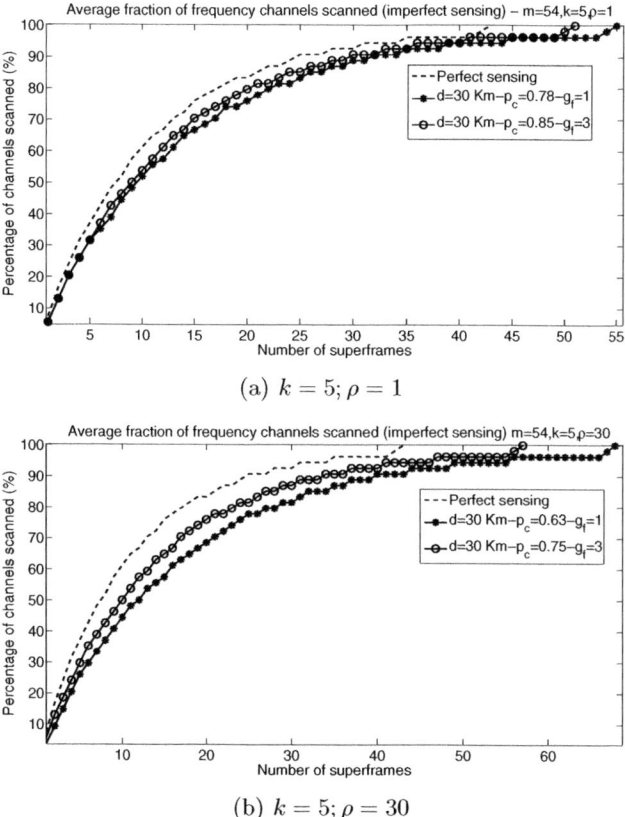

(a) $k = 5; \rho = 1$

(b) $k = 5; \rho = 30$

Fig. 6. Average number of frequency channels sensed vs. time measured in number of superframes

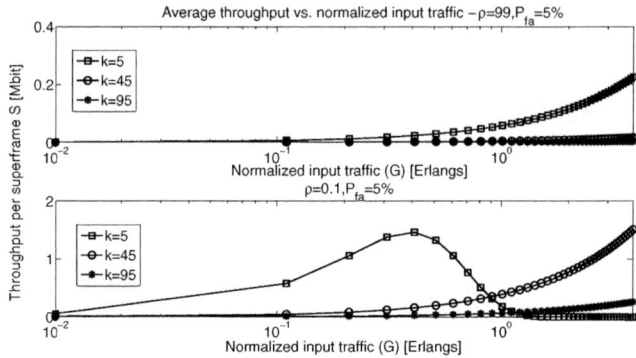

Fig. 7. Average throughput vs. normalized channel input traffic

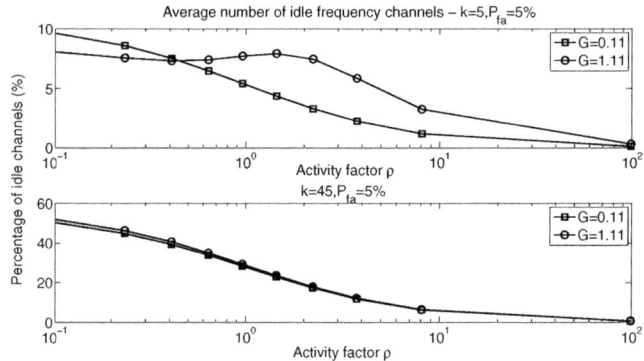

Fig. 8. Average number of channels sensed idle vs. activity factor of the PU

Fig. 6 shows the average convergence time T_c (see Proposition 1) that is required to sense at least once all the frequency channels using the aforementioned random selection scheme. The average observation time lays below 80 superframes ($\sim 10s$). Thus, in case the PU is not highly dynamic, the CRN could be able to estimate the system state by means of observations, without requiring complex inference techniques.

Fig. 7 shows the average throughput computed with (17) versus the normalized input traffic G. As the population size increases, the traffic generated by each device decreases. Since a pair of devices can reserve one frequency channel for exchanging data, for a high value of the activity factor ($\rho = 99$) the throughput of the CR network is low, as many devices do not have opportunity to transmit. Instead, when $\rho = 0.01$, the throughput is higher but for the case $k = 5$ we can observe a bottleneck when approaching channel capacity.

Fig. 8 shows the average number of idle frequency channels computed with (18). As the traffic in the network increases, the knowledge of channels occupation by the devices is improved. However, as the size of the population increases, the contribution of sensing information to the overall knowledge of the the number of idle channels becomes predominant. The figure shows that for small values of the activity factor ρ (i.e., a frequency channel is mainly idle), the CRN is able to retrieve well knowledge of the idle channels by means of sensing.

7   Conclusions

In this paper we have addressed the problem of CR devices that opportunistically exploits unused idle channels to exchange data in TV white spaces. We have considered CR devices able to combine GEO-location and spectrum sensing techniques. We have proposed a MAC protocol based on the Standard ECMA-392 to manage the network in distributed fashion. For our proposed MAC protocol we have defined a proprietary method to gain network membership whereas data are exchanged in FDMA fashion.

We have applied a random selection policy to retrieve information of the frequency channels. Furthermore, we presented an innovative approach to analyze the cognitive network based on the general framework given by the urn occupancy problems. In particular, we have considered a network that does not rely on inference techniques to estimate channels occupation patterns of the PU but relying only on sensing information. Our results show that in scenarios where the PU is not highly dynamic (as it is expected for TV white spaces), CR devices might have the opportunity to acquire sufficient information to exchange useful data.

References

1. Mitola, J.: Cognitive Radio: an integrated agent architecture for software defined radio, PhD Dissertation Royal Institute of Technology KTH, Stockholm, Sweden (2000)
2. Federal Communications Commission, Unlicensed operation in the TV broadcast bands and additional spectrum for unlicensed devices below 900 MHz in the 3 GHz band, Recommendation ET-Docket No. 04-186 (2004)
3. ECMA International, Standard ECMA-92: MAC and PHY for Operation in TV White Space, Standard Cognitive Network Alliance (2009)
4. Wang, J., Myung, S.S., Santhiveeran, S., Lim, K., Ko, G., Kim, K., Hwang, S.H., Ghosh, M., Gaddam, V., Challapali, K.: First Cognitive Radio Networking Standard for Pesonal/Portable Devices in TV White Spaces. In: IEEE DySPAN 2010, Singapore, pp. 1–12 (2010)
5. Cognitive Networking Alliance, http://www.cognea.org
6. Drmota, M., Gardy, D., Gittenberger, B.: A Unified Presentation of Some Urn Models, Algorithmica, San Diego, California, vol. 29, pp. 120–147 (2001)
7. Luo, L., Roy, S.: Analysis of Search Schems in Cognitive Radio, Special Section: Seismic Acquisition, the Leading Edge, San Diego, California, pp. 647–654 (2007)
8. Zhao, Q., Tong, L., Awami, A., Chen, Y.: Decentralized Cognitive MAC for Opportunistic Spectrum Access in Ad Hoc: A POMDP Framework. IEEE Journal on Selected Areas in Communications 25 (2007)

9. Nekovee, M.: Quantifying the Availability of TV White Spaces for Cognitive Radio Operation in the UK. In: 2010 IEEE Symposium on New Frontiers in Dynamic Spectrum, Singapore, pp. 120–147 (2010)
10. Hohlfeld, O., Ciucu, F.: Viewing Impaired Video Transmissions From a Modeling Perspective. ACM SIGMETRICS Performance Evaluation Review 37(2) (September 2009)
11. Poikonen, J., Paavola, J., Ipatov, V.: Aggregated Renewal Markov Processes With Applications in Simulating Mobile Broadcast Systems. IEEE Transactions on Vehicular Technology 58(1) (January 2009)
12. McDougall, J., Miller, S.: Sensitivity of Wireless Network Simulations to a Two-State Markov Model Channel Approximation. In: Global Telecommunications Conference GLOBECOM, vol. 2, pp. 697–701 (2003)

BPS-MAC: Backoff Preamble Based MAC Protocol with Sequential Contention Resolution

Alexander Klein

Network Architectures and Services - Institute for Informatics
Technische Universität München, Germany
klein@net.in.tum.de

Abstract. Contention resolution represents a performance critical task in dense wireless networks since many Medium Access Control (MAC) protocols solely rely on the carrier-sense capabilities of the transceivers. Typical transceivers require a large amount of time to detect a busy radio channel. Especially, in the case that the transceiver has been switched off or has to be switched from receive to transmit mode. It is thus not able to sense the media during the switching phase, which leads to a large number of collisions in dense networks with correlated event-driven traffic load. In this paper the Backoff Preamble Sequential (BPS) MAC protocol is introduced which uses a sequential contention resolution to reduce the number of competing nodes step by step.

Keywords: Random access, wireless, reliable, networks.

1 Introduction

Clear Channel Assessment (CCA) is a logical function that returns the current state of the wireless medium. It is provided by almost any low power transceiver for WSNs in order to support Carrier Sense Multiple Access (CSMA) functionality to the MAC layer. However, the transceivers require a certain amount of time to reliably determine the state of the medium. Moreover, the time that a transceiver requires to switch from receive to transmit mode represents a vulnerable period for protocols that rely on the CSMA functionality since transceivers are not able to detect any transmissions that start during the switching period.

The CCA delay becomes the dominating performance limitation factor [1] for low power transceivers. Transceivers, like the CC2400 and the CC2520 from Texas Instruments or ATMEL´s AT86RF231, have to listen to the medium for a duration of 8 symbol periods to reliably detect an ongoing transmission. They average the Received Signal Strength Indication (RSSI) over the last 8 symbols in order to decide whether the channel is assumed to be busy or idle.

The reliability of CSMA based protocols can be increased if a backoff algorithm is used to smooth the peak traffic load. Backoff algorithms may only reduce the collision probability to some extend since the possibility to reduce the peak utilization strongly depends on the overall traffic load. They have to be configured very carefully to achieve the desired trade-off between reliability

C. Sacchi et al. (Eds.): MACOM 2011, LNCS 6886, pp. 39–50, 2011.

and delay [2]. Event suppression techniques [3,4] could be implemented to reduce the average number of nodes that compete for the medium access. Some MAC protocols, like SIFT [5], need to know the number of competing nodes in advance in order to achieve their maximum performance.

The introduced protocol was originally designed for Structural Health Monitoring applications with periodic and event-driven traffic. The target application had high requirements in terms of reliability under varying traffic load which could not be achieved with standard CSMA based protocols due to high node density, correlated traffic, and limited sensing capabilities of the transceiver. For that reason, we decided to focus on a completely different approach which is based on preamble transmission and sequential backoff resolution mechanism.

This paper is organized as follows. In Section 2, we describe the access mechanism of the BPS-MAC protocol and analyze the collision probability in case of simultaneous medium access of several nodes. Moreover, the performance of the sequential contention resolution depending on the number of sequences and the applied backoff distribution is analyzed. An overview of related work is given in Section 3. Finally, we conclude with our future work in Section 4.

2   BPS-Mac

The BPS-MAC protocol is optimized for reliability in scenarios with a high node density and highly correlated event-driven data traffic. It does not require synchronization or a large amount of memory which makes the protocol most applicable for sensor nodes with low computational power and limited transceiver sensing capabilities. A collision occurs if two or more nodes try to access the medium within a time interval that is shorter than the CCA delay of the used transceiver. Backoff algorithms are only able to reduce the collision probability by spreading the traffic load. Nevertheless, a node can never know whether another node is starting its transmission due to the fact that it cannot listen to the air interface while switching from rx to tx mode.

The introduced protocol follows a new approach in order to deal with the problem of CCA delay and the rx/tx switching. The basic idea of the protocol is to send a backoff preamble with variable length before transmitting the data. The length of the preamble has to be a multiple of the CCA delay to maximize the reliability of the protocol. The protocol uses a slotted contention resolution since the backoff preamble is a multiple of the CCA delay. In the case that two nodes send a preamble with different length, the node with the shorter preamble is able to detect the occupation of the medium by the other node.

2.1   Protocol Description

First, a closer look is taken on the contention resolution as used by the standard BP-MAC protocol [6]. In the following, the term slot is used instead of CCA delay duration since it is more related to the context of contention resolution. Moreover, the term collision probability represents the probability that two or more nodes start their data transmission simultaneously after backoff transmission which represents an unsuccessful contention resolution. A node senses the medium for duration of three backoff slots if it wants to transmit a packet. The transceiver is switched from rx to tx in the case that the medium is free for three consecutive slots in order to transmit the backoff preamble. The duration of the preamble is chosen according to a uniform distribution between two and a maximum backoff window. The preamble covers the function of a reservation signal. Thus, a longer preamble increases the probability of gaining access to the medium.

The node senses the medium after the transmission of the preamble. If the medium is busy after the transmission, the node waits between two and maximum backoff window number of slots until it restarts the access procedure described above. Otherwise, the node is allowed to access the medium. Thus, it switches its transceiver from rx to tx mode which takes duration of one backoff slot. As a consequence, the medium is idle for duration of two slots after the transmission of a backoff preamble. For that reason, a node senses the medium for the duration of three slots in order to be sure that there is no ongoing contention resolution.

In [6] it was shown that the average number of transmissions which are part of a collision in a single backoff preamble sequence is given by the fraction of n and m where n is the duration of the preamble in number of slots while m corresponds to the number of nodes that start their preamble transmission simultaneously. This fact encouraged us to think about a new sequential backoff resolution called BPS-MAC which is described and analyzed in the following paragraphs of this section. Short consecutive backoff preambles are able to reduce the number of competing nodes step by step. Therefore, just a small number of nodes will compete in the last backoff preamble sequence for the medium access. The proposed sequential contention resolution procedure is shown in Figure 1.

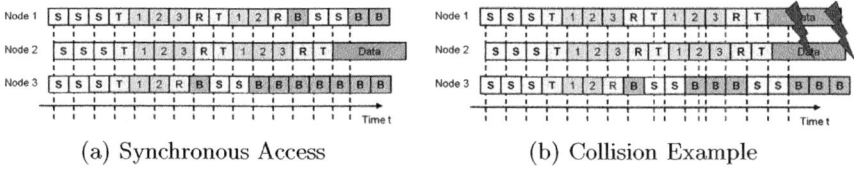

(a) Synchronous Access   (b) Collision Example

Fig. 1. Sequential Contention Resolution

Competing nodes switch their transceivers to rx after the transmission of the first backoff preamble. If they sense a busy channel, the nodes abort their current medium access process and wait between zero and EBW slots before sensing the medium again. In the case of an idle channel, the nodes switch their transceivers back to tx and transmit the next backoff preamble. Thus, collisions may only occur if two or more nodes start their medium access procedure within one CCA delay interval and choose the same number of backoff slots in every backoff sequence. The maximum duration of each backoff preamble sequence and the number of sequences defines the maximum medium access delay for a single contention resolution.

Let y be the medium access delay in number of backoff slots and s the number of sequences. The EBW of sequence i is denoted as n_i. Furthermore, it is assumed that a node has to sense the medium for three slots before it switches its transceiver to tx mode - which requires an additional duration of one slot - in order to start the preamble transmission. The maximum access delay can be calculated according to Equation 1 provided that the gap between two consecutive backoff preambles is two slots.

$$y \leq 4 + \sum_{i=1}^{s} n_i + 2s \tag{1}$$

The minimum medium access delay is achieved if a node chooses the first backoff slot in every backoff sequence while no other node is competing for the medium access. Therefore, the lower bound of the access delay is given by Equation 2.

$$y \geq 4 + 3s \tag{2}$$

Many applications for WSNs need guarantees in respect to maximum medium access delay since the generated data is often mission critical. In the following it is assumed that a certain number of nodes have to transmit a small amount of data if they recognize an event. Thus, the maximum allowed medium access delay in number of backoff slots can be calculated if the amount of data per node, the transmission rate, and the maximum number of nodes that respond to an event are known in advance. The BPS-MAC protocol can be easily optimized for a particular application in the case that the maximum allowed medium access delay is known. First, the boundaries of the number of backoff sequences have to be specified according to the maximum allowed delay. The boundaries of the number of backoff sequences can be calculated according to Equation 3 provided that the smallest allowed value of the EBW is two slots.

$$1 \leq s \leq \frac{y}{4} - 1, s \in N \tag{3}$$

The next question that has to be answered is that of defining the length n_i of each individual backoff sequence. The length of the individual backoff sequences n_i has to be chosen such that $\prod_{i=1}^{s} n_i$ is maximized since the average number of collisions per backoff sequence is given by the fraction of competing nodes m and the length of the backoff sequence n_i. Therefore, the duration of each backoff sequence should be selected as short as possible to maximize the product. The highest probability of a successful contention resolution is achieved if n is a multiple of four. Due to the gaps between two consecutive backoff sequences, a length of four slots represents the best trade-off between overhead and success probability. In the following it is assumed that n is always a multiple of four.

Figure 2 shows the probability of successful contention resolution depending on the number of competing nodes and the number of backoff sequences. The results shown in Figure 2 are very promising, especially in the case that

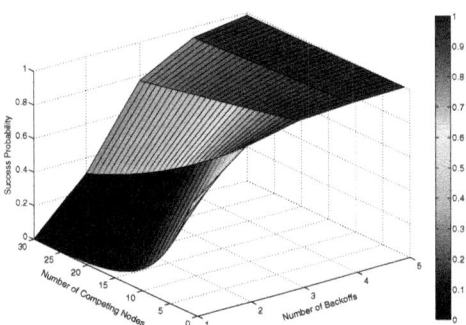

Fig. 2. Uniform Distribution - Probability of Successful Contention Resolution depending on the Number of Competing Nodes

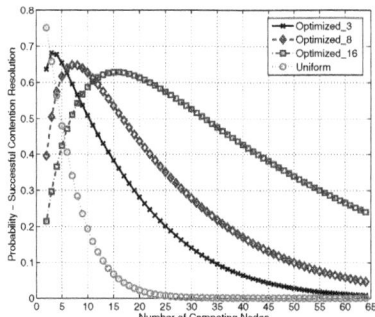

Fig. 3. Probability of Successful Contention Resolution for a four Slot Backoff Procedure depending on the Number of Competing Nodes

three or more backoff sequences are available. However, in some cases it is only possible to use up to two sequences in order to maintain within given medium access delay boundaries. A solution for this problem is given by Tay et al. [10] which evaluated the performance of non-uniform distributions for slotted contention resolution. They introduced an algorithm which calculates the optimum distribution for a given number of backoff slots provided that the number of competing nodes is known in advance. Their optimized solution only achieves a high success probability if the number of competitors does not differ much from the assumed number of competitors. Thus, they recommend using a truncated geometric distribution which performs similar to the optimized distribution but is less affected by the number of competitors. Figure 3 shows the probability of successful contention resolution for a single backoff sequence with maximum backoff duration of four slots depending on the used distribution from Table 1 and the number of competitors. The results of Figure 3 point out that the uniform distribution represents the best choice if only two nodes compete for the medium access. Nonetheless, the probability of successful contention resolution decreases rapidly with the increasing number of competitors. Therefore, the

Table 1. Distributions - Backoff Slot Selection

Distribution / Probability	Slot 1	Slot 2	Slot 3	Slot4
Optimimized_3	0.534	0.217	0.148	0.101
Optimimized_8	0.766	0.086	0.078	0.070
Optimimized_16	0.884	0.040	0.039	0.037
Uniform	0.250	0.250	0.250	0.250

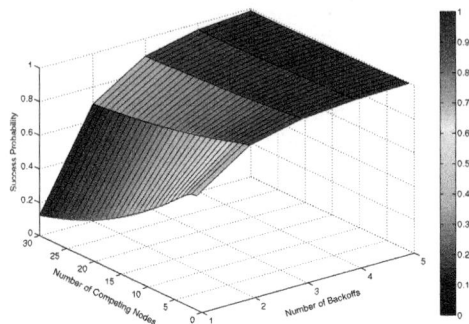

Fig. 4. Optimized_3 - Probability of Successful Contention Resolution depending on the Number of Competing Nodes and the Number of Backoff Sequences

uniform distribution is not the first choice for networks with high node density and correlated traffic. The truncated geometric distribution can be optimized for a fix number of competitors. However, the optimization of the distribution for more than three nodes is not really practical since the performance degrades significantly if the number of competing nodes is overestimated. This behavior becomes clear by taking a look at the different distributions shown in Table 1.

The optimized distributions achieve a high success probability of the contention resolution due to their skewness. As a consequence of the skewness, the majority of the competing nodes choose one of the first slots while the minority of the nodes competes in the rest of the available slots. This explains the high success probability of the optimized distributions even in the case that the number of competitors is under estimated. Nevertheless, the skewness reduces the success probability if the number of nodes is smaller than the number for which the distribution is optimized. It has to be kept in mind that the number of competing nodes always decreases from a maximum - which depends on the node density and the traffic pattern - to one. For that reason, an optimized distribution for three competing nodes represents the best choice for most scenarios. An underestimation of the number of competitors only has a small impact on the packet loss in contrast to an overestimation which increases the collision probability in a significant way. The success probability of the Optimized_3 distribution for an EBW of four depending on the number of competing nodes and the number of backoff sequences is shown in Figure 4. The results of Figure 4 point out that the success probability for the Optimized_3 distribution for the first two backoff

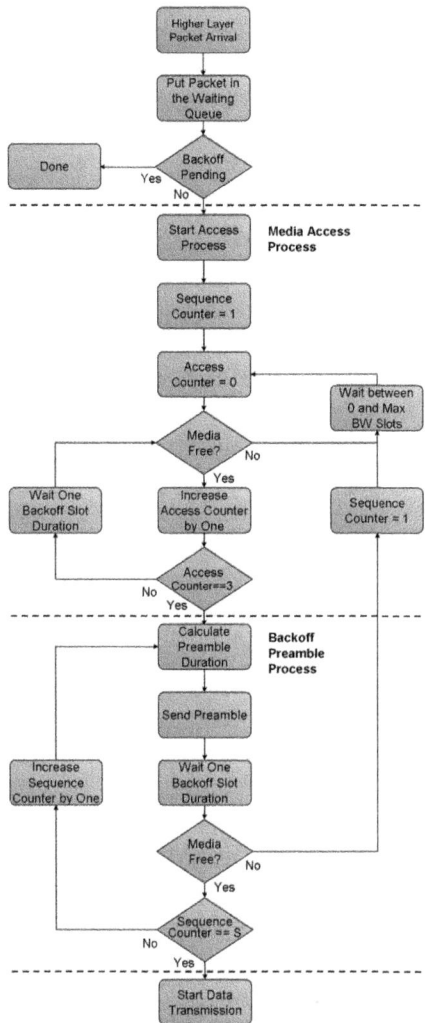

Fig. 5. Flow Diagram of the Medium Access Process of the BPS-MAC Protocol

sequences is much higher compared to the uniform distribution shown in Figure 2. However, the difference becomes smaller with an increasing number of backoff sequences. The uniform distribution even represents a slightly better solution if the number of sequences exceeds four and the number of competing nodes is less than 32. This behavior is the consequence of the stepwise reduction of the number of competing nodes. The probability that only two nodes compete in a single backoff sequence increases with an increasing number of backoff sequences. Due to the fact that the uniform distribution is the optimum distribution for the case of two competing nodes, its performance increases more with the number of backoff sequences than the performance of the Optimized_3 distribution.

2.2   Medium Access Process

In the following the medium access process of the BPS-MAC protocol shown in Figure 5 is described in detail. Higher layer packets are put into the waiting queue if a backoff is already pending. In the case that no backoff is pending the medium access process is started. The protocol initializes a sequence counter and an access counter. The access counter is used to count the number of free consecutive backoff preamble slots while the sequence counter represents the number of transmitted backoff preambles. Furthermore, the access counter starts with an initial value of zero in contrast to the sequence counter which starts with an initial value of one. After the initialization of the counters is completed, the protocol switches the transceiver to receive mode and starts to sense the medium. If the medium is busy, the node waits between zero and EBW slots before the medium is sensed again. In addition, the access counter is set back to zero. The transceiver might be switched off during the waiting period depending on the energy constraints of the node. The access counter is increased by one if the medium is idle and checks whether the counter is equal to three which indicates that the medium has been idle for duration of three consecutive backoff slots. If the value of the access counter is smaller than three the protocol waits one backoff slot until it follows the procedure described above. The protocol calculates the preamble duration depending on the sequence counter and starts to send the backoff preamble after the medium has been idle for duration of three backoff slots. This mechanism allows the modification of each backoff sequence e.g. a different EBW size or a different backoff distribution. Then it switches the transceiver back to receive mode which requires the duration of one backoff slot. If the node senses a busy channel after the preamble transmission, it resets the access and the sequence counter and waits between 0 and EBW slots before it senses the medium again in order to restart the access process. In the case that the medium is idle after the backoff transmission, the node checks whether the sequence counter has reached the maximum number of backoff sequences S. If the value is smaller than S, the counter is increased by one and the preamble process is started again. The node is allowed to start its data transmission if the medium is idle after the transmission of S backoff preambles.

2.3   Performance Analysis

A closer look is taken on the average number of collisions per backoff. Note, a distribution may achieve a higher success probability than another distribution but it may have a higher packet loss if the average number of nodes that are part of a collision is higher. Thus, the question is, how many nodes are part of a collision in case of an unsuccessful contention resolution depending on the backoff distribution and the number of backoff sequences.

Let c_0 be the number of nodes that compete for the medium access in the first backoff preamble sequence and c_i the number of nodes that collide in the ith sequence. Moreover, n_i represents the number of backoff slots in the ith backoff sequence while s represents the number of backoff sequences. The function $p(var_1, var_2, var3)$ is an extension of probability mass function introduced in [6] whereas the parameters n, m, and c are freely configurable. Variable var_1 corresponds to the maximum number of backoff slots n while variable var_2 represents the number of competing nodes m. The number of nodes c that are part of a collision is indicated by var_3. Thus, the average number of nodes that are part of a collision after s backoff sequences can be calculated according to Equation 4 by using Equation 1.

$$E[C,1] = \sum_{c_1=2}^{c_0} c_1 p(n_1, c_0, c_1)$$

$$E[C,2] = \sum_{c_1=2}^{c_0} \sum_{c_2=2}^{c_1} c_2 p(n_1, c_0, c_1) p(n_2, c_1, c_2)$$

$$\vdots \qquad \vdots \qquad \qquad \vdots$$

$$E[C,s] = \sum_{c_1=2}^{c_0} \cdots \sum_{c_s=2}^{c_{s-1}} c_s p(n_1, c_0, c_1) \cdots p(n_s, c_{s-1}, c_s)$$

$$(4)$$

Figure 6 shows the average number of collisions per backoff for the optimized distributions for three and eight competing nodes as well as for the uniform distribution. The Opt3_Uniform graphs represent the results of a hybrid approach where the Optimized_3 distribution from Table 1 is used in the first backoff sequence while the uniform distribution is used in the consecutive sequences.

The first thing that can be mentioned for the results of the single backoff sequence shown in Figure 6(a) is that the average number of collisions per backoff increases linearly with the number of competing nodes for the uniform distribution. The uniform distribution only offers the best performance for two competing nodes while the Optimized_3 distribution represents the best solution for three to 10 competing nodes. If the number of competing nodes exceeds 10 the Optimized_8 distribution shows a better performance. It is interesting to notice that the Optimized_8 distribution does not achieve the lowest packet loss for eight competing nodes though its success probability is optimal for 8 competing nodes. The answer is given by the Optimized_8 distribution function. Due to the high probability of the first slot there is a noticeable probability that all nodes choose the first backoff slot in one sequence. Therefore, the average number of collisions increases in a significant way. Figure 6(b) shows that the average number of collisions can be approximately quartered if the BPS-MAC protocol uses two consecutive backoff preambles to resolve the contention. This affect can be recognized for the uniform, Optimized_3 and Opt3_Uniform distributions. The performance of the Optimized_8 distribution does not represent a good solution for scenarios with less than 32 competing nodes. As a consequence of its heavy-tailed characteristic, the probability is high that less than 8 nodes compete for the medium access in the second backoff preamble sequence. Thus, there is a high chance that the remaining competitors collide in one of the first slots in the second backoff sequence.

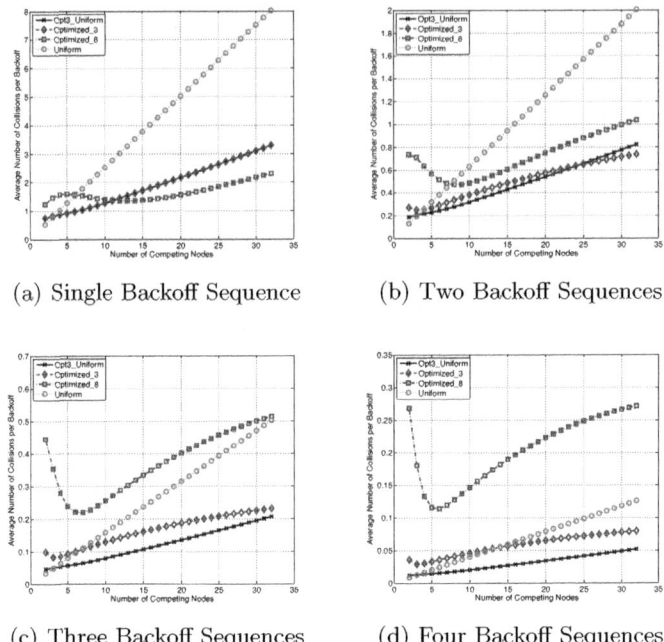

(a) Single Backoff Sequence   (b) Two Backoff Sequences

(c) Three Backoff Sequences   (d) Four Backoff Sequences

Fig. 6. Average Number of Nodes that are Part of a Collision

If the BPS-MAC protocol uses three consecutive backoff preamble sequences the performance of the Optimized_8 distribution degrades even more which is shown by the results of Figure 6(c). The highest reliability for scenarios with more than three competitors is achieved by the Opt3_Uniform approach. The Optimized_3 distribution reduces the number of competing nodes in the first sequence such that uniform distribution becomes the best choice for the consecutive backoff sequences. The Opt3_Uniform approach should be used for these scenarios since it offers the highest reliability which is indicated by the results of Figure 6(d).

3   Related Work

A large number of different types of MAC protocols for WSNs were introduced in the past few years. Most of them are optimized in respect to energy consumption [14], delay or throughput. However, the majority of these MAC protocols requires synchronization and are too complex to be practical for WSNs. The performance evaluation of the protocols often neglect or simplify many issues of wireless communication. The assumptions that are made, e.g. bi-directional links or circular transmission area, may have a large impact on the results as shown in Kotz et al. [7] and Langendoen [8]. Moreover, technical aspects, like the CCA delay of low power transceivers, are usually disregarded. The problem of

CCA delay is only addressed by a small number of papers since standard models from network simulators, e.g. ns-2 or OPNET, simply assume a transceiver that does not need any time to sense the radio channel or to switch between rx and tx mode. The impact of CCA delay on IEEE 802.15.4 networks is described by Kiryushin et al. [1]. The focus of their work lies on real world performance of WSNs and describes the impact of different kinds of communication aspects. Bertocco et al. [9] have shown that the performance of a wireless network can be improved by minimizing the CCA threshold. Nevertheless, the minimization of the threshold requires great knowledge of the radio channel since a too small threshold will result in false positives. Another very interesting approach is followed by Tay et al. [10] which use optimized distributions to select the number of backoff slots in order to reduce the collision probability. The same research group introduced the SIFT [5] MAC protocol which uses non-uniform backoff distribution and achieves a very high performance provided that the number of competing nodes is known in advance. A small number of MAC protocols make use of preamble transmissions in order to wake up neighbor nodes [11] or to reserve the radio channel [12,13,14]. However, their contention resolution is based on standard CSMA mechanisms. Thus, their performance is affected by the CCA capability of the wireless transceiver which limits their performance in dense networks with event-driven traffic.

4 Conclusion

In this work we introduced the BPS-MAC protocol which uses a new sequential backoff preamble mechanism to minimize the number of competing nodes step by step. It is able to deal with a very high number of competing nodes due to the stepwise contention resolution. Its medium access procedure is independent from the CCA delay of the transceiver and can thus be applied on any platform.

Furthermore, the protocol will take more advantage out of next generation transceivers compared to CSMA based protocols since its performance in terms of medium access delay is directly affected by the duration of CCA delay. We are currently working on different Quality of Service (QoS) mechanisms in order to make the protocol attractive for heterogeneous networks and for those which require priority based medium access.

References

1. Kiryushin, A., Sadkov, A., Mainwaring, A.: Real World Performance of Clear Channel Assessment in 802.15.4 Wireless Sensor Networks. In: Proc. Second International Conference on Sensor Technologies and Applications SENSORCOMM 2008, pp. 625–630 (August 2008)
2. Vinel, A., Zhang, Y., Lott, M., Turlikov, A.: Performance Analysis of the Random Access in IEEE 802.16. In: Proc. of the 16th Annual IEEE International Symposium on Personal, Indoor and Mobile Radio Communications, IEEE PIMRC 2005, pp. 1596–1600 (2005)

3. Silberstein, A., Braynard, R., Yang, J.: Constraint Chaining: On Energy-efficient continuous Monitoring in Sensor Networks. In: Proc. of the ACM SIGMOD 2006, pp. 157–168 (2006)
4. Meng, X., Li, L., Nandagopal, T., Lu, S.: An Effivient and Robust Mechanism for Tasks in Sensor Networks, Technical Report TR-040018, UCLA (2004)
5. Jamieson, K., Balakrishnan, H., Tay, Y.C.: Sift: A MAC protocol for event-driven wireless sensor networks. In: Römer, K., Karl, H., Mattern, F. (eds.) EWSN 2006. LNCS, vol. 3868, pp. 260–275. Springer, Heidelberg (2006)
6. Klein, A., Klaue, J., Schalk, J.: BP-MAC: A high Reliable Backoff Preamble MAC Protocol for Wireless Sensor Networks. Electronic Journal of Structural Engineering(EJSE): Special Issue of Sensor Networks for Building Monitoring: From Theory to Real Application, 35–45 (December 2009)
7. Kotz, D., Newport, C., Gray, R.S., Liu, J., Yuan, Y., Elliott, C.: Experimental Evaluation of Wireless Simulation Assumptions. In: Proc. of the 7th ACM International Symposium on Modeling, Analysis and Simulation of Wireless and Mobile Systems, pp. 78–82 (2004)
8. Muneb, A., Saif, U., Dunkels, A., Voigt, T., Römer, K., Langendoen, K., Polastre, J., Uzmi, Z.A.: Medium Access Control Issues in Sensor Networks. SIGCOMM Comput. Commun. Rev. 36(2), 33–36 (2006)
9. Bertocco, M., Gamba, G., Sona, A.: Experimental Optimization of CCA Thresholds in Wireles Sensor Networks in Presence of Interference. In: Proc. of IEEE EMC Europe 2007 Workshop on Electromagnetic Compatibility (June 2007)
10. Tay, Y.C., Jamieson, K., Balakrishnan, H.: Collision-minimizing CSMA and its Applications to Wireless Sensor Networks. IEEE Journal on Selected Areas in Communications 22(6), 1048–1057 (2004)
11. El-Hoiydi, A.: Aloha with Preamble Sampling for Sporadic Traffic in Ad Hoc Wireless Sensor Networks. In: Proc. IEEE International Conference on Communications (ICC), pp. 3418–3423 (May 2002)
12. Firoze, A.M., Ju, L.Y., Kwong, L.M.: PR-MAC A Priority Reservation MAC Protocol For Wireless Sensor Networks. In: Proc. Int. Conf. Electrical Engineering ICEE 2007, pp. 1–6 (2007)
13. Cano, C., Bellalta, B., Sfairopoulou, A., Barcelo, J.: A low Power Listening MAC with Scheduled Wake up after Transmissions for WSNs. IEEE Communication Letters 13(3), 221–223 (2009)
14. El-Hoiydi, A., Decotignie, J.D.: WiseMAC: An Ultra Low Power MAC Protocol for the Downlink of Infrastructure Wireless Sensor Networks. In: Proc. of Ninth International Symposium on Computers and Communications (ISCC), pp. 244–251 (June 2004)

Collision-Free Operation in Wireless Ad-Hoc Networks

Jaume Barcelo[1], Boris Bellalta[2], Miquel Oliver[2], and Albert Banchs[1]

[1] Universidad Carlos III de Madrid,
Av. de la Universidad, 30, 28911 Leganés, Madrid, Spain
{jbarcelo,banchs}@it.uc3m.es
[2] Universitat Pompeu Fabra,
C. de Tànger 122-140, 08018, Barcelona, Catalunya, Spain
{boris.bellalta,miquel.oliver}@upf.edu

Abstract. In some wireless ad-hoc networks it is not possible to rely on carrier-sense mechanisms to prevent collisions. In this article we suggest a MAC protocol that reaches collision-free operation in sparse ad-hoc wireless networks when all the stations are saturated. The basic idea is to use a random backoff after failed transmissions and a deterministic backoff after successful transmissions. Each of the participating stations can configure its own backoff parameter after collecting information from its neighborhood. Then the system enters in a transient state until collision-free operation is reached. We assess the duration of the transient state and other performance metrics for an example scenario and finally we discuss two options to incorporate reception acknowledgements.

Keywords: Medium access control, wireless ad-hoc networks, collision-free operation.

1 Introduction and Motivation

Wireless local area networks (WLANs) can be found in homes, campuses, public buildings and enterprises. They are a convenient broadband last-hop alternative, specially for portable and mobile devices. Most of current deployments consist of one or several wireless access points that are connected to a wired network.

Nevertheless, there is substantial interest in extending the coverage of such wireless networks by means of multi-hop wireless links. As an example, multi-hop networks can be used to provide coverage on the streets. The manufacturers offer sturdy outdoor access points that can be placed on lampposts. Light poles have power supply but no network connection, and therefore the access points have to create a mesh network to provide a connection to the Internet.

Another example of the use of multi-hop wireless networks are grassroots community networks. Some of these networks support thousands of users and consist of thousands of mesh in a geographical area spanning several hundreds of kilometers. This alternative is particularly attractive in rural areas where broadband is expensive or non-existent [1].

C. Sacchi et al. (Eds.): MACOM 2011, LNCS 6886, pp. 51–62, 2011.

Most of the currently deployed mesh networks, which belong to the broad family of ad-hoc networks, use WiFi hardware due to its availability and affordability. As a result, WLAN protocols are also used in mesh networks. The promise of highly-configurable WiFi firmware [2] and the possibility to develop tailored medium access control (MAC) protocols for different kinds of networks motivates us to explore a simple MAC protocol that is appropriate for ad-hoc networks.

In this article we study some of the characteristics of ad-hoc networks that make them intrinsically different from WLANs. In particular, in section 2 we describe three specific problems that arise in ad-hoc networks. These issues warrant the study of new protocols which are tailored to the distinctive properties of ad-hoc networks. In section 2, we also briefly mention work that is closely related and relevant for the subsequent discussion, and we define the scope and the goal of our work. We are interested in a distributed protocol that can achieve collision-free operation in ad-hoc networks, without requiring network-wide synchronization.

The protocol itself is described in section 3 and relies on a very simple idea: the use of a deterministic backoff after successful transmissions and a random backoff after failures. In commonly encountered topologies, this approach guarantees that collision-free operation can be reached in a finite time and the network converges to a periodic, deterministic collision-free schedule.

Then, we propose a distributed approach that allows each node to configure its own contention parameter in section 4. In section 5, we use a simple example scenario to explain that there is a trade-off that involves the duration of the transient state and the efficiency that it is obtained in the steady state. Section 6 is devoted to a protocol comparison that includes different performance metrics. Two different options to accommodate the acknowledgements of correct receptions are outlined in 7 and finally some conclusions remarks are offered in 8.

2   Open Challenges and Related Work

When contention protocols are used in wireless communications, collisions can occur. Different wireless terminals might simultaneously access the channel and the receivers may have difficulties decoding the packets when different transmissions overlap in time. It is not unlikely that one or more of those packets that overlap in time are lost.

In the design and study of MAC protocols for WLANs, it is common to assume that all the different stations are in each other's transmission range. This is a fair assumption since WLANs are often confined to a limited area. Under this assumption, the contending stations can rely on carrier-sense mechanisms to avoid collisions. If the participating stations transmit only when the channel is sensed idle, the likelihood of collisions is greatly reduced. In general, the availability of carrier-sense information allows for high channel efficiency in the case of carrier sense multiple access with collision avoidance (CSMA/CA).

Unfortunately, the assumption that all the stations can hear all the transmissions is no longer valid in multi-hop wireless networks. The reason that we need multi-hop is, very often, the fact that there are at least two stations that do not hear each other and therefore they need the help of the other stations to relay the messages in a multi-hop fashion. Even for those stations that can hear each other, carrier sense may fail due to long propagation times. This is the case of long radio-links typically used in rural community wireless networks, that can easily be in the order of tens of kilometers with the help of directive antennas.

Unsurprisingly, the absence of carrier-sense information breaks the operation of CSMA/CA. We will provide three examples of the undesirable effects of using a CSMA/CA protocol as the one included in the IEEE 802.11 [3] suite of standards.

1. Hidden terminal effect: This term describes the interference caused by the simultaneous transmission of nodes that cannot carrier sense each other as shown in Fig. 1.(a). More details on the hidden terminal effect and its negative interaction with the upper layers of the protocol stack in a real mesh network deployment can be found in [4].
2. Exposed terminal effect: as illustrated in 1.(b), two senders B and C want to transmit to two receivers A and D respectively. B and C are in each other's transmission range, but their transmissions do not interfere because A is much closer to B than it is to C and, similarly, B and D are far away. In this situation the simultaneous transmission of B and C would not result in a collision. Still, the carrier-sense mechanism prevents the simultaneous transmission of B and C.
3. Fig. 1.(c) shows two stations, E and F that are far away. Still, they can communicate thanks to the use of directional antennas. Even though they are in each other's transmission range, the propagation delay interferes with the carrier-sense mechanism. The propagation delay introduces a vulnerability interval in which one of the stations is transmitting while the other senses the channel idle. More details on the impact of large propagation delay on the performance of IEEE 802.11 can be found in [5].

As a consequence of the above described effects, it is apparent that a carrier-sense medium access control is not appropriate when carrier-sense information is not available or reliable. For this reason, many mesh network deployments have resorted to multi-channel solutions. When budget and spectrum availability is not a concern, the first two of the aforementioned problems (hidden and exposed terminal) can be trivially solved by assigning a different channel to each radio-link. The third problem may still increase the probability of collision, but it is a minor issue if the distance is not too long.

Assigning different channels to different links requires that each station is equipped with multiple radios, which increase the price of the device. In this paper we will study the (challenging) case in which, due to either budgetary or spectrum constraints, each of the stations is equipped with a single radio, and the three problems of multi-hop wireless communications (hidden, exposed and distant terminal) need to be addressed at the MAC layer.

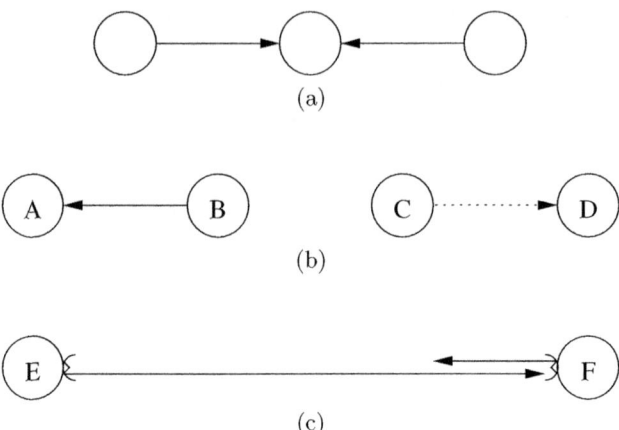

Fig. 1. Problems arising when using CSMA in ad-hoc and long-distance wireless networks. (a) the hidden terminal effect. (b) the exposed terminal effect. (c) the distant terminal effect.

2.1   Related Work

A survey on modeling and performance analysis of multihop packet radio networks is presented in [6]. A theoretical advance was presented in [7] where it was shown that it was possible to analyze the problem of offering proportional fairness in ad-hoc Aloha networks using local information. Under certain assumptions, the transmission rate of each station can be computed by knowing some information about the neighbors and the two-hop neighbors. This approach is valid for both slotted Aloha and pure Aloha networks. In slotted Aloha, it is required that all the stations synchronize to the beginning of the slots.

The possibility of collision-free operation has been studied in, e.g., [8,9,10,11]. All these references assume that the network time is slotted, and some of them refer to those protocols that can potentially learn a collision-free schedule as learning protocols. In the present work we present two protocols that can learn a collision-free schedule even in the absence of slot synchronization. The first one, l-Aloha, assumes previous knowledge of the topology and communication graph. In the second one, scl-Aloha, the nodes can self-configure using information collected from their neighborhood.

3   L-Aloha: Deterministic Backoff After Successes in Ad-Hoc Networks

In this section we will propose a protocol that can achieve collision-free operation in ad-hoc networks where carrier-sense information is incomplete or unavailable. For the sake of tractability, we will rely on several simplifications:

- We will ignore the complexities of radio propagation and assume a graph-based interference model. I.e., two nodes perfectly hear each other or they do not hear each other at all (ideal channel).

- There is no capture effect. It is not possible to decode overlapping packets.
- The stations are saturated, which means that they always have a packet ready to be transmitted.
- The duration of a transmission is fixed and normalized to one. The protocol that we are suggesting in this paper can also be extended to work in networks where the packet length is variable and upper-bounded.
- Initially, acknowledgement packets will not be explicitly considered. This discussion is postponed to section 7.

Since we use a graph-based interference model, we can represent the topology of the network as an undirected graph $G = (S, L)$ where S represents the set of stations and L is the set of links. If a link exists between two stations s_i and s_j in S, then these two stations can communicate with each other and also interfere with each other. We define the set of neighbors K_i of a station s_i as those stations that have a link connecting to s_i, i.e. $K_i = \{s_j : (s_i, s_j) \in L\}$.

The fact that two stations are in each other's transmission range does not necessarily mean that they are exchanging data. We will say that there is a data *flow* between a station s_i and a station s_j when s_i is transmitting data to s_j. This is a directed edge (s_i, s_j) between the two stations and we call the set of all flows F.

We will use the simple topology presented in Fig. 2 for exemplifying purposes. In this topology we have three different stations $(S = \{s_1, s_2, s_3\})$, two links $(L = \{l_1, l_2\}; l_1 = (s_1, s_2); l_2 = (s_2, s_3))$ and three flows $(F = \{f_1, f_2, f_3\}; f_1 = (s_1, s_2); f_2 = (s_2, s_1); f_3 = (s_3, s_2))$.

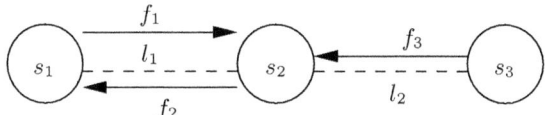

Fig. 2. Topology of a simple ad-hoc network

From the topology description in Fig. 2 we can derive the interference graph in Fig. 3. This is a directed graph where and edge from f_2 to f_3 means that a transmission of f_3 will be lost if it overlaps in time with a transmission from f_2. In contrast, the transmission in f_2 is unaffected by the transmission of f_3.

In this example, the interference graph is strongly connected. This means that the graph contains a directed path from f_i to f_j and a directed path from f_j to f_i for any pair of vertices f_i and f_j.

For given set of flows, a schedule σ defines which of the flows are active at any given time. The period of the schedule is T_σ and we are interested in a collision-free schedule that satisfies the following conditions:

- When a node is active, the destination node must be silent, i.e. s_k must be silent when flow $f_i = (s_j, s_k)$ is active.

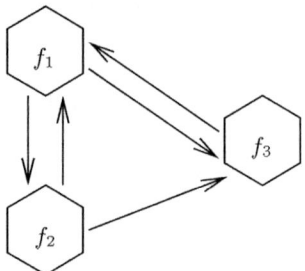

Fig. 3. Interference graph of a simple ad-hoc network

– The neighbors of the destination node must also be silent for the duration of the transmission. I.e, when $f_i = (s_j, s_k)$ is active, all nodes belonging to K_k must remain silent.

For any given topology, it exists a minimum schedule period which we call T_σ^{min} that can accommodate a collision-free schedule. In our particular example in Fig. 3, $T_\sigma^{min} = 3$ because there are three flows and the simultaneous transmission of any two flows would result in collision. We suggest a distributed protocol that satisfies that, for any topology with a strongly connected interference graph, and a given schedule duration T_σ which is strictly greater than T_σ^{min}, a collision-free schedule is reached in a finite time. We will use a value $T_\sigma = T_\sigma^{min}(1 + \epsilon)$ where ϵ is a positive real value arbitrarily close to one.

The idea is to use a random backoff after failed transmissions and a deterministic backoff after successful transmissions. The random backoff is exponentially distributed with parameter $\lambda = (T_\sigma)^{-1}$. The random backoff starts to count at the end of the unsuccessful transmission. The deterministic backoff after successes is equal to T_σ, with the particularity that in this case the backoff time starts to count at the beginning of the successful transmission. In other words, T_σ is the time elapsing from the beginning of a successful transmission to the beginning of the next transmission attempt. The goal is that, in the collision-free mode of the operation, the behavior of each station is periodic with period equal to T_σ.

This is a key difference from our previous work in slotted networks and therefore deserves some additional explanation. Since the network that we are considering in the present paper is not slotted, the backoff period (and the length of the schedule) is continuous and has to be expressed in units of time, not in slots. Moreover, the time elapsing between a successful transmission and the next transmission has to be independent of the packet length. This is an important property that makes it possible to extend our approach to networks in which the packet length is variable.

We will use Fig. 4 for exemplifying purposes. It represents two stations that run our proposed protocol and the rounded shapes are the stations' transmissions. The two stations collide in their first transmission attempt and therefore compute an exponentially distributed backoff that is measured from the end of

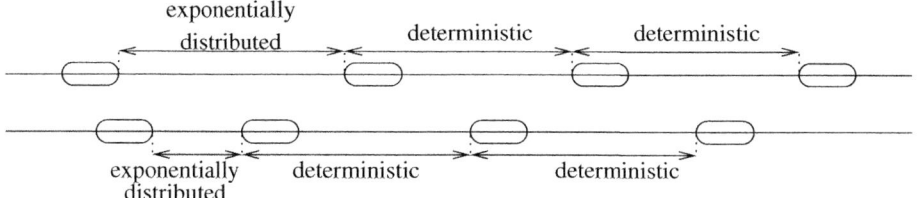

Fig. 4. A deterministic backoff is used after successful transmissions and a random backoff is used after collisions

a transmission to the beginning of the next transmission. The two stations successfully transmit in their next transmission attempt, and consequently choose a deterministic backoff value that starts at the beginning of the successful transmission. At this point the behaviour of the system is completely deterministic. Note that in the hypothetical case that one of the stations transmitted a shorter packet after reaching collision-free operation, the duration of the packet transmission would not affect the global schedule.

In a topology with a strictly connected interference graph, any station that is not settled in a collision-free schedule can trigger a chain of collisions that can potentially reach all the other stations. All the stations that suffer a collision will choose their backoff at random and there is a finite possibility that they choose a global collision-free schedule.

4   Scl-Aloha: Distributed Self-configuration

An attractive property of the solution presented in [7] is the possibility of distributed self-configuration. In that reference, the transmission rate of each Aloha station can be computed using locally gathered information. The idea is that each station broadcasts some *hello* messages containing information about the number of incoming and outgoing flows. Each node collects the *hello* messages from its neighbors and uses this information to decide its own transmission rate. The advantage is that a node does not need to know the whole network topology in order to self-configure.

In this section we suggest a similar self-configuration approach that will make it possible to reach collision-free operation using the information provided by neighboring nodes. We use the name scl-Aloha to refer to this self-configuring learning Aloha. Each node i gathers information about its number of incoming flows $|I_i|$ and outgoing flows $|O_i|$ and distributes this information to its immediate neighbors using broadcast *hello* messages. Therefore, each station knows the number of incoming flows of each of its neighbors and also its number of incoming flows. At, this point, each station s_i computes the duration of its schedule as:

$$T_{\sigma_i} = 2^{\left\lceil \log_2\left(\sum_{k \in K_i} |I_k| + |O_k|\right)\right\rceil}(1 + \epsilon), \tag{1}$$

which is the smallest power of two that it is larger than the sum of all flows in the one-hop neighborhood multiplied by a number which is slightly larger than one.

The $\lceil \cdot \rceil$ operator is the ceiling operator. And the value of ϵ has to be common for all the stations of the network.

With this approach, it is possible that different nodes obtain a different schedule length. The global schedule T_σ is the largest of all T_{σ_i}. Those stations that use a schedule which is an integer fraction of the global schedule, will transmit multiple times in each global schedule.

The performance of scl-Aloha is compared to l-ahola in Table 1 in section 6. Since the global schedule is restricted to be a power of two multiple of $(1+\epsilon)$, the length of the schedule that we obtain with scl-Aloha is longer than in l-Aloha (for a fixed value of ϵ). Therefore, the performance metrics that are achieved by scl-Aloha in the steady state are not as good as the ones that can be attained with l-Aloha. Nevertheless, the use of a longer schedule has the advantage of having a much shorter transient state duration, as we will see in the next section.

5   Transient State Duration

The learning protocols presented in the present article require some time to reach collision-free operation, which is the steady state. The time to reach collision-free operation is a random variable and its distribution depends on the topology. We will analyze the same topology that we have already discussed in section 3 and we will use simulations to measure the average time that is required for the system to reach collision-free operation.

We have used a custom simulator in c (the source code is available upon request) that implements only the MAC layer. The simulator adopts all the assumptions that we have used in our previous discussion of the protocol. Averages are computed across 100,000 simulation runs and the standard error of the mean is below 5%.

The schedule length T_σ is the time that elapses from the start of a successful transmission to the start of the following transmission. This very same value is the parameter of the exponential random distribution that is used to choose the random backoff after a failed transmission. Remember that the random backoff time starts at the end of an unsuccessful transmission, while the deterministic backoff is measured from the beginning of the successful transmission (See Fig. 4).

In our example scenario, the schedule length T_σ has to be larger than three in order to accommodate three stations transmitting in a collision-free fashion. Therefore, we take schedule length values from 3.25 up to 15.75 and we evaluate two performance metrics: the steady state aggregated traffic and the time required to reach collision-free operation.

The results are presented in Fig. 5, which shows that our two metrics of interest decrease as we increase the schedule length T_σ. Therefore, there is a design trade-off which is controlled by the choice of the schedule length or, equivalently, the parameter ϵ in Table 1 in the next section. If we want to attain a high aggregated throughput in the steady state, we should be ready to accept a long transient state.

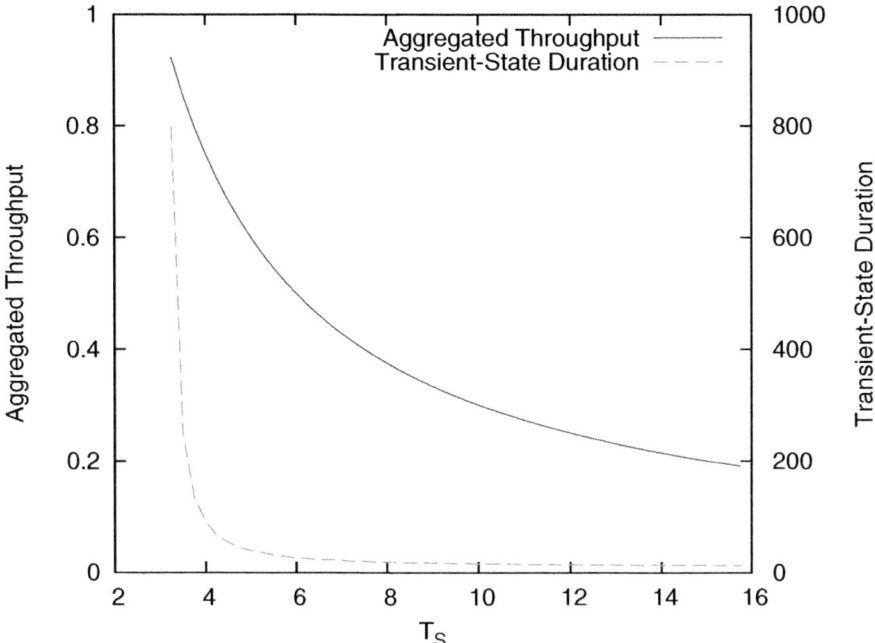

Fig. 5. This plot shows the aggregated throughput and the time required to reach collision-free operation in the example topology of Fig. 2 for different values of the schedule length T_σ

6 A Performance Comparison

This section compares the steady state performance of our proposed protocols (l-Aloha, scl-Aloha) with the performance of Aloha. The results are summarized in Table 1, where log denotes the natural logarithm.

The first three columns (τ_1, τ_2, τ_3) show the transmission rate of the three stations, which is the average fraction of time that each of the stations devotes to transmission. The transmission rate of the Aloha protocol has been computed in such a way that maximizes proportional fairness [7]. The transmission rate for l-Aloha and scl-Aloha is simply $\frac{1}{T_\sigma}$. Note that knowledge of the global topology is assumed in Aloha and $T_\sigma = 3(1 + \epsilon)$. In scl-Aloha, the schedule length is locally computed and we obtain $T_\sigma = 4(1 + \epsilon)$.

The following three columns $(\theta_1, \theta_2, \theta_3)$ represent the throughput attained by each of the stations, which is the time devoted to successful transmission by each of the stations. The derivation of the throughput for optimum Aloha is detailed in the Appendix.

The last three columns represent three different performance metrics: Jain's Fairness index $(JF = \frac{(\theta_1 + \theta_2 + \theta_3)^2}{3(\theta_1^2 + \theta_2^2 + \theta_3^2)})$, aggregated throughput $(AT = \theta_1 + \theta_2 + \theta_3)$ and proportional fairness $(PF = \log\theta_1 + \log\theta_2 + \log\theta_3)$.

It is remarkable that, for a sufficiently small value of ϵ, l-Aloha outperforms Aloha in the three metrics that are considered in this particular comparative. We can observe that l-Aloha achieves perfect fairness and that, by taking a sufficiently small value of ϵ, the aggregate throughput can be increased to a value arbitrarily close to one.

Table 1. Performance Comparison

Contention	Tx rate			Throughput			Performance		
	τ_1	τ_2	τ_3	θ_1	θ_2	θ_3	JF	AT	PF
Aloha	$\frac{\sqrt{\frac{3}{2}}-1}{\sqrt{\frac{3}{2}}}$	$\frac{\sqrt{\frac{3}{2}}-1}{\sqrt{\frac{3}{2}}}$	$\frac{\sqrt{2}-1}{\sqrt{2}}$	0.056	0.120	0.108	0.921	0.283	-7.234
l-Aloha	$\frac{1}{3(1+\epsilon)}$	$\frac{1}{3(1+\epsilon)}$	$\frac{1}{3(1+\epsilon)}$	$\frac{1}{3(1+\epsilon)}$	$\frac{1}{3(1+\epsilon)}$	$\frac{1}{3(1+\epsilon)}$	1	$\frac{1}{1+\epsilon}$	$-3.296 - 3\log(1+\epsilon)$
scl-Aloha	$\frac{1}{4(1+\epsilon)}$	$\frac{1}{4(1+\epsilon)}$	$\frac{1}{4(1+\epsilon)}$	$\frac{1}{4(1+\epsilon)}$	$\frac{1}{4(1+\epsilon)}$	$\frac{1}{4(1+\epsilon)}$	1	$\frac{3}{4(1+\epsilon)}$	$-4.159 - 3\log(1+\epsilon)$

7   Reception Acknowledgements

In order to make it possible to compare our protocol with Aloha, we have not discussed the presence of acknowledgements in the previous sections. Nevertheless, acknowledgements play a critical role in wireless networks in general, and in our proposed protocols in particular. Both l-Aloha and scl-Aloha use a deterministic backoff after successful transmissions and a random backoff otherwise. Therefore the stations need to know whether a transmission has been successful or not. It should be noted that the acknowledgement is transmitted in the reverse direction of the data transmission, and therefore the interference graph for the acknowledgements is different than the one for data packets.

There are two possible approaches to accommodate acknowledgements, and both of them have some detrimental effect on performance. The first approach is to modify Eq. 1 to account for the flows of two-hop neighbors to guarantee that a collision-free schedule also exists in the reverse path. As a result, the schedule will be longer and the steady state performance will be lower. A second approach is to require all the flows to be bidirectional and piggyback the acknowledgements in data packets. This solution is much more efficient in the steady state but requires a longer transient state since the random backoff has to be longer than T_σ to give time to the correspondent node to transmit its data packet.

8   Conclusions

In this paper we have studied the possibility of reaching collision-free operation in ad-hoc networks by using a deterministic backoff after successful transmissions.

We have considered a simple example scenario in which collision-free operation results in a performance improvement when the collision-free schedule is learned by all nodes after a transient state. Finally, we have proposed a mechanism that the stations can use to self-configure their contention parameter using information that is gathered from the neighboring nodes.

Acknowledgements. V. Mancuso provided several corrections and ideas to improve an earlier version of the manuscript. This work has been partially supported by the Spanish Government (TEC2008-0655, Plan Nacional I+D), (CSD2008-00010, Consolider-Ingenio Program) and by the Catalan Government (SGR2009#00617).

References

1. Oliver, M., Zuidweg, J., Batikas, M.: Wireless Commons Against the Digital Divide. In: IEEE International Symposium on Technology and Society ISTAS, New South Wales, Australia (2010)
2. Gringoli, F., Nava, L.: OpenFWWF: OpenFirmWare for WiFi networks (2010), http://www.ing.unibs.it/~openfwwf/ (accessed March 25, 2011)
3. IEEE 802.11: Wireless LAN Medium Access Control (MAC) and Physical Layer (PHY) Specification (2007)
4. Gurewitz, O., Mancuso, V., Shi, J., Knightly, E.: Measurement and Modeling of the Origins of Starvation of Congestion-Controlled Flows in Wireless Mesh Networks. IEEE/ACM Transactions on Networking 17, 1832–1845 (2009)
5. Lopez-Aguilera, E., Casademont, J., Cotrina, J.: Propagation Delay Influence in IEEE 802.11 Outdoor Networks. Wireless Networks 16(4), 1123–1142 (2010)
6. Tobagi, F.: Modeling and performance analysis of multihop packet radio networks. Proceedings of the IEEE 75(1), 135–155 (1987)
7. Kar, K., Sarkar, S., Tassiulas, L.: Achieving Proportional Fairness Using Local Information in Aloha Networks. IEEE Transactions on Automatic Control 49(10), 1858–1863 (2004)
8. He, Y., Yuan, R., Sun, J., Gong, W.: Semi-Random Backoff: Towards Resource Reservation for Channel Access in Wireless LANs. In: IEEE ICNP, pp. 21–30 (2009)
9. Barcelo, J., Bellalta, B., Cano, C., Sfairopoulou, A., Oliver, M.: Towards a Collision-Free WLAN: Dynamic Parameter Adjustment in CSMA/E2CA. EURASIP Journal on Wireless Communications and Networking (to appear, 2011)
10. Fang, M., Malone, D., Duffy, K., Leith, D.: Decentralised Learning MACs for Collision-free Access in WLANs. Arxiv preprint arXiv:1009.4386v2 (2011)
11. Yi, Y., De Veciana, G., Shakkottai, S.: MAC Scheduling With Low Overheads by Learning Neighborhood Contention Patterns. IEEE/ACM Transactions on Networking (2010)

Appendix: Aloha throughput in the Simple Example Ad-Hoc Network

In this appendix we derive the throughput of the stations 1 to 3 in the example scenario that is presented in Fig. 2. We will use the notation s_i for $i \in \{1, 2, 3\}$ to name the stations. Each station s_i transmits fixed-length packets with a transmission duration normalized to one and then backs off for an exponentially distributed time. The parameter of this exponential distribution is λ_i.

We follow the steps in [7] and model the transmissions as a renewal process. The expected time interval that elapses between two consecutive transmission epochs is the sum of the transmission time and the exponentially distributed backoff, totalling $1 + 1/\lambda_i$. And the throughput obtained by station s_i will be computed as $S_i = \phi_i P_i$, where ϕ_i denotes the fraction of time that station s_i devotes to transmissions and P_i is the probability that one transmission by station s_i succeeds. Since station s_i transmits during one unit of time in each transmission epoch, the fraction of time devoted to transmissions is simply $\phi_i = \frac{1}{1+\lambda_i}$.

Particularizing now for our example scenario, we need that two conditions are satisfied for a transmission by s_1 to be successful. First, both s_2 and s_3 have to be silent when the transmission by s_1 starts and, second, both s_2 and s_3 have to remain silent for one unit of time. The probability that a station s_i is silent at any given time is $1 - \phi_i$ and the probability that a station that is silent remains silent for one unit of time is $e^{-\lambda_i}$. Consequently,

$$P_1 = (1 - \phi_2)(1 - \phi_3)e^{-\lambda_2}e^{-\lambda_3} = \frac{1}{(1 + \lambda_2)(1 + \lambda_3)}e^{-(\lambda_2+\lambda_3)}. \tag{2}$$

And finally, we can compute the throughput obtained by s_1 as

$$S_1 = \phi_1 P_1 = \frac{\lambda_1}{1 + \lambda_1}\frac{1}{(1 + \lambda_2)(1 + \lambda_3)}e^{-(\lambda_2+\lambda_3)}. \tag{3}$$

We repeat the same steps to compute the throughput of s_2 (taking into account that only transmissions from s_1 disrupt transmissions from s_2)

$$S_2 = \frac{\lambda_2}{1 + \lambda_2}\frac{1}{1 + \lambda_1}e^{-\lambda_1}, \tag{4}$$

and the throughput of s_3

$$S_3 = \frac{\lambda_3}{1 + \lambda_3}\frac{1}{(1 + \lambda_2)(1 + \lambda_1)}e^{-(\lambda_2+\lambda_1)}. \tag{5}$$

The expressions derived in this appendix are used to compute the throughput in Table 1.

Closed-Loop Adaptive IEEE 802.11n with PHY/MAC Cross-Layer Constraints

Gabriel Martorell, Felip Riera-Palou, and Guillem Femenias

Mobile Communications Group
University of the Balearic Islands, Spain
{gabriel.martorell,felip.riera,guillem.femenias}@uib.es

Abstract. This paper presents a comprehensive performance study of closed-loop fast link adaptation (FLA) in the context of IEEE 802.11n, spanning the physical (PHY) and medium-access control (MAC) layers. In particular, a semi-analytical model is derived for the widely used basic access scheme of the distributed coordination function (DCF), that applies to both, open- and closed-loop strategies. Numerical results serve to demonstrate the accuracy of the proposed model and the superiority of FLA in terms of MAC goodput in comparison to open-loop policies. Realistic operating conditions such as outdated feedback information and the use of statistical packet length distributions, issues not treated in previous studies, have also been considered. Moreover, it is shown how the inclusion of a time-out mechanism in the FLA scheme that weighs down the influence of channel information as this becomes outdated is a useful strategy to counteract its deleterious effects.

Keywords: FLA, DCF, 802.11n, AMC, basic access mechanism.

1 Introduction

Over the last decade the IEEE 802.11 standard for wireless local area network (WLAN) has become the prevalent technology for indoor wireless Internet access. More recently, and in response to the growing demands for higher capacity, the IEEE standards committee has published the final version of IEEE 802.11n [1] as a new amendment of IEEE 802.11. Compared to previous specifications, this new norm allows much higher throughputs to be achieved while being able to fulfill more stringent quality of service (QoS) requirements. This amendment specifies enhancements to the IEEE 802.11 physical layer (PHY) and the medium access control (MAC) sublayer, most notably, the use of multiple-antenna technology (so-called MIMO) and frame aggregation, respectively. Additionally, it incorporates a feedback control channel from the receiver (Rx) to the transmitter (Tx) that enables the implementation of closed-loop adaptive mechanisms.

Adaptation plays a crucial role in dealing with the time varying nature of the wireless channel. Adaptive mechanisms allow the reconfiguration of system parameters in order to exploit the available instantaneous channel capacity while satisfying QoS constraints. One of the most widely used reconfiguration techniques is adaptive modulation and coding (AMC), which selects an appropriate

C. Sacchi et al. (Eds.): MACOM 2011, LNCS 6886, pp. 63–74, 2011.

modulation and coding scheme (MCS) in response to changes in the environment or system behaviour. AMC algorithms can be broadly categorized as closed- or open-loop, depending on whether an explicit feedback channel between Rx and Tx is used or not. Open-loop setups operate in an heuristic manner and their rate of adaptation tends to be slow with respect to channel changes, thus compromising the fulfilment of QoS constraints. In contrast, closed-loop mechanisms track more accurately the channel behavior and they are more reactive to rapid channel variations.

Most IEEE 802.11-based systems employ the distributed coordination function (DCF) at the MAC sublayer and adopt open-loop AMC policies such as automatic rate fallback (ARF) [2] or one of its variants (e.g. CARA [3], SARA [4]). Owing to its simplicity, ARF is by far the most popular algorithm in use. However, the DCF scheme does not differentiate between collisions and transmission failures caused by poor channel conditions. Consequently, when the system experiences a high collision probability, ARF tends to use the lowest transmission rate even if the channel conditions are favorable to use much higher transmission modes (see for example, [3,5,6,7]). Other adaptive strategies have been proposed to solve this issue, but they may require frame format modifications [8], different transmission schemes (RTS/CTS) [3], or the use of channel quality indicators (e.g. signal strength indicator) [6,8] and, in fact, none of them has achieved widespread use in current WLAN systems [9].

Analytical models for DCF-based WLANs that do not make use of AMC have been known since long ago [10], however, the inclusion of AMC in the theoretical framework has only been recently addressed [11,12]. These studies have demonstrated that, in the context of IEEE 802.11n, the use of closed-loop techniques such as fast link adaptation (FLA) offers important benefits in terms of physical layer throughput. Nevertheless, current literature does not consider how this improvement reflects on the MAC goodput of a FLA-based system. This paper presents a semi-analytical model that can be used to assess the goodput performance at the MAC layer of both, open- and closed-loop adaptive schemes targeting IEEE 802.11n. The proposed model expands the one presented by the authors in [13] by modelling the retry limits and the anomalous slot performance reported in [14]. Additionally, issues that may affect very significantly the practical implementation of closed-loop strategies such as having to cope with delayed (possibly outdated) feedback information and the possible utilization of different packet lengths are also considered in this study. Lastly, a novel strategy for the FLA-based scheme that minimises the effects of delayed feedback is presented and validated.

The rest of the paper is structured as follows. Section 2 describes the system model under consideration. Section 3 briefly reviews the two adaptive schemes covered in this work. In Section 4 the analytical framework used to analyze the system goodput is presented. In section 5 the simulation tool features are described and the numerical results comparing the performance of open- and closed-loop schemes are presented under different configurations. Finally, in Section 6, the main conclusions of this study are summarized.

2 System Overview

Physical layer description. Without loss of generality, our study focuses on the IEEE 802.11n standard [1], whose PHY layer is based on MIMO-OFDM. The MIMO component enables the use of different transmission techniques (e.g., space-time block coding (STBC), space division multiplexing (SDM), cyclic delay diversity (CDD) and/or combinations of them) in order to increase the system capacity and/or reliability [15]. At the transmitter side, information bits are first encoded with a $\frac{1}{2}$-rate convolutional encoder with generator polynomials [133, 171] and then punctured to one of the possible coding rates $R_m \in \{1/2, 2/3, 3/4, 5/6\}$. Depending on the selected MIMO configuration, the resulting bits are demultiplexed into N_s spatial streams. For each stream, the coded bits are interleaved and then assigned to symbols from one of the allowed signal constellations (BPSK, QPSK, 16-QAM or 64-QAM). According to the chosen MIMO mode, the symbols are then either STBC encoded or antenna mapped on the available N_T transmit antennas. The resulting symbols are finally supplied to a conventional OFDM modulator consisting of an IFFT (inverse fast fourier transform) and the addition of a guard interval. For simplicity of exhibition, this paper focuses on a 2×2 MIMO system ($N_T = N_R = 2$), implying that MCSs with $N_s = 1$ and $N_s = 2$ spatial streams employ STBC [16] and SDM [17], respectively.

At the receiver side, Alamouti decoding or Minimum Mean Square Error (MMSE) detection is applied depending on whether STBC or SDM has been employed. In either case, the detector extracts soft information in the form of log-likelihood ratios (LLRs) that, after suitable de-interleaving/de-parsing, can be exploited by a soft Viterbi decoder [12].

MAC layer description. The IEEE 802.11 standard specifies three different MAC mechanisms for WLANs, namely the DCF, the point coordination function (PCF) and the hybrid coordination function (HCF). The DCF is the mandatory MAC mechanism for the IEEE 802.11 standard [1]. It is a random access scheme based on the carrier sense multiple access with collision avoidance (CSMA/CA) protocol that incorporates a binary exponential backoff (BEB) algorithm to manage the retransmission of collided and erroneous packets.

The basic access technique is the most extensively used access scheme in DCF [3] and the one central to the study presented in this contribution. In basic access, a station (STA) transmits one data packet at its BEB scheduled slot and waits for its packet-acknowledgement (ACK-control frame) from the receiver. If no reply arrives during a predefined time interval, the STA interprets the transmission as erroneous and the packet is retransmitted in the next BEB scheduled slot or discarded if the number of packet retransmissions exceeds the maximum number of allowed retransmissions, which will be denoted by R.

Timing of DCF events. According to the basic access technique of DCF, the elapsed time for a successful transmission of an L-bit MAC packet data unit (MPDU) using MCS m is

$$T_s(m, L) = T_{Tr}(m, L) + t_{SIFS} + T_{ACK+HTC}(m) + t_{DIFS}, \tag{1}$$

where t_{SIFS} (short interframe space) and t_{DIFS} (distributed interframe space) are 802.11n time constants defined in [1]. The time elapsed in the MPDU transmission, $T_{Tr}(m, L)$, is defined as

$$T_{Tr}(m, L) = t_{Preamble} + N_{Sym}(L)t_{Sym}, \tag{2}$$

with $t_{Preamble}$ representing the PLCP preamble duration, t_{Sym} denoting the OFDM symbol period and

$$N_{Sym}(L) = m_{STBC} \left\lceil \frac{L + 22}{m_{STBC} N_{DBPS}(m)} \right\rceil, \tag{3}$$

being the number of OFDM symbols involved in the transmission of a complete MPDU, where $N_{DBPS}(m)$ is the quantity of bits forming each OFDM symbol as defined by MCS m, $\lceil z \rceil$ denotes the smallest integer greater than or equal to z, and $m_{STBC} = 2$ if STBC is used and $m_{STBC} = 1$ otherwise. Similarly, the time required for the transmission of an ACK+HTC frame[1] using PHY mode m is given by

$$T_{ACK+HTC}(m) = t_{Preamble} + N_{Sym}(20 \cdot 8)t_{Sym}. \tag{4}$$

A collision occurs whenever two or more STAs transmit on the same slot, finishing t_{EIFS} (extended interframe space) after the end of the longest transmission of the collided STAs. That is, its duration depends on the MCS and MPDU length corresponding to the longest transmission, denoted by m^* and L^*, respectively. Therefore, the collision duration can be mathematically expressed as

$$T_c(m^*, L^*) = T_{Tr}(m^*, L^*) + t_{EIFS}, \tag{5}$$

where

$$t_{EIFS} = t_{SIFS} + T_{ACK}(m = 0) + t_{DIFS}. \tag{6}$$

The MPDU error transmission duration $T_e(m, L)$ is the time elapsed in a transmission that experiences errors without collisions, and it can be expressed as

$$T_e(m, L) = T_{Tr}(m, L) + t_{EIFS}. \tag{7}$$

In this model, due to its negligible probability of occurrence, we have not considered the possibility of an error in the ACK transmission. The ACK transmission takes place under the same system conditions than the packet being acknowledged, i.e., using the same MCS and suffering similar channel conditions. However, its packet size is considerably smaller than that of the information packets and therefore, its error probability can be safely considered insignificant.

---

[1] Wrapper control frame that encapsules the ACK and the high throughput (HT) control field required to feedback the MCS selection.

3   Adaptive Modulation and Coding Strategies

ARF. This algorithm adapts the transmission rate according to the number of consecutive transmission failures and successes, both reported by the ACK mechanism. The transmission rate is decreased after two consecutive transmission failures and increased after either ten consecutive successful packet transmissions or a timeout. In order to improve the system adaptation during long intervals of inactivity, this timeout counter is reset after a transmission rate change or after a transmission failure [2]. Acceptable timeout values lie in the range of 50-200 ms [18]. Note that, following a rate increase, the next data transmission is deemed as a probing transmission for the new mode. If an ACK is not received for this probing packet the system falls back to the previous data rate.

In order to implement ARF in IEEE 802.11n it is necessary to determine the available rates in the MCS set, denoted by $\mathcal{M}$. In contrast to previous IEEE 802.11 standards, in 802.11n different MCSs $\in \mathcal{M}$ can provide the same transmission rate, but only one of them can be used by the ARF algorithm. For this reason, the MCSs in $\mathcal{M}$ are reordered according to their transmission rate [12]. For those rates that can be attained using either SDM or STBC, only the STBC MCS is kept as it can be shown to be more robust against channel variations [16]. The reordered and pruned MCS set will be denoted by $\overline{\mathcal{M}}$.

FLA. Fast link adaptation is a closed-loop technique that relies on the availability of a feedback channel from the receiver to the transmitter. The main idea behind FLA is that the receiver, thanks to an accurate knowledge of the channel response, can compute a reliable prediction of the error rate for all available MCSs and choose the one maximising the instantaneous throughput while satisfying QoS constraints in the form of outage packet error rate probability. The selected MCS can then be communicated to the transmitter via the feedback channel. In this work we assume the use of the methodology presented in [12], where link performance prediction for each MCS is based on the exponential effective SNR mapping (EESM). Using this approach, the EESM for a given MCS can be easily associated to packet error rate (PER) using look-up tables that have been previously computed during an off-line calibration phase.

In crowded scenarios, the delay between the MCS selection at the receiver and its use at the transmitter can be very large, very often exceeding the channel coherence time and significantly affecting the FLA operation. In DCF, all STAs have an equal long term probability of accessing the medium. Therefore, successive transmissions from a given STA are intertwined with transmissions from the other contending STAs with the time between successive transmissions increasing with the MCS feedback delay. This delay becomes critical for FLA when it approaches the channel coherence time, indicating that the provided MCS has been determined for a channel response that is almost uncorrelated to the current channel response. This mismatch between current and prior channel state can increase the error probability due to a mistakenly selected or expired MCS, causing several consecutive errors in the next retransmissions prior to packet discard.

In order to counteract the effects of using stale feedback MCSs, we propose that the STA decreases the transmission mode when the MCS feedback delay exceeds a fixed timeout. The STA will decrease again the MCS in all the subsequent packet retransmissions (if any) until the packet is successfully transmitted. The timeout is configured to a value close to the channel coherence time, assuring in this way that the current channel response is similar to the one that the receiver has used to determine the feedback MCS. As it will be shown in the numerical results section, this strategy reduces the error probability without considerably affecting the goodput and fulfilment of QoS constraints.

4   Goodput Analysis

Following the well established model presented in [10] and then refined in [14], the goodput analysis presented in this paper focuses on the saturation region, defined as the operation point where each STA has always new packets to transmit. The system saturation goodput S can be defined as

$$S = \frac{E\{\text{payload information in a slot}\}}{E\{\text{duration of a slot}\}}, \tag{8}$$

where $E\{\cdot\}$ denotes statistical expectation. The duration of a slot refers to the time interval between two consecutive backoff counter decrements.

In any given slot, one out of four events can occur: a successful packet transmission (s), an error packet transmission (e), a collision (c) or an idle slot (i). From the point of view of the BEB algorithm, error transmissions and collisions are undistinguishable. The conditional probability of the union of these events can be computed as

$$p = 1 - (1 - \zeta_u)(1 - \tau)^{n-1}, \tag{9}$$

where n is the number of active STAs in the scenario, ζ_u is the user error transmission probability for the considered AMC algorithm, averaged on a per-user basis, and τ is the stationary probability that a particular STA transmits in a given slot. This transmission probability can be obtained as

$$\tau = \frac{1}{1 + \frac{1-p}{2(1-p^{R+1})}\left[\sum_{j=0}^{R} p^j \cdot (2^{min(j,m_{max})}W - 1) - (1 - p^{R+1})\right]}, \tag{10}$$

where $W = CW_{min} + 1$, and m_{max} is the maximum backoff stage. Notice that p and τ can be obtained by solving the nonlinear system formed by eqs. (9) and (10).

Using τ, the probability that only one STA transmits on a given slot is

$$P_s = n\tau(1 - \tau)^{n-1}. \tag{11}$$

Furthermore, the probability that a given slot is idle is given by

$$P_i = (1 - \tau)^n. \tag{12}$$

Among all possible events, only the successful packet transmission increases the payload information while any other event leads to a goodput degradation. Consequently, combining the goodput expression in [19, eq. (50)] with [14, eq. (18)], and taking into account the use of multiple transmission modes, the system goodput can be expressed as

$$S = \frac{(1 - \zeta_s)P_s\overline{L_p}\left[\frac{W}{W-1}\right]}{P_i\sigma + (1 - \zeta_s)P_s\overline{T_s^{(n,L)}} + \zeta_s P_s\overline{T_e^{(n,L)}} + (1 - P_s - P_i)\overline{T_c^{(n,L)}}}, \tag{13}$$

where $\overline{L_p} = E\{L_p\}$, with $L_p = L - L_h$ representing the packet payload length and L_h denoting the MAC sublayer overhead, ζ_s denotes the average system packet error probability for a given slot, σ is the idle slot duration [1], and the time values $\overline{T_s^{(n,L)}}$, $\overline{T_c^{(n,L)}}$ and $\overline{T_e^{(n,L)}}$ represent the average elapsed time for successful, colliding and error transmissions, respectively. These time values are determined by simulation considering the effects of the feedback delay. Notice that $\overline{L_p}$ is multiplied by $\left[\frac{W}{W-1}\right]$ in order to account for the additional information transmitted in anomalous slots[2] [14].

5   Numerical Results

In order to validate our semi-analytical model and compare the performance of FLA and ARF under different system configurations, an IEEE 802.11n system-level Matlab simulator has been implemented using the link-level parameters derived in [12]. It should be stressed that this model is considerably more realistic than the one proposed by Tinnirello et al. in [14], since it allows the treatment of AMC, statistical packet length distribution and non-ideal closed-loop FLA strategies, at the expense of relying on some semi-analytic parameters. In this paper we concentrate on the performance evaluation of the uplink scenario where, nevertheless, MAC control frame transmissions from access point (AP) to STA are also accounted for. Different scenarios have been generated by uniformly distributing n static users in a circular area of radius R_{max} centered around the AP and then determining the individual channel response from each user to the AP. To this end, the MIMO channel generation tool presented in [20], parameterized with each user's distance to the AP, has been employed. The maximum radius R_{max} has been set to 30 m, a value that ensures the avoidance of the hidden terminal problem and precludes the utilization of the no transmission mode (available in FLA). For all STAs, transmit power has been set to 20 dBm and receiver noise power to -80 dBm. The physical layer uses only the first 16 MCS modes of IEEE 802.11n (MCS0-MCS15), achieving date rates of up to 130 Mbps [1]. The ARF timeout has been set to 60 ms [18] and the FLA outage constraint for a PER objective (not including collisions) of 10^{-1} has been configured to 10%. The corresponding CSI feedback overhead has also

---

[2] Slot with a lower probability to be accessed than the average (see [14] for more details).

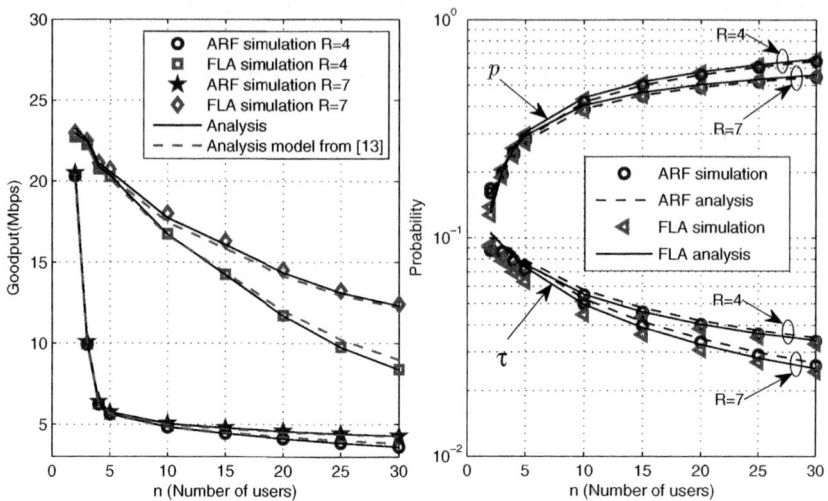

Fig. 1. Semi-analytic and simulated system performance of goodput, τ and p using $R = 4$ and $R = 7$ retransmissions

been considered in FLA. In order to obtain an accurate estimate of the average system performance $N_{sim} = 100$ simulation runs of duration $t_{sim} = 22$ seconds have been generated for each value of n.

The left and right plots of Fig. 1 show the goodput performance and the conditional probabilities p and τ, respectively, as a function of the number of STAs and for a fixed packet length of $L_p = 1500$ bytes. A very accurate match between the semi-analytical and simulated system performance metrics for FLA- and ARF-based schemes can be appreciated. The left plot of Fig. 1 also reports the goodput performance obtained using the proposed semi-analytical model compared to the previous proposal[3] presented in [13], where the anomalous slot performance and the packet retry limit were not considered. Although the previous model provides valuable approximations to the simulation performance, the new semi-analytical model results in improved modelling accuracy, especially when the system uses $R = 4$. The left plot in Fig. 1 also illustrates that regardless of the retry limit, FLA-based schemes outperform ARF-based strategies in terms of goodput performance. This is because a lower retry limit leads to a lower average backoff contention window, thus increasing the transmission probability (τ) and, consequently, the collision and error probability (p).

The top plot of Fig. 2 shows the goodput performance of FLA under the assumptions of ideal CSI and non ideal CSI with different timeout values (t_{out}) when using $R = 7$. A priori, ideal FLA could be expected to provide the maximum goodput, however it is outperformed by FLA with $t_{out} = \infty$. Remarkably, as it can be observed in the bottom left plot of Fig. 2, this goodput improvement

---

[3] Configured to $m_{max} = 4$ or $m_{max} = 6$ in order to be compared to the new model using $m_{max} = 6$ with $R = 4$ or $R = 7$, respectively.

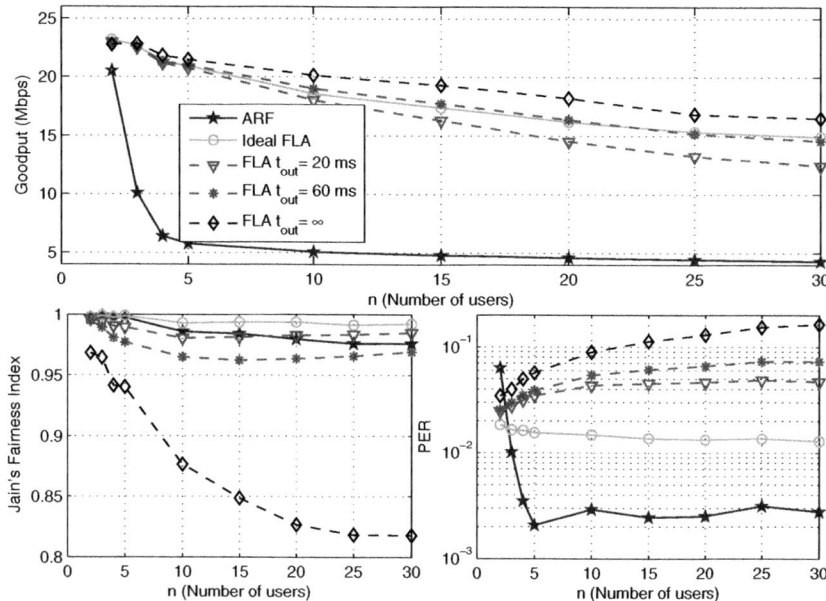

Fig. 2. Goodput, Jain's fairness index and PER of ARF and FLA strategies using $R = 7$

is at the expense of a loss in the Jain's fairness index measured in terms of the per-STA transmission opportunity[4]. This loss in fairness is mainly due to two facts:

1. The STAs with very good channel conditions (high SNR) mostly use the highest throughput MCS and, on average, they are granted the channel more frequently than the other STAs. This is because their conditions are so favorable that their probability of error is very small, regardless of the MCS feedback delay.
2. Due to the MCS feedback delay, the rest of STAs experience an increased error rate and consequently, the DCF mechanism reduces their probability of accessing the medium.

The combination of these two facts results in an overall system goodput improvement due to a more frequent use of the highest rate MCS, and despite the higher error probability for configurations employing a finite time-out value (see bottom-right plot of Fig. 2). Under the constraint of maximum system fairness, the ideal FLA can be considered as the benchmark system from a goodput point of view. Nevertheless, ideal FLA is not implementable due to the 802.11n MCS

---

[4] The Jain's fairness measure used in this paper is calculated as $I = \frac{\left(\sum_i^n \beta_i\right)^2}{n \sum_i^n \beta_i^2}$ where β_i denotes the number of transmissions for STA i. Note that $I = \frac{1}{n}$ implies an unfair system and $I = 1$ reflects a completely fair system.

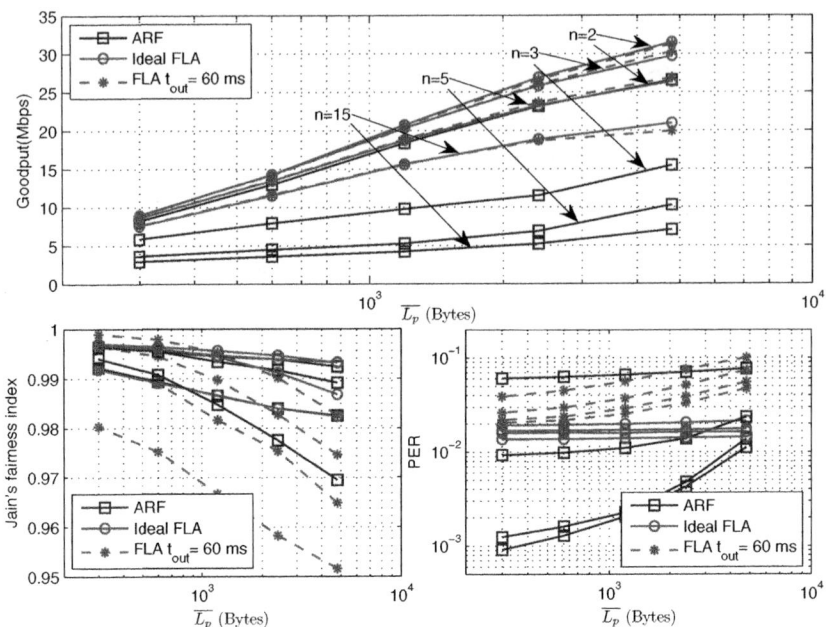

Fig. 3. Goodput, Jain's fairness index and PER system performance as a function of $\overline{L_p}$ and n

feedback mechanism, which invariably introduces some delay in its transmission. In order to improve the FLA performance for those STAs that experience large MCS delays, the FLA algorithm proposed in this paper lowers the MCS rate after the expiration of a finite timeout. Although the timeout should be set according to the channel coherence time, experimental results show that FLA with $t_{out} = 60$ ms performs similarly to ideal FLA in terms of goodput, while preserving a high fairness index and satisfying PER-based QoS constraints (see bottom-left and -right plots of Fig. 2, respectively).

In Fig. 3, the performance of FLA and ARF is shown for a packet length (L_p) modelled as a doubly truncated exponential distribution between 40 and 10.000 bytes. When using FLA, it is assumed that the receiver knows the length of the next packet to be transmitted when determining the most suitable MCS for the next packet transmission. This assumption is quite realistic since there exists a high L_p correlation between consecutive packet lengths sent from the same STA in typical WLAN environments.

The top plot of Fig. 3 presents the goodput performance of ARF, ideal FLA and FLA (FLA with $t_{out} = 60ms$), for different average packet sizes ($\overline{L_p}$). Due to the large overhead introduced by the DCF mechanism, the adoption of long $\overline{L_p}$ values improves the DCF protocol efficiency and consequently, the system goodput increases, especially for the FLA cases. Note that FLA is still outperforming ARF for any $\overline{L_p}$ and number of users, most notably for those cases where more than two users are contending for the medium. As previously observed, the goodput performance of FLA with $t_{out} = 60$ ms is similar to ideal FLA for the whole range of $\overline{L_p}$ values and number of users under consideration (see the top plot of Fig. 3). Furthermore, it keeps Jain's fairness index high (see the left bottom plot of Fig. 3) and fulfills the PER QoS constraint for all the considered configurations (see the right bottom plot of Fig. 3). Note that the system PER performance of FLA increases for large packets as a consequence of the obvious increment of the average MCS feedback delay. For completeness, left and right bottom plots of Fig. 3, also present fairness and PER performance, respectively, for ARF and ideal FLA.

6 Conclusions

This paper has presented a semi-analytical framework for the performance modelling of MIMO-OFDM WLANs when using the basic access scheme of DCF at the MAC layer. Unlike previous works, the proposed model is able to incorporate the effects of channel errors, the possibility of using open- or closed-loop transmission mode adaptation, the effect of the retry limit at the MAC layer and the use of outdated MCS feedback information. A complete study of FLA over 802.11n PHY/MAC in terms of goodput, fairness and system PER performance for a wide range of number of users and packet sizes has been presented and contrasted to those obtained using ARF. Noteworthy, the influence of feedback delay in FLA has been assessed. It has been found that the degradation caused by an outdated MCS information can be largely compensated with the use of a time-out strategy that weighs down the influence of the received feedback. Numerical results clearly show that as the number of users in the system grows, the FLA-based adaptation proves to be much more robust to collisions than ARF even when employing outdated MCS information. This effect is clearly demonstrated by the fact that whereas ARF-based schemes suffer a dramatic reduction in goodput for more than 2 users, the FLA-based strategy exhibits a very graceful degradation thanks to a more accurate rate selection in the presence of collisions. Overall it can be concluded that FLA yields a goodput that more than trebles the one of ARF for most system loads, while keeping a large degree of fairness and satisfying prescribed PER-based QoS constraints.

Acknowledgements. This work has been partially funded by MEC and FEDER through project COSMOS (TEC2008-02422) and Conselleria d'Economia, Hisenda i Innovació del Govern de les Illes Balears through a PhD grant.

References

1. IEEE, Part 11: Wireless LAN Medium Access Control (MAC) and Physical Layer (PHY) Specifications Amendment 5: Enhancements for Higher Throughput. IEEE Std 802.11n-2009 (2009)
2. Kamerman, A., Monteban, L.: WaveLAN®-II: a high-performance wireless LAN for the unlicensed band. Bell Labs Technical Journal 2(3), 118–133 (1997)

3. Kim, S., Verma, L., Choi, S., Qiao, D.: Collision-aware rate adaptation in multi-rate wlans: Design and implementation. Computer Networks 54(17), 3011–3030 (2010)
4. Joshi, T., Ahuja, D., Singh, D., Agrawal, D.: Sara: stochastic automata rate adaptation for IEEE 802.11 networks. IEEE Transactions on Parallel and Distributed Systems 19(11), 1579–1590 (2008)
5. He, J., Kaleshi, D., Munro, A., McGeehan, J.: Modeling Link Adaptation Algorithm for IEEE 802.11 Wireless LAN Networks. In: IEEE ISWCS, Valencia, Spain (September 2006)
6. Zhang, J., Tan, K., Zhao, J., Wu, H., Zhang, Y.: A Practical SNR-Guided Rate Adaptation. In: IEEE INFOCOM, Phoenix, AZ (April 2008)
7. Jung, H., Kwon, T., Choi, Y., Seok, Y.: A scalable rate adaptation mechanism for IEEE 802.11e wireless. In: IEEE FGCN, Jeju-Island, Korea (December 2007)
8. Holland, G., Vaidya, N., Bahl, P.: A rate-adaptive MAC protocol for multi-Hop wireless networks. In: ACM MobiCom., pp. 236–251 (2001)
9. Choi, J., Na, J., Lim, Y., Park, K., Kim, C.: Collision-aware design of rate adaptation for multi-rate 802.11 WLANs. IEEE Journal on Selected Areas in Communications 26(8), 1366–1375 (2008)
10. Bianchi, G.: Performance analysis of the IEEE 802.11 distributed coordination function. IEEE Journal on Selected Areas in Communications 18(3), 535–547 (2000)
11. Martorell, G., Riera-Palou, F., Femenias, G.: Cross-layer link adaptation for IEEE 802.11n. In: IEEE IWCLD, Palma, Spain (June 2009)
12. Martorell, G., Riera-Palou, F., Femenias, G.: Cross-layer fast link adaptation for MIMO-OFDM based WLANs. Springer Wireless Personal Communications 56(3), 599–609 (2011)
13. Martorell, G., Riera-Palou, F., Femenias, G.: DCF performance analysis of open- and closed-loop adaptive IEEE 802.11n networks. In: IEEE ICC, Kyoto, Japan (June 2011)
14. Tinnirello, I., Bianchi, G., Xiao, Y.: Refinements on IEEE 802.11 Distributed Coordination Function Modeling Approaches. IEEE Transactions on Vehicular Technology 59(3), 1055–1067 (2010)
15. Goldsmith, A.: Wireless Communications. Cambridge University Press, Cambridge (2005)
16. Choi, Y.-S., Alamouti, S.: A pragmatic PHY abstraction technique for link adaptation and MIMO switching. IEEE Journal of Selected Areas in Communications 26(6), 960–971 (2008)
17. Foschini, G.: Layered space-time architecture for wireless communication in a fading environment when using multi-element antennas. Bell Labs Technical Journal 1(2), 41–59 (1996)
18. Holland, G., Vaidya, N., Bahl, P.: A rate-adaptive MAC protocol for multi-hop wireless networks. In: ACM MobiCom., Rome, Italy (2001)
19. Bing, B.: Emerging Technologies in Wireless LANs: Theory, Design, and Deployment. Cambridge University Press, Cambridge (2007)
20. Kermoal, J., Schumacher, L., Pedersen, K., Mogensen, P., Frederiksen, F.: A stochastic MIMO radio channel model with experimental validation. IEEE Journal of Selected Areas in Communications 20(6), 1211–1226 (2002)

Throughput-Optimal Distributed Probabilistic Medium-Access in MPR-Capable Networks

Majid Ghanbarinejad[1] and Christian Schlegel[2]

[1] Department of Electrical and Computer Engineering
[2] Department of Computing Science
University of Alberta, Edmonton, Canada
madjid@ece.ualberta.ca, schlegel@cs.ualberta.ca

Abstract. Enabling multipacket reception (MPR) at the physical layer is a promising way to achieve higher bandwidth efficiency while reducing the complexity of the medium-access control layer in distributed networks. We study distributed probabilistic access where transmitting nodes access the shared wireless medium with a probability optimized based on the node's information about the aggregate traffic offered by the network. We model bursty traffic by rate-controlled two-state Markov sources and introduce a parameter that describes the "burstiness" level of the offered traffic. The throughput-optimal medium-access strategy utilizing limited feedback is then described and its performance is examined for traffic with different levels of burstiness. It is shown that the bursty nature of the traffic in data networks allows for further improvement of the bandwidth efficiency. Bounds for the system throughput are proposed and queuing delay is analyzed.

Keywords: Probabilistic Access, Multipacket Reception, On/Off Source, Bursty Traffic, Forward Algorithm, Queuing Delay.

1 Introduction

Medium-access control (MAC) in wireless networks dates back to Abramson's random access protocol ALOHA [1]. The original ALOHA protocol allows a node to send a packet as soon as the packet is ready for transmission. If a transmission fails, the packet is backlogged and the node retransmits the backlogged packet with some retransmission probability $p_r < 1$ to avoid loading up the system. In [11], the term "delayed first transmission" (DFT) was used for the case where nodes try the first transmission with a probability $p < 1$. We use the term "probabilistic access" for the general case where a node accesses the medium with some probability $p < 1$ without deterministic coordinations with other nodes.

The low throughput of ALOHA [2] led to other proposals for multiple access such as the carrier-sense multiple-access (CSMA) [8] family of protocols followed by proposals for collision detection and collision avoidance mechanisms. These protocols have served as the basis for the medium access control (MAC) protocol

C. Sacchi et al. (Eds.): MACOM 2011, LNCS 6886, pp. 75–86, 2011.

of several worldwide standards including the original IEEE 802.3 (Ethernet) and IEEE 802.11 (WiFi) standards.

Despite their popularity, legacy carrier-sense protocols still suffer from low bandwidth efficiency and fairness issues using conventional collision and capture channels especially in ad hoc wireless networks. On the other hand, the advent of new physical (PHY) layer technologies such as spread-spectrum and multiple-antenna communications has provided the opportunity to implement receivers capable of receiving multiple concurrent transmissions. This capability, known as multipacket reception (MPR), and the ever-decreasing costs of implementing complex receivers paint a promising picture for a more efficient optimization of the PHY-MAC interplay that provides the opportunity of higher bandwidth efficiency.

It was shown in [10, 7] that MPR can profoundly improve the bandwidth efficiency of the probabilistic access; for example, if we let K denote the maximum number of concurrent transmissions that can be decoded by the receiver, slotted probabilistic access affords utilization of up to 70% of the bandwidth with $K = 30$ [5]. The bandwidth efficiency can be improved, in theory, to 100% asymptotically if we let $K \to \infty$. Since the associated queuing system is inherently unstable, however, the maximum efficiency is achieved when mechanisms are devised to control the traffic at the medium-access level.

The performance of probabilistic control of packet transmissions in MPR-capable networks was examined in [7]. Numerical analysis and simulations showed that low system throughput in the heavy traffic regime can be avoided with *perfect* information about the instantaneous offered traffic. Controlled probabilistic access with *imperfect* information was examined in [6]. It was shown that the method of updating the Bayesian "belief" about the network traffic state has the potential to approach optimal performance.

In this paper, we model *bursty* traffic as the aggregate of N transmitters with on/off packet-generating sources. We introduce a parameter for representing the degree of burstiness of the traffic generated by each node. Selection of the optimal transmission probability based on nodes' belief about the offered traffic is modeled as a partially-observable Markov decision process. The proposed MAC scheme utilizes the traffic burstiness and limited feedback to predict the traffic in the future and take the optimal action accordingly. Bounds on the throughput performance are given and the queuing delay is analyzed.

The rest of the paper is organized as follows. Sect. 2 describes the system model studied in this paper. The model is analyzed and a probabilistic MAC scheme is proposed in Sect. 3. Throughput and delay performance of the system is studied in Sect. 4 and simulation results are provided. Finally, Sect. 5 concludes the paper.

2   System Model

We focus on *slotted* medium access in this paper. Packets have identical length at the medium-access level, each taking one time slot to be transmitted. We neglect the propagation time and assume the nodes to be slot-synchronized. These assumptions allow us to use a discrete time index $t \in \mathbb{N} \cup \{0\}$.

A *single-hop* distributed wireless network consisting of a receiver and $M \leq \infty$ transmitters is considered. M may represent either the total number of nodes in the vicinity, or the number of currently admitted nodes if connections follow a call-admission control (CAC) mechanism. The latter case offers a better representation of the network model of this paper as we will later assume that the traffic rate and "burstiness" of the nodes are known. This assumption is well accommodated in a network with CAC.

Receivers are capable of MPR with the model described by

$$N^{\text{tx}} = \begin{cases} N^{\text{rx}} & \text{if } N^{\text{tx}} \leq K \\ 0 & \text{otherwise} \end{cases},$$

where $K \geq 1$ is the *joint decoding capability* of a receiver, and N^{tx} and N^{rx} denote the number of concurrently transmitted and successfully received packets, respectively.

Packets originated from transmitters are generated by on/off Markov sources [3] as depicted in Fig. 1. An on/off Markov source S is in the *active* state when it generates a new packet, and is in the *idle* state otherwise. The probabilities α and δ together with the slot duration determine/model the packet generation rate of the source as well as its level of "burstiness" – when α and δ are small, the source shows a more bursty behavior in general, resulting in more *inertia* at the source to remain in a given state. This increases the predictability of the source and, as we will see, can be utilized in estimating network traffic. This will be explained in more detail in Sect. 4.

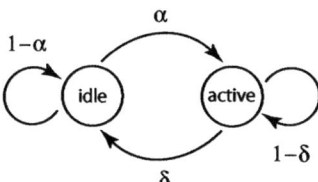

Fig. 1. On/off Markov source used in this paper to model packet generation

Finally, we propose a model for the transmitting nodes. The model is illustrated in Fig. 2. Each transmitting node has an on/off Markov source with parameters α and δ generating packets that enter a queue and wait to be serviced. At each time slot, if the queue is occupied, TX transmits a queued packet with probability p, and immediately receives feedback informing the node if the transmission was successful. In case of success, the packet is removed from the queue. Otherwise, the packet is backlogged. Similarly to the definitions of active and idle for a *source*, we call a *node* active if its queue is occupied, and we call it idle otherwise.

To avoid the problem of unbounded queuing delay, we suppose that the source's transitions between the idle and active states are synchronized with

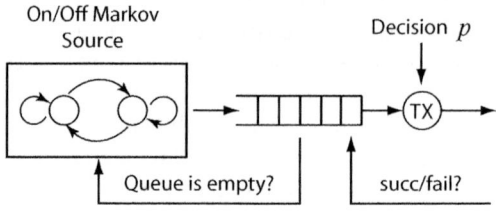

Fig. 2. Abstract model of a transmitter

the time slots. Furthermore, the source pauses when it is in the idle state and the queue is occupied. This, in part, guarantees that the source does not start a new burst of packets before the previously queued burst is completely serviced. This models mechanisms of adaptive flow control in the higher layers of the network architecture. Moreover, it transfers the Markovian behavior of the source to the output of TX for the sake of tractability.

3   System Analysis

3.1   Probabilistic Access with Imperfect Information

We examine controlled probabilistic access [7,6] as follows. At the beginning of a time slot, an active node starts transmitting a packet or postpones transmission according to the outcome of a bernoulli experiment with parameter $0 < p \leq 1$. This parameter is called the transmission probability and is, in general, calculated based on the node's information of the network state, quality-of-service demands/constraints, etc.

The goal is for nodes to cooperate to maximize total system throughput of the network. With N active nodes each transmitting with probability p, the total system throughput[1] is given by

$$R_K(N,p) = \mathsf{E}\left[N^{\mathrm{rx}} \mid N, p\right] = \sum_{n=1}^{\min(N,K)} n \binom{N}{n} p^n (1-p)^{N-n}, \qquad (1)$$

If N is known to the nodes, the throughput-optimal p is obtained as

$$p_K^*(N) \triangleq \arg\max_p R_K(N,p) . \qquad (2)$$

We have $p_K^*(N) = 1$ for $N \leq K$. For $N > K$, however, information about N is central to the calculation of (2). We call N the network "state" in this context.

The performance of probabilistic access with the above optimization was examined in [7] and analyzed in [5]. It was shown that total throughput of the optimally-controlled probabilistic access remains large, for receivers with sufficiently large decoding capability K, even as the average packet rate λ offered to

---

[1] In this paper, throughput is measured in packets per slot duration.

the medium increases. The asymptotic throughput for $\lambda \to \infty$ was shown to be equal to the maximum throughput of ALOHA with Poisson traffic [5].

While it may be costly or infeasible in practice (for example in ad hoc networks) to update nodes with perfect information of the network state N, nodes may still be able to acquire estimates of N by observing the medium, e.g., overhearing signals transmitted in the vicinity, or by receiving some sort of limited feedback from the receiver(s). We study the case where each node keeps a belief vector of the network state of the form $\mathbf{b} = (b_0, b_1, \cdots, b_M)$ where

$$b_i = \Pr\{N = i \mid \mathcal{H}, \Omega\}$$

is the Bayesian belief of N given the history of observations $\mathcal{H}$ as well as the node's prior information Ω of network parameters. Then, the node's optimal selection of p, in the sense of total expected system throughput, is

$$p_K^*(\mathbf{b}) \triangleq \arg\max_p R_K(\mathbf{b}, p), \tag{3}$$

where

$$R_K(\mathbf{b}, p) \triangleq \sum_{N=1}^{M} b_N R_K(N, p) . \tag{4}$$

This approach has been shown to possess the potential to approach optimal (i.e., the "genie-aided") performance in MPR-capable netwokrs [6].

The rest of this section describes the underlying model of controlled probabilistic access with the network model described in Sect. 2, followed by a MAC scheme that utilizes traffic characteristics known at the nodes as well as limited feedback in order to update $\mathbf{b}$ and take the optimal action accordingly.

3.2   A Decision-Theoretic Description

Let us look at the statistics of the traffic generated by the M nodes. If $M \leq K$, the receiver's MPR capability is always sufficient to receive packets no matter how many nodes are active. That is to say, the persistent-transmission strategy ($p = 1$) is optimal. In this case, the number of active nodes N forms a *stationary* Markov chain with the state space $\{0, 1, \cdots, M\}$.

If $M > K$, however, the probability of N exceeding K is non-zero, packets become backlogged eventually, and the optimal decision $0 < p \leq 1$ in general. As a result, the network state follows a Markov process with the transition probability matrix[2]

$$\mathbf{T} = \mathcal{T}(\alpha, \delta, M, K, p), \tag{5}$$

which is non-stationary since it is a function of the nodes' *decision* on p.

The resulting model is a partially-observable Markov decision process [9], i.e., a Markov decision process with *hidden* states. State transitions of an individual transmitter in this system are similar to that of a source, depicted in Fig. 1, where transition probabilities corresponding to the active state are changed to $pP_{\text{succ}}\delta$ and $1 - pP_{\text{succ}}\delta$. We focus on the short-term throughput-optimal decision of (3), which achieves near-optimal performance with little complexity.

---

[2] The tedious equations describing the matrix are omitted in this paper.

3.3   Belief Update and Access Control

In the proposed MAC scheme, nodes receive feedback $\mathcal{F}_t$ at the end of every time slot t informing them of the outcome of the transmissions in that slot.[3] A typical example is binary success/failure feedback through ACK/NACK messages from the receiver. The type of feedback depends, in general, on the application, signal processing capability of the receiver, bandwidth of the feedback channel, etc. Examples of feedback types are introduced and studied in Sect. 4. Having received $\mathcal{F}_t$, nodes compute the updated belief vector $\mathbf{b}_t$.

Given a hidden Markov process and a sequence of observations (i.e., limited feedback), what is the probability of the process being in a given state at a given time instant? The forward-backward algorithm [4] solves this problem. The algorithm consists of two stages: a forward pass which is executed in the forward time direction and is used to update posterior marginal beliefs based on previous observations, and a backward pass to smooth the beliefs by considering future observations as well. In our application, we only implement the forward pass, a.k.a. the forward algorithm, as smoothing beliefs of the past time slots does not affect a node's current decision.

Forward Algorithm (FA): Suppose that the hidden Markov process is stationary, and let state space $\mathcal{S}$ and event space $\mathcal{E}$ denote, respectively, the set of all possible hidden states and the set of all possible events observed from the underlying process. Let $\mathbf{T}$ be the $|\,\mathcal{S}\,| \times |\,\mathcal{S}\,|$ transition probability matrix whose entry τ_{ij} is the probability of the next state j given the current state i. Also, let the entry ϵ_{ij} of the $|\,\mathcal{S}\,| \times |\,\mathcal{E}\,|$ event matrix $\mathbf{E}$ be the *posterior* probability of observing event j when the process is in state i. We use the discrete time index t to distinguish quantities in different time slots. For a stationary process, the belief-update output of the FA can be summarized as

$$\mathbf{b}_t = \kappa_t^{-1} \mathbf{b}_{t-1} \mathbf{T} \, \mathrm{diag}\left(\epsilon_{\mathcal{F}_t}\right), \tag{6}$$

where $\mathrm{diag}\,(\mathbf{x})$ denotes the diagonal matrix taking vector $\mathbf{x}$ on its diagonal, and $\epsilon_{\mathcal{F}_t}$ is the column of $\mathbf{E}$ indexed by the observation $\mathcal{F}_t \in \mathcal{E}$ at time t. The normalization factor κ_t^{-1} is to ensure $\sum_i \mathbf{b}_{t,i} = 1$.

We use the FA and adapt it to accommodate the non-stationarity of the underlying decision process. Suppose a node is active at the beginning of time slot t. The node's current belief is $\mathbf{b}_{t-1}$ and was last updated after the transmissions at $t-1$. To take into account possible changes of the network state from $t-1$ to t, the node adjusts its belief by using the constant matrix $\mathbf{A}$ defined by

$$\mathbf{A} \triangleq \mathcal{T}\left(\alpha, \delta, M, K, 0\right), \tag{7}$$

that is, the transition probability matrix with no transmission ($p = 0$). The optimal decision is therefore obtained as

$$p_t := p_K^*(\mathbf{b}_{t-1}\mathbf{A}) \ . \tag{8}$$

---

[3] Generalization of the algorithm to cases of less frequent feedback is straightforward.

After transmissions, nodes receive $\mathcal{F}_t$ from which $(\epsilon_t)_{\mathcal{F}_t}$ is computed as a function of p_t. Note that in order to reduce computational effort, it is sufficient to compute only the $\mathcal{F}_t$th column of $\mathbf{E}_t$ as the matrix changes over time. Finally, beliefs are updated as

$$\mathbf{b}_t = \kappa_t^{-1}\mathbf{b}_{t-1}\mathbf{T}_t \operatorname{diag}\left((\epsilon_t)_{\mathcal{F}_t}\right), \qquad (9)$$

where $\mathbf{T}_t = \mathcal{T}(\alpha, \delta, M, K, p_t)$. Nodes may initialize $\mathbf{b}_0$ with the uniform probability vector or the steady state probability vector corresponding to

$$\mathbf{T} = \mathcal{T}\left(\alpha, \delta, M, K, p_K^*\left(\frac{M\alpha}{\alpha+\delta}\right)\right) .$$

4 Performance Analysis and Simulation Results

4.1 Rate/Burstiness Description of a Source

We examine the throughput performance of the MAC scheme proposed in the previous section. As mentioned before, *burstiness* of the traffic increases the predictability of the traffic, which can be utilized in updating the beliefs. In the following, we translate the transition probabilities α and δ into parameters that distinguish packet generation rate and burstiness level. The packet generation rate of a source S equals the steady state probability of S being active, i.e., $\lambda_S \triangleq \alpha/(\alpha+\delta)$. It is sensible to assume that $\alpha \leq 1 - \delta$, which gives $\lambda_S \geq \alpha$.

We need a second parameter, in addition to λ_S, in order to describe an on/off Markov source. Here, we introduce a quantity called the burstiness overhead γ of the source S defined as

$$\gamma \triangleq \frac{\log(\alpha+\delta)}{\log \alpha}, \qquad (10)$$

which gives $\lambda_S = \alpha^{1-\gamma}$.

Note that the pair (λ_S, γ) uniquely describes an on/off Markov source. For $\gamma = 0$ we have $\lambda_S = \alpha$, which corresponds to the simple case where the generation of packets are i.i.d. Bernoulli experiments with parameter $\alpha = 1 - \delta$.[4] However, as $\gamma \to 1$, we have $\lambda_S \to 1$ showing that the tendency of the source to generate packets in bursts increases the rate by $\alpha^{-\gamma}$.

4.2 Simulation and Numerical Results

We simulate a system with $K = 5$ and $M = 10$. The average rate offered by each source is set to $\lambda_S = 0.44$ for the best achievable throughput given the aforementioned values of K and M.

Figure 3 shows the throughput performance of running the proposed algorithm with three types of feedback: (i) binary feedback $\mathcal{E} = \{\text{fail}, \text{succ}\}$, i.e. where the receiver reports the decoding success or failure, (ii) $\mathcal{E} = \{0, 1, \cdots, K\} \cup \{\text{fail}\}$, i.e. where the receiver reports the number of successfully-decoded packets, and (iii) $\mathcal{E} = \{0, 1, \cdots, M\}$. Two more cases are examined as baselines:

---

[4] Poisson traffic with average rate λ is obtained by $M \to \infty$ and $\alpha = 1 - \delta = \lambda/M$.

- The case where nodes obtain perfect information of the current network state, called the genie-aided (GA) case. This case can intuitively achieve the best (short-term) throughput via (2).
- The case of constant transmission probability (CTP), i.e., where no feedback is considered and the *a priori* information, is used to numerically calculate

$$p^*_{\text{const}} = \max_p R_{\text{ss}}\big(T(\alpha, \delta, M, K, p)\big),$$

where $R_{\text{ss}}(\mathbf{T})$ denotes the steady-state throughput of the network with the stationary transition probability matrix $\mathbf{T}$, which can be calculated *a priori* if α, δ and M are known.

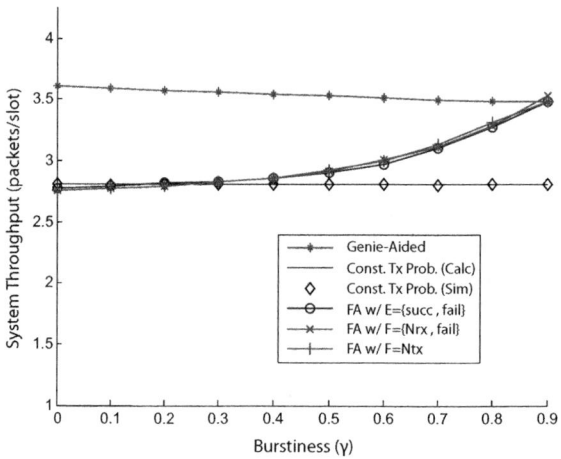

Fig. 3. Throughput of the proposed scheme with different types of feedback versus the throughput by the state-aware genie and constant transmission probability

It can be seen that for the system with the given parameters: (i) different feedback types result in almost the same performance, and (ii) increasing γ improves the throughput performance, starting from the CTP performance for $\gamma = 0$ and increasing to the GA performance. These values, which turn out to remain almost constant for fixed λ_S and variable γ, can be used as approximate[5] bounds for the throughput of probabilistic access with limited feedback. The above results make sense because, with non-bursty traffic, the information conveyed by feedback about the network state in the subsequent time slots is low and the resulting performance is approximately equal to the case where no instantaneous information about the state N_t is available, while this information increases as γ approaches 1. Indeed, for γ very close to 1 nodes rarely change their states and,

---

[5] The bounds are not exact (e.g., see the results for $\gamma = 0, 0.1, 0.9$ in Fig. 3) because (3) optimizes the expected throughput of the *current* time slot, which may be slightly different from the long-term-optimal decision on p.

hence, N_t remains almost constant from slot to slot, leaving sufficient time for the nodes to learn N.

It is observed that the bounds remain almost constant as γ varies. Let us fix γ to an arbitrary value to evaluate the bounds for different values of λ_S. The result is illustrated in Fig. 4. It can be seen that the lower bound monotonically increases while the upper bound increases up to a maximum and then converges with the lower bound. The two bounds meet at $\lambda_S = 0$ and $\lambda_S = 1$, i.e., where the traffic behavior of the nodes are perfectly known *a priori*.

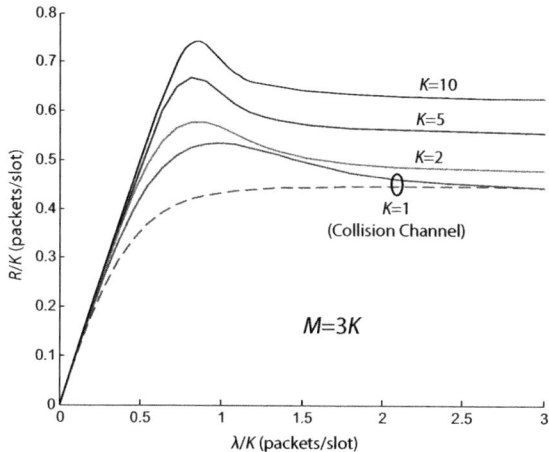

Fig. 4. Bounds on the bandwidth efficiency (R/K) for $K = 1, 2, 5, 10$, $M = 3K$, $\gamma = 0.2$. The total offered rate $\lambda = M\lambda_S$ is normalized by a factor of $1/K$. Some lower bounds are omitted for clarity.

Figure 4 also shows the bounds on the throughput for different values of K. It is clear that devising a larger joint decoding capability increases the maximum achievable system throughput. Note that K is normally a design specification of the receiver(s) and possibly a function of the network's application and/or environment, and therefore is assumed to be constant during operation.

Figure 5 illustrates the effect of M on the maximum achievable throughput. It can be seen that smaller numbers of admitted nodes are generally better in terms of the total system throughput providing that this number can offer sufficient amount of traffic load to avoid bandwidth under-utilization. From this figure, we can conclude that admission control plays a positive role in optimizing the bandwidth efficiency. Furthermore, it is evident that the transport layer can also shape the offered traffic to induce more burstiness and approach the upper bound. This, however, is not without cost. The cost of shaping the traffic as such is increasing delay. This is addressed in the next subsection.

4.3 Queuing Delay

Let $P_s = pP_{\text{succ}}$ denote the service probability of a packet in a time slot, i.e., the probability that a packet is transmitted *and* successfully received in a time

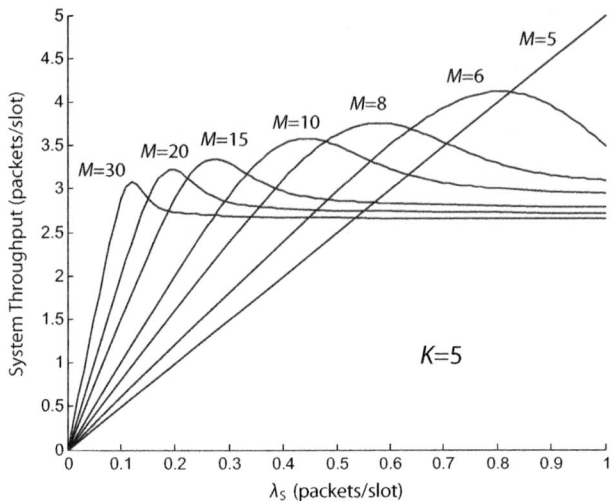

Fig. 5. Upper bound on the throughput for $K = 5$ and different values of M. Smaller M allows to achieve higher throughput providing that each transmitter offers sufficient traffic.

slot when the queue is occupied. We approximate this quantity by its average obtained by

$$(1 - P_{\text{empty}})P_{\text{s}} = \frac{R}{M}, \tag{11}$$

where P_{empty} is the probability of the queue being empty, and R/M is a node's share of the total system throughput R. The average service time of TX is $1/P_{\text{s}}$. In order to calculate P_{empty}, note that

$$\mathsf{E}\left[T_{\text{queued}}\right] = \frac{1}{\delta P_{\text{s}}}, \quad \mathsf{E}\left[T_{\text{empty}}\right] = \frac{1}{\alpha}, \tag{12}$$

where T_{queued} (resp. T_{empty}) denotes the average time that a queue is occupied (resp. empty); note that the second equality is ensured by the flow control mechanism. Using a renewal theory argument, we have

$$P_{\text{empty}} = \frac{T_{\text{empty}}}{T_{\text{empty}} + T_{\text{queued}}} = \frac{\delta P_{\text{s}}}{\delta P_{\text{s}} + \alpha}. \tag{13}$$

From (11) and (13), we obtain

$$P_{\text{s}} = \frac{R\alpha}{M\alpha - R\delta}. \tag{14}$$

Let $P_{\text{B}}(m)$ be the probability that a generated packet is the mth in the current burst, which is equal to the probability that the "reverse" chain of an on/off Markov source (Fig. 1), starting at the active state, generates a burst of exactly m packets. Since the on/off Markov chain is equivalent to its reverse, we have

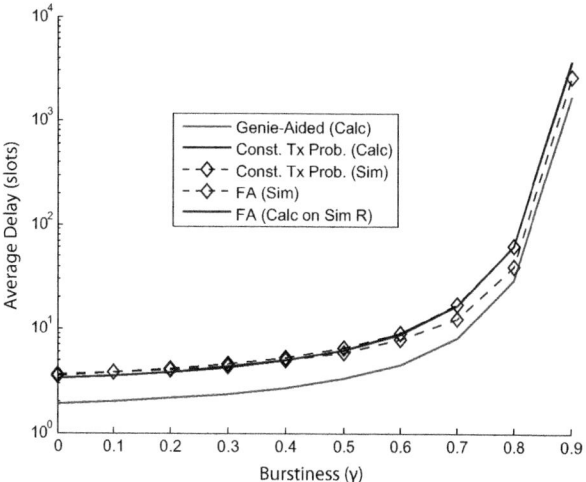

Fig. 6. Average queuing delay versus burstiness. The results are obtained for $K = 5$, $M = 10$, $\lambda_S = 0.44$, and $\mathcal{E} = \{0, 1, \cdots, K, \text{fail}\}$.

$$P_{\text{B}}(m) = (1 - \delta)^{m-1}\delta \ .$$

Also, define $P_{\text{Q}}(n)$ the probability that a packet is the nth in the queue upon its entrance to the queue. For this to occur, if the packet is the mth one generated in the current burst, TX must have already serviced exactly $m - n$ packets out of the previous $m - 1$ packets, and must have delayed the queue for exactly $n - 1$ slots. Therefore,

$$P_{\text{Q}}(n) = \sum_{m=n}^{\infty} P_{\text{B}}(m) \binom{m-1}{m-n} P_{\text{s}}^{m-n}(1 - P_{\text{s}})^{n-1}$$
$$= \frac{(1 - \delta)^{n-1}\delta(1 - P_{\text{s}})^{n-1}}{(1 - P_{\text{s}} + P_{\text{s}}\delta)^n} \ .$$

It can be easily verified that $\sum_n P_{\text{Q}}(n) = 1$. Finally, the average queuing delay is obtained by

$$\bar{D} = \sum_{n=1}^{\infty} n \left(\frac{1}{P_{\text{s}}}\right) P_{\text{Q}}(n) = \frac{1 - P_{\text{s}}}{P_{\text{s}}\delta} + 1 = \frac{M\alpha - R(\alpha + \delta)}{R\alpha\delta} + 1 \quad \text{slots}, \quad (15)$$

where (14) is used in the last equality. Note that we have $\bar{D} = 1$ with $P_{\text{s}} = 1$.

Figure 6 shows the average queuing delay that a packet experiences. It is observed that the delay increases dramatically as γ approaches one.

5   Conclusion

Throughput performance of controlled probabilistic access in MPR-capable networks was examined in this paper. It was shown that bursty nature of the packetized data traffic can be utilized to improve the prediction of the traffic. A Markov decision model was described for the network and the throughput-optimal MAC scheme was examined to update the nodes' belief about the network state. It was shown that as traffic becomes more bursty, nodes improve their estimates and achieve better performance.

References

1. Abramson, N.: The aloha system–another alternative for computer communications. In: Proc. Fall Joint Comput. Conf., Houston, TX (November 1970)
2. Abramson, N.: The throughput of packet broadcasting channels. IEEE Trans. Comm. COM-25(1), 117–128 (1977)
3. Adas, A.: Traffic models in broadband networks. IEEE Comm. Magazine 35(7), 82–89 (1997)
4. Baum, L.E., Petrie, T., Soules, G., Weiss, N.: A maximization technique occurring in the statistical analysis of probabilistic functions of markov chains. The Annals of Mathematical Statistics 41(1), 164–171 (1970)
5. Ghanbarinejad, M., Schlegel, C.: Analysis of controlled probabilistic access with multipacket reception. Submitted to Globecom 2011 (2011)
6. Ghanbarinejad, M., Schlegel, C.: Controlled random access with multipacket reception and traffic uncertainty. In: Proc. IEEE Globecom 2010 Workshops, Miami, FL (December 2010)
7. Ghanbarinejad, M., Schlegel, C., Gburzynski, P.: Adaptive probabilistic medium access in mpr-capable ad-hoc wireless networks. In: Proc. IEEE Globecom 2009, Honolulu, HI (November/December 2009)
8. Kleinrock, L., Tobagi, F.A.: Packet switching in radio channels: Part i–carrier sense multiple-access modes and their throughput-delay characteristics. IEEE Trans. Comm. COM-23(12), 1400–1416 (1975)
9. Monahan, G.E.: A survey of partially observable markov decision processes: Theory, models, and algorithms. Management Science 28(1), 1–16 (1982)
10. Nagaraj, S., Truhachev, D., Schlegel, C.: Analysis of a random channel access scheme with multi-packet reception. In: Proc. IEEE Globecom 2008, New Orleans, LA (November/December 2008)
11. Tobagi, F.A.: Analysis of a two-hop centralized packet radio network–part i: Slotted aloha. IEEE Trans. Communications COM-28(2), 196–207 (1980)

On Gaussian Multiple Access Channels with Interference: Achievable Rates and Upper Bounds

Anas Chaaban[1], Aydin Sezgin[1], Bernd Bandemer[2], and Arogyaswami Paulraj[2]

[1] Institute of Telecommunications and Applied Information Theory, Ulm University,
89081 Ulm, Germany
{anas.chaaban,aydin.sezgin}@uni-ulm.de*
[2] Information Systems Lab, Stanford University, Packard Building, 350 Serra Mall,
Stanford, CA 94305-9510, U.S.A.
{bandemer,apaulraj}@stanford.edu**

Abstract. We study the interaction between two interfering Gaussian 2-user multiple access channels. The capacity region is characterized under mixed strong–extremely strong interference and individually very strong interference. Furthermore, the sum capacity is derived under a less restricting definition of very strong interference. Finally, a general upper bound on the sum capacity is provided, which is nearly tight for weak cross links.

Keywords: Gaussian MAC, capacity, bounds, strong interference, very strong interference.

1 Introduction

A scenario where several transmitters each want to deliver a message to a common receiver is known as the multiple access channel (MAC). This setup models mobile users that want to communicate with a central base station in a cellular network, for example. The MAC capacity region is known since 1971 [1,2].

Another intensively studied model in information theory is the interference channel (IC). In this model, two transmit-receive pairs want to communicate while causing interference to each other. First proposed in 1978 [3], the interference channel is still not fully understood. Its capacity is known only in special cases, e.g., the very-strong interference regime [4], the strong interference regime [5], and the noisy interference regime [6,7,8] where only its sum-capacity is known. The sum-capacity of the interference channel with mixed interference was analyzed in [9].

---

* The work of A. Chaaban and A. Sezgin is supported by the German Research Foundation, Deutsche Forschungsgemeinschaft (DFG), Germany, under grant SE 1697/3.
** The work of B. Bandemer is supported by an Eric and Illeana Benhamou Stanford Graduate Fellowship.

C. Sacchi et al. (Eds.): MACOM 2011, LNCS 6886, pp. 87–96, 2011.

The MAC and the IC are the two building blocks of the model considered here. We consider a setup that models two interfering 2-user MACs. This is a very practical situation which occurs frequently in cellular networks, where multiple mobile stations communicate with the base stations in their respective cells. The degrees of freedom of this setup were studied in [10] and [11]. We follow the naming in [11] where the interfering multiple access channel was called the IMAC. We study this model and obtain new capacity results.

The capacity region of the IMAC is derived for a case of mixed strong–extremely strong interference. That is, when at each receiver, one interferer satisfies a strong interference condition and the other interferer satisfies an extremely strong interference condition. In this case, we show that the capacity region of the IMAC is bounded by the capacity region of the MAC formed by the two desired signals and the strong interfering signal at each receiver. This region is achievable by using Gaussian codes, decoding the extremely strong interferer first and subtracting it from the received signal, and then using the capacity achieving scheme for the resulting MAC to decode the remaining three signals.

A condition for individually very strong interference is derived, and when this condition is satisfied, interference does not decrease the *capacity region* of each of the interfering MACs, i.e., their interference free *capacity region* can be achieved. Furthermore, another condition is derived (very strong combined interference), under which interference does not decrease the *sum capacity* of each of the interfering MACs, i.e., their interference-free *sum capacity* can be achieved.

The simple scheme of treating interference as noise at each receiver gives a sum capacity lower bound for the IMAC. Using a genie aided approach similar to [6], we obtain a sum capacity upper bound which, although not coinciding with the lower bound of treating interference as noise, is fairly tight if the interference power is low.

2   System Model

We consider the *interfering MAC (IMAC)* channel depicted in Figure 1, in which two 2-user multiple access channels use the same transmission resource and therefore interfere with each other. In this channel, transmitters 1 and 2 would like to send independent messages to receiver 1, while transmitters 3 and 4 have independent messages for receiver 2. Each of the two receiver nodes observes the combination of two desired and two interfering signals.

We constrain our attention to the symmetric real-valued memoryless Gaussian setting, where the channel inputs X_i, controlled by the corresponding transmit node i, are subject to the average power constraints

$$\mathbb{E}[X_1^2] \leq P_1, \qquad\qquad \mathbb{E}[X_3^2] \leq P_3 = P_1,$$
$$\mathbb{E}[X_2^2] \leq P_2, \qquad\qquad \mathbb{E}[X_4^2] \leq P_4 = P_2.$$

The channel inputs are real numbers, the observation noise is additive Gaussian, and at each time instance, the channel outputs Y_i are given by

$$Y_1 = X_1 + X_2 + h_1 X_3 + h_2 X_4 + Z_1, \tag{1}$$
$$Y_2 = h_1 X_1 + h_2 X_2 + X_3 + X_4 + Z_2. \tag{2}$$

Here, h_1 and h_2 denote the channel coefficients of the undesired cross-links. The noise terms Z_1, Z_2 are independent unit variance Gaussian random variables. The channel is therefore completely symmetric with respect to exchanging the two multiple-access channels. It is parameterized by the tuple (P_1, P_2, h_1, h_2). The symmetry is assumed for simplicity of exposition, the results can easily be extended to the general asymmetric case.

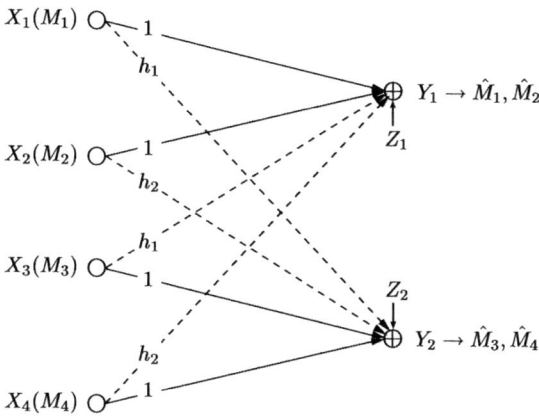

Fig. 1. Multiple access channel with interference. Users 1 and 2 want to communicate with receiver 1, while users 3 and 4 want to communicate with receiver 2.

A $(n, 2^{nR_1}, 2^{nR_2}, 2^{nR_3}, 2^{nR_4})$ code for the IMAC consists of message sets $\mathcal{M}_i = \{1, \ldots, 2^{nR_i}\}$, four encoding functions $f_i : \mathcal{M}_i \to \mathbb{R}^n$ (one for each transmitting node), and four decoding functions $g_i : \mathbb{R}^n \to \mathcal{M}_i$ (two for each receiving node). The probability of decoding error for the code c is

$$P_e^{(n)} = P(\hat{M}_i \neq M_i \text{ for some } i), \tag{3}$$

where the messages M_i are uniformly and independently drawn from the message sets, and $\hat{M}_i$ are the detected messages at the receivers, resulting from applying the decoding functions g_i.

A rate tuple (R_1, R_2, R_3, R_4) is achievable in the IMAC if there exists a sequence of $(n, 2^{nR_1}, 2^{nR_2}, 2^{nR_3}, 2^{nR_4})$ codes such that $P_e^{(n)} \to 0$ as $n \to \infty$. The capacity region $\mathcal{C}$ of the IMAC is the closure of the set of all achievable rate tuples. The sum capacity is the largest achievable sum-rate

$$C_\Sigma = \max_{(R_1, R_2, R_3, R_4) \in \mathcal{C}} R_1 + R_2 + R_3 + R_4. \tag{4}$$

3   Main Results

Before we state the main results of this paper, we need the following definition for simplicity of exposition. Consider the MAC channels that are contained in the IMAC.

Definition 1. *Let* $M(\mathcal{S}, j, N)$ *denote the multiple access channel (MAC) from transmitters* $i \in \mathcal{S} \subseteq \{1, 2, 3, 4\}$ *to receiver* $j \in \{1, 2\}$ *with additive Gaussian noise of variance* N. *Let* $\mathcal{C}^M(\mathcal{S}, j, N)$ *be the capacity region of this MAC.*

It is well-known [12] that $\mathcal{C}^M(\mathcal{S}, j, N) \subseteq \mathbb{R}_+^{|\mathcal{S}|}$ is specified by the inequalities

$$\sum_{i \in \mathcal{T}} R_i \leq \frac{1}{2} \log \left(1 + \sum_{i \in \mathcal{T}} h_{ij}^2 P_i / N \right), \quad \forall \mathcal{T} \subseteq \mathcal{S},$$

where $h_{ij} \in \{1, h_1, h_2\}$ is the channel coefficient from the ith transmitter to the jth receiver.

When convenient, we abbreviate $M(\mathcal{S}, j, 1)$ as $M(\mathcal{S}, j)$ and $\mathcal{C}^M(\mathcal{S}, j, 1)$ as $\mathcal{C}^M(\mathcal{S}, j)$. The following lemma will be useful in the proof of subsequent theorems.

Lemma 1. *The capacity of the IMAC* $\mathcal{C}$ *is included in* $\overline{\mathcal{C}}$, *i.e.*

$$\mathcal{C} \subseteq \overline{\mathcal{C}}$$

where $\overline{\mathcal{C}} =$

$$\left\{ \begin{array}{l} R_i \geq 0: \\ (R_1, R_2) \in \mathcal{C}^M(\{1, 2\}, 1) \\ (R_3, R_4) \in \mathcal{C}^M(\{3, 4\}, 2) \\ (R_1, R_2, R_3) \in \mathcal{C}^M(\{1, 2, 3\}, 1) \text{ if } h_1^2 \geq 1 \\ (R_1, R_2, R_4) \in \mathcal{C}^M(\{1, 2, 4\}, 1) \text{ if } h_2^2 \geq 1 \\ (R_1, R_3, R_4) \in \mathcal{C}^M(\{1, 3, 4\}, 2) \text{ if } h_1^2 \geq 1 \\ (R_2, R_3, R_4) \in \mathcal{C}^M(\{2, 3, 4\}, 2) \text{ if } h_2^2 \geq 1 \end{array} \right\} \tag{5}$$

Proof. The bound on (R_1, R_2) is trivial since $M(\{1, 2\}, 1)$ is the interference-free version of the first MAC, and the presense of interference cannot improve the rates. Similarly $(R_3, R_4) \in \mathcal{C}^M(\{3, 4\}, 2)$. For the other bounds, assume that $h_1^2 \geq 1$, and consider a rate tuple in $\mathcal{C}$. Since the rate tuple is in $\mathcal{C}$, then the first receiver is able to decode both M_1 and M_2. If we give M_4 to the first receiver as genie information, it can construct $\tilde{Y}_2^n$, a less noisy version of Y_2^n from its own observation Y_1^n as follows

$$\tilde{Y}_2^n = \frac{1}{h_1}(Y_1^n - X_1^n - X_2^n - h_2 X_4^n) + h_1 X_1^n + h_2 X_2^n + X_4^n \tag{6}$$

$$= h_1 X_1^n + h_2 X_2^n + X_3^n + X_4^n + \frac{1}{h_1} Z_1^n, \tag{7}$$

which is less noisy than Y_2^n since $h_1^2 \geq 1$. Therefore, for a rate tuple in $\mathcal{C}$, since M_3 can be reliably decoded from Y_2^n, it can also be relaibly decoded from $\tilde{Y}_2^n$. Hence, a code for the genie aided IMAC with $h_1^2 \geq 1$ is also a code for the MAC from transmitters 1, 2, and 3 to receiver 1. Thus, we obtain the outer bound $(R_1, R_2, R_3) \in \mathcal{C}^M(\{1, 2, 3\}, 1)$. The other bounds are obtained similarly.

3.1 Capacity with Mixed Strong–Extremely Strong Interference

Consider the following special case of the IMAC.

Definition 2. *The IMAC has mixed strong–extremely strong interference* $MSES(i, j)$ *if for* $i, j \in \{1, 2\}$, $i \neq j$, *we have*

$$h_j^2 \geq 1 + P_1 + P_2 + h_i^2 P_i, \tag{8}$$
$$h_i^2 \geq 1. \tag{9}$$

where h_i *represents the strong interference channel, and* h_j *the extremely strong one.*

The capacity region then follows from this theorem.

Theorem 1. *The capacity region of the IMAC with mixed strong–extremely strong interference* $MSES(1, 2)$ *is given by*

$$\mathcal{C} = \left\{ \begin{array}{l} (R_1, R_2, R_3, R_4) \in \mathbb{R}_+^4 : \\ (R_1, R_2, R_3) \in \mathcal{C}^M(\{1, 2, 3\}, 1) \\ (R_1, R_3, R_4) \in \mathcal{C}^M(\{1, 3, 4\}, 2) \end{array} \right\} \tag{10}$$

Note that due to symmetry in the channel, the sets $\mathcal{C}^M(\{1, 2, 3\}, 1)$ and $\mathcal{C}^M(\{1, 3, 4\}, 2)$ are in fact equal. A similar result holds for the other case $MSES(2, 1)$.

Proof (Proof Sketch). The outer bound is obtained from Lemma 1. The inner bound is obtained using the following scheme. Receivers decode the extremely strong interfering signal first while treating all other signals as noise. That is, X_4^n is decoded first at receiver 1 while treating X_1^n, X_2^n, and X_3^n as noise, and X_1^n is decoded first at receiver 2 while treating X_2^n, X_3^n, and X_4^n as noise. This is reliably possible due to condition (8). Then the receivers remove the contribution of the decoded interference from their received signal, and decode the remaining signals in a MAC fashion, achieving the outer bound.

3.2 Capacity with Individually Very Strong Interference

Inspired by the interference channel with very strong interference [4], where the presence of cross-links does not impair the capacity region, we now consider the following special case of the IMAC.

Definition 3. *The IMAC has individually very strong interference if*

$$h_1^2, h_2^2 \geq 1 + P_1 + P_2, \tag{11}$$

We call this *individually very strong*, since both cross-link gains have to satisfy separate conditions.

Theorem 2. *The capacity region of the IMAC with individually very strong interference is*

$$\mathcal{C} = \left\{ \begin{array}{l} R_i \geq 0 : \\ (R_1, R_2) \in \mathcal{C}^M(\{1, 2\}, 1), \\ (R_3, R_4) \in \mathcal{C}^M(\{3, 4\}, 2), \end{array} \right\} \tag{12}$$

As in the case of the interference channel, the capacity region is not impaired by the presence of cross-links, i.e., the interference-free capacity is achieved. Note that because of symmetry in the channel, the sets $\mathcal{C}^M(\{1, 2\}, 1)$ and $\mathcal{C}^M(\{3, 4\}, 2)$ are in fact equal.

Proof (Proof Sketch). The outer bound is given by Lemma 1. This outer bound is achievable as follows. Transmitters use Gaussian codebooks. Each receiver decodes both interfering signals first while treating both desired signals as noise. Reliable decoding of interference is possible if $(R_1, R_2) \in \mathcal{C}^M(\{1, 2\}, 2, 1+P_1+P_2)$ and $(R_3, R_4) \in \mathcal{C}^M(\{3, 4\}, 1, 1+P_1+P_2)$. Then, each receiver subtracts the contribution of the interfering signals, and decodes the desired signals interference free. Reliable decoding of the desired signals is possible if $(R_1, R_2) \in \mathcal{C}^M(\{1, 2\}, 1)$ and $(R_3, R_4) \in \mathcal{C}^M(\{3, 4\}, 2)$. Now if condition (11) holds, then $\mathcal{C}^M(\{1, 2\}, 1) \subseteq \mathcal{C}^M(\{1, 2\}, 2, 1 + P_1 + P_2)$ and $\mathcal{C}^M(\{3, 4\}, 2) \subseteq \mathcal{C}^M(\{3, 4\}, 1, 1 + P_1 + P_2)$ and hence the regions $\mathcal{C}^M(\{1, 2\}, 1)$ and $\mathcal{C}^M(\{3, 4\}, 2)$ are achievable.

As shown in Figure 2, condition (11) guarantees that the region $\mathcal{C}^M(\{3, 4\}, 2)$ (solid blue) is completely contained in $\mathcal{C}^M(\{3, 4\}, 1, 1 + P_1 + P_2)$ (dashed red). The intuition is that the first receiver can decode the messages from transmitters 3 and 4 even under the additional noise caused by the first two transmitters.

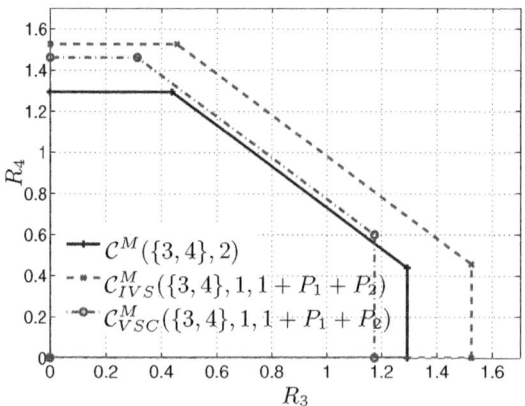

Fig. 2. The interference-free MAC $M(\{3, 4\}, 2)$ as compared to $M(\{3, 4\}, 1, 1+P_1+P_2)$ under the scenarios of Theorem 2 (individually very strong, IVS) and Theorem 3 (very strong combined, VSC).

3.3   Sum Capacity with Very Strong Combined Interference

Now consider a weaker condition than (11).

Definition 4. *The IMAC has very strong combined interference if*

$$h_1^2 P_1 + h_2^2 P_2 \geq (P_1 + P_2)(1 + P_1 + P_2), \tag{13}$$

We call this the very strong combined interference regime because the condition is on the sum of the interference powers at each receiver. It is clear that individually very strong interference implies very strong combined interference. The converse, however, does not hold.

This special case permits the following result.

Theorem 3. *The sum capacity of the IMAC with very strong combined interference is*

$$C_\Sigma = \log(1 + P_1 + P_2). \tag{14}$$

This means that the sum capacities of the interference-free MACs $M(\{1,2\},1)$ and $M(\{3,4\},2)$, namely $1/2 \cdot \log(1 + P_1 + P_2)$ each, are achievable in the IMAC.

Proof (Proof Sketch). From the outer bound in Lemma 1, we know that the sum capacity is upper bounded by $\log(1 + P_1 + P_2)$. Now, by using the scheme in the proof of Theorem 2, we show that the following region is achievable

$$\underline{\mathcal{C}} = \left\{ \begin{array}{l} (R_1, R_2, R_3, R_4) \in \mathbb{R}_+^4 : \\ (R_1, R_2) \in \mathcal{C}^M(\{1,2\},1) \cap \mathcal{C}^M(\{1,2\}, 2, 1 + P_1 + P_2) \\ (R_3, R_4) \in \mathcal{C}^M(\{3,4\},2) \cap \mathcal{C}^M(\{3,4\}, 1, 1 + P_1 + P_2) \end{array} \right\}$$

Under condition (13), the maximum of the sum of the achievable rates in $\underline{\mathcal{C}}$ is $\log(1 + P_1 + P_2)$ which is equal to the upper bound.

An example is shown in Figure 2. Although $\mathcal{C}^M(\{3,4\}, 1, 1 + P_1 + P_2)$ (dot-dashed green) is not a superset of $\mathcal{C}^M(\{3,4\},2)$ (solid blue), it still does not constrain the sum rate to a value below the sum capacity of $\mathcal{C}^M(\{3,4\},2)$. Therefore, the overall sum rate of the IMAC is not impaired by the presence of cross-links.

Notice that the achievable rate region $\underline{\mathcal{C}}$ in the proof above is a cartesian product, i.e., it does not contain conditions that couple the two constituent MACs. We therefore do not expect this region to be optimal in general.

Figure 3 shows the channel parameter range where the *capacity regions* of the interference free MACs $M(\{1,2\},1)$ and $M(\{3,4\},2)$ are achievable, as compared to the parameter range where their *sum capacities* are achievable.

3.4   Sum Capacity Upper Bound for the IMAC

In this subsection, we provide an upper bound on the sum capacity of the symmetric IMAC. In [6,7,8], a genie aided technique was used to obtain a sum

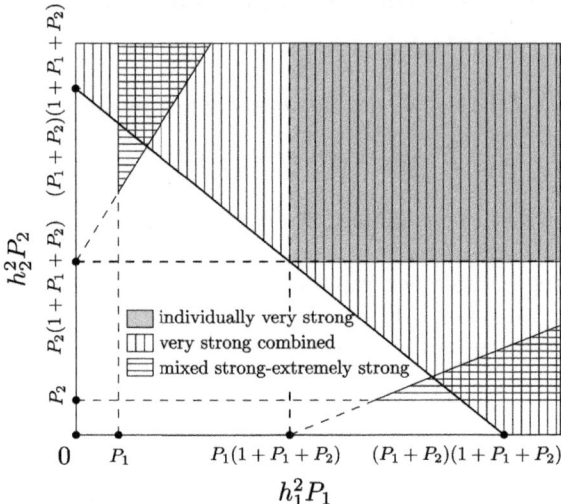

Fig. 3. In the parameter range within the shaded area (see (11)), the capacity region of the interference free MACs $M(\{1,2\},1)$ and $M(\{3,4\},2)$ is achievable simultaneously, while in the range within the vertically dashed area (see (13)), this holds only for the sum capacities. The horizontally dashed area denotes the parameter range with mixed strong–extremely strong interference.

capacity upper bound for the IC that coincides with the simple lower bound of treating interference as noise. Thus the sum capacity of the IC in the so-called noisy interference regime was obtained. We use a similar technique to that used in [6] to obtain an upper bound for the IMAC. This upper bound is stated in the following theorem.

Theorem 4. *The sum capacity of the IMAC is upper bounded by $\overline{C}_\Sigma$,*

$$C_\Sigma \leq \overline{C}_\Sigma \triangleq \min_{\substack{\rho \in [-1,1], \\ \eta^2 \leq 1 - \rho^2}} \log\left(1 + \frac{1}{\eta^2}\left(\mathsf{INR} + \frac{A}{1 - \rho^2 + \mathsf{INR}}\right)\right) \qquad (15)$$

where $\mathsf{INR} = h_1^2 P_1 + h_2^2 P_2$, *and*

$$A = P_1(\eta - \rho h_1)^2 + P_2(\eta - \rho h_2)^2 + P_1 P_2(h_1 - h_2)^2.$$

Proof (Proof sketch). We bound $R_1 + R_2$ and $R_3 + R_4$ by using a genie aided approach similar to [6]. We give receiver 1 the genie signal $S_1^n = h_1 X_1^n + h_2 X_2^n + \eta_1 W_1^n$ and receiver 2 $S_2^n = h_1 X_3^n + h_2 X_4^n + \eta_2 W_2^n$ where $W_i \sim \mathcal{N}(0,1)$ and $\mathbb{E}[W_i Z_i] = \rho_i$, $i = 1, 2$. The parameters η and ρ are introduced to control the quality of the side information provided by the genie, to allow the optimization of the upper bound. Namely, ρ controls the correlation between the genie noise and the noise at the receivers, and η controls the variance of the genie noise.

After adding the bounds, we observe that their sum is maximized by Gaussian inputs if $\eta_i^2 \leq 1 - \rho_j^2$, $j \neq i$. By evaluating the upper bound for Gaussian inputs, we obtain the desired expression.

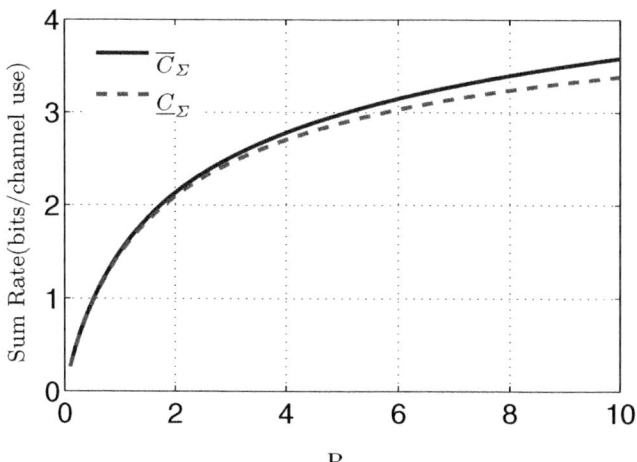

Fig. 4. Sum Capacity upper bound and lower bound for an IMAC with $P_1 = P_2 = P$, $h_1 = 0.3$, and $h_2 = 0.15$

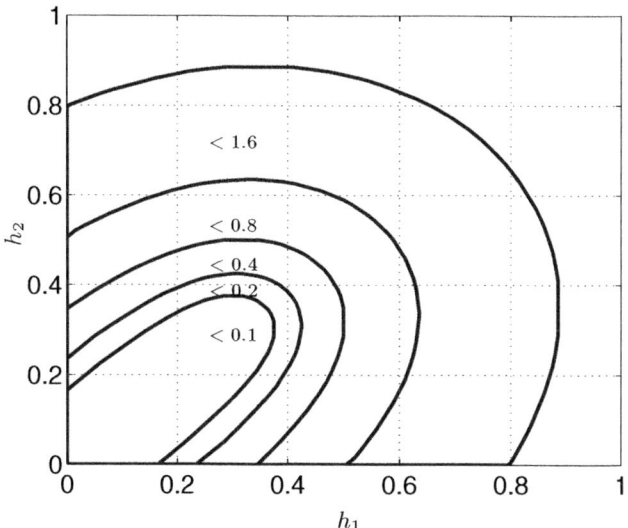

Fig. 5. This plot shows the gap $\overline{C}_\Sigma - \underline{C}_\Sigma$ as a function of h_1 and h_2 when $P_1 = P_2 = 5$. Each region denotes a set of pairs (h_1, h_2) where the gap is smaller than the indicated value 0.1, 0.2...

A sum capacity lower bound is obtained by using Gaussian codes and treating interference as noise, namely

$$C_\Sigma \geq \underline{C}_\Sigma = \log\left(1 + \frac{P_1 + P_2}{1 + h_1^2 P_1 + h_2^2 P_2}\right). \tag{16}$$

In Figure 4, we plot the upper bound $\overline{C}_\Sigma$ and the lower bound $\underline{C}_\Sigma$ for an IMAC with $P_1 = P_2 = P$, $h_1 = 0.3$, and $h_2 = 0.15$. Notice that this upper bound is nearly tight up to some value of P. Intuitively, this means that below some threshold value of INR, treating interference as noise achieves sum rate very close to the sum capacity C_Σ.

Figure 5 shows the gap between $\overline{C}_\Sigma$ and $\underline{C}_\Sigma$ in bits per channel use for an IMAC with $P_1 = P_2 = 5$ versus h_1 and h_2.

4   Conclusion

In this paper, progress has been made towards understanding the interfering MACs (IMAC) channel. The capacity region was characterized under various special cases, namely mixed strong–extremely strong interference, individually very strong interference, very strong combined interference. In the opposite extreme, when the interference is weak, a genie-based upper bound was obtained which is asymptotically tight and nearly tight for reasonably weak cross links.

References

1. Ahlswede, R.: Multi-way communication channels. In: Proceedings of 2nd International Symposium on Information Theory, Tsahkadsor, Armenian S.S.R (September 1971)
2. Liao, H.H.J.: Multiple access channels. Ph.D. dissertation, Department of Electrical Engineering. University of Hawaii, Honolulu (September 1972)
3. Carleial, A.B.: Interference channels. IEEE Transactions on Information Theory 24(1), 60–70 (1978)
4. Carleial, A.B.: A case where interference does not reduce capacity. IEEE Transactions on Information Theory IT-21(1), 569–570 (1975)
5. Sato, H.: The capacity of the Gaussian interference channel under strong interference. IEEE Transactions on Information Theory IT-27(6), 786–788 (1981)
6. Annapureddy, V.S., Veeravalli, V.V.: Gaussian interference networks: Sum capacity in the low interference regime and new outer bounds on the capacity region. IEEE Transactions on Information Theory 55(7), 3032–3050 (2009)
7. Shang, X., Kramer, G., Chen, B.: A new outer bound and the noisy-interference sum-rate capacity for Gaussian interference channels. IEEE Transactions on Information Theory 55(2), 689–699 (2009)
8. Motahari, A.S., Khandani, A.K.: Capacity bounds for the Gaussian interference channel. IEEE Transactions on Information Theory 55(2), 620–643 (2009)
9. Weng, Y., Tuninetti, D.: On Gaussian interference channels with mixed interference. In: Proceedings of the 2008 Information Theory and Applications Workshop (ITA), San Diego, CA USA (January 2008)
10. Cadambe, V.R., Jafar, S.A., Wang, C.: Interference alignment with asymmetric complex signaling - settling the Host-Madsen-Nosratinia conjecture. IEEE Transactions on Information Theory 56(9), 4552–4565 (2010)
11. Suh, C., Tse, D.: Interference alignment for cellular networks. In: Proceedings of 40th Annual Allerton Conference on Communication, Control and Computing (September 2008)
12. Cover, T., Thomas, J.: Elements of information theory. John Wiley and Sons, Chichester (1991)

Low Complexity Time Domain Equalization for Cyclic Prefix Multicode CDMA

Daniela Valente, Ernestina Cianca, Marina Ruggieri, and Ramjee Prasad

Center for TeleInFrastruktur (CTIF)-Italy
University of Rome Tor Vergata - Italy
{daniela.valente,ernestina.cianca,ruggieri}@uniroma2.it
Center for TeleInFrastruktur (CTIF)
Aalborg University - Denmark
prasad@es.aau.dk

Abstract. This paper presents a low complexity time-domain equalization approach for a novel multicode CDMA scheme. The novel multicode CDMA scheme is inherently characterized by lower ICI and the paper shows how the analysis of the ICI of this cyclic prefixed multicode CDMA suggests a novel way to equalize this scheme. The paper presents the novel low complexity equalization where the IFFT/FFT operations can be skipped and results show that the multicode scheme with the novel equalization performs almost like an OFDMA scheme.

Keywords: Multicode DS-CDMA, Equalization, FDE, Multipath, FFT (Fast Fourier Transform).

1 Introduction

The 3GPP Long Term Evolution (LTE) is the latest step in cellular 3G services. The main drivers for the evolution towards LTE are needs for high-speed data and media transport as well as high-capacity voice support [1]. Demand for higher data-rate is leading to the utilization of wider transmission bandwidth but a main challenge for high-speed broadband cellular wireless access systems is the dominant propagation impairment due to multipath effects in the terrestrial radio channel which cause inter-symbol interference (ISI). For high data-rate transmissions, the complexity and required digital processing speed become prohibitive, and the more traditional time domain equalization (TDE) approach becomes unattractive. LTE advanced foresees a FDE (Frequency Domain Equalization) approach both in the downlink, where OFDMA (Orthogonal Frequency Domain Multiple Access) has been chosen as transmission technique, and in the uplink, where SC-FDMA (Single Carrier - Frequency Domain Equalization) has been chosen. FDE approach allows to get the required performance with lower complexity than TDE receivers in very frequency-selective channels. The equalization step is less complex (one-tap equalizer) and most of the complexity is in the FFT/IFFT operations. In case of OFDMA, one Inverse-FFT

C. Sacchi et al. (Eds.): MACOM 2011, LNCS 6886, pp. 97–106, 2011.

(IFFT) and one FFT are done at the TX, in case of SC-FDMA they are both done at the TX. At the same time, other studies on the use of DS-CDMA (Direct Sequence - Code Division Multiple Access) with frequency domain equalization based on the minimum mean square error (MMSE) criterion have been conducted [2]. The main problem is that the residual inter-chip interference (ICI) is present after MMSE-FDE and this limits the BER performance improvement. In [3], Authors proposed a frequency-domain ICI cancellation for the DS-CDMA downlink and showed that frequency-domain ICI cancelation can bring the BER performance very close to the theoretical lower-bound. In [4], a novel multicode CDMA scheme has been proposed which is inherently characterized by lower ICI, as shown in [5]. In this paper we show how the analysis of the ICI of the novel cyclic prefixed multicode CDMA suggests a novel way to equalize the proposed scheme. The paper presents the novel low complexity equalization where the IFFT/FFT operations can be skipped. Results show that the multicode scheme with the novel equalization performs almost like an OFDMA scheme. In [4], Authors have proposed a special type of multicode-CDMA with FDE which has performance very close to that ones of an OFDMA scheme. With respect to a normal DS-CDMA scheme with FDE [2], the new structure of the transmission signal allows to drastically reduce the inter-chip interference, as it is shown in [5] and gets performance very close to an OFDMA system. In this paper, we show that the proposed cyclic prefixed multicode scheme can be equalized with a very low complexity receiver without need of using FFT/IFFT processing. This powerful result is a consequence of the observation that if symbols are sent in parallel as in a OFDMA system it is possible to equalize the received signal in time domain using the same approach which the OFDMA scheme applies in the frequency domain. This paper presents the new receiver architecture and simulations show that the proposed equalization scheme performs like OFDMA.

The paper is organized as follows: Section 2 describes the system model for multicode CDMA with FDE outlining the differences in the transmitted signal structure with respect to DS-CDMA with FDE; the proposed low complexity equalization approach for Multicode CDMA is derived in Section 3; Section 4 shows numerical examples of the proposed low complexity equalization approach for multicode CDMA in comparison with Frequency Domain Equalization over Rayleigh fading channels. Conclusions are drawn in Section 5.

2   System Model

It is assumed block-level transmission with cyclic prefix insertion: the block unit is supposed to be N-chip long where N is the number of points of the Fast-Fourier Transform at the receiver. M is the spreading gain for both the systems and N/M is the number of data symbols that each user sent within the transmission block.

During each transmission, the maximum number of allocated users is $U = M$. T_c denotes the chip interval, T_s the data symbol interval and T_b the block interval; therefore, each parallel transmission within the block contains $N = T_b/T_c$ chips.

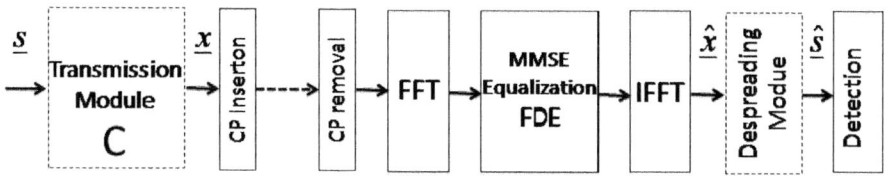

Fig. 1. Common System Model for the downlink transceiver of both Multicode CDMA and DS-CDMA with FDE

Each u-th user transmits N/M information symbols per block that are collected in the vector:

$$\mathbf{s} = [s_u(0), \dots, s_u(N/M - 1)] \tag{1}$$

Fig. 2 and Fig. 3 show how one transmission block is built for DS-CDMA with FDE and multicode CDMA with FDE, respectively.

DS-CDMA with FDE

In order to obtain a DS-CDMA transmission block (Fig. 2), each data symbol $s_u(i)$ where $i \in \{0, \dots, N/M - 1\}$ is extended by a M-chip long Walsh-Hadamard code $\mathbf{c}_u$ assigned to each u-th user.

The block of N/M consecutive information symbols can be written as:

$$\boldsymbol{x}_u = [s_u(0)\mathbf{c}_u, \dots, s_u(N/M - 1)\mathbf{c}_u] \tag{2}$$

with $\mathbf{c}_u = [c_u(0), c_u(1), \dots, c_u(M - 1)]$.

Multicode CDMA with FDE

In case of multicode CDMA with FDE (Fig. 3), each information symbol within the block is spread by a N-chip long Walsh-Hadamard code to form a $N \times 1$ chip block. In this case:

$$\boldsymbol{x}_u = \mathbf{s}\boldsymbol{C}_u \tag{3}$$

where $\boldsymbol{C}_u$ denotes the $N/M \times N$ spreading matrix of the u-th user.

$$\boldsymbol{C}_u = \begin{pmatrix} c_u^{(0)}(0) & c_u^{(0)}(1) & \dots & c_u^{(0)}(N-1) \\ c_u^{(1)}(0) & c_u^{(1)}(1) & \dots & c_u^{(1)}(N-1) \\ \dots & \dots & \dots & \dots \\ c_u^{(N/M-1)}(0) & c_u^{(N/M-1)}(1) & \dots & c_u^{(N/M-1)}(N-1) \end{pmatrix} \tag{4}$$

with $c_u^{(i)}(n)$ the i-th code assigned to the u-th user, where $i \in \{0, \dots, N/M - 1\}$ and $n \in \{0, \dots, N - 1\}$ is the chip index.

The main difference with DS-CDMA with FDE is that in case of multicode approach, each symbol is first time-extended up to N/M times and then multiplied by one of the N-chip long code of the set of N/M codes assigned to the u-th user. In comparison with the multicode CDMA presented in [2], the block

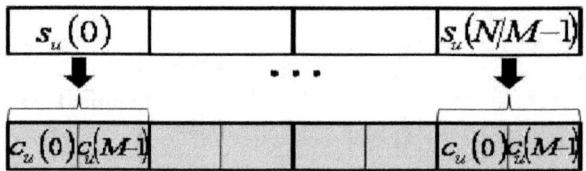

(a) Single-user data symbols transmission within the transmission block

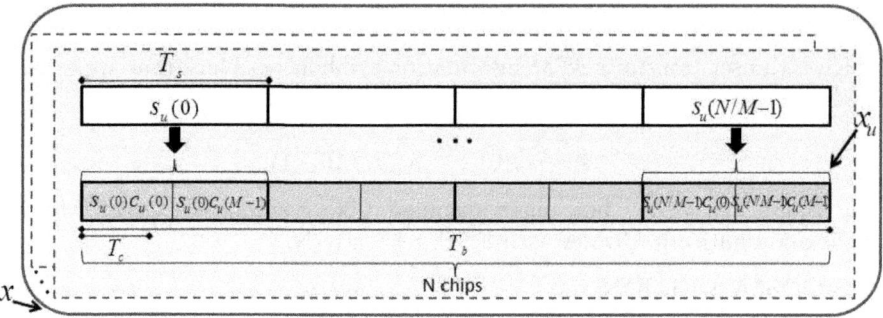

(b) Transmission block considering users multiplexing

Fig. 2. DS-CDMA with FDE

length N is function of both the number of data symbols of each user N/M and the total number of users $U = M$ assigned to the system; in this way it is possible to see the OFDMA as a special case of this multicode CDMA with FDE if the used code set is the one made by complex exponentials. Moreover, DS-CDMA is also an instance of our multicode CDMA, but symbols of one user are transmitted in serial over the physical channel.

However, even if the codes are N-chip long, there is an implicit time duration extension therefore the actual spreading factor is still M as for the equivalent DS-CDMA with FDE symbol transmission. In the following, the length of the specific spreading code is addressed with the common notation SF meaning that in case of DS-CDMA its value is M while in case of multicode it is N. For synchronous transmissions, the sums of all users' chip sequences is:

$$\mathbf{x} = \sum_{u=0}^{U-1} \mathbf{x}_u \qquad (5)$$

The multiuser chipblock $\mathbf{x}$ is then extended with a Cyclic Prefix (CP) of length G, longer than the maximum excess delay of the channel to accommodate the inter-symbol interference.

At the receiver, for both the systems, the received block after removal of cyclic prefix can be formulated as:

$$\mathbf{r} = \mathbf{x}\mathbf{H}_t + \mathbf{n} \qquad (6)$$

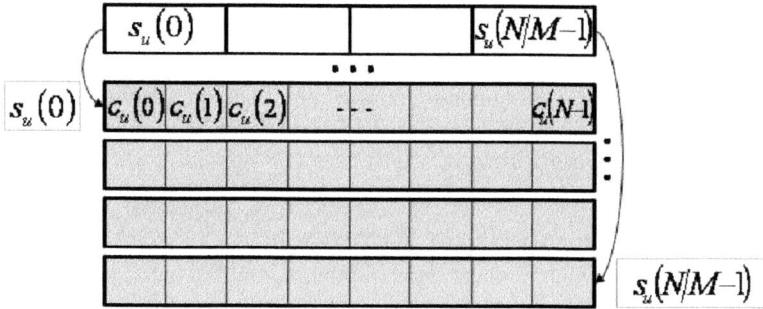

(a) Single-user data symbols transmission within the transmission block.

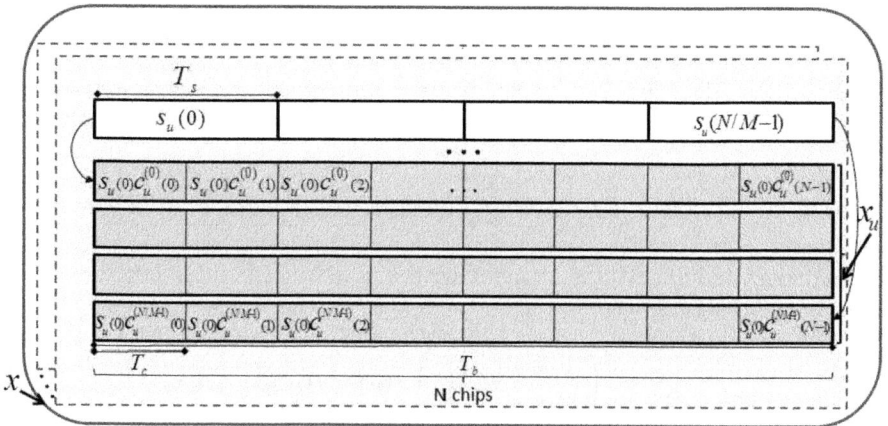

(b) Transmission block considering users multiplexing.

Fig. 3. Multicode CDMA with FDE

where **x** is the block of transmitted spread symbols or chips prior to insertion of cyclic prefix, given in eq. (5), **n** is the Additive White Gaussian Noise (AWGN) vector and $\mathbf{H}_t$ is the NxN circulant channel matrix formed by the impulse response channel coefficients $(h_0, h_1,.....,h_{L-1})$ as follows:

$$\mathbf{H}_t = \begin{pmatrix} h_0 & 0 & \ldots \ldots \ldots \ldots & h_2 & h_1 \\ h_1 & h_0 & \ldots \ldots \ldots \ldots & h_3 & h_2 \\ \ldots & \ldots & \ldots \ldots \ldots \ldots \ldots & \ldots \\ h_{L-2} & h_{L-3} & \ldots \ldots \ldots \ldots & 0 & h_{L-1} \\ h_{L-1} & h_{L-2} & \ldots \ldots \ldots \ldots & 0 & 0 \\ 0 & h_{L-1} & \ldots \ldots \ldots \ldots & 0 & 0 \\ \ldots & \ldots & \ldots \ldots \ldots \ldots & h_0 & 0 \\ 0 & 0 & \ldots \ldots \ldots \ldots & h_1 & h_0 \end{pmatrix} \tag{7}$$

The Rayleigh fading channel model includes the physical channel as well as transmit and receive filter. After the Discrete Fourier Transform (DFT), we have the signal:

$$\mathbf{Wr} = \mathbf{WxH}_t + \mathbf{Wn} \tag{8}$$

where $\mathbf{W}$ is the NxN normalized DFT matrix. The signal $\mathbf{Wr}$ is first equalized by using a one-tap FD (Frequency Domain) equalizer and then it goes through the IDFT block. We assume to use an FDE based on Minimum Mean Squared Error (MMSE) combining criteria.

3   Proposed Equalization Approach

In this section, we describe a new low complexity approach in time domain to equalize at the receiver the multicode signal. In case of multicode transmission, we have parallel transmission of user's spread symbols and hence it is possible to express the user symbol to detect in a useful way for the equalization and detection processing.

In order to describe the new equalization approach, it is convenient to consider the signal $\hat{\mathbf{x}}$ in Fig 4(a), after the N-point IFFT transform applied to the signal $\hat{\mathbf{X}}$:

$$\hat{x}(n) = \frac{1}{N} \sum_{k=0}^{N-1} \hat{X}(k) \exp\left(j2\pi nk/N\right) \tag{9}$$

k frequency-index and n time-index with $k, n = 0 \sim (N-1)$. The signal in (9) can be rewritten as:

$$\hat{x}(n) = \left(\frac{1}{N} \sum_{k=0}^{N-1} \hat{H}_f(k)\right) x(n) + I\hat{C}I(n) + \hat{n}(n) \tag{10}$$

where $x(n)$ is the transmitted chip at the time instant n, $I\hat{C}I(n)$ is the residual time-domain inter-chip interference component after FDE and $\hat{n}(n)$ is the time-domain noise component after equalization. $\hat{H}_f(k)$ is the frequency channel response after frequency domain equalization and *plain* $H_f(k)$ is the k-th subcarrier component of the channel gain:

$$H_f(k) = \sum_{l=0}^{L-1} h_l \exp\left(-j2\pi k \frac{\tau_l}{N}\right) \tag{11}$$

with h_l and τ_l the complex-valued path gain and time delay of the l-th path ($l = 0 \sim (L-1)$), respectively. Therefore the frequency channel response after FDE is:

$$\hat{H}_f(k) = m_f(k)H_f(k) \tag{12}$$

where $m_f(k)$ is the FDE MMSE equalization weight for the k-th subcarrier. The u-th user's decision variable $\hat{s}_u(i)$ after despreading of $\hat{\mathbf{x}}$ is:

$$\hat{s}_u(i) = \frac{1}{SF} \sum_{n=iSF}^{(i+1)SF-1} \hat{x}(n) c_u^{(i)*}(n) \tag{13}$$

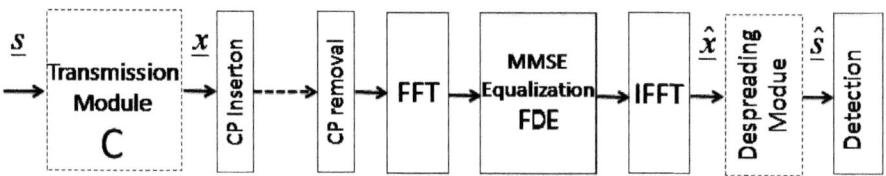

(a) System model for the multicode CDMA with Frequency Domain Equalization, as in Fig. 1

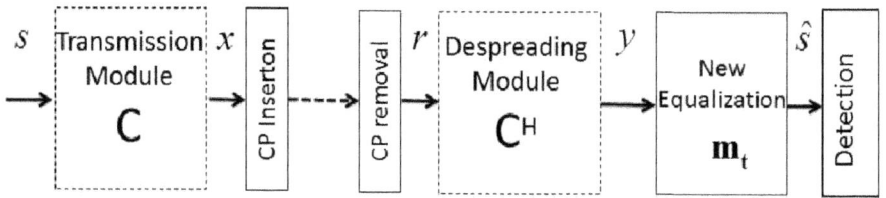

(b) System model for the multicode CDMA with the new equalization technique in time domain

Fig. 4. Comparison of equalization techniques for multicode transmission scheme

i data symbol-index, with $i \in \{0, 1, \ldots, N/M-1\}$. Therefore, also according analysis in [3], the u-th user's inter-chip interference component after despreading reads:

$$
I\tilde{C}I_u(i) = \frac{1}{SF} \sum_{n=iSF}^{(i+1)SF-1} c_u^{(i)*}(n) \frac{1}{N} \sum_{k=0}^{N-1} \hat{H}_f(k)
$$
$$
\times \left[\sum_{\substack{\tau=0 \\ \neq n}}^{N-1} x(\tau) \exp\left(j2\pi k(n - \tau)/N\right) \right]
\tag{14}
$$

Expression in eq. (14) is the general expression of the inter-chip interference component valid for both DS-CDMA and multicode block transmission with FDE. It can be rewritten in a easier way for multicode transmission, because in this case we have parallel transmission of users's symbols instead of serial one as in case of DS-CDMA with FDE.

Hence the inter-chip component for multicode has the following expression with $SF = N$:

$$
I\tilde{C}I_u(i) = \frac{1}{N^2} A_s \sum_{k=0}^{N-1} \hat{H}_f(k) \sum_{n=iN}^{(i+1)N-1} \sum_{\substack{\tau=0 \\ \neq n}}^{N-1} c_u^{(i)}(n) c_u^{(i)*}(\tau)
$$
$$
\times \exp\left(j2\pi k(n - \tau)/N\right)
\tag{15}
$$

where $A_s = \sum_{u=0}^{U-1} \sum_{i=0}^{N/M-1} s_u(i)$ with $U = M$.

Therefore, the u-th user's decision variable $\hat{s}_u(i)$ on the i-th information symbol for the multicode CDMA scheme is given by:

$$\hat{s}_u(i) = \frac{1}{N^2} s_u(i) \sum_{k=0}^{N-1} \hat{H}_f(k) + I\hat{C}I_u(i) + \tilde{n}(i) \tag{16}$$

where $\tilde{n}(i)$ is the noise component after despreading.

Observing eq. (16), we have realized the possibility to skip FDE processing in order to detect the transmitted data symbol $s_u(i)$ in eq. (16) and this is the first step towards the new equalization approach. Assuming that the FDE equalization weights are equal to 1 for each k-th subcarrier (i.e. $m_f(k) = 1$ for all k), we have $\hat{H}_f(k) = H_f(k)$ and therefore it is possible to rewrite eq. (16) as follows:

$$\hat{s}_u(i) = \frac{1}{N^2} s_u(i) \sum_{k=0}^{N-1} H_f(k) + I\bar{C}I_u(i) + \bar{n}(i) \tag{17}$$

with $I\bar{C}I_u(i)$ and $\bar{n}(i)$ residual time-domain inter-chip interference and noise component in case of FDE equalization weights equal to 1. We notice that in this case, the signal vector $\hat{s}$ in scheme in Fig. 4(a) is equivalent to the signal vector $\mathbf{y}$ in scheme in Fig. 4(b) because the MMSE equalization vector is unitary and FFT and IFFT compensate each other, $\mathbf{W}^H \mathbf{W} = \mathbf{I}$. Therefore, it is possible to pass from scheme in Fig. 4(a) to scheme in Fig. 4(b) and the u-th user's signal $y_u(i)$ on the i-th information symbol can be expressed as:

$$y_u(i) = \frac{1}{N^2} s_u(i) \sum_{k=0}^{N-1} H_f(k) + I\bar{C}I_u(i) + \bar{n}(i) \tag{18}$$

and this is true if FDE is not introduced (i.e. $m_f(k) = 1$ for all k). Therefore, it is evident that to extract the desired signal $s_u(i)$ from eq. (18) it would be enough to divide $y_u(i)$ by a term which is $\sum_{k=0}^{N-1} H_f(k)$ using a zero-forcing equalization approach. Moreover, instead of using the zero-forcing approach, we can introduce a MMSE equalization approach which takes in consideration also the presence of interference and noise while calculating the equalization coefficients. It is also worth noting that in case of multicode CDMA transmission the ICI contribution is less in comparison with the DS-CDMA with FDE approach due to the parallel transmission of user's symbols [5]. MMSE combining criteria is applied to obtain the vector $\mathbf{m}_t$ of equalization coefficients in time domain; the received vector $\mathbf{y}$ after despreading will be processed by this equalization vector $\mathbf{m}_t$, as in scheme in Fig. 4(b):

$$\mathbf{m}_t = E[\mathbf{s}\mathbf{y}^H] E[\mathbf{y}\mathbf{y}^H]^{-1} \tag{19}$$

where $\mathbf{s}$ is the true data vector or block of user information symbols and $\mathbf{y}$ is the observation vector. After straight forward algebra to apply the MMSE combining criteria, the equalization vector $\mathbf{m}_t$ reads:

$$\mathbf{m}_t = (\mathbf{C}^H \mathbf{H}^H \mathbf{C})(\mathbf{C}^H \mathbf{H} \mathbf{C} \mathbf{C}^H \mathbf{H}^H \mathbf{C} + SNR^{-1}\mathbf{I})^{-1} \tag{20}$$

where $\mathbf{C}$ is the spreading Matrix and $\mathbf{H}_t$ the circular channel matrix in time domain.

4   Numerical Examples

In this section, a performance comparison among the multicode CDMA scheme, with the new low complexity equalizer and with FDE, DS-CDMA with FDE and OFDMA is shown; full load conditions and same bandwidth for each scheme are assumed. The channel coefficients are assumed to be known at the receiver. The parameters of Monte Carlo simulations are shown in table 1.

Table 1. Simulation parameters

SIMULATION PARAMETERS	
Modulation scheme	QPSK
FFT dimension (N)	256
Effective spreading factor (M)	16
CP length (G)	32
n. channel paths (L)	16

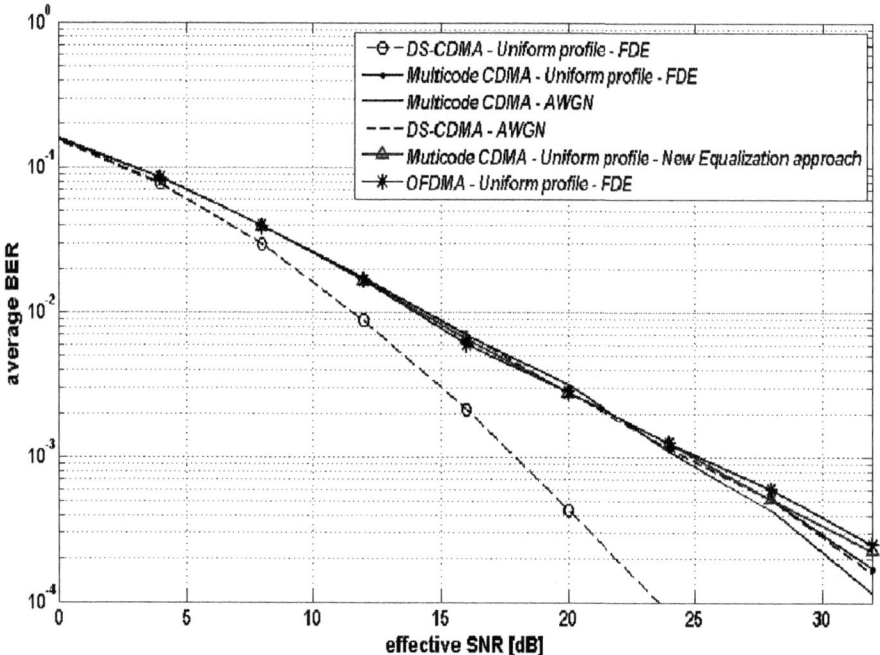

Fig. 5. BER comparison between FDE and the new equalization technique in time domain for a frequency selective Rayleigh fading channel with uniform power delay profile

For multicode CDMA scheme and DS-CDMA, Walsh-Hadamard orthogonal codes are assumed. The number of FFT points is $N = 256$ for all schemes. The spreading factor is $SF = 16$. A quasi-static Rayleigh fading channel is examined: a channel with uniform power delay profile with $L = 16$ paths; each path has a time delay separation of one FFT sample. Unitary energy for each data-modulated symbol after despreading and unitary average power spread over the L paths are assumed.

Computer simulations in Fig. 5 show how the multicode system with the new equalization approach in time domain has similar performance in comparison with the classical FDE and OFDMA. It is worth noting that the new approach has a significant reduction of the receiver complexity without need of using FFT and IFFT processing.

5   Conclusions

This paper presents a very low complexity receiver without need of using FFT/ IFFT processing for cyclic prefixed multicode scheme which uses the parallel transmission of symbols as in a OFDMA system. The proposed low complexity receiver works in time domain and this means that the block received signal does not need to be transformed in the frequency domain but it is despread and then equalizes in time domain, directly with drastic computational complexity reduction. The paper presents the new receiver architecture and simulations show that the proposed equalization scheme performs like OFDMA.

References

1. Zyren, J.: Overview of the 3GPP Long Term Evolution Physical Layer (July 2007) (White Paper)
2. Adachi, F., Sao, T., Itagaki, T.: Performance of multicode DS-CDMA using frequency domain equalisation in frequency selective fading channel. Electronics Letters 39(2), 239–241 (2003)
3. Takeda, K., Adachi, F.: Frequency-Domain Interchip Interference cancelation for DS-CDMA Downlink Transmission. IEEE Transactions on Vehicular Technology 56(3) (May 2007)
4. Cianca, E., Valente, D., Prasad, R.: A modified multicode CDMA scheme with FDE and its equivalence with OFDMA. In: Proc. IEEE 19th International Symposium on Personal, Indoor and Mobile Communications 2008, PIMRC 2008 (September 2008)
5. Valente, D., Cianca, E., Ruggieri, M., Prasad, R.: Interchip Interference and PAPR of a Novel Multicode CDMA with FDE. In: WPMC, Proceedings of Wireless Personal Multimedia Communications Symposia (October 2010)

Resource Allocation in Cooperative Relaying for Multicell OFDMA Systems

Abdelhalim Najjar[1], Noureddine Hamdi[2], and Ammar Bouallegue[1]

[1] Communication Systems Lab, ENIT
Manar University, Tunisia
[2] Departement of Computer Science and Mathematics, INSAT
Carthage University, Tunisia
abdelhalim.najjar@gmail.com,
noureddine.hamdi@ept.rnu.tn,
ammar.bouallegue@enit.rnu.tn

Abstract. In this paper, we propose an allocation algorithm that minimizes the base station (BS) transmit power of broadcast link OFDMA cellular networks and satisfies the user rate requirements. By minimizing the base station transmitted power, the co-channel cell interference (CCI) can be reduced effectively. To perform the mitigation of the CCI, a fixed amplify and forward relay station (RS) that assists the BS to broadcast data to mobiles in the cell edge region, has been adopted. Numerical results are used to show the improvement of the proposed optimal cooperative scheme compared to the performance of similar scheme without relays.

Keywords: Resource Allocation, Cooperative Relaying, OFDMA.

1 Introduction

Recently, intense interest has focused on OFDMA as an attractive multiple access technique for broadband wireless applications. One of the biggest advantages of OFDM systems is the ability to allocate power and rate optimally among subcarriers. Several works have been proposed to perform ressource allocation such as in [1] where an efficient technique is based on a min-max formulation of the optimization problem and is adopted to adhoc networks environment. The authors of [2] and [3] investigate the issue of power control and subcarrier assignment in a sectorized two-cell downlink OFDMA system impaired by co-channel cell interference (CCI). Also, frequency hopping (FH) associated with OFDM modulations offers the advantage of averaging interference as in CDMA system and enables us to adopt a frequency reuse factor (FRF) equal to 1 between co-channel cell in multicell context [4], [5]. Through FH and assuming that the channels are random frequency selective, the authors of [6] propose an allocation algorithm that computes the optimum number of subcarrier per user that satisfies the rate requirement of all users and minimizes the total transmitted power.

In this paper, we perform the general problem for resource allocation proposed in [6] by introducing the cooperative relaying which was addressed in

C. Sacchi et al. (Eds.): MACOM 2011, LNCS 6886, pp. 107–118, 2011.
© Springer-Verlag Berlin Heidelberg 2011

our previous work [7]. For simplicity, we consider a sectored two-cell downlink OFDMA system where a single RS by sector is placed at the edge region of each cell. Downlink cooperation is triggered with the Non orthogonal Amplify and Forward (NAF) cooperation protocol with one relay and two time slots [8]. Numerical results show that the proposed optimal cooperative scheme appreciably outperforms the non-cooperative scheme presented in [6].

2   System Model

In order to simplify our problem, the network is supposed to be one dimensional cellular system that consists of a linear regular array of cells. We assume that a given user is only subject to interference from the nearest interfering cell. Thus we focus on two interfering sectors of two adjacent cells, say cell A and cell B as shown in Fig.1. We denote by D the radius of each cell . A single RS by sector is placed at the edge region of each cell. We denote by N the total number of users in the cell, by W the channel bandwidth and by M the number of available subcarriers. We denote by α_n, the sharing factor associated with user n. Thus, the number of subcarriers modulated by user n is equal to $\alpha_n M$.

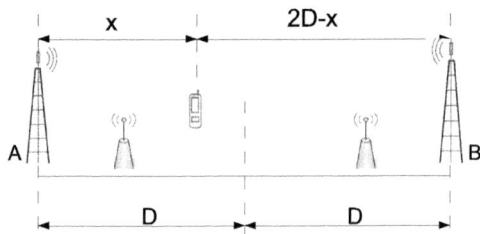

Fig. 1. Two-cell system model

3   Resource Allocation

3.1   Single Cell Context

We denote by R_n the rate requirement for a given user n. For any modulate subcarrier m of the OFDM symbol k, we denote by $e_n = E(|s_n(k,m)|^2)$ the energy transmitted for a given user n. Similarly we define $p_n = \alpha_n e_n$ the average power transmitted to user n. Denoting by $P_A = \sum_{n=1}^{N} p_n$ the average power spent by base station A during one OFDM block. Our aim is then the following: given a rate vector $R = [R_1, ..., R_N]^T$, find the power $\{p_n\}_{n \in \{1,...,N\}}$ such that the total transmitted power P_A is minimum. Furthermore, as we shall study a multicell environment, it is legitimate to limit the interference produced by base station A. Consequently, the power P_A should not exceed a certain nuisance value ν which is assumed to be a predefined constant imposed by system's requirements. To be able to reach the capacity, we approximate the multi-cell interference as a

Gaussian random variable as shown in several studies [2]. The ergodic capacity in the whole bandwidth is given by

$$C_n(\alpha_n, p_n) = \alpha_n E[log(1 + g_n \frac{p_n}{\alpha_n} z)] \tag{1}$$

where g_n is the channel gain-to-noise ratio of user n. The single cell resource allocation problem can be formulated as follow.

•$Minimize$ P_A with respect to $\{\alpha_n, p_n\}_{n \in \{1,...,N\}}$ under the following constraints

$$R_n \leq C_n, \ n = 1, ..., N. \tag{2}$$

$$\sum_{n=1}^{N} \alpha_n = 1 \tag{3}$$

$$\sum_{n=1}^{N} p_n \leq \nu \tag{4}$$

Since the resource parameters of users in cell A are fixed, it is straitforward to show that the ergodic capacity $C_n(\alpha_n, p_n)$ given by (1) is concave function of α_n and p_n (and hence $-C_n(\alpha_n, p_n)$ is convex). Thus the single cell resource allocation problem is convex in $\{\alpha_n, p_n\}_{n \in \{1,...,N\}}$ and can be solved using the Lagrange Karush-kuhn-Tuker (KKT) conditions. At first, we define the Lagrangian L associated with the proposed problem as

$$L(\alpha_n, p_n) = P_A + \sum_{n=1}^{N} \beta_n(R_n - C_n) + \lambda(\sum_{n=1}^{N} \alpha_n - 1) + \xi(\sum_{n=1}^{N} p_n - \mu) \tag{5}$$

where β_n, $n = 1, .., N$ are the Lagrange multipliers associated with constraints (2), the positives numbers λ and ξ are the Lagrange multipliers associated with the constraint (3) and (4) respectively. Considering the vector parameter $X = [P_A^T, \alpha^T]$ where $P_A = [p_1, ..., p_N]^T$ and $\alpha = [\alpha_1, ..., \alpha_N]^T$ The Lagrange(KKT) conditions are then written as

$$\nabla_X L(\alpha_n, p_n) = 0 \Longleftrightarrow \tag{6}$$

$$\nabla_X P_A - \sum_{n=1}^{N} \beta_n \nabla_X C_n + \lambda \nabla_X (\sum_{n=1}^{N} \alpha_n) + \xi \nabla_X (\sum_{n=1}^{N} p_n) = 0 \tag{7}$$

where ∇_X denotes the gradient operator with respect to the vector x. The equation(7) can be rewritten as the set of $2N$ equations given by $\frac{\partial L(\alpha_n, p_n)}{\partial p_n} = 0$ and $\frac{\partial L(\alpha_n, p_n)}{\partial \alpha_n} = 0$ for $n = 1, 2, ...N$. The development of these equations leads to

$$E(\frac{z}{1 + g_n \frac{p_n}{\alpha_n} z}) = \frac{1 + \xi}{\beta_n g_n} \tag{8}$$

$$\beta_n E[log(1 + g_n \frac{p_n}{\alpha_n} z) - \frac{g_n \frac{p_n}{\alpha_n} z}{1 + g_n \frac{p_n}{\alpha_n} z}] = \lambda \tag{9}$$

We define the following function on $\mathbb{R}$

$$\mathcal{F}(x) = \frac{E[log(1+xz)]}{E[\frac{z}{1+xz}]} - x \tag{10}$$

using (8) and (10), (9) can be rewritten as

$$\frac{1+\xi}{g_n}\mathcal{F}(g_n e_n) = \lambda \tag{11}$$

thus e_n can be formulated as

$$e_n(\lambda, \xi) = \frac{1}{g_n}\mathcal{F}^{-1}(\frac{g_n\lambda}{1+\xi}) \tag{12}$$

where $\mathcal{F}^{-1}$ defined in $[0, +\infty[$ is the inverse of $\mathcal{F}$ with respect to composition. Define for each $x \geq 0$

$$L(x) = E[log(1+\mathcal{F}^{-1}(x)z)] \tag{13}$$

the sharing factors α_n, $n = 1, ..., N$, are given by

$$\alpha_n(\lambda, \xi) = \frac{R_n}{L(\frac{g_n\lambda}{1+\xi})} \tag{14}$$

or from constraint (3) we have

$$\sum_{n=1}^{N} \alpha_n(\lambda, \xi) = 1 \tag{15}$$

so λ and ξ verify the following equation

$$\sum_{n=1}^{N} \frac{R_n}{L(\frac{g_n\lambda}{1+\xi})} = 1 \tag{16}$$

The average power transmitted to user n is given by

$$p_n(\lambda, \xi) = \alpha_n(\lambda, \xi)e_n(\lambda, \xi) \tag{17}$$
$$= \frac{R_n}{g_n}\frac{\mathcal{F}^{-1}(\frac{g_n\lambda}{1+\xi})}{L(\frac{g_n\lambda}{1+\xi})}$$

Finally, the expression of P_A can be formulated as

$$P_A = \sum_{n=1}^{N} \frac{R_n}{g_n}\frac{\mathcal{F}^{-1}(\frac{g_n\lambda}{1+\xi})}{L(\frac{g_n\lambda}{1+\xi})} \tag{18}$$

The solution to the single cell allocation problem is unique and can be solved using the following algorithm.

• *Algorithm*:

$\xi \leftarrow 0$.

Repeat

$\lambda \leftarrow$ unique solution to (17).

$P_A \leftarrow \sum_{n=1}^{N} \frac{R_n}{g_n} \frac{\mathcal{F}^{-1}(\frac{g_n\lambda}{1+\xi})}{L(\frac{g_n\lambda}{1+\xi})}$.

if $P_A > \nu$ **then**

Increase ξ

end if

until $P_A \leq \nu$

return λ, ξ

3.2   Asymptotic Regime

As shown in [6], the asymptotic regime is characterized by •$N \to \infty$, •$W \to \infty$ and •$\frac{N}{W} \to \varrho$ where ϱ is a positive constant. The cell can be identified with a compact $I = [\epsilon, D]$ included in $\mathbb{R}_+$ since the cell is considered one dimensional variable. ϵ is a real number which can be chosen as small as needed. It is useful to model g_n as being directly related to the location x_n by

$$g_n = \frac{|x_n|^{-s}}{N_0} \qquad (19)$$

where $|x_n|$ is the distance between the mobile and base station and s is the pathloss component. We denote by $t(x) = \frac{|x|^{-s}}{N_0}$ is a continuous function defined on I to $\mathbb{R}_+^*$. In the following, we denote by $r_n = R_n W$ the required rate for user n in $nats/s$. Without restriction, we assume that for each user n, $r_n \in [r_{min}, r_{max}]$ where r_{max} can be chosen as large as needed. The implementation of equation (18) needs two parameters of user n: R_n and g_n which can be described by the couple (r_n, x_n). Thus, the distribution of the set of couples $\{(r_n, x_n)\}_{n \in \{1,\dots,N\}}$ can be interpreted by the following measure $\mu^{(N)}$ defined on the Borel sets of $\mathbb{R}_+ \times \mathbb{R}_+$ as follows:

$$\mu^{(N)}(U, V) = \frac{1}{N} \sum_{n=1}^{N} \delta_{r_n, x_n}(U, V) \qquad (20)$$

where U and V are any intervals of $\mathbb{R}_+$ and δ_{r_n, x_n} is the Dirac measure at point (r_n, x_n). In order to have a clear idea on the meaning of this measure, $\mu^{(N)}(U, V)$ is equal to Ω/N where Ω is the number of users located in V and requiring a rate (in $nats/s$) in interval U. By replacing R_n by $\frac{r_n}{W}$ in (18), we obtain:

$$P_A^{(N)} = \frac{1}{W} \sum_{n=1}^{N} \frac{r_n \mathcal{F}^{-1}(\frac{t(x_n)\lambda^{(N)}}{1+\xi^{(N)}})}{t(x_n) L(\frac{t(x_n)\lambda^{(N)}}{1+\xi^{(N)}})} \qquad (21)$$

$$= \frac{N}{W} \int_{r_{min}}^{r_{max}} \int_{\epsilon}^{D} \frac{r}{t(x)} \frac{\mathcal{F}^{-1}(\frac{t(x_n)\lambda^{(N)}}{1+\xi^{(N)}})}{L(\frac{t(x_n)\lambda^{(N)}}{1+\xi^{(N)}})} d\mu^{(N)}(r, x)$$

The new notations $P_A^{(N)}$ and $\lambda^{(N)}$ are used to indicate the dependency of the results on the number of users N. Intuitively, the asymptotic power per channel use $lim_{N\to\infty}P_A^N$ can be obtained by replacing, N/W by ϱ, $\lambda^{(N)}$ by λ, $\xi^{(N)}$ by ξ and the distribution $\mu^{(N)}$ by the asymptotic distribution μ of couples (r_n, x_n) as $N\to\infty$. For more details on the convergence of measure, we can refer to [3]. The convergence of $P_A^{(N)}$ will come from the following assumption.

• $Assumption1$: The measure $\mu^{(N)}$ converges weakly to a measure μ as $N\to\infty$. In order to further simplify the expression of the asymptotic power, it is realistic to assume that the limit joint distribution μ of rates distribution times a limit location distribution. This assumption come from the fact that in practice, the rate requirement r_n of a given user n is independent of its location x_n.
• $Assumption2$: The measure μ satisfies $d\mu(r, x) = d\vartheta(r) \times d\varsigma(x)$ where ϑ is the limit distribution of rates and ς is the limit distribution of the users' locations. Here $\times$ denotes the product of measures. Using these two assumptions, $P_A^{(N)}$ converges to a constant P_A^∞ defined by the following theorem
• $Theorem1$: Assume $N\to\infty$ in such a way that $\frac{N}{W}\to\varphi > 0$ and that measure μ^N satisfies assumption 1 and assumption 2. Assume that $t(x)$ is continuous and satisfies $t(x) > 0$ on $[\epsilon, D]$. The total power spent by the network $P_A^{(N)}$ converges to a constant P_A^∞ given by the following form:

$$P_A^\infty = \bar{r} \int_\epsilon^D \frac{\mathcal{F}^{-1}(\frac{t(x)\lambda}{1+\xi})}{t(x)L(\frac{t(x)\lambda}{1+\xi})} d\varsigma(x) \tag{22}$$

where $\bar{r}$ represents the average rate requirements per channel use in cell A given by

$$\bar{r} = \varrho \int_{r_{min}}^{r_{max}} r d\vartheta(r) \tag{23}$$

and (λ, ξ) is the unique solution of

$$\bar{r} \int_\epsilon^D \frac{d\varsigma(x)}{L(\frac{t(x)\lambda}{1+\xi})} = 1 \tag{24}$$

3.3   Multicell Context

For each $c \in \{A, B\}$, we denote by $\bar{c}$ the adjacent cell. We denote by $P_c^{(i)}$, the total required power per channel use transmitted by base station c at the ith moment. The sequence $\left\{P_c^{(i)}\right\}_{\{i\geq 0\}}$ is defined as follows:

• $P_c^{(0)} = 0$: For simplicity and without loss of generality, we initialize the total transmitted power to 0
• $P_c^{(1)} = P_A^\infty = P_B^\infty$: At the moment 1, we execute the allocation algorithm and each BS will transmit a signal with the power P_A^∞.
• $P_c^{(i)} = \Phi(P_{\bar{c}}^{(i-1)}, \bar{r})$ is the power delivered by BS c obtained by iterating at moment i. $\Phi(P_{\bar{c}}^{(i-1)}), \bar{r})$ is the total power per channel use a cell c needs to

transmit to reach the mean rate of $\bar{r}$ nats per channel use when the neighboring cell $\bar{c}$ transmits at power $P_{\bar{c}}^{(i-1)}$. It is given by the following expression:

$$\Phi(P_{\bar{c}}^{(i-1)}, \bar{r}) = \bar{r} \int_{\epsilon}^{D} \frac{\mathcal{F}^{-1}\left(\frac{T_{\bar{c}}(x)\lambda(P_{\bar{c}}^{(i-1)}, \bar{r})}{1+\xi(P_{\bar{c}}^{(i-1)}, \bar{r})}\right)}{T_{\bar{c}}(x)L\left(\frac{T_{\bar{c}}(x)\lambda(P_{\bar{c}}^{(i-1)}, \bar{r})}{1+\xi(P_{\bar{c}}^{(i-1)}, \bar{r})}\right)} d\varsigma(x) \tag{25}$$

where $(\lambda(P_{\bar{c}}^{(i-1)}, \bar{r}), \xi(P_{\bar{c}}^{(i-1)}, \bar{r}))$ is the unique solution to the equation

$$\bar{r} \int_{\epsilon}^{D} \frac{d\varsigma(x)}{L\left(\frac{T_{\bar{c}}(x)\lambda(P_{\bar{c}}^{(i-1)}, \bar{r})}{1+\xi(P_{\bar{c}}^{(i-1)}, \bar{r})}\right)} = 1 \tag{26}$$

and

$$T_{\bar{c}}(x) = \frac{|x|^{-s}}{P_{\bar{c}}^{(i-1)}|2D - x|^{-s} + N_0} \tag{27}$$

The convergence of the sequence

$$P_c^{(i)} = \Phi(P_{\bar{c}}^{(i-1)}, \bar{r}) \tag{28}$$

is treated by [6] and given by the following theorem

- *Theorem2:* define $\varphi(r)$ in $]0, +\infty[$ as

$$\varphi(r) = r \int_{\epsilon}^{D} \frac{\mathcal{F}^{-1}\left(\frac{T(x)\theta(r)}{1+\rho(r)}\right)}{T(x)L\left(\frac{T(x)\theta(r)}{1+\rho(r)}\right)} d\varsigma(x) \tag{29}$$

where $T(x)$ is a continuous function that satisfies $T(x) > 0$ in I given by

$$T(x) = \frac{|x|^{-s}}{|2D - x|^{-s} + N_0} \tag{30}$$

and $(\theta(r), \rho(r))$ is the unique solution of:

$$r \int_{\epsilon}^{D} \frac{d\varsigma(x)}{L\left(\frac{T(x)\theta(r)}{1+\rho(r)}\right)} = 1 \tag{31}$$

For any value of $P_c^{(0)} \geq 0$, there is a real $r_{th} > 0$ unique solution of $\varphi(r) = 1$ that satisfies

1. $\left\{P_c^{(i)}\right\}_{\{i \geq 0\}}$ converge if $\bar{r} < r_{th}$.
2. $\left\{P_c^{(i)}\right\}_{\{i \geq 0\}}$ diverge if $\bar{r} \geq r_{th}$.

If we compare the expressions of the solutions given by equations (22) and (25), to the results of [6], we can see the presence of the term $(1 + \xi)$ which does not exist in [6]. This is explained by the constraint (4) which is not taken into account by [6].

4   Cooperative Scheme with Fixed Relaying

4.1   Broadcasting Phase

The received signal at the mobile n directly from BS A and B during the broadcasting phase can be given by

$$r_{1,n}(t) = \sum_{c \in \{A,B\}} \sum_{l=0}^{L-1} h_l^{(c)} s_n(t - v_l^{(c)}) + Z_1(t) \qquad (32)$$

$h_l^{(c)}$ is the channel impulse of the lth path within the cell $c \in \{A,B\}$ and $v_l^{(c)}$ is the corresponding time delay. $Z_1(t)$ is the noise component. The demodulator output of the kth OFDM symbol at subcarrier m for user n is formulated by

$$R_{1,n}(k,m) = \sum_{c \in \{A,B\}} H_{1,n}^{(c)}(k,m) s_{n,m}^{(c)} + z_{1,m} \qquad (33)$$

where $H_{1,n}^{(c)(k,m)}$, $c \in \{A,B\}$ is the channel transfer function of the kth $OFDM$ symbol for mobile n at subcarrier m. In the following and without loss of generality, we denote by $H_{1,n}^{(c)(k,m)}$, as $H_{1,n,m}^{(c)}$.

For each $c \in \{A,B\}$, the received signal at the relay within cell c is given by

$$y_{1,r}^{(c)}(t) = \sum_{l=0}^{L-1} c_l^{(c)} s_n^{(c)}(t - \tau_{l,r}^{(c)}) + c_l^{'(\bar{c})} s_n^{(\bar{c})}(t - \tau_{l,r}^{'(\bar{c})}) + z_r^{(c)}(t) \qquad (34)$$

where $c_l^{(c)}$ is the channel impulse between BS c and the corresponding relay. $c_l^{'(\bar{c})}$ is the channel impulse between BS $\bar{c}$ and the relay within the cell c. $\tau_{l,r}^{(c)}$ and $\tau_{l,r}^{'(\bar{c})}$ are respectively the times delay of the channel impulse $c_l^{(c)}$ and $c_l^{'(\bar{c})}$. In our study, we consider a free space loss (FSL) model characterized by a path-loss exponent $s = 2$. The basic equation for path-loss in decibels are

$$FSL : PL_{dB}(d_{km}) = 20 log_{10}(d_{km}) + 97.5 \qquad (35)$$

where d_{km} is the distance in kilometers between the serving BS and the mobile. The average channel gain between the serving BS A and the mobile n on subcarrier m can be written as:

$$G_{1,n,m}^{(A)} = 10^{-PL_{dB}(d_n^{(A)}/10)} E(|H_{1,n,m}^{(A)}|^2) \qquad (36)$$

The received $SINR$ for mobile n on subcarrier m during the first time slot can be expressed as:

$$\gamma_{1,n,m} = \frac{G_{1,n,m}^{(A)} P_{n,m}^{(A)}}{G_{1,n,m}^{(B)} P_B^{\infty} + N_0} \qquad (37)$$

4.2 Relaying Phase

Each relay amplifies and forwards its received signal while all the BS are silent. Consequently, the received signal at the mobile n from the relays during the relaying phase can be developed as

$$r_{2,n}(t) = \sum_{c \in \{A,B\}} \sum_{l=0}^{L-1} \beta^c q_l^{(c)} y_{1,r}(t - \mu_l^{(c)}) + Z_2(t) \tag{38}$$

$$= \sum_{c \in \{A,B\}} \sum_{l=0}^{L-1} \beta^c q_l^{(c)} [c_l^{(c)} s_n^{(c)}(t - \tau_{l,r}^{(c)} - \mu_l^{(c)})$$

$$+ c_l^{'(\bar{c})} s_n^{(\bar{c})}(t - \tau_{l,r}^{'(\bar{c})} - \mu_l^{(c)}) + z_r^{(c)}(t - \mu_l^{(c)})] + Z_2(t) \tag{39}$$

where $q_l^{(c)}$ is the channel impulse of the lth between BS c and the mobile n. $\mu_l^{(c)}$ is the corresponding time delay. β^c is the amplification factor used at the RS within cell c and given by the following expression

$$\beta^{(c)} = \frac{1}{\sqrt{\sum_{l=0}^{L-1} |c_l^{(c)}|^2 + \frac{N_0}{E_s T_s}}}, \tag{40}$$

E_s denotes the average energy per transmitted symbol and T_s is the symbol duration. The demodulated signal sample of the kth OFDM symbol at subcarrier m for user n can formulated by:

$$R_{2,n}(k,m) = H_{2,n,m}^{(A)} s_{A,n,m} + H_{2,n,m}^{(B)} s_{2,n,m} + z_{2,m} \tag{41}$$

where

$$H_{2,n,m}^{(A)} = \beta^{(A)} Q_{n,m}^{(A)} C_{r,m}^{(A)} \tag{42}$$

$$H_{2,n,m}^{(B)} = \beta^{(A)} Q_{n,m}^{(A)} C_{r,m}^{(B)} + \beta^{(B)} Q_{n,m}^{(B)} C_{r,m}^{(B)} \tag{43}$$

For $c \in \{A,B\}$, $C_{r,m}^{(c)}$ denotes the channel transfer function between BS c and its RS on subcarrier m. $Q_{n,m}^{(c)}$ is the channel transfer function between the relay of BS c and mobile n on subcarrier m. The channel gain between the relay of cell (c) and mobile n on subcarrier m can be expressed as

$$G_{2,n,m}^{(c)} = 10^{-PL_{dB}(d_{r,n}^{(c)}/10)} E(|H_{2,n,m}^{(c)}|^2) \tag{44}$$

$d_{r,n}^{(c)}$ denotes the distance between mobile n and the relay of cell (c). During the second time slot, the SINR for mobile n on subcarrier m is given by the following formula

$$\gamma_{2,n,m} = \frac{G_{2,n,m}^{(A)} p_{n,m}^{(A)}}{G_{2,n,m}^{(B)} P_B^{\infty} + N_0} \tag{45}$$

The received SINR at the mobile n on subcarrier m in broadcasting phase and relaying phase are maximum ratio combined (MRC) as follows

$$\gamma_{n,m} = \gamma_{1,n,m} + \gamma_{2,n,m} \tag{46}$$

5   Scheduling

To enhance the performance of the proposed scheme, the proportional fair scheduling (PFS) algorithm is considered in this paper. In mathematical terms, the PF scheduling decision at the time slot t may be expressed as .

$$n_s = \underset{n}{\mathrm{argmax}}\,(\frac{a_{n,m}(t)}{\bar{a}_n(t)}) \tag{47}$$

where $a_{n,m}(t)$ is given by

$$a_{n,m}(t) = log_2(1 + \gamma_{n,m}(t)) \tag{48}$$

$\bar{a}_n$ is an estimate average rate for user n in a past window of t_c slots, and it is updated each time slot according to:

$$\bar{a}_n(t+1) = (1 - \frac{1}{t_c})\bar{a}_n(t), n \neq n_s \tag{49}$$

$$\bar{a}_{n_s}(t+1) = (1 - \frac{1}{t_c})\bar{a}_{n_s}(t) + \frac{a_{n_s,m}(t)}{t_c} \tag{50}$$

6   Numerical Results

In Fig.2, we compute the total power $P_A^\infty W$ required by base station A to reach a mean rate $\bar{r} = 2Bits/Sec/Hz$ and $\bar{r} = 1Bits/Sec/Hz$ per channel use, versus the cell radius. Asymptotic approximations provided by (22), (23), (25) and (26) are considered. We can deduce from theses curves that the required power increases with the cell radius and the average rate. Also, the required power in multicell environment is greater than the single cell context. This increase is caused by multicell interference that disturbs each base station. Fig.3 illustrates the received SINR versus the distance between the serving BS (A) and the considered mobile n for the proposed scheme and the scheme proposed in [6]. As shown in this figure, the proposed cooperative scheme gives better performance than the non-cooperative scheme [6]. The obtained gain compared to [6] is about $10dB$

Table 1. Simulation parameters

Parameters	Values
channel bandwidth	5 MHz
Carrier frequency	1.8 GHz
Number of subcarriers	300
White noise power density	-174 dBm/Hz
Relay transmit power	33dBm (2W)
Minimum mobile to BS distance	100m
Distance between BS and Relay	800m

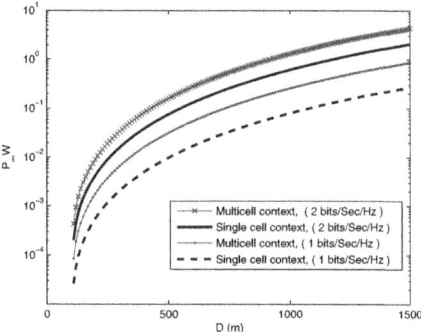

Fig. 2. Required power versus cell radius D

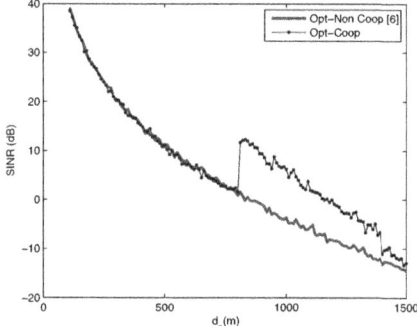

Fig. 3. The received SINR versus the distance between user and the BS

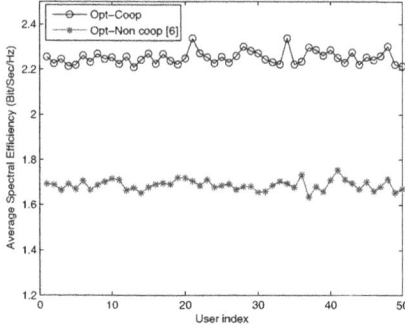

Fig. 4. The average spectral efficiency versus the number of users with tc = 100 slots

in the cell edge. In Fig.4, we evaluate the performance of the proposed optimal cooperative scheme in terms of average spectral efficiency versus the number of users in the cell A. As seen in this figure, the proposed optimal scheme with fixed relaying performs much better than the optimal scheme without cooperation. We notice a performance improvement of about $O.7$ bits/Sec/Hz in comparison with scheme presented in [6].

7   Conclusion

In this paper, we have investigated the resource allocation problem in cooperative relaying for sectorized downlink OFDMA system. In multicell context, asymptotic algorithm can provides a tractable expression of the minimal power which depends only on the global rate requirement. Minimizing the total transmitted power assisted by fixed relays is a powerful solution for interference avoidance in the edge of the cell.

References

1. Wiczanowski, M., Stanczak, S., Boche, H.: Providing quadratic convergence of decentralized power control in wireless networks-The method of min-max functions. IEEE Trans. Signal Process. 56(8), 4053–4068 (2008)
2. Ksairi, N., Bianchi, P., Ciblat, P., Hachem, W.: Resource allocation for downlink sectorized cellular OFDMA systems: Part I-Optimal allocation. IEEE Trans. Signal Process. 58(2), 720–734 (2010)
3. Ksairi, N., Bianchi, P., Ciblat, P., Hachem, W.: Resource Allocation for Downlink Cellular OFDMA Systems Part II: Practical Algorithms and Optimal Reuse Factor. IEEE Trans. Signal Process. 58(2), 720–734 (2010)
4. Stamatiou, K., Proakis, J.: A performance analysis of coded frequency-Hopped OFDMA. In: Proc. IEEE Wireless Commun. Networking Conf., pp. 1132–1137 (2005)
5. Laroia, R., Uppala, S., Li, J.: Designing a mobile broadband wireless access network. IEEE Signal Process Mag., 20–28 (September 2004)
6. Gault, S., Hachem, W., Ciblat, P.: Performance Analysis of an OFDMA Transmission System in a Multicell Environment. IEEE Transaction on Communications 55(4) (April 2007)
7. Najjar, A., Hamdi, N., Bouallegue, A.: Fractional Frequency Reuse Scheme in Cooperative Relaying For Multi-cell OFDMA Systems. In: Vinel, A., Bellalta, B., Sacchi, C., Lyakhov, A., Telek, M., Oliver, M. (eds.) MACOM 2010. LNCS, vol. 6235, pp. 199–210. Springer, Heidelberg (2010)
8. Nabar, R.U., Bolcskei, H., Kneubuhler, F.W.: Fading relay channels: performance limites and space-time signal design. IEEE Journals on Sel. Areas in Telecommun. 22(6), 1099–1109 (2004)

SDR Implementation of a Low Complexity and Interference-Resilient Space-Time Block Decoder for MIMO-OFDM Systems

Morris Filippi[1], Andrea F. Cattoni[2], Yannick Le Moullec[2], and Claudio Sacchi[1,*]

[1] University of Trento, Department of Information Engineering and Computer Science,
Via Sommarive 5, I-38123 Trento, Italy
`morris.filippi@hotmail.it, sacchi@disi.unitn.it`
[2] Aalborg University, Aalborg DK-9220, Denmark
`{afc,ylm}@es.aau.dk`

Abstract. In the recent wireless systems, MIMO technologies are largely used to increase data throughput. Many efficient solutions have been proposed for the classical 2 transmitting and 2 receiving antennas (2x2) configuration, such as: the Spatial Multiplexing (SM) and the Alamouti's Space Time Block Coding (STBC). The extension of these techniques in terms of antennas number is a key topic in MIMO signal processing. In these cases, the computational burden increases due to the large number of elementary operations. Moreover, additional interference due to the non-perfect orthogonality of space-time coding may affect the decoder. In this paper an SDR implementation of a 4x4 STBC configuration for MIMO-OFDM systems is considered. The aim is to introduce a low-complexity algorithm which reduces the interference due to the Quasi-Orthogonality of the STBC decoding. In the literature, feedback techniques have been proposed to solve this problem. However, the algorithm introduced in this paper has been conceived in order to avoid the transmission feedback, by estimating the interference factors and removing them. The related STBC decoder has been implemented on FPGA. The considered algorithm exhibits a low computational complexity and complies with the requirements of HW feasibility, considering the execution time/area occupation trade-off.

Keywords: MIMO, OFDM, Space-Time Block Coding, Software-Defined Radio, MIMO signal processing.

1 Introduction

Nowadays, wireless systems allow connecting people in almost every place in the world. By means of a mobile device it is also possible to surf the Web and to access many more services. The main issues to be tackled are related to the limitation in terms of functionality and speed involved by the difficulty of effectively managing the scarce available power and spectrum resources. Therefore, the objective of the

---

* Corresponding author.

C. Sacchi et al. (Eds.): MACOM 2011, LNCS 6886, pp. 119–129, 2011.

designers is to propose advanced technical solutions that can improve those functionalities. A valuable solution consists of the introduction of advanced digital signal processing techniques based on Multiple Input – Multiple Output (MIMO) concept. The key feature of MIMO is the capability to increase channel capacity without increasing transmitted power and RF bandwidth [1]. Nowadays, MIMO techniques present some well-promising applications in wireless standards like IEEE 802.11n and IEEE 802.16x (WiMax). Different space-time processing techniques have been proposed in the literature in order to fully exploit potentialities of MIMO systems. The most popular one is Space-Time Coding [2], in which the time dimension is complemented with the spatial dimension inherent to the use of multiple spatially-distributed antennas. Commonly used ST coding schemes are ST-trellis codes and ST block codes (STBC). A well-known example of conceptually simple, computationally efficient and mathematically elegant STBC scheme has been proposed by Alamouti in [3]. Substantially, Alamouti's coding is an orthogonal ST block code where two successive symbols are encoded in an orthogonal 2x2 matrix. The columns of the matrix are transmitted in successive symbol periods, but the upper and the lower symbols in a given column are sent simultaneously through the first and the second transmit antennas, respectively.

The alternative solution to ST coding is represented by Spatial Multiplexing (SM) [4]. Spatial multiplexing is a space-time modulation technique whose core idea is to send independent data streams from each transmit antenna. This is motivated by the spatially white property of the distribution which achieves capacity in MIMO i.i.d. Rayleigh matrix channels [5]. SM is addressed to push up link capacity rather than to exploit spatial diversity.

The switch between Diversity (i.e.: Space-Time coding) and Multiplexing (i.e.: SM) has been theoretically studied by Heath and Paulraj in [5] and some simulation results have been shown for a switch criterion based on the minimum Euclidean distance of the received codebook. Such a criterion has been considered in [5], because this measure reveals dependencies on the channel realization and provides an approximate measure of error-rate performances.

In our opinion, the practical implementation of switchable MIMO systems able to adaptively select different transmission modalities and to dynamically reconfigure the MIMO receiver depending on the selected mode is a very interesting topic in the framework of "4G and beyond" communication standards. In such a framework, Software Defined Radio (SDR) can provide relevant and innovative answers in order to efficiently implement receiver architectures characterized by modularity and adaptive reconfiguration capability with respect to channel conditions [6].

In the current paper, a practical solution for the implementation of a SDR-based Space-Time Block Decoder for a 4x4 MIMO-OFDM transmission system is proposed and tested. This kind of SDR implementation is really challenging and presents some issues to be solved. The most relevant ones are related to the efficient implementation of the space-time diversity combiner at the receiver side. Such a block is very critical as in the 4x4 MIMO configuration it should be implemented by means of a pseudo-inversion of the channel matrix that is computationally expensive and may provide poor performance due to the noise increasing. Therefore, a computationally-affordable and interference-robust subtractive combiner is considered for the conceived receiver. In this work, the SDR-based implementation of the subtractive combiner is motivated and discussed, and results are shown in terms of FPGA resource requirements and real-time execution capabilities.

The paper is structured as follows: in Section 2 some related works about SDR-based MIMO implementation are presented. Section 3 is devoted to describing the signal processing architecture of the proposed SDR-based STBC MIMO system. Section 4 focuses on the hardware implementation of the diversity combiner. Section 5 aims at presenting and discussing experimental results. Section 6 draws paper conclusions.

2   Related Works

The SDR-based implementation of MIMO systems has recently become a hot topic of R&D in wireless communications. One of the first works dealing with SDR MIMO-OFDM prototyping has been proposed by Gupta, Forenza and Heat in [7]. The prototyping approach was targeted to the rapid deployment of a "ready-to-market" architecture based on flexible SDR and commercially available hardware. The software design of all main receiver functionalities added a great flexibility and ease of use to the designed architecture, at the price of throughput expense. Very recent works like [8] and [9] are explicitly targeted at mapping the SDR architectural design of MIMO systems onto efficient commercial HW platforms able to support real-world wireless applications. In [8], the utilization of GNU Radio has been considered to program the PHY and DATA LINK layers of Universal Software Radio Peripheral (USRP) consisting of a motherboard for baseband processing, two daughter boards for RF frontend processing and an embedded Intel Core General Purpose Processing (GPP) unit hosting Linux OS. Using such a platform a variety of multimedia delivery applications can be effectively supported on MANETs. In [9], a 40 MHz MIMO OFDM system with Space Division Multiplexing has been mapped onto a multi-processor SDR platform using two instances of state-of-the-art ADRES embedded processor. It has been shown in [9] that when the parallelization is wisely performed, it is possible to achieve the theoretical gain factor of two with respect to the single-processor system.

Another interesting work has been proposed by Pan et al. in [10]; its authors considered the implementation of reconfigurable antennas in multi-radio platform. The antenna developed in [10] is characterized by a high degree of reconfigurability and general-purpose features, to enable SDR cognitive radio, MIMO and phased-array antennas. By this preliminary state-of-the-art scanning, we can say that the emphasis of R&D in SDR-based MIMO systems is on the implementation of SW receiver architectures characterized by flexibility, adaptivity and high degree of reprogrammability, with the clear objective of achieving high performances while keeping hardware costs reasonably low.

Our work is perfectly inserted in this state-of-the-art framework. In fact, in this work, the problem of the implementation of a MIMO receiver has been addressed from a practical viewpoint, considering commercial HW platforms, characterized by a good tradeoff between efficiency and cost.

3 OFDM-MIMO Signal Processing

The MIMO-OFDM system considered in this paper is based on the IEEE 802.16d standard [11], extended with the MIMO section. The IEEE 802.16 is the telecommunication standard on which the Worldwide Interoperability for Microwave Access (WiMAX) and the Wireless Metropolitan Area Network (WMAN) are based. These two are wireless technologies which provides high bit rate to the system. In particular, the paper is focused on the IEEE 802.16d-2004, based on OFDM transmission with TDMA as multiple access. In particular, the analysis carried out relies on different parts: the first one is related to software simulations and the second one to the hardware implementation and co-simulation. The simulation work deals with the test of MISO/MIMO encoding and decoding algorithms. The work done on the hardware focuses on the receiver side (decoder) and in particular considers the MIMO mode which has best simulation results between those treated (see Fig.1).

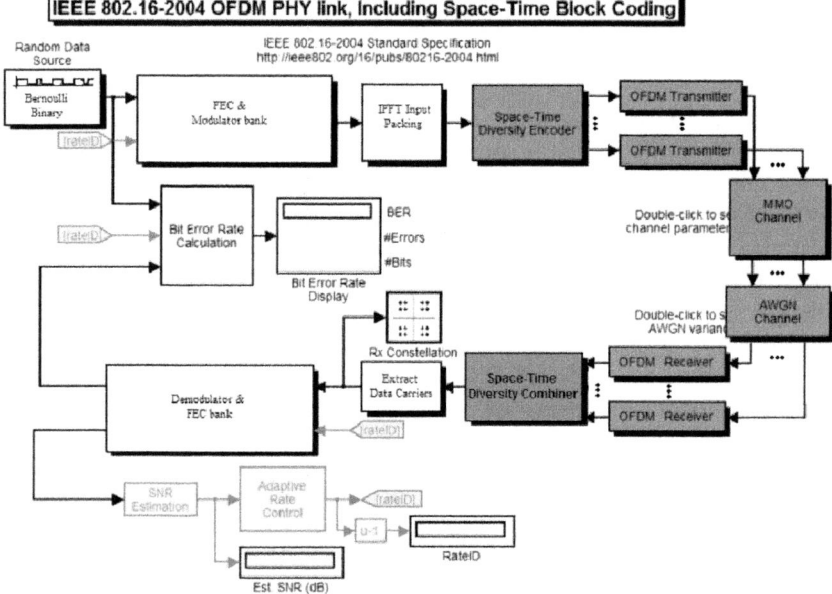

Fig. 1. IEEE 802.16-2004 OFDM PHY-layer SIMULINK scheme: the green blocks have been simulated and implemented on hardware; the blue blocks have been developed for the software simulations

In Fig. 2 a 4x4 MIMO system with Alamouti STBC algorithm is shown. The MIMO channels are shown in four colors to split them into four groups. The choice of a 4x4 MIMO instead of usual 2x1 or 2x2 is motivated by the necessity of increasing diversity in the space domain (and therefore robustness against fading effects) together with the spectral efficiency. Nowadays, a 4-element MIMO array can be implemented with affordable cost and the yielded performance improvement in terms of spectral efficiency may justify such an additional (non-prohibitive) cost.

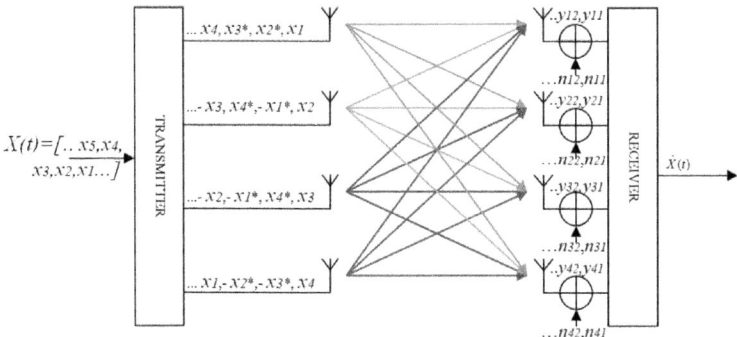

Fig. 2. The 4x4 MIMO-STBC system

The signal received during a MIMO symbol period is given as follow [12]:

$$Y = HX + N \qquad (1)$$

where H denotes the non-squared channel matrix composed of 16 rows and 4 columns, X the 4x4 Alamouti STBC matrix containing the space-time encoded OFDM symbols as seen in (2), and finally N the noise matrix, made of independent and identically-distributed Gaussian noise samples.

As the channel matrix is not square, the direct matrix inversion cannot be employed in order to perform the space-time combining at the receiver side. However, the pseudo-inversion can be computed [12] even for a non-squared matrix by using H^H, the *Hermitian channel matrix* (i.e.: the transposed complex conjugate channel matrix). However, the computation of the pseudo-inverse is computationally expensive (it includes a matrix inversion involving a 16x16 matrix) and the performance may degrade due to the increase of the noise level generated by the multiplication of the noise matrix by the pseudo-inverse channel matrix [12].

A computationally-lighter combining method is the subtractive combiner proposed in [14] and [15]. The subtractive combiner is based on the utilization of the Hermitian channel matrix in order to combine the received signal, as shown in (5).

$$\tilde{X} = \frac{1}{\alpha}H^HY = \frac{1}{\alpha}H^HHX + \frac{1}{\alpha}H^HN = \tilde{I} \cdot X + \frac{1}{\alpha}H^HN \qquad (2)$$

The matrix resulting by the product of the channel matrix with its Hermitian will be quasi-identical, as shown in (3):

$$\tilde{I} = \begin{bmatrix} 1 & 0 & 0 & \beta/\alpha \\ 0 & 1 & -\beta/\alpha & 0 \\ 0 & -\beta/\alpha & 1 & 0 \\ \beta/\alpha & 0 & 0 & 1 \end{bmatrix} \qquad (3)$$

with α and β defined as in (4) and (5).

$$\alpha = |h_{11}|^2 + |h_{12}|^2 + |h_{13}|^2 + |h_{14}|^2 + |h_{21}|^2 + |h_{22}|^2 + |h_{23}|^2 + |h_{24}|^2 + $$
$$+ |h_{31}|^2 + |h_{32}|^2 + |h_{33}|^2 + |h_{34}|^2 + |h_{41}|^2 + |h_{42}|^2 + |h_{43}|^2 + |h_{44}|^2 \tag{4}$$

$$\beta = 2 \cdot \mathrm{Re}\left(h_{11}^* h_{41} - h_{21} h_{31}^* + h_{12}^* h_{42} - h_{22} h_{32}^* + h_{13}^* h_{43} - h_{23} h_{33}^* + h_{14}^* h_{44} - h_{24} h_{34}^*\right) \tag{5}$$

The new decision vector is then defined as in (6).

$$\begin{bmatrix} \underline{x}_1 + \beta/\alpha \cdot \underline{x}_4 \\ \underline{x}_2 - \beta/\alpha \cdot \underline{x}_3 \\ \underline{x}_3 - \beta/\alpha \cdot \underline{x}_2 \\ \underline{x}_4 + \beta/\alpha \cdot \underline{x}_1 \end{bmatrix} = \frac{1}{\alpha} \mathrm{H}^H \mathrm{Y} = \begin{bmatrix} x_1 + \beta/\alpha \cdot x_4 \\ x_2 - \beta/\alpha \cdot x_3 \\ x_3 - \beta/\alpha \cdot x_2 \\ x_4 + \beta/\alpha \cdot x_1 \end{bmatrix} + \frac{1}{\alpha} \mathrm{H}^H \mathrm{N} \tag{6}$$

Assuming the knowledge of the Hermitian channel matrix (as done till now), the estimated symbols $\underline{x}_1, \underline{x}_2, \underline{x}_3$, and $\underline{x}_4$ can be computed by solving a simple linear system of equations.

The two different algorithms described above, i.e. channel pseudo-inversion and subtractive combining have been tested by means of intensive simulation trials in the MATLAB-SIMULINK environment and the simulation results are shown in Fig.3. The IEEE 802.16-2004 system of Fig.1 has been simulated over a Rayleigh fading MIMO channel, characterized by the following parameters: delay spread 10^{-6} sec. and Doppler spread 0.5 Hz. The simulation results are related to 100 average trials for each signal-to-noise ratio values. Given the extremely reduced number of simulated samples, what is relevant for the investigation is the trend of the results more than the absolute value obtained.

As a matter of fact Fig.3 presents some absolute numbers which are not fully consistent; nevertheless it is clear from the trend that subtractive combining provides much better results with a reduced computational burden. For this reason, we decided to select this solution for the practical SDR-based implementation.

4   Emulated SDR Implementation of the 4x4 Subtractive MIMO Combiner

There are several valuable approaches to implement the subtractive presented in Section 3. In this paper, an efficient solution from a computational viewpoint is presented. The architecture is designed by considering as cost function parameters the execution time and the FPGA resources. Finding a suitable solution is a matter of trading off these two parameters. The proposed solution exploits the maximum operation parallelism in order to reduce the execution time. On the other hand, to minimize the number of required resources, basic real operators are used, such as multipliers, adders, and CORDIC dividers [16]. Moreover, the use of integrated processors and high accuracy operators is avoided to preserve the initial trade-off.

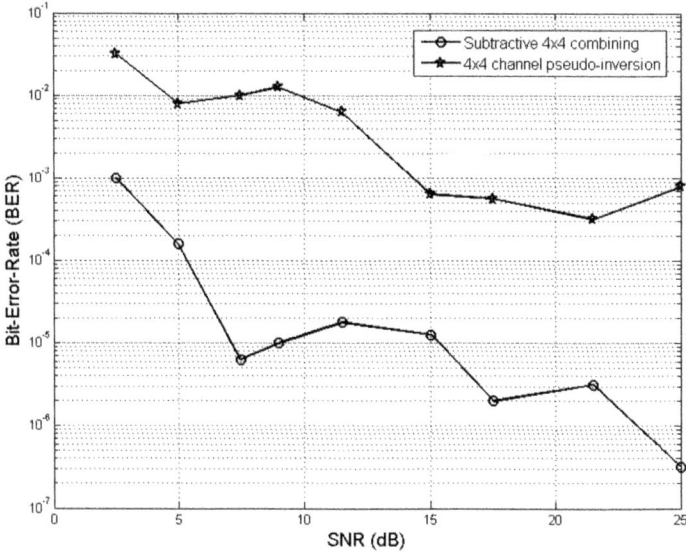

Fig. 3. Comparative simulations in terms of BER for Subtractive 4x4 MIMO combining and 4x4 channel pseudo-inversion combining using the IEEE 802.16-2004 simulator of Fig.1

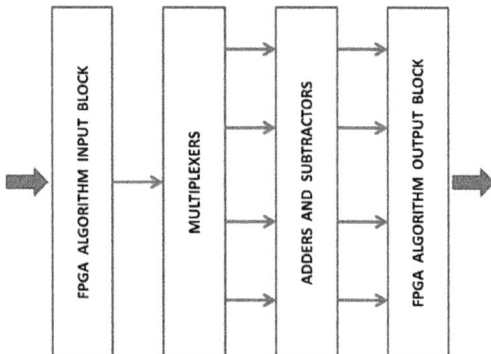

Fig. 4. The STBC 4x4 subtractive combiner scheme which has been implemented in SysGen blocks

The inputs of the system are the received signal matrix Y and the estimated channel matrix H. All the signals are complex variables, so real operators must be combined to perform this operation. This is done minimizing the operators, such as avoiding complex divisions (which would need a large amount of resources), by replacing them with complex multiplications followed by real divisions.

The architecture includes the parallel operators which compute the decoding operation of (5) and the coefficients α and β of (7) and (8). The final outputs are the interference-free decoded OFDM symbols obtained by solving the linear system of (9). In order to evaluate the implementation of the subtractive 4x4 OFDM-MIMO combiner considered in this paper, a Xilinx Virtex 5 xc5vsx50t-1ff1136 FPGA has been used. For the specification, synthesis, and implementation, Xilinx ISE and System Generator have been used.

The OFDM-MIMO main scheme shown in Fig.1 has been adapted to provide the 4x4 transmission data to the MIMO combiner which has been implemented by means of System Generator.

In Fig. 4 the block scheme of the System Generator implementation is shown. The inputs are the received signals coming from the 4-antennas OFDM receivers, and the MIMO channel estimations. In order to allow the interface between System Generator and standard MATLAB blocks, the signals must be splitted from floating point complex values into real-imaginary parts. Note that here the System Generator input ports reduce the accuracy to 8-bit. This choice is due to the limited number of available I/O ports (480) and of slices in the FPGA. Moreover, note that the full amount of I/O ports is used with the aim of parallelizing the architecture, and thus it is necessary to avoid serial inputs.

The banks at the top of Fig. 4 execute the matrix product between the received signal and the channel estimation. The operators used here maintain the 8-bit accuracy and their delays are set to exploit a pipelined cascade. The weighs for the interference cancellation are implemented by the blocks on the bottom of Fig. 4. Finally, the two parts computations are combined to obtain the final symbol estimation.

The System Generator MIMO combiner is synthesized and the generated bitstream file is loaded on the FPGA. In order to manage the system in real time, a HW/SW co-simulation environment is set. The data transmitted from the computer to the FPGA are serialized by a point-to-point Ethernet connection. This testing environment allows a direct comparison between the software and the FPGA results.

5   Experimental Results

The 4x4 MIMO decoder has been specified in Simulink via Xilinx System Generator and the corresponding HDL code has been generated with the same tool. Then, the design has been synthesized, placed, and routed using Xilinx ISE. Finally, the bistream file has been generated using the same tool.

The HW/SW co-simulation is supported by the following tools:

- MATLAB version 7.6.0.324 (R2008a);
- SIMULINK 7.1.1. (R2008a+);
- Xilinx ISE Design Suite 11.1 (including System Generator for DSP 11.1);
- ML506 board with a Virtex 5 xc5vsx50t-1ff1136 (see Fig.5a);
- Ethernet cable (for the HW/SW co-simulation);
- USB-JTAG cable (for programming the FPGA);
- Power supply;
- Computer from the Embedded Systems Laboratory of the Department of Electronic Systems, AAU (2 GHz single core, 1 GB RAM) (see Fig.5b, showing the complete co-simulation setup).

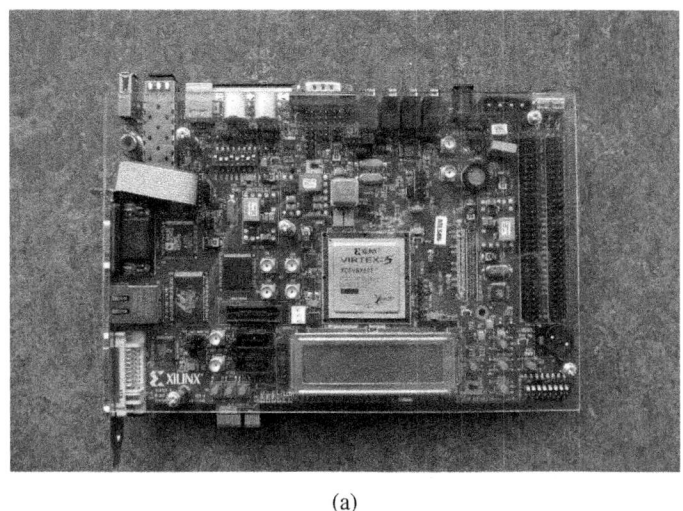

(a)

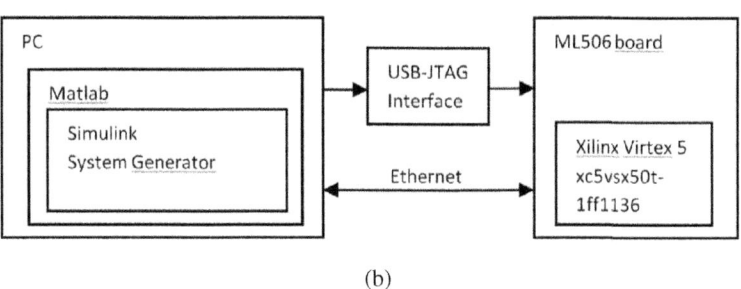

(b)

Fig. 5. (a) ML506 board picture, (b) co-simulation setup scheme

Device Utilization Summary			
Slice Logic Utilization	**Used**	**Available**	**Utilization**
Number of Slice Registers	464	32,640	1%
Number of occupied Slices	4,688	8,160	57%
Number of LUT Flip Flop pairs used	13,965		
Number used as logic	13,136	32,640	40%
Number used as Memory	128	12,480	1%
Number of bonded IOBs	385	480	80%
Number of DSP48Es	256	288	88%
Number of BUFG/BUFGCTRLs	1	32	3%

Fig. 6. Snapshot of the synthesis results. The resources considered are the number of slice/slice registers, Flip-Flops, Memory usage, bits of I/Os, Embedded multipliers (DSP48E) and Buffers.

In Fig.6, a snapshot of the synthesis results is shown; looking at the numbers it is possible to conclude that the design fits into the targeted FPGA, with 57 % of area occupation (slices). The most critical value, as expected, is the number of bonded I/Os, which is at 80% of utilization. This could be problematic if the hardware implementation should be extended. The number of DSP48E embedded multipliers is at 88 % but it is not so critical, because the multipliers can be implemented also by standard slices (of which ca. 40% are still available), so the number of multipliers can be reasonably incremented.

Another typical parameter is the working frequency of the system on FPGA. The co-simulation generation tool has allowed using a 10 ns FPGA clock period, the maximum available in System Generator for the given FPGA board.

The longest path of the system implemented on FPGA falls within the allowed limit:

- FPGA clock period (co-simulation) = 10 ns;
- Longest path = 9.986 ns.

The time slack, i.e. the difference between the longest available period (here 10 ns) and the required period for the design (here 9.986 ns) is just 14 ps, which means that it is most likely impossible to cascade other combinatorial operators without introducing intermediate registers.

Regarding this point, it can be useful to analyze the trade-off between latency and delay. The latency is the time needed to complete a cascade of combinatorial operations (in this case equal to the longest path). The delay is the additional time introduced by sequential elements (as registers). By analyzing this trade-off it could be possible to reduce the total execution time, depending on the targeted application and its constraints.

6 Conclusion

This paper has proposed an optimized implementation of a 4x4 decoder for OFDM-MIMO systems by means of a rapid prototyping approach for FPGA. The innovative design allows reducing the execution time and preserving the number of resources, as compared with other state-of-the-art implementations. The parallel computation allows minimizing the clock period and the pipelining of the operations. The final results illustrate that a FPGA-based hardware implementation is feasible. The proposed solution could also be implemented on ASIC or DSPs (in that case the clock frequency/execution time/resource usage would be different as compared to the FPGA implementation); moreover, the proposed solution allows a possible scalability of the system for instance by increasing the number of antennas.

References

1. Paulraj, A.J., Papadias, C.B.: Space-Time Processing for Wireless Communications. IEEE Sig. Process. Mag., 49–83 (November 1997)
2. Gesbert, D., Shafi, M., et al.: From Theory to Practice: An Overview of MIMO Space-Time Coded Wireless Systems. IEEE J. Sel. Areas in Comm. 21(3), 281–301 (2003)

3. Alamouti, S.M.: A simple transmit diversity tecnique for wireless communications. IEEE J. Sel. Areas in Comm. 16(8), 1451–1458 (1998)
4. Foschini, G.J.: Layered Space-Time Architecture for Wireless Communication in a Fading Enviroment when using Multi-Element Antennas. Bell Labs Tech. Jour. 1(2), 41–59 (1996)
5. Heath, R.V., Paulraj, A.J.: Switching between Diversity and Multiplexing in MIMO Systems. IEEE Trans. on Comm. 53(6), 962–968 (2005)
6. Mitola III, J.: Software Radio Architecture. Wiley, New York (2000)
7. Gupta, A., Forenza, A., Heat, R.W.: Rapid MIMO-OFDM Software Defined Radio System Prototyping. In: Proc. of 2004 IEEE Workshop on Signal Processing Systems (SIPS 2004), Austin (TX), October 13-15, pp. 182–186 (2004)
8. Li, X., Hu, W., Yousefi'zadeh, H., Qureshi, A.: A Case Study of a MIMO SDR Implementation. In: Proc. of IEEE MILCOM 2008 Conf., San Diego (CA), November 16-19, pp. 1–7 (2008)
9. Palkovic, M., Capelle, H., Glassee, M., Bougard, B., Van der Perre, L.: Mapping of 40 MHz MIMO SDM-OFDM Baseband Processing on Multi-Processor SDR Platform. In: Proc. of 11th IEEE Workshop on Design and Diagnostics of Electronic Circuits and Systems (DDECS 2008) (April 16-18, 2008); available on CD-ROM
10. Pan, H.K., Tsai, J., Golden, S., Nair, V.K., Bernhard, J.T.: Reconfigurable Antenna Implementation in Multi-radio Platform. In: Proc. of IEEE Antennas and Propagat. Symp. (AP-S 2008), San Diego, CA (July 5-11, 2008); CD ROM available
11. IEEE Standard 802.16-2004, Part 16: Air interface for fixed broadband wireless access systems (October 2004), http://ieee802.org/16/published.html
12. Kaiser, T., Bourdoux, A., et al. (eds.): Smart Antennas – State of the Art. In: EURASIP Series on Signal Processing and Communications, Hindawi (2005)
13. Press, W.H., Teukolsky, S.A., Vetterling, W.T., Flannery, B.P.: Numerical Recipes in C, 2nd edn. Cambridge University Press, Cambridge (1992)
14. Kim, J., Ariyavistajul, S.L., Seshadri, N.: STBC/ SFBC for 4 Transmit Antennas with 1-bit Feedback. In: Proc. of IEEE ICC 2008 Conf., pp. 3493–3497 (2008)
15. Badic, B., Rupp, M., Weinrichter, H.: Adaptive Channel-Matched Extended Alamouti Space-Time Code Exploiting Partial Feedback. ETRI Journal 26(5) (October 2004)
16. Volder, J.E.: The CORDIC Trigonometric Computing Technique. IRE Trans. on Electronic Computers 8, 330–334 (1959)

Transmission Power Control in Single-Hop and Multi-hop Wireless Sensor Networks

Mahir Meghji and Daryoush Habibi

Centre for Communications Engineering Research, School of Engineering,
Edith Cowan University, Perth, WA, 6027, Australia
mmeghji@our.ecu.edu.au, d.habi@ecu.edu.au
http://www.ecu.edu.au

Abstract. A major challenge in wireless sensor networks (WSNs) deployment is to minimize sensor node's energy consumption to prolong the lifetime of the finite-capacity batteries. Power control is one of the main techniques used to conserve energy in wireless sensor networks, particularly in star topology/cellular networks. In this paper we provide a study on transmission power control (TPC) in multi-hop and single-hop wireless sensor networks using typical Telosb platform parameters, which is IEEE 802.15.4 standard compliant. We offer a new approach to test TPC in multihop networks at the physical layer, and provide energy consumption performance results via simulation and numerical model. Our simulation and numerical model results illustrate that energy spent to send packets using short-range multi-hop path instead of single-hop does not necessarily save energy as suggested by some of the earlier research. However, in single-hop networks, we found that we can save energy by transmitting at lower transmission power levels while still maintaining reliable connectivity, resulting in up to 23% reduction in energy consumption.

Keyword:wireless sensor network, energy efficiency, transmission power control.

1 Introduction

Sensor networks are distributed networks made up of small sensing devices equipped with a processor, memory and the capability for short-range wireless communication. Recently, ad-hoc WSNs have gained tremendous attention in research communities and commercial applications. This has been partly due to ad-hoc wireless networks' capability to establish connectivity without the need for pre-existing infrastructure, and the fact that these networks are envisioned to support a wide range of embedded applications. It is also worth mentioning that the decrease in the size and cost of sensors has also played a part in increasing the use of WSNs for applications that would not have been considered feasible previously.

The capability of setting up networks without pre-existing infrastructure provides a significant benefit in rapid sensor nodes deployment, and a reduction

C. Sacchi et al. (Eds.): MACOM 2011, LNCS 6886, pp. 130–143, 2011.

in the cost of setting up and maintaining networks. Wireless sensor networking can offer a wide range of potential monitoring and control applications in areas such as security surveillance, rescue missions in inhospitable terrain, traffic surveillance, environmental monitoring, health care, robotic exploration, inventory tracking, home appliances, and farming [1,2].

Whilst ad-hoc networks have been the subject of a significant research and development, currently, the emerging field of WSN research combines numerous disciplines and poses a combination of challenges facing modern computer science, wireless communication and mobile computing [3].

Sensor networks may consist of a large number of tiny, energy constrained distributed nodes that collect information via their sensors and forward this information to a user or a general data sink for processing/reporting. Due to the node's limited transmission range, information collected by a particular node will most likely go through intermediate nodes (multi-hop path) to reach its destination/data sink.

A major challenge in sensor networks protocol design is to minimize nodes' energy consumption to prolong the network's operational lifetime, while still maintaining effective communication. Conserving node's power will prolong node's lifetime and network's lifetime as a whole. We expect the emerging WSNs to be more energy-efficient, given that nodes in these networks will most likely have a limited power source. Furthermore, the shrinking size and increasing density of future wireless devices imply greater constraints on battery capacities.

There are several techniques for minimizing energy consumption to prolong WSN's lifespan. These techniques can roughly be categorized into four groups: efficient data aggregation, efficient routing, MAC layer power management and topology management using transmission power control.

In this paper we concentrate on TPC, which is one of the promising and effective techniques for minimizing interference and improving sensor nodes' energy consumption. TPC is based on techniques through which a transmitter can dynamically adjust the transmission output power to the minimum level, depending on the receiver proximity, and still maintaining a reliable link. TPC has been widely studied in the literature, particularly in cellular networks and IEEE 802.11 networks. Our work is based on 802.15.4 physical layer, using the fact that all sensor nodes have adjustable transmission power levels that can be utilized to minimize sensor nodes' power consumption and therefore prolong the lifespan of nodes. A review of the literature reveals several published work in cellular TPC algorithms in cellular networks, but to the best of my knowledge, there is no comprehensive published work which compares energy efficiency in multi-hop communication for the same distance from source to sink. Although some articles suggest that short-range multi-hop communication is more energy-efficient [4,5,6], our simulation and numerical results differ from these studies.

The main contribution of this paper is to illustrate by numerical model and by simulation, the performance comparison of transmission power control in a single-hop and multi-hop communication using real sensor node hardware parameters (Telosb) [7,8]. We provide a new well controlled approach to test TPC in multi-hop networks at physical (PHY) layer. This approach can be used to test 802.15.4 standards and related protocols. Our results illustrate that TPC in multi-hop communication does not necessarily save energy as suggested in some of the literature [4,5,6]. In addition, we found that by using TPC in single-hop networks, we can save battery life by up to 23%.

The rest of the paper is organized as follows. In section 2, we provide a literature review. In section 3 we present an overview of IEEE 802.15.4 standard, on which our work is based. In section 4, we introduce important power control parameters, and derive energy consumption numerical model. Section 5 presents performance evaluation of multi-hop and single-hop TPC and a discussion of results. Finally, conclusions are drawn in section 6.

2   Related Work

There are several earlier studies that have sought to improve WSN performance (throughput, power consumption, etc.) by varying transmission power. In[9,10,11], the focus is on the power control in 802.11 standard as a mechanism to increase the channel efficiency rather than a mechanism to increase battery life. Their work is based on RTS/CTS protocols and consider the issues of exposed and hidden terminals in networks. Most of these studies are based on 802.11 standard. However 802.11 is power-hungry and therefore unsuitable for WSN applications, but these studies can be extrapolated and used for WSN protocol design.

In [12,13], the authors use transmission range adjustment to avoid overlapped sensing area but still maintain effective coverage. Their main objective is to minimize energy consumed by sensing function and not due to communication. In our paper, we look at the amount of energy consumed to transmit information from source to destination.

Zhao [4] suggests that multi-hop communication can be more energy-efficient than single-hop communication. He derives an expression to show the power advantage of a N-hop transmission verses a single-hop transmission over the same distance. This model is somewhat too simplified, leading to favoring the multi-hop scenario and presenting it to be more energy-efficient. Monks [6] and Kai [5]suggest that information from a source should go through one or more intermediate hops to reach its destination in order to achieve desired power savings.

Bandai [14], uses Friis transmission equation suggesting that shorter distance hop greatly decreases transmission power.

The work by Liu [15] considered a variable Physical carrier sense (PCS) based on background noise to minimize collision and therefore minimize energy consumption. Using our approach, results presented in this paper can be related to those found in [16].

Our derived energy model presented in this paper and used to obtain numerical results is based on the research of Heinzehman [17]. We look at transmission power control at lowest general PHY layer and therefore our findings can be used in implementation of MAC or network layer. We consider typical sensor nodes that are in the market (Telosb), whereby PCS cannot be changed. In practice there is only a limited number of power levels, and therefore the optimum value can only be the value close to one of the available power levels. Most of the transmission power optimization research consider continuous power levels as a linear function. However, in this work we consider discrete power levels and therefore an optimal value can only be one of the available power levels.

3   An Overview of IEEE 802.15.4

The IEEE 802.15.4 standard describes the physical layer (PHY) and the medium access control (MAC) sublayer specifications for wireless communication, particularly for low-rate, low-power consumption wireless personal area networks (LR-WPANs) [18]. The standard has been designed to offer low complexity, low-cost and low power wireless connectivity, which makes it one of the most anticipated enabling technologies for WSNs.

3.1   Physical Specification

IEEE 802.15.4 physical layer is responsible for data transmission and reception using a certain radio channel and according to specific modulation/demodulation and spreading/de-spreading technique . The standard also provides other common provisions such as receiver sensitivity, the ability to adjust transmitter power, ability to dynamically select channel, a channel scan function in search of a beacon, activation and deactivation of radio transceiver, ability to measure received packet energy known as energy detection (ED) , the ability to measure the quality of the received signal for each packet known as link quality indicator (LQI) and the ability to check for activity in the medium known as clear channel assessment (CCA) [18].

3.2   Network Topologies

Depending on the application requirements, the IEEE 802.15.4 standard supports two network topologies: star and peer-to-peer . In our work we consider the peer-to-peer topology since it allows more complex networks such as mesh topology to be implemented, and it offers more flexibility. In peer-to-peer networks, devices can communicate with one another as long as they are within the range of one another [18].

3.3   IEEE 802.15.4 MAC Layer

The IEEE 802.15.4 medium access control (MAC) sublayer controls the access to the radio channel using Carrier Sense Multiple Access with Collision Avoidance (CSMA/CA) mechanism. This is achieved through supported IEEE 802.15.4 modes of operation: beacon enable mode and non beacon enable mode. A particular mode of operation is selected by central node, i.e. PAN coordinator. In non beacon enable mode, MAC is ruled by a simple non-slotted CSMA/CA protocol that require a constant reception of possible incoming data. In beacon enabled mode, MAC is ruled by modified slotted CSMA/CA protocol[18].

The 802.15.4 is also responsible for flow control via acknowledgment frame delivery, frame validation as well as maintaining network synchronization, handles network association and dissociation, administering device security and scheming the guaranteed time slot mechanism.

3.4   The CSMA/CA Algorithm

In CSMA, a node wishing to send information first listens to the channel for a predetermined amount of time to check for any activity on the channel. If the channel is sensed "idle" then the node is permitted to send. If the channel is sensed as "busy" the node has to defer its transmission for a random interval. This is the essence of both CSMA/CA and CSMA/CD, in order to gain access to the channel and to reduce the probability of collisions.

Every node in a PAN uses the CSMA/CA algorithm for every new data or MAC frame transmission during contention access period (CAP). Based on whether beacons are used or not, the CSMA/CA will choose either a slotted/non-slotted procedure. In beacon enabled mode, the MAC sublayer uses the slotted version of the CSMA/CA algorithm for transmission in the CAP of the superframe. If beacons are not used then non-slotted version of CSMA-CA algorithm is used. The non-slotted procedure is also used in the case beacons are not detected in the PAN. Fig. 1 depicts the flowchart describing non-slotted CSMA/CA mechanism.

3.5   Data Transmission Procedures

Based on IEEE 802.15.4 standard supported network topologies, three types of data transmission exist: transmission from a coordinator to a device, transmission from a device to a coordinator and transmission between any two peer devices.

The nature of data transfer will depend as to whether the network supports transmission of beacons (star topology) or not (peer-to-peer topology). Fig. 2 shows the transmission protocol for non beacon enabled data transfer for downlink and uplink.

4   Essential Power Control Parameters and Related Models

4.1   Radio Propagation Model

Radio channel plays an important role in the performance of wireless systems, particularly when dealing with power control. When a signal propagates, the signal strength or energy level decays as the distance from the source to destination increases. In this paper, we take into account both the free space model (direct path) and the multipath fading model (reflection path), depending on the distance between transmitter and receiver [19]. If the distance between transmitter

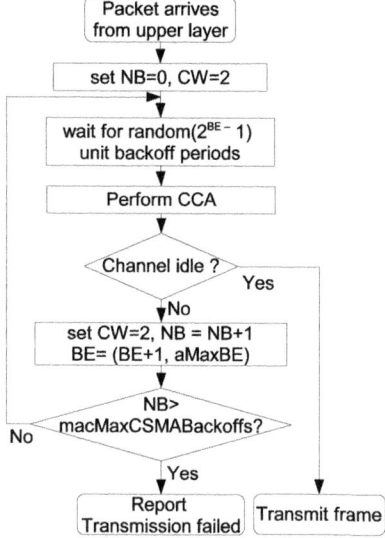

Fig. 1. Unslotted CSMA/CA algorithm

and receiver is less than a certain distance known as the cross-over distance, then the Friis free space model is used, and if the distance is greater than the cross-over distance, then the two-ray ground propagation model is used. The cross-over distance is defined as follows:

$$d_{xover} = \frac{4\pi h_r h_t \sqrt{L}}{\lambda} \tag{1}$$

For example, in our study we use 2.45GHz carrier frequency, therefore the cross over distance is approximately 103 meters.

If the distance between transmitter and receiver is less than d_{xover}, that is $d < d_{xover}$, then the received signal power at the receiver is modeled using the

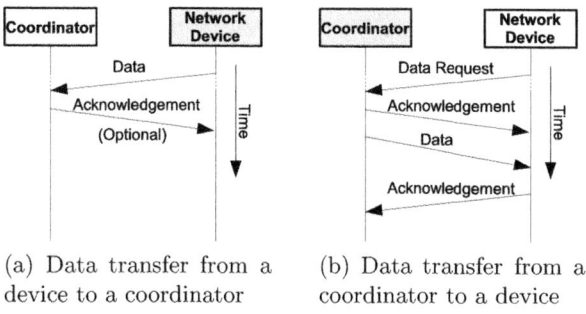

(a) Data transfer from a device to a coordinator

(b) Data transfer from a coordinator to a device

Fig. 2. Communication in a non beacon enabled PAN

Friis freespace model:

$$P_r\left(d\right) = \frac{P_t G_t G_r \lambda^2}{\left(4\pi\right)^2 d^2 L} \tag{2}$$

If the distance between transmitter and receiver is greater than d_{xover}, that is $d > d_{xover}$, then the received signal power at the receiver is modeled using the two-ray ground model:

$$P_r\left(d\right) = \frac{P_t G_t G_r h_t^2 h_r^2}{d^4 L} \tag{3}$$

where $P_r(d)$ is the received power for a transmitter-receiver separation of d, $L \geq 1$ is the system loss factor not related to propagation, h_t and h_r are the heights of the transmitter and receiver antennas above the ground respectively, G_t and G_r are the antenna gains, and λ is the wavelength of the carrier signal.

Taking into account the propagation model, a receiver can successfully receive a packet with acceptable error rate only if the received signal power is greater than receiver sensitivity threshold (RXthresh_) and the signal to noise ratio (SNR) is above a threshold.

4.2   Physical Layer Energy Model

Here we describe the energy numerical model that was used in our work. To understand and optimize physical energy consumption, we use an energy model like that used by Heinzelman [17] and Holger [3]. The energy consumption for transmitting one packet, E_p, is made up of two parts: the energy consumed by the transmitter when sending a packet E_{tx} and receiver energy consumption for receiving the packet, E_{rx}. That is, $E_p = E_{tx} + E_{rx}$.

In general, the energy consumed by a transmitter has two components. The first is the energy dissipation due to RF signal generation, and this depends mostly on the modulation technique used and the distance from the source to the destination. Power control can be used by setting the power amplifier to ensure certain power at the receiver. Here, energy consumed, depends on the transmission power, that is, the power radiated by the antenna.

The second component, is the energy consumed by electronic components necessary for frequency synthesis, frequency conversion, filters and others. This will remain constant depending on the electronic components used.

The sensor node transmission energy consumption can be modeled as the sum of constant electronic components energy consumption and an amplifier energy proportional to the receiver distance. Thus, the energy required for a node to transmit a packet of length l bits over a distance d is:

$$E_{tx}(l, d) = E_{tx-elect}(l) + E_{tx-amp}(l, d) \tag{4}$$

$$E_{tx}(l, d) = (\beta + \mu d^n)l \tag{5}$$

Where β is constant energy consumed by electronics, μd^n accounts for radiated power necessary to transmit over a distance d , between two nodes(source and destination) and n is the path loss index. The parameter μ is proportional constant that will depend on the receiver sensitivity and the receiver noise figure, therefore transmit power needs to be adjusted so that the power at the receiver is above a certain threshold.

The energy consumed by the receiver is consumed by receiver electronics $E_{rx}(l) = E_{rx-elec}(l)$, given by:

$$E_{rx}(l) = lE_{elec} \tag{6}$$

Considering the discussion in previous subsection, relating (5) and propagation models, we get:

$$E_{tx}(l,d) = \begin{cases} (E_{elect} + \mu_{friss-amp}d^2)l & : d < d_{xover} \\ (E_{elect} + \mu_{two-ray-amp}d^4)l & : d \geq d_{xover} \end{cases} \tag{7}$$

If the radio bit rate is R_b, then the transmit power, P_t, is equal to the transmit energy per bit multiplied by the bit rate:

$$P_t = E_{tx-amp}(1,d)R_b \tag{8}$$

Now if we consider only the radiating part of (7) and substituting the value of $E_{tx-amp}(1,d)$, we have:

$$P_t = \begin{cases} \mu_{friss-amp}R_b d^2 & : d < d_{xover} \\ \mu_{two-ray-amp}R_b d^4 & : d \geq d_{xover} \end{cases} \tag{9}$$

Using the propagation model described previously, and solving received power as receiver threshold power, we determine:

$$\mu_{friss-amp} = \frac{P_{r-thresh}(4\pi)^2}{R_b G_t G_r \lambda^2} \tag{10}$$

$$\mu_{two-ray-amp} = \frac{P_{r-thresh}}{R_b G_t G_r h_t^2 h_r^2} \tag{11}$$

In our experiments, receiver threshold remains constant, -94dBm. Substituting values used in our experiments, that is, $G_r = G_t = 1$, $h_r = h_t = 1.5$, $R_b = 250kbps$ and 2450MHz frequency into (10) and (11) we get:

$$\mu_{friss-amp} = 1.6771 \times 10^{-14} J/bit/m^2$$

and

$$\mu_{two-ray-amp} = 3.1455 \times 10^{-19} J/bit/m^4$$

5   Performance Evaluation and Discussion

To observe the impact of transmission power control in multi-hop and single-hop scenarios, we use simulation and numerical model to obtain the average

Table 1. Simulation Parameter Settings

Parameter	Value
Channel carrier frequency	2450 MHz
Data packet size	100 bytes, 28 bytes
Data rate	12 kbps
RXthresh_	-94 dB
Max Queue length	256
Radio propagation model	Freespace and reflection
Transmission power (Pt_)	0,-1,-3,-5,-7,-10,-15,-25 dB
Pt_consume, Pr_consume, P_idle	according to Telosb [8]
Antenna gain	0dB
Simulation area	250m x 250m
Simulation time	24,000 seconds

energy consumed per packet per node, taking into account all nodes involved in sending packets from a source node to a data sink node. For example, in a 2 hops communication, three nodes exist i.e. one source node, one relaying node, and node destination/sink node. We also obtain the percentage contribution of energy spent due to the radiation and electronic components.

5.1   Simulation Environment

Our radio model uses characteristics similar to Telosb interface and using ad-hoc routing. Telosb uses CC2420 chip [8], supporting eight different transmission power levels. Energy consumption for different transmission power levels can be calculated using Table 2 values. To simulate the typical Telosb energy model in NS-2, we calculate the energy consumption by each power level, using Table 2 values, whereby energy is the product of power and time ($E = Pt$), and power is the product of the voltage and current drained at that particular power level ($P = VI$). Table 1 shows our simulation parameters. Likewise, we obtain numerical approximation results, using our derived numerical energy model (Section 4), considering the constant receiver energy consumption for all power levels, different transmission power levels energy consumption (Table 2), number of hops and number of nodes, and the time to transmit/receive a packet (packet size divide by data rate/average packet delay).

5.2   Experiment 1: Multi-hop

We simulate a basic chain topology,where the distance from a source node to a destination node (sink) is kept constant at 120 meters. We also use the same traffic load from the source to the destination. First we simulate two nodes transmitting at maximum power (0dBm) for single-hop communication, and measure energy consumption for each node. We then reduce transmission power to one of the supported Telosb, CC2420 chip power levels. This will reduce the node's communication range. To maintain the link between the source and the sink

Table 2. Telosb Transmission Power and Current

PA_level	Output power(dBm)	Current drained (mA)
31	0	17.4
27	-1	16.5
23	-3	15.2
19	-5	13.9
15	-7	12.5
11	-10	11.5
7	-15	9.4
3	-25	8.5

which are 120 meters apart, a node is strategically placed between the source and sink, and transmission powers are adjusted to establish a two hop communication link (Fig. 3). This process is repeated for other lower power level values and more intermediate nodes are strategically placed between the source and the sink, thus increasing the number of hops between them. The range between nodes, and transmission power levels, can be approximated using propagation models, whereby P_r is the node constant receiver sensitivity (-94dBm).

This is a basic topology but it is quite sufficient to show the basic characteristics of transmission power control in multi-hop case.

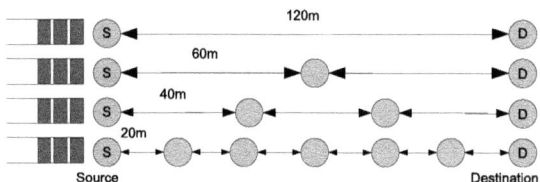

Fig. 3. Chain ad-hoc scenario

5.3 Experiment 2: Single-Hop

We simulate a pair of transmitter-receiver nodes, such that the distance from the transmitter to the receiver is small enough to enable the use of the lowest power level (Table 2) to transmit packets. and therefore the radiation part remains constant. Using the same traffic load and same Tx/Rx range, we measure energy consumption for sending packets at different power levels. Here, the radiation part will remain constant. The energy consumption using lowest level will obviously be minimum, however, we want to find by how much this will contribute to the energy savings and compare our simulation and numerical results.

5.4 Results

Fig. 4 shows numerical and simulation results for average energy consumed per packet for each node as the number of hops increases. This shows that using TPC

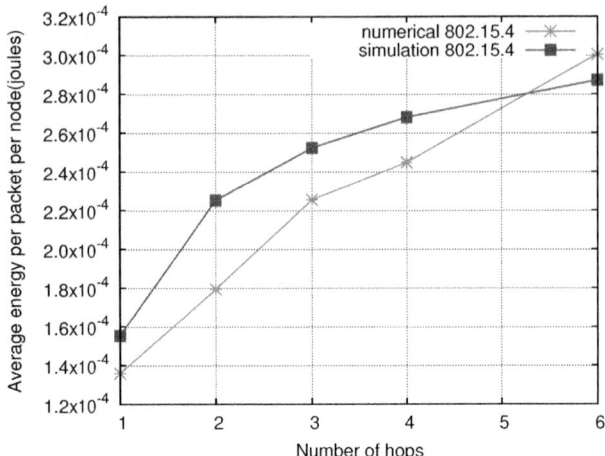

Fig. 4. Multi-hop average energy consumption (packet size 28 bytes, data rate 12kbps)

short-range multihop instead of single hop does not prolong nodes' lifespan in this case.

Among other advantages of multi-hop communication, using multi-hop will increase coverage due to limited sensor nodes ranges at the cost of energy but not as an alternative to save energy (Fig. 4). They can be several reasons why multi-hop short-range fail to reduce the power consumption. Some of these reasons include: energy is consumed by node's electronics not only when sending packets but also when receiving packets; the International Organization for Standardization (ISO) communication stack and layered protocols interactions as the packet transverse from one node to another, for example, the CSMA/CA in MAC sub-layer is performed per packet and per hop basis as packets go through several hops. Furthermore, by increasing number of hops, we increase the number of nodes contending to the channel and number of nodes that cannot hear one another, this increases the chance of packet collisions due to hidden terminals.

Fig. 5 shows average amount of energy consumed per packet for each node as a function of transmission power. clearly, single-hop power control optimization can offer better energy savings than using fixed transmission power, this is not new, it has been published and known for many years. From this Fig. 5, if we compare energy spent when sending at the maximum power level (0dBm) and the lowest power level (-25dBm), it shows that we can save energy by up to 23% compared to the normally used single level maximum transmission power. Fig. 6 shows the amount of energy contributed by radiation and electronics part using different transmission power levels. These results suggest that a better topology would be a cluster based (hybrid topology) or similar topologies whereby instead of having every node relay the information, specific nodes would be responsible for relaying the information and sensor nodes will pass the message in one hop to the cluster head/relaying node which will not have the same energy restrictions

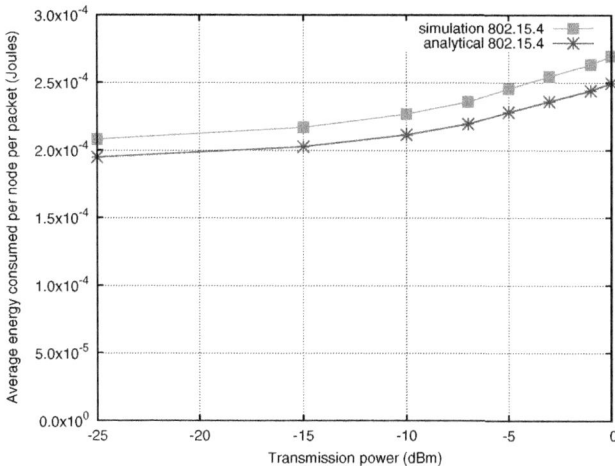

Fig. 5. Average energy consumption per node per packet (data rate 64kbps, packet size 100 bytes)

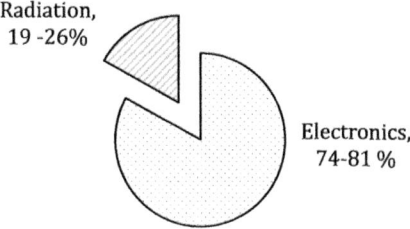

Fig. 6. Radiation energy percentage

as the sensors nodes. Each node associated with cluster head/relaying node will control transmission power based on its distance from the cluster head/relaying node.

6 Conclusion

In this paper, a new approach to transmission power control was presented for multi-hop and single-hop WSNs. While some researchers have suggested that short-range multi-hop communication can extend sensor node's lifespan, our results, both numerical and simulation, show that this is not the case. We have shown that if the distance between source and destination is fixed, then the total energy consumption in the WSN increases as we increase the number of hops and reduce the transmission power for each hop. Our results indicate that in our simulation scenario when a single-hop is used in conjunction with optimization of the transmission power, the node's energy consumption decreases by up to 23%. The difference between our results and the published literature is due to the fact that we consider all components of energy consumption and not just the component related to the radiating power from antennas. Furthermore, we used a basic simulation scenario that is effectively maintained to test TPC in multi-hop communication.

References

1. Akyildiz, I.F., Weilian, S., Sankarasubramaniam, Y., Cayirci, E.: A survey on sensor networks. IEEE Communications Magazine 40(8), 102–114 (2002); 0163-6804
2. Wei, Y., Heidemann, J., Estrin, D.: An energy-efficient mac protocol for wireless sensor networks. In: Proceedings of 21st -First Annual Joint Conference of the IEEE Computer and Communications Societies, INFOCOM 2002, vol. 3, pp. 1567–1576. IEEE, Los Alamitos (2002)
3. Holger, K., Andreas, W.: Protocols and Architectures for Wireless Sensor Networks. John Wiley & Sons, Chichester (2005); 1076303
4. Zhao, F., Leonidas, G.: Wireless Sensor Networks: An Information Processing Approach. Morgan Kaufmann, San Francisco (2004)
5. Kai, W., Wei, G., Jun, l.: A novel transmission power control algorithm based on position in wireless ad hoc networks. In: Proceedings of 2006 6th International Conference on ITS Telecommunications , pp. 675–679 (2006)
6. Monks, J.P., Ebert, J.P., Wolisz, A., Hwu, W.W.: A study of the energy saving and capacity improvement potential of power control in multi-hop wireless networks. In: Proceedings of 26th Annual IEEE Conference on Local Computer Networks, LCN 2001, pp. 550–559 (2001)
7. Polastre, J., Szewczyk, R., Culler, D.: Telos: enabling ultra-low power wireless research. In: Fourth International Symposium on Information Processing in Sensor Networks, IPSN 2005, pp. 364–369 (2005)
8. 2.4 ghz ieee 802.15.4 / zigbee-ready rf transceiver. Chipcon Products from Texas Instruments (May 2011), http://focus.ti.com/lit/ds/symlink/cc2420.pdf
9. Monks, J.P., Bharghavan, V., Hwu, W.M.W.: A power controlled multiple access protocol for wireless packet networks. In: Proceedings of Twentieth Annual Joint Conference of the IEEE Computer and Communications Societies, INFOCOM 2001, vol. 1, pp. 219–228. IEEE, Los Alamitos (2001)
10. Shih-Lin, W., Yu-Chee, T., Jang-Ping, S.: Intelligent medium access for mobile ad hoc networks with busy tones and power control. IEEE Journal on Selected Areas in Communications 18(9), 1647–1657 (2000); 0733-8716
11. Eun-Sun, J., Nitin, H.V.: A power control mac protocol for ad hoc networks. Wirel. Netw. 11(1-2), 55–66 (2005); 1160105
12. Jie, W., Shuhui, Y.: Coverage issue in sensor networks with adjustable ranges. In: Proceedings of International Conference on Parallel Processing Workshops, ICPP 2004, pp. 61–68 (2004)
13. Zalyubovskiy, V., Erzin, A., Astrakov, S., Choo, H.: Energy-efficient area coverage by sensors with adjustable ranges. Sensors 9(4), 2446–2460 (2009)
14. Bandai, M., Nakayama, S., Watanabe, T.: Energy efficient route construction scheme with continuous and discrete power control in ad hoc sensor networks. In: IEEE 63rd Vehicular Technology Conference, VTC 2006-Spring, vol. 3, pp. 1082–1086 (2006)

15. Liu, A., Yu, H., Guo, J., Li, H., Wang, X.: A strategy for self-configuring physical carrier sensing threshold in wireless sensor networks. In: International Conference on Wireless Communications, Networking and Mobile Computing, WiCom 2007, pp. 2650–2653 (2007)

16. Jaein, J., Culler, D., Jae-Hyuk, O.: Empirical analysis of transmission power control algorithms for wireless sensor networks. In: Fourth International Conference on Networked Sensing Systems, INSS 2007, pp. 27–34 (2007)

17. Heinzelman, W.B.: Application specific protocol architectures for wireless networks. Ph.D. dissertation, Massachusetts Institute of Technology, Department of Electrical Engineering and Computer Science, 932370 Supervisor - Anantha P. Chandrakasan Supervisor - Hari Balakrishnan (2000)

18. IEEE std 802.15.4, Wireless Medium Access Control (MAC) and Physical Layer (PHY) Specifications for Low-Rate Wireless Personal Area Networks (WPANs), IEEE Standard Association Std

19. Rappaport, T.S.: Wireless Communications: Principles and Practice. Prentice-Hall PTR, Englewood Cliffs (2002)

A Preamble-Based Approach for Providing Quality of Service Support in Wireless Sensor Networks

Alexander Klein and Lothar Braun

Network Architectures and Services - Institute for Informatics
Technische Universität München, Germany
{klein,braun}@net.in.tum.de

Abstract. Medium Access Control (MAC) protocols for Wireless Sensor Networks (WSN) are usually designed as random access protocols that apply different kinds of backoff strategies since Time Division Multiple Access (TDMA) based protocols with admission control are very complex and require mechanisms for synchronization. Without such mechanisms, fair or priority based medium access with Quality of Service (QoS) guarantees can hardly be achieved by existing protocols. Therefore, we developed a random access protocol which uses a new preamble based medium access strategy that enables high reliable priority based access. In this paper we introduce different QoS strategies and their use cases. All strategies can be easily integrated in our protocol to meet the requirements of different target applications. Furthermore, we compare the performance of the strategies with a typical carrier-sense based protocol.

Keywords: random access, wireless, quality of service.

1 Introduction

A trend towards heterogeneous sensor networks can be recognized which is driven by the large number of applications with different QoS requirements [1], e.g. light and temperature sensing for autonomous home networks, structural health monitoring of stressed components or multimedia applications. Thus, nodes in such wireless networks typically consist of heterogeneous hardware which suits the requirements of the target application in terms of computational power, memory, and energy constraints.

Dense wireless networks with high utilization or correlated traffic represent a challenging environment for random access MAC protocols due to the shared characteristic of the medium. The fact that nodes cannot send and receive at the same time limits the number of strategies which can be applied to achieve a reliable priority based access. For this reason, carrier sense multiple access with collision resolution, as used by the Controller Area Network (CAN), is not an option. TDMA protocols can solve the problem of priority based access. However, they require time synchronization which represents another complex

C. Sacchi et al. (Eds.): MACOM 2011, LNCS 6886, pp. 144–155, 2011.

task. As a consequence of the heterogeneous hardware TDMA protocols have to deal with communication issues such as different transmission ranges, clock drift, and unreliable links and sleep schedule of energy constraint nodes.

It has been shown that carrier-sense based MAC protocols require additional mechanisms in order to solve the problem of contention resolution [8] and QoS support [1]. Therefore, we decided to follow a new approach [9] which is based on the transmission of preambles which cover the function of reservation signals and contention resolution. Existing MAC protocols, like the Low Power Listening (LPL) [12] and XMAC [13], only use the preamble transmission to make sure that the destination is listening to the channel. An exception is represented by the PR-MAC protocol [6] which uses preamble transmissions for channel reservation, but still requires carrier-sense based backoff mechanisms for contention resolution. However, no one has yet used the transmission of preambles in the wireless domain to schedule the medium access. In this work, we extend our previous approach and show that the transmission of consecutive preambles can be used to solve contention on the radio channel while providing priority based medium access.

This paper is organized as follows. A brief description of the BPS-MAC protocol, which represents the basis framework for our approach, is given in Section 2. Furthermore, we outline how static and dynamic QoS strategies can be integrated in the protocol to suit the requirements of different target applications in terms of fairness and delay. In Section 3, we propose different QoS strategies and describe how to integrate them into our approach. The performance of the different strategies in the context of challenging scenarios is discussed in Section 4. Finally, we draw our conclusion in Section 5.

2   BPS-Mac

The introduced approach is based on the BPS-MAC protocol [3] which was originally designed to overcome the hardware limitations of low-power transceivers, namely the Clear Channel Assessment (CCA) delay and the rx-tx switching time. In dense WSNs with event-driven data traffic, typical Carrier Sense Multiple Access (CSMA) based protocols cannot achieve high performance since nodes are not able to reliably detect the transmission of other nodes if the transmission has started within duration that is shorter than the CCA delay [7][11]. Thus, the CCA delay represents a critical time-period which has to be taken into account when applying CSMA based protocols. Recall, that state-of-the-art low-power transceivers, like the CC2400 and the CC2520 from Texas Instruments or ATMEL´s AT86RF231, require $128\mu s$ to sense the medium. Therefore, high fractions of lost packets in dense WSNs result from the limited sensing capabilities. However, it is obvious that this fraction strongly depends on the node density, the traffic load and the traffic pattern. First, a brief description of the BPS-MAC protocol is given before we introduce our QoS-aware medium access extension.

2.1 Protocol Description

The BPS-MAC protocol has been introduced in [3]. It applies a preamble based medium access procedure which is not directly affected by the channel sensing capabilities of the transceiver. The protocol uses the transmission of preambles with variable length to schedule medium access. The preamble covers the function of a reservation signal in order to notify other nodes that there is a competition for the medium access. The node which sends the longest preamble gains access to the medium. Competing nodes switch there transceiver to receive mode after they have transmitted their preamble. If they detect an occupied channel, they assume that other nodes are still competing for the access which means that they have lost the competition and thus have to postpone their medium access. However, the problem of CCA delay is not yet solved since two nodes can still start their transmission at the same time. For this reason, the duration of the preamble has to be a multiple of the CCA delay in order to distinguish preambles of different length. BPS-MAC defines the term slot for duration which corresponds to the CCA delay since it is more related to the context of contention resolution. A collision can still occur if two or more nodes start their preamble transmission at the same time and choose the same preamble length. As a consequence, the nodes would start their data transmission synchronously due to the fact that they would sense an idle channel after their preamble transmission. A longer maximum preamble length in terms of slots results in a lower packet loss since the probability decreases that two nodes choose the same number of slots. The collision probability can even be further decreased if multiple short preambles are transmitted since a collision only occurs in the unlikely event that competing nodes start their preamble transmission within duration shorter than the CCA delay and choose the same number of slots in every sequence, as shown in Figure 1(a). A detailed description of the sequential contention resolution of the protocol can be found in [3].

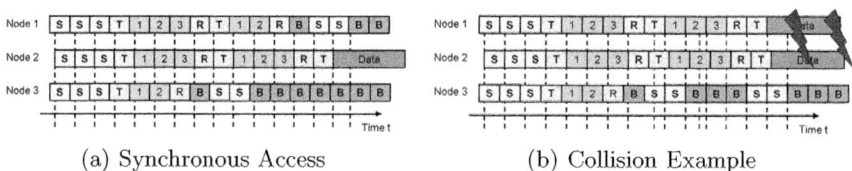

(a) Synchronous Access   (b) Collision Example

Fig. 1. Sequential Contention Resolution

2.2 QoS Extension of the BPS-MAC Protocol

QoS strategies can be applied in many ways to meet the requirements of the target application [2]. However, even the best QoS-support mechanism is affected by the unpredictable nature of the wireless links. No strategy can provide a "'one-size-for-all"' solution since the mechanisms either focus on delay-bounded and reliable data delivery or on fairness. The QoS strategies that are introduced in

Section 3 were selected with respect to this trade-off in terms of fairness and priority based medium access.

The BPS-MAC protocol uses two or more preamble sequences to resolve the contention on the channel. A node assumes to have control of the radio channel if it senses an idle medium after the transmission of its own preamble. Thus, the node with the longest preamble in every sequence gets access to the medium. Instead of using all preamble sequences for contention resolution, we encode the priority of the medium access on the duration of the first preamble. The first preamble covers the function of a priority indicator while the consecutive preambles are used to resolve contention among nodes with the same priority. The modification of the length of the first preamble is the simplest way to provide priority based medium access and can be used to integrate various strategies.

The number of preamble sequences and their length can be freely configured to achieve the desired reliability and medium access delay. Simulations and first testbed results have shown that three to four preamble sequences, each having duration of four slots, represents the best trade-off for most scenarios. In this work, we focus on protocol configurations with three preamble sequences where the first sequence reflects the priority while the two following sequences are used for contention resolution.

Static Medium Access Priority
Priority based medium access strategies can be divided into two groups. The first group is represented by static priorities, e.g. priority for a certain traffic type or network. The advantage of static priorities is that the behavior of the network is more predictable since the node with the highest priority is able to access the medium immediately in case of a free radio channel or after the current transmission if the channel is busy. Thus, it is even possible to calculate medium access delay boundaries for the node with the highest priority if the longest preamble duration and maximum packet length are known. However, we recommend to assign static priorities to groups rather than individual nodes due to the fact that the number of preamble slots should be as small as possible in order to minimize the protocol overhead and medium access delay. Moreover, group based priority assignment can improve the collective QoS [2] in terms of collective latency, collective packet loss, and information throughput.

Dynamic Medium Access Priority
Dynamic priority strategies are based on changing conditions, e.g. remaining energy, waiting queue length, data rate, buffer level, and distance to the root or number of neighbors. They typically result in a more complex network behavior which requires a detailed understanding of the encoded priority metric. Basically, dynamic access strategies are used to balance or shift the load in the network or to guarantee fair medium access. Metrics which consider the traffic load and buffer level of nodes are of particular interest in WSNs since nodes are very limited in terms of energy and memory.

3   QoS Strategies

QoS in WSNs represents a challenging issue due to unreliable links and time varying channel conditions [10]. Moreover, many established QoS-support mechanisms, like IntServ [4] and DiffServ [5], can hardly be applied in the context of WSNs since nodes have severe resource constraints in terms of computational power, memory and bandwidth. For these reasons, the proposed QoS strategy should be as simple as possible while meeting the requirements of the target applications. In the following, we introduce different scenarios where priority-based medium access can significantly improve the network performance.

3.1   Topology-Aware

Typical WSNs consist of two types of nodes: few powerful nodes with little energy constraints form a backbone for many smaller and more constraint devices. However, the backbone nodes and their smaller and less powerful counterparts access the shared medium and therefore compete for medium access. Thus, mechanisms should be employed to prioritize the medium access for backbone nodes in order to improve the overall network performance. By assigning a high priority to the backbone nodes, the medium access delay of these nodes is reduced and the delivery ratio is increased since the number of nodes with high access priority is very small. Furthermore, this strategy gives the backbone nodes control of the medium access which improves the support for data aggregation mechanisms.

3.2   Network-Aware

The self-organizing capability of WSNs have made the technology an attractive solution for monitoring tasks since nodes can be randomly placed in a field or in areas which are or become hardly accessible, e.g. due to radioactive contamination. In some scenarios, nodes cannot be replaced or removed which represents a problem due to the shared characteristic of the medium. In addition, asymmetric links or partitioning of the network can make reprogramming or remote shut down of the nodes impossible. This can limit the performance of later deployed networks which operate on the same radio channel, especially if nodes frequently transmit data until their batteries are drained. A priority based medium access strategy which employs network IDs can mitigate the problem of co-existing networks. Network IDs can be used to represent the medium access priority of the WSNs: a higher ID corresponds to a higher access priority and vice versa. One the one hand, this strategy allows the deployment of a new high priority WSNs on top of an already deployed sensor network, which could not be removed or shut down. On the other hand, a new low priority WSN can be placed within the area of another sensor network without having a large impact on the performance of the already deployed network.

3.3   Traffic-Aware

More and more sensor networks perform different tasks at the same time. Traffic-awareness within the MAC protocol is required if the tasks have different priorities. Assume a WSN in which nodes generate traffic with different priorities, e.g. the stress and strain measurements of a structural health monitoring application, which has high QoS requirements, and temperature measurements which can be transmitted as best effort traffic. Thus, the traffic of the structural health monitoring application should have a higher medium access priority than that of the temperature application.

3.4   Service-Aware

Virtualization of networks and services has become very popular in recent years. The first implementations for sensor networks are already available [14]. They allow several users to access the nodes and their sensors in a shared manner. Resource allocation for each user, e.g. computational power, memory, sensors, is not a challenging issue in general, since it represents a well investigated field of research. However, as soon as the medium access has to be taken into account, the consideration of user priorities becomes a challenging task. The scheduling of packets at a single node can be easily done by applying pre-defined user priorities. Nevertheless, the best scheduling is useless if a node does not get access to the medium in order to transmit the queued packets. Therefore, the MAC protocol should be able to consider the user priority for the medium access.

3.5   Distance-Aware

Measured data is typically transmitted to a small number of data sinks in the WSN which evaluate and process the data or simply function as a gateway. The topology of these networks is often arranged in a tree structure [15]. Such a tree topology allows taking advantage from data aggregation and data processing mechanisms. However, medium access plays a critical role in this task due to the fact that the traffic load increases towards data sinks. A priority based medium access procedure which takes the distance to the sink into account can support the data aggregation mechanisms and decrease the energy consumption of the sensing nodes. If nodes that are closer to the sink have a higher priority, the delay in event-based WSNs can be reduced since the node which is triggered by the event and is closest to the sink has the highest priority. Thus, it can immediately access the medium to transmit its data. Furthermore, the priority of the transmitted packets further increases on the path towards the sink, which results in a low delay. If energy consumption is the major constraint, rather than high delay, a medium access strategy should be preferred which gives nodes further away from the sink a higher priority than nodes closer to the sink. This medium access strategy reduces the energy consumption since nodes that are furthest away from the sink can transmit their data immediately and turn off their transceiver at the end of the transmission. Furthermore, it improves the potential of data aggregation due to the fact that all children of a node in the tree have a higher medium access priority than their parent. As a result, the children can transmit their data to the parent before the parent gains access to the media in order to forward the data.

3.6   Energy-Aware

Wireless sensor nodes have very limited power supplies. Therefore, designers of communication protocols try to minimize the energy consumption as much as possible while meeting the requirements of the target application. Routing protocols, which take energy consumption into account, typically try not to forward traffic via nodes that have only a small amount of energy left. Such mechanisms have proven to balance the traffic load and to prolong the lifetime of WSNs. However, the access to the medium can become costly as well in terms of energy if a node requires several attempts. For this reason, nodes which run low on power should have a high medium access priority in order to reduce the average number of access attempts.

3.7   Buffer-Aware

The limited amount of memory of wireless sensor nodes becomes a serious problem if the nodes should be able to support the Internet Protocol (IP). Especially, fragmentation of data packets and forwarding of packets leads to high memory consumption. It has to be kept in mind that most sensor nodes, e.g. TelosB, T-Mote and Mica, only have 8KB or 10KB of ram which makes buffering of multiple large packets almost impossible. Furthermore, the event-driven traffic patterns in WSNs lead to temporary high network load. Routing protocols with load-balancing support can mitigate the impact of this issue in multi-hop networks. However, the MAC protocol can further improve the performance by taking the length of the waiting queue into account. Thus, nodes that have more packets stored in their waiting queue should have a higher medium access priority. As a consequence, the maximum waiting queue length and the percentage of dropped packets due to buffer overflows could be decreased. This strategy also improves the fairness in dense single hop networks provided that the nodes generate traffic at the same data rate.

3.8   Data-Rate Aware

The latest generation of routing protocols for WSNs, e.g. the Collection Tree Protocol (CTP) [15], apply adaptive mechanisms to cope with frequent topology changes. In general, these protocols increase their beacon transmission rate if they detect changes in their neighborhood. Topology changes usually result from interference or mobility of the nodes. The latter may lead to frequent topology changes which significantly increase the routing overhead. In dense networks, the routing overhead can even result in temporary congestion of the network. Temporary congestion can also be caused by applications which generate event-driven traffic, e.g. intruder detection or structural health monitoring applications. For these kinds of applications, it is important to receive information from all nodes which have detected the event to gain more precise information and to minimize false positives. The priority of the medium access should depend on the transmission rate of the nodes. A fair medium access can be achieved if a higher transmission rate results in a lower access priority and vice versa. Thus, nodes which rarely transmit traffic have a high probability of gaining access to the medium immediately. However, nodes that frequently transmit traffic can utilize the whole bandwidth as long as no other nodes need access to the medium.

3.9 Combined Strategy

Depending on the target scenario and application, a combined strategy could further improve the performance, e.g. a combination of a traffic-aware and buffer-aware strategy. Such a strategy would represent a trade-off between delay of high priority packets and packet loss of packets due to buffer overflows.

4 Performance Evaluation

In this section, we take a closer look on the performance of a static and a dynamic priority QoS strategy in terms of delay. Furthermore, we compare their performance with the standard BPS-MAC protocol as defined in [3]. The majority of sensor networks uses the IEEE 802.15.4 standard since it is supported by almost every state-of-the-art transceiver. Therefore, we decided to compare its performance with our approach even though the protocol does not support QoS.

The performance of MAC protocols is mainly affected by the number of competing nodes, traffic pattern, and utilization of the medium and characteristics of the radio channel. Especially, asymmetric links and non-circular transmission and/or interference range have to be taken into account. These issues do not allow reproducibility of measurements in multi-hop wireless sensor testbeds. Thus, we decided to evaluate the performance of the strategies and protocols in a controlled single hop simulation scenario instead of employing them on real sensor nodes to avoid distortion caused by interference or other side effects.

We focus on the default configuration of the BPS-MAC protocol and IEEE 802.15.4 standard since most users deploy the sensor nodes without modifying the configuration of the link layer. The results of IEEE 802.15.4 standard are marked with the 'CSMA' tag. The BPS-MAC protocol uses three backoff preamble sequences. Each sequence has a maximum length of four slots. The graphs marked with the 'NONE' tag represent the performance of the standard protocol without any modification. The only difference between the standard protocol and our approach is represented by the way nodes chose the length of the first preamble sequence. The static priority QoS strategy, which is marked with the 'TRAFFIC' tag, uses fix preamble length of four slots for high priority traffic and a preamble length of two slots for low priority traffic. The length of the consecutive preambles is chosen as specified in the standard protocol. The dynamic QoS strategy, which is marked by the 'WQL' tag, takes the fill level of the buffer into account to determine the length of the first preamble. A preamble length of one slot is used if the buffer fill state is below 25%. A fill state between 25% and 50% results in a two slot preamble while a fill stat between 50% and 75% is represented by preamble duration of three slots. The maximum preamble duration of four slots is used if the buffer fill state exceeds 75%. We set the maximum buffer size to 16 packets. Thus, the buffer thresholds correspond to a fill state of 4, 8 and 12 packets.

The OPNET Modeler network simulator is used to simulate the performance of the protocols. However, we use a self-developed wireless sensor framework 3 which considers hardware limitations of low-power transceivers such as CCA delay. A CCA delay of $128\mu s$ is applied to reflect the limited sensing capabilities of the sensor hardware. The data rate is set to 256 kb/s. The simulated scenario should include all aspects of typical WSNs, e.g. event-driven traffic with high priority and periodic traffic with low priority. For this reason, we simulate two different kinds of traffic pattern which are shown in Table 1. The first pattern is used to simulate event-driven traffic, e.g. stress and strain measurements. This burst-like pattern is triggered approximately every 10 seconds. It generates packets every 20 milliseconds with a packet size of 1024 bit for duration of 2 seconds resulting in 100 packets per burst. Thus, the average data rate of this pattern is 10 kb/s while its peak rate is 50 kb/s. The second traffic pattern is used to reflect periodic tasks, like temperature or humidity measurements. Nodes, applying this traffic pattern, generate one packet with a size of 1024 bit approximately every second. Both traffic patterns start with a uniform distributed offset between 0 and 1 second to avoid exact synchronization. For the same reason, the burst inter-arrival time of the first pattern and the packet inter-arrival time of the second pattern are also chosen according to a uniform distribution. The simulated scenario consists of two nodes which generate traffic according the burst traffic pattern. The number of nodes, which generate traffic according to the single traffic pattern, is increased from 10 to 100 in steps of 10 nodes to simulate the performance of the different protocols and QoS strategies under different traffic load. The simulation results represent the average from 30 simulation runs with duration of 1100 seconds. Statistics are collected after 100 seconds to avoid the transient phase. Due to the low variance of the simulation results, we use the average instead of error bars.

In order to evaluate the performance of our approach, we take a closer look on the delay of the periodic and the burst traffic. The nodes which generate traffic according to the periodic traffic pattern are in the following referred to as low traffic nodes while their counterparts are referred to as high traffic nodes. Figure 2 shows the average delay of the periodic traffic depending on the number of low traffic users. The results point out a slight delay increase of the delay for the non-modified BPS-MAC protocol as well as for the WQL strategy and the IEEE 802.15.4 standard. The increase is the consequence of the higher traffic load due to the higher number of low traffic users. Moreover, the increase of delay is on a comparable level which indicates that the network is not congested. However, the average delay of the periodic traffic in the TRAFFIC scenario shows a significant increase which results from the fact that the periodic traffic is assigned a low priority. As a consequence, transmissions of high traffic nodes use a longer preamble which prevents the medium access of the low traffic nodes. Thus, the periodic traffic is delayed while the delay of the burst traffic is kept

Table 1. Traffic Pattern

Pattern Name	Parameter	Distribution	Range / Values
Burst	Burst IAT	uniform	[9.9; 10.1] s
	Packets per Burst	constant	100
	Packet IAT	constant	0.02 s
	Packet Size	constant	1024 bit
	Number of Sources	-	2
	Offset	uniform	[0; 1] s
Single	Packet IAT	uniform	[0.9; 1.1] s
	Packet Size	constant	1024 bit
	Number of Sources	-	[10;20;30;40;50; 60;70;80;90;100]
	Offset	uniform	[0; 1] s

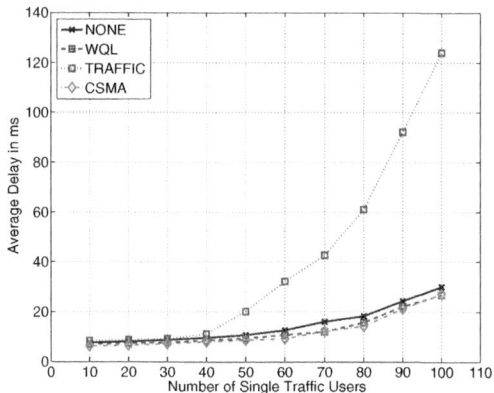

Fig. 2. Delay of periodic traffic depending on the employed QoS strategy

at a minimum, as shown in Figure 3. Only a slight delay increase of the burst traffic can be recognized for the TRAFFIC QoS solution if the number of low traffic nodes increases. The increase results from the fact that it becomes more likely that the medium is already occupied. Thus, the high traffic nodes have to wait until the medium becomes idle in order to transmit their first preamble. The graph of the IEEE 802.15.4 standard points out that the CSMA-based protocols only provide a good performance up to a certain utilization of the radio channel. A high utilization often leads to idle periods since the backoff duration is doubled if a busy medium was sensed. The standard BPS-MAC protocol achieves a better performance than the IEEE 802.15.4 standard, but has a much higher delay compared to the TRAFFIC QoS strategy. In addition, the variance of the delay of the standard BPS-MAC protocol can lead to rare buffer overflows in this scenario which affects the overall delay as a result of the lower traffic load. The WQL QoS strategy shows a high performance up to 70 low traffic users before a significant increase of the delay can be recognized. The

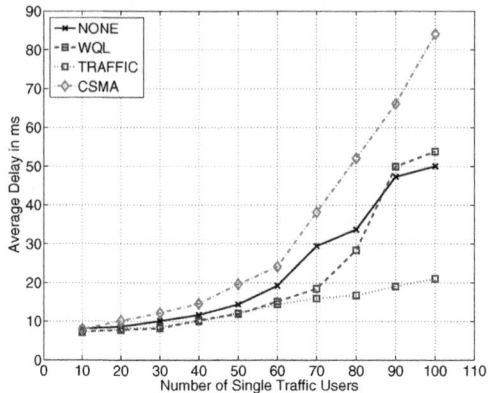

Fig. 3. Delay of burst traffic depending on the employed QoS strategy

dynamic medium access priority of the WQL QoS approach is the only simulated solution which minimizes the delay of the low and high traffic. Therefore, it represents an optimal choice for scenarios which require fair medium access.

5   Conclusion

In this work, we introduced a new comprehensive approach for priority-based medium access with QoS support for WSNs. The approach offers a high level of flexibility to suit the requirements of a wide range of target applications. It uses the transmission of short preambles to indicate the priority of a transmission and to resolve contention on the radio channel.

We implemented a static and a dynamic medium access strategy with our approach and compared their performance with the standard BPS-MAC protocol and the IEEE 802.15.4 standard in a one hop scenario with periodic and event-driven traffic. Our results have shown that our approach can be used to minimize delay and buffer utilization, e.g. by employing a dynamic QoS strategy which takes the buffer fill state into account. Moreover, static medium access priorities can be used to minimize the delay of a certain traffic type or to deploy a high priority network on top of an existing network.

References

1. Yigitel, M.A., Incel, O.D., Ersoy, C.: QoS-aware MAC Protocols for Wireless Sensor Networks: A Survey. Comput. Netw. 55, 1982–2004 (2011)
2. Chen, D., Varshney, P.K.: QoS Support in Wireless Sensor Networks: A Survey. In: Proc. of the International Conference on Wireless Networks (ICWN), USA (June 2004)
3. Klein, A.: Performance Issues of MAC and Routing Protocols in Wireless Sensor Networks, PhD thesis, University of Wuerzburg, Germany (December 2010)

4. Braden, R., Clark, D., Shenker, S.: Integrated Srvices in the Internet Architecture - An Overview. IETF RFC 1663 (June 1994)
5. Blake, S., Black, D., Carlson, M., Davies, E., Wang, Z., Weiss, W.: An Architecture for Differentiated Services. IETF RFC 2475 (December 1998)
6. Firoze, A.M., Ju, L.Y., Kwong, L.M.: PR-MAC A Priority Reservation MAC Protocol For Wireless Sensor Networks. In: Proc. Int. Conf. Electrical Engineering ICEE 2007, pp. 1–6 (2007)
7. Kiryushin, A., Sadkov, A., Mainwaring, A.: Real World Performance of Clear Channel Assessment in 802.15.4 Wireless Sensor Networks. In: Proc. Second International Conference on Sensor Technologies and Applications SENSORCOMM 2008, pp. 625–630 (August 2008)
8. Vinel, A., Zhang, Y., Lott, M., Turlikov, A.: Performance Analysis of the Random Access in IEEE 802.16. In: Proc. of the 16th Annual IEEE International Symposium on Personal, Indoor and Mobile Radio Communications, IEEE PIMRC 2005, pp. 1596–1600 (2005)
9. Klein, A., Klaue, J., Schalk, J.: BP-MAC: A high Reliable Backoff Preamble MAC Protocol for Wireless Sensor Networks. Electronic Journal of Structural Engineering(EJSE): Special Issue of Sensor Networks for Building Monitoring: From Theory to Real Application, 35–45 (December 2009)
10. Muneb, A., Saif, U., Dunkels, A., Voigt, T., Römer, K., Langendoen, K., Polastre, J., Uzmi, Z.A.: Medium Access Control Issues in Sensor Networks. SIGCOMM Comput. Commun. Rev. 36(2), 33–36 (2006)
11. Bertocco, M., Gamba, G., Sona, A.: Experimental Optimization of CCA Thresholds in Wireles Sensor Networks in Presence of Interference. In: Proc. of IEEE EMC Europe 2007 Workshop on Electromagnetic Compatibility (June 2007)
12. El-Hoiydi, A.: Spatial TDMA and CSMA with Preamble Sampling for Low Power Ad Hoc Wireless Sensor Networks. In: Proc. Seventh International Symposium on Computers and Communications ISCC 2002, pp. 685–692 (2002)
13. Buettner, M., Yee, G.V., Anderson, E., Han, R.: X-MAC: A Short Preamble MAC Protocol for Duty-Cycled Wireless Sensor Networks. In: SenSys 2006: Proceedings of the 4th International Conference on Embedded Networked Sensor Systems, pp. 307–320. ACM, New York (2006)
14. Donovan, B.C., Mclaughlin, D.J., Zink, M., Kurose, J.: Western Massachusetts Off-the-Grid Radar Technology Testbed. In: Proc. IEEE Int. Geoscience and Remote Sensing Symp., IGARSS 2008, vol. 5 (2008)
15. Gnawali, O., Fonseca, R., Jamieson, K., Moss, D., Levis, P.: Collection Tree Protocol. In: SenSys 2009: Proceedings of the 7th ACM Conference on Embedded Networked Sensor Systems, pp. 1–14. ACM, New York (2009)

Evaluating the LWT-MAC Performance in Query-Driven WSNs Using Data-Centric Routing

Anna Sfairopoulou, Cristina Cano, Eduard Bonada, and Boris Bellalta

Department of Technology, Universitat Pompeu Fabra,
c/ Roc Boronat 138, 08018, Barcelona, Spain
anna.sfairopoulou@upf.edu

Abstract. Data-centric routing is a new paradigm of routing mechanism adapted for Wireless Sensor Networks (WSNs), where the data request and collection is done based on data attributes rather than node IDs and using only local interactions. An example of data-centric routing protocol is Directed Diffusion, in which sinks disseminate queries in order to collect data from a specific area. Both query dissemination as also data collection in case of event detection imply an increase of the network load, which can seriously compromise the WSN performance in terms of reliability, delay and energy consumption. In this study we examine how the previously proposed Low power listening with Wake up after Transmissions MAC protocol (LWT-MAC), designed to react and manage sporadic load increases, is also well suited for data-centric WSNs. The obtained results demonstrate that LWT-MAC is able to cope with the higher load produced by the operation of Directed Diffusion, showing a notably better performance when compared to basic Low Power Listening (LPL) MAC protocols.

Keywords: Wireless Sensor Networks, Low Power Listening MAC protocols, query-driven traffic, Directed Diffusion.

1 Introduction

Wireless Sensor Networks (WSNs) are networks formed by small and low-capability devices able to sense environmental metrics and communicate them wirelessly to one or more central units (known as sinks) [1]. There is a large range of potential applications in industrial, military, environmental, health and home automation areas, among others, that can take profit of using WSNs to collect data.

Data collection in WSNs can be done in different ways: triggered by events (*event-based*), in a periodic manner in monitoring applications (*periodic*) or as a response to queries initiated by the sink (*query-based*). Each mode of operation has different demands. For example, in monitoring applications, WSNs work at low traffic loads, due to the small amount of required information per unit of time. However, in other applications it can also be necessary to report specific

C. Sacchi et al. (Eds.): MACOM 2011, LNCS 6886, pp. 156–167, 2011.

events to the sink or to disseminate/reply a query. In such situations, the traffic load considerably increases and the delay to report the event or to reply a query becomes critical.

WSNs have thus a high application dependence [1], and the different requirements and constraints are directly imposed by the application to be provided. This issue complicates the design of a general protocol stack to be used in different deployments and leads to the definition of distinct approaches; a different routing or MAC protocol can make a big difference considering the concrete scenario where it will be used.

In general, traditional routing protocols designed for wireless ad-hoc networks are not optimal for WSNs due to the special characteristics of them. First of all, traditional routing protocols do not take into consideration that the sensor nodes are usually battery based and thus limited in energy. Energy consumption is a very important constraint of WSNs since many times these are deployed in large, difficult to access areas, and batteries cannot be easily replaced. The limitation on the energy resources is one of the most important as it directly affects the network lifetime. Therefore, it is important to design mechanisms that address the reduction of energy consumption. Additionally, most traditional routing protocols usually request data from a specific node with a concrete node identifier. In WSNs, sensor nodes may not have a unique global identifier and requests for data are usually based on certain attributes, not on node IDs. To give a simplified example, a common request for a WSN can be "nodes of this area should report back as soon as their temperature is higher than 40°C" rather than "node X tell me your temperature". This is called data-centric routing [2] and it is commonly used in query-based scenarios.

Directed Diffusion [3], is one of the most known data-centric routing protocol for WSNs. In this, sinks inject a query at the network which is disseminated by the sensors until it reaches the destination area of interest. During this process routes are created dynamically towards the sink and when an event is detected data responses are drawn towards the sink using these paths. The protocol is explained briefly in section 2. Directed Diffusion can save a lot of energy by avoiding unnecessary operations at network layer routing and eliminating the need for an addressing scheme as all communications are based on local interactions. At the same time though, these local interactions create various alternative paths and loops which, if not handled properly, can become inefficient and lead to an increase in traffic load, or even cause network saturation resulting in high packet losses, high delay and high battery consumption.

Of crucial importance for handling the network traffic and also for reducing the energy consumption in WSNs is the MAC layer, since it directly controls the operation of the transceiver, the most consuming component of a sensor node. The most common technique in WSNs is to put sensor nodes into sleep mode to save energy. In order to ensure that a sensor node is awake to receive the data, several proposals have been defined. The proposed approaches can be divided in three main categories [4]: TDMA-like channel access, protocols with Common Active Periods and asynchronous MAC protocols. Among these, asynchronous protocols and specifically Low Power Listening (LPL) protocols (also known as preamble sampling) [5], [6], [7] have gained special attention. This is caused by the fact that they are extremely simple, do not require synchronization and, even more important, can provide considerable low levels of energy consumption when the network load is low, which is the common situation in WSNs used for monitoring. However, they do not respond equally well in higher network load or in the presence of hidden terminals [8].

With the goal to improve the network performance when the traffic load increases, like in event-based or query-driven WSNs, the Low power listening with Wake up after Transmissions MAC (LWT-MAC) was defined in [8]. This protocol aims at consuming few amounts of energy, comparable to the basic preamble sampling, but at the same time, being able to switch to a CSMA-like operation when the traffic load increases. The basic operation of LWT-MAC is explained in section 3.

In this study, we evaluate the benefits of using the LWT-MAC protocol, designed for working best with sporadic traffic increases, in a query-driven scenario using the Directed Diffusion routing protocol. We expect that in this scenario, LWT-MAC will also be able to efficiently cope with the traffic load increase produced by the operation of Directed Diffusion.

2   Directed Diffusion

Directed Diffusion [3] is a data-centric routing mechanism for coordination between sensor nodes. It is data-centric in the sense that all communication is for named data, all data generated by sensor nodes is named by attribute-value pairs. It is also a reactive routing protocol since the routes are not preconfigured but they are established on demand, when there is a need (i.e. query) for data. There are several elements defined in the Directed Diffusion protocol: interests, gradients, data messages and reinforcements. These are very briefly explained next. For more details the reader should refer to [3].

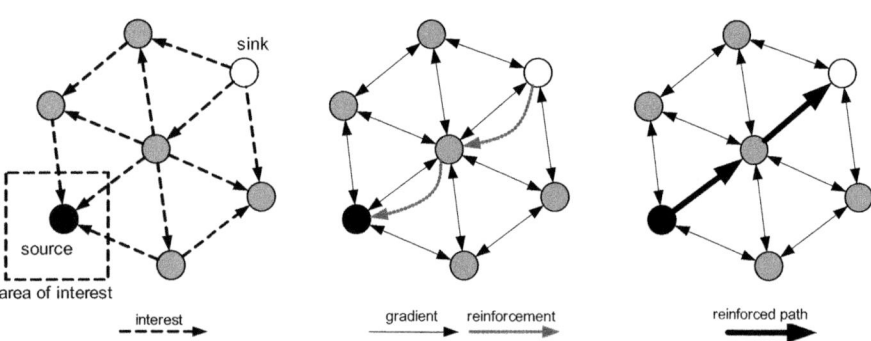

Fig. 1. Directed Diffusion: a) Interest propagation, b) Gradient establishment and Reinforcement and c) Reinforced path

A node, usually called *sink*, creates and sends to all its neighbors an initial query for data, called an *interest* (Fig. 1.a). In this, the sink specifies the type of data that it is interested in and an *interest area* from which it wants to draw data at a specific data rate, also specified in the interest. When a sensor node receives the interest it forwards it to all its neighbors, until it reaches the sensors that are inside the area of interest, known as *sources*. At the same time, each sensor creates an interest cache where the interest is stored together with a field indicating from which neighbor the interest came from and the desired data rate of responses. In this way, each node creates backward links towards its neighbors, known as *gradients*, forming paths towards the sink (Fig. 1.b). Interest cache also serves for detection of duplicated interests in case of loops.

When an event is detected, sources start to generate data at the requested data rate and send the data back through the formed gradients, thus data are drawn back to the sink the same way that the interest arrived. Data are stored in a data cache at each node, which can be later used for detection and avoidance of duplicated packets. However, this interest propagation mechanism is very energy consuming since it creates many simultaneously active paths, which lead to loops. The interest is initially flooded throughout the network and due to local interactions two-way gradients are formed between each pair of neighbors. Many alternative paths that connect the sources with the sink are created and the nodes retransmit the data messages to all the possible paths. Thus, in each hop, the number of data messages transmitted at the network is multiplied.

In order to avoid this, a mechanism called *reinforcement* is used (Fig. 1.b). The sink, after receiving the first data messages from the sources (also knows as *exploratory data*), can decide and choose one (or more) of the possible paths to reinforce, so as to draw quality data faster. In order to do that, the sink re-sends to one of its neighbors a reinforcement interest: the same interest only with higher data rate defined. The intermediate sensors that receive this reinforcement, must also reinforce one of their neighbors, until the reinforcement reaches the sources, which will then start creating data responses at this faster data rate and send it back through the reinforced path (Fig. 1.c). The rules for choosing the best neighbor to reinforce are not defined and can be changed according to the application and the concrete WSN deployment. There are various possibilities, for example, the sink can choose to reinforce the neighbor from which new data arrived first, thus intuitively choose to reinforce the fastest path. It is important to point out here the significance of the reinforcement procedure on loop removal, since, as we will see later, failures of this procedure can severely degrade the performance of the network.

Other mechanisms specified in the Directed Diffusion specification, like in-network data aggregation [9] for the case of multiple sources and negative reinforcement for eliminating loops or broken paths, can also be very useful. However, in this paper, we have not considered the implementation of these additional mechanisms and their effects in collaboration with available MAC mechanisms are left for further study.

3   The LWT-MAC Protocol

Low Power Listening MAC protocols is a category of MAC protocols designed for WSNs, taking into account the energy constraint of them. In LPL, nodes sleep and wake up periodically to sample the channel. If the channel is found empty they return to sleep, otherwise they remain awake. A sensor node willing to send data has to send a long preamble that overlaps with the channel sampling time of the receiver before transmitting the packet. It can be easily observed that when there is a low load in the network, these protocols considerably reduce the energy consumption because the time needed to sample the channel is extremely short. However, as soon as the network load starts to increase, collisions of long preambles cause a performance degradation that can be intensified by the presence of hidden terminals (common in multihop environments) [10].

The LWT-MAC protocol [8] is based on the basic preamble sampling technique and tries to improve its performance by reacting more efficiently to instantaneous load increases and managing better the hidden terminal problems, while maintaining the simplicity and energy consumption low, comparable to this of basic preamble sampling. Its main difference lies on defining that after a transmission all sensor nodes that have overheard this must wake up and are allowed to transmit. Since all nodes that have overheard the last transmission are awake, the long preamble is not needed for the following transmissions. In this sense, the LWT-MAC protocol is able to amortize the long preamble across several transmissions.

Moreover, in order to alleviate hidden terminal problems, the RTS/CTS access is used in the *scheduled* phase (when all nodes that have overheard a transmission wake up to transmit or receive). This feature allows us to cope with hidden terminal problems that become noticeable when the network load increases (i.e., in event detection, when more than one packet need to be transmitted by a set of neighbors in a short time interval). A schematic representation is provided in Fig. 2.

In addition to this behavior, a non-aggressive retransmission procedure is defined. When a packet transmission fails, instead of immediately retrying transmission, sensor nodes wait a Collision Avoidance (CA) Timer before transmitting. During the CA Timer (set to the duration of a long preamble and packet transmission) sensor nodes keep listening to the channel. The goals of the CA Timer are the following: *i)* allow other transmissions to finish, *ii)* increase the probability of overhearing a packet of an ongoing transmission and get *synchronized* (wake up at the end) to it and *iii)* reduce the consecutive collisions that can happen among hidden terminals. Moreover, in case of a data packet failure in the *unscheduled* phase (when the long preamble is used), an RTS is immediately sent. This mechanism, called *RTS if DATA fails*, aims at increasing the probability of at least receiving the last RTS of a partial overlapping collision among hidden terminals.

Observe that the LWT-MAC protocol maintains a simplicity similar to basic LPL as no synchronization is needed. It also provides a reduced energy consumption when the network load is low. Apart from that, it is able to reduce the

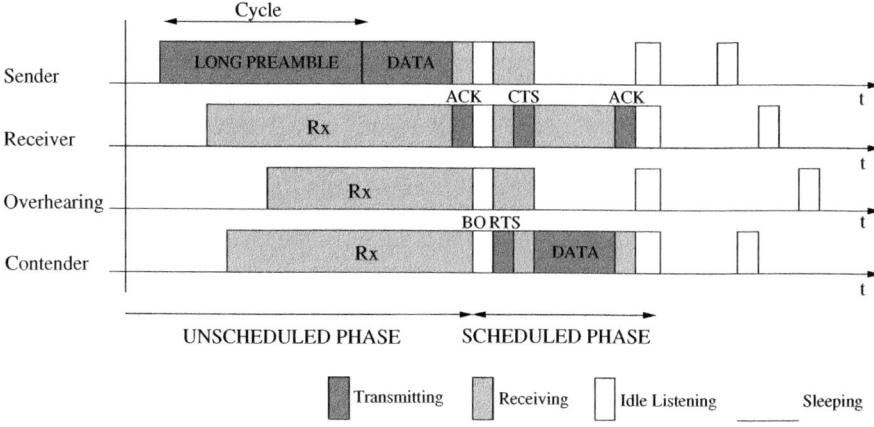

Fig. 2. LWT-MAC Protocol

sleep delay when several packets need to be transmitted, independently if they are generated at the same or different sensor nodes. And, finally, it takes hidden terminal problems into account and implements specific mechanisms to alleviate them.

Some similar mechanisms have been also defined in order to address the same problem. For instance, the multi-hop streaming capability defined in the SCP-MAC protocol [11] that increases the duty cycle upon a message reception in order to reduce the end-to-end delay. Another example is described in [12] where the sender of a message activates a *send more* bit in the header of the packet indicating that there is more data pending to be transmitted. The destination of the message stays awake at the end of the transmission to receive the packet, thus eliminating the need of the long preamble transmission. An extension to this approach is the Stay Awake Promise defined in [13]. It defines that when a sensor node receives a message with the more bit set to 1, it replies with an ACK with the stay awake promise bit also set. By doing this, other nodes willing to transmit to the same destination can contend for the channel just after the current data transmission.

All these mechanisms differ from the LWT-MAC approach in the sense that in LWT-MAC *every* node that has overheard a transmission is allowed to transmit at the end to any other node, not only the sender or the recipient of the last transmission. This approach improves the performance when the traffic load of the network increases, as in the case of an event detection, where a set of nearby nodes try to transmit a packet to inform the sink about the event occurrence.

The LWT-MAC protocol can notably improve the performance of the network but at the same time it has some limitations that should be identified. The first one is the increase of energy consumption at low loads. Sensor nodes wake up at the end of each transmission to listen to the channel, however when the traffic load is low the probability that a node has something to transmit during that time is also low. As a result there is an increase of energy consumption compared to basic LPL. Nevertheless, it should be considered that although there is an increase in energy consumption, it is usually low as it accounts for the energy waste of being in idle mode only during the maximum back-off duration. Another limitation of the protocol is the impossibility of assuring that a neighbor will be awake in the scheduled phase. Waking up all sensor nodes that overheard a transmission does not guarantee that all the neighbors of a specific node were able to overhear the transmission. This affects the delivery rate and forces the enabling of retransmissions to cope with this problem.

4   Evaluation Scenarios and Results

We have studied three different scenarios: a) increasing the density of sensor nodes under the same field area, b) increasing the area of sensor field while maintaining the network density and c) increasing the number of sources (interest area) while maintaining the same density and field area. In all of them, the sink position has been fixed in the upper right corner of the area while the source (or sources in the third scenario) was placed at the bottom left corner of the area, a worst case scenario in terms of distance between sink and source. These scenarios have allowed us to evaluate two important metrics of the WSNs, the delay of the data messages (crucial for event detection) and the energy consumption of each sensor node. The results of this study are presented in detail next.

For the evaluation we have used the SENSE simulator [14] and implemented the basic LPL MAC protocol, the LWT-MAC protocol and the basic version of Directed Diffusion mechanism as previously explained. The basic parameter set seen in Table 1 has been used, most of these values have been taken from the Mica2 motes specification [15]. The MAC protocol backoff time has been assumed uniformly distributed in the range of [0-CW]. The carrier sense range has been considered equal to the receiving range, while no transceiver issues like turnaround time and Clear Channel Assesment (CCA) delay were considered in the simulator.

The sink injects an interest to the network at the beginning of the simulation, requesting data at an exploratory interval, set to $20s$ and for a duration equivalent to the duration of the simulation ($500s$). Event is generated and detected by the source at random time after the interest arrival, with mean average $T = 10s$ uniformly distributed, which triggers the creation of data messages at the predefined interval. When (and if) the reinforcement arrives to the source, it start sending data at a higher rate, switching to the lower interval of data creation defined at the reinforcement (reinforcement interval, set to $5s$ in the simulation). As an addition to the simulation results, a real testbed implementation using Mica2 motes is under development.

4.1   Effect of Network Density

In this scenario we test the performance of the LWT-MAC protocol against variations in the network density in a query-driven scenario using basic Directed Diffusion routing. We maintain the network area at 200x200 m^2 while increasing

Table 1. Simulation Parameters

Parameter	Value
Number of Trials	500
Sim. Duration	500 s
Packet length	30 bytes
Transmission Range	43 m
Data rate	20 kbps
Exploratory Interval	20 s
Reinforcement Interval	5 s
MAC listen/sleep time	2.45/97.55 ms
Contention Window	128

the number of nodes from 50 to 200. We consider one sink and one source at the two opposite corners of the area. As the network density increases, so does the number of neighbors (and thus the number of gradients) per node. This leads to more data messages being retransmitted at each hop, causing saturation and an increase in number of collisions.

When network density is higher than $25 \cdot 10^{-4}$ nodes per m^2, the benefits of LWT-MAC mechanism are intensified since more neighbors overhear each transmission and stay awake in case there is another transmission following, thus more sensors are synchronized and can transmit in the scheduled mode without using the long preamble. As a consequence, using LWT-MAC reduces the duration of each transmission, causing an important reduction in both energy (Fig. 3.a) and delay (Fig. 3.b) compared to basic LPL.

At the same time, there are more hidden terminals as the network density increases, which is more harmful when using the basic LPL protocol that uses the long preamble before each transmission [10]. As we have previously explained, the LWT-MAC protocol, using additional mechanisms like RTS/CTS in the scheduled mode and CA Timer can help alleviate this effect and thus obtain a further decrease in delay and energy consumption. We also observe in Fig. 3.c that reliability is maintained to almost 100% in the case of LWT-MAC, meaning all created data messages arrive to the sink, while with basic LPL MAC up to 50% of the messages are lost when network density is high.

Due to the high number of gradients per node at high density, the cases where reinforcement is not successful (i.e. no unique path from source to sink is chosen) are more critical. As we see in Fig. 3.d the source is rarely reinforced (reinforcement packets are lost with a very high probability), especially as the traffic load increases. This in turn causes persistent loops and a further increase in the transmitted data messages, thus bringing the network to saturation conditions. The main cause for this is the high amount of traffic produced by the initial exploratory data messages flooded through the network, which saturate the sensors queues and cause the loss of reinforcements, especially when density is high. In the few trials that reinforcement successfully reaches the source, we have observed that the difference in the delay results is huge, with delay being around 2 seconds for both studied MAC protocols, even at high network density.

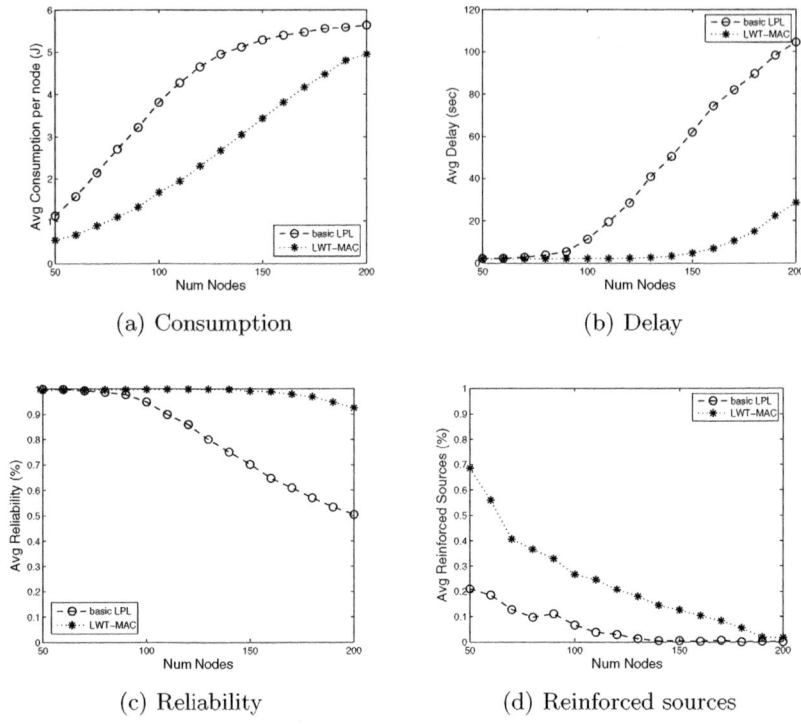

(a) Consumption

(b) Delay

(c) Reliability

(d) Reinforced sources

Fig. 3. Effect of network density

This proves the importance of the reinforcement procedure and the necessity to prioritize reinforcement packets or establish a procedure for recovery from failed reinforcement.

4.2 Effect of Network Size

We have also tested the LWT-MAC protocol against various network sizes, maintaining a fixed density of nodes and one sink with one source at the two opposite corners of the area. We have started with an area of 100x100 m^2 and 20 sensors and increased the number of nodes by 20 until reaching 200 sensors, increasing accordingly the network area so that the density of nodes per m^2 is maintained constant (equal to $20 \cdot 10^{-4}$ nodes per m^2).

By increasing the network size, the number of hops from the source to the sink grows, causing a proportional increase to the end-to-end delay of the data messages. At the same time, more hops mean more data transmissions. LWT-MAC is again found more efficient in handling higher traffic load as it reduces the duration of these transmissions and thus the total delay (Fig. 4.a) and consumption (Fig. 4.b). Reliability, for this tested degree of density, was found to be around 100% in all cases and for both protocols, thus it is not affected from the increase in network size as significantly as from the increase in nodes density.

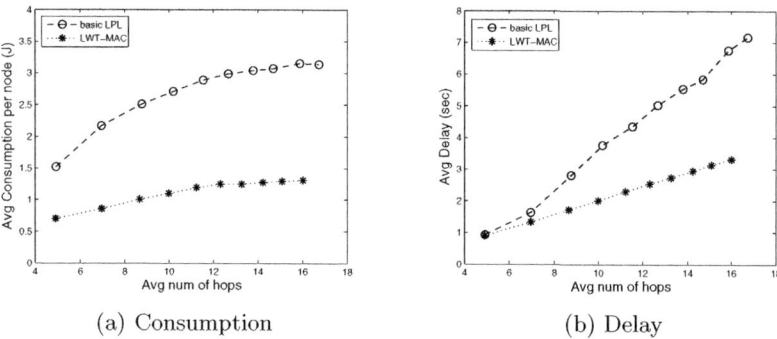

(a) Consumption   (b) Delay

Fig. 4. Effect of increasing the network size, from 100x100m^2 to 316x316m^2

4.3   Effect of Number of Sources

We use four different interest areas all placed at the bottom left corner of the sensor field: 10x10, 20x20, 30x30, 40x40 m^2 in a total field area of 200x200 m^2 with 80 nodes. Increasing the interest area increases the total number of sources and thus the created data messages and amount of traffic load. Each node has

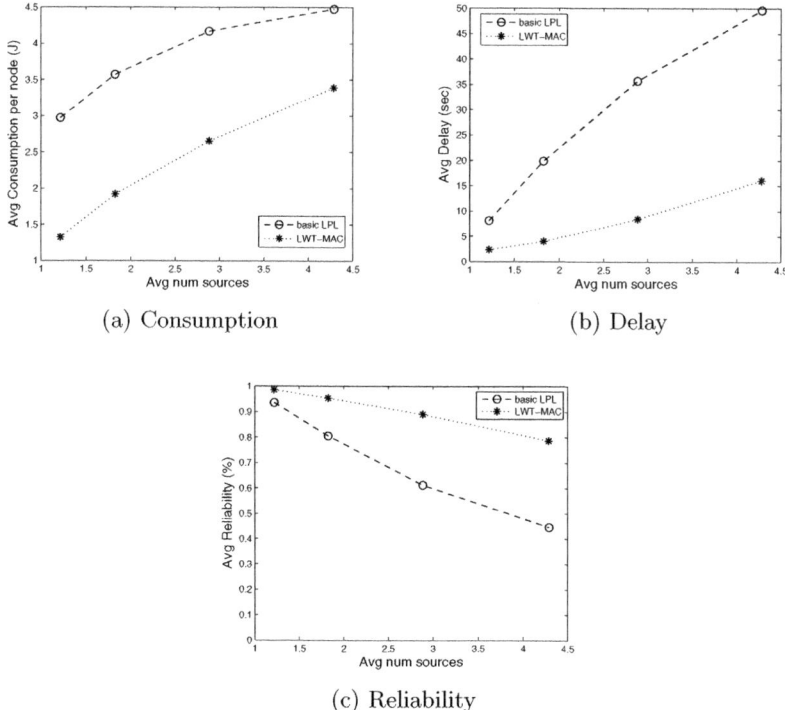

(a) Consumption   (b) Delay

(c) Reliability

Fig. 5. Effect of number of sources

more data to transmit and thus the energy consumption per node increases with the number of sources. LWT-MAC is again able to react better to increases of traffic load, putting all overhearing nodes to a scheduled, CSMA-like mode and decreasing the collisions, which is visible in the lower delay and reduction of consumption (Figures 5.a and 5.b).

Observe again that reliability (Fig. 5.c) is reduced when increasing the number of sources, as higher traffic causes more collisions and packet losses. In the case of LWT-MAC, reliability is kept over 85% even as the number of sources increases, while with basic LPL MAC this goes down to 45%.

5   Conclusions

In this paper, we have used a basic implementation of Directed Diffusion in order to evaluate the previously proposed LWT-MAC protocol in query-driven scenarios with data-centric routing. We have seen that data-centric routing can increase sporadically the network traffic load, either due to its normal procedures of queries and responses dissemination or due to inefficient operation when reinforcement is lost. In these cases, LWT-MAC protocol outperforms the basic LPL MAC algorithms, since it is specially designed to handle in a more efficient way the increases in the network load.

When network density is high and many gradients per node are created, the initial operation of query dissemination and exploratory data responses can cause an increased number of transmission due to many alternative active paths and a high probability of reinforcement being lost, leading to persistent loops. LWT-MAC can handle efficiently also these cases, achieving a high reliability with a reduced delay and energy consumption compared to basic LPL MAC, by using the local synchronization of the sensors and reducing the transmission duration.

Finally, with this study as a starting point, we have identified various issues of Directed Diffusion which can be optimized with a closer collaboration with the MAC protocols. As a next step, we want to implement data-aggregation and see how this affects the performance of the two protocols. Additionally, due to the importance of the reinforcement procedure it is essential to establish mechanisms for recovery when this fails, which are currently not well defined in the protocol.

References

1. Akyildiz, I.F., Su, W., Sankarasubramaniam, Y., Cayirci, E.: A survey on sensor networks. IEEE Communications Magazine 40(8), 102–114 (2002)
2. Akkaya, K., Younis, M.: A survey on routing protocols for wireless sensor networks. Ad hoc networks 3(3), 325–349 (2005)
3. Intanagonwiwat, C., Govindan, R., Estrin, D., Heidemann, J., Silva, F.: Directed diffusion for wireless sensor networking. IEEE/ACM Transactions on Networking 11(1), 2–16 (2003)
4. Bachir, A., Dohler, M., Watteyne, T., Leung, K.K.: MAC Essentials for Wireless Sensor Networks. IEEE Communications Surveys & Tutorials 12(2), 222–248 (2010)

5. El-Hoiydi, A.: Aloha with Preamble Sampling for Sporadic Traffic in Ad hoc Wireless Sensor Networks. In: Proceedings of the IEEE International Conference on Communications (ICC 2002), vol. 5, pp. 3418–3423 (2002)
6. Hill, J., Culler, D.: Mica: A Wireless Platform for Deeply Embedded Networks. IEEE Micro, 12–24 (2002)
7. Polastre, J., Hill, J., Culler, D.: Versatile low power media access for wireless sensor networks. In: Proceedings of the 2nd International Conference on Embedded Networked Sensor Systems, pp. 95–107. ACM, New York (2004)
8. Cano, C., Bellalta, B., Sfairopoulou, A., Barceló, J.: A low power listening mac with scheduled wake up after transmissions for wsns. IEEE Communications Letters 13(4), 221–223 (2009)
9. Intanagonwiwat, C., Estrin, D., Govindan, R., Heidemann, J.: Impact of network density on data aggregation in wireless sensor networks. In: Proceedings of 22nd International Conference on Distributed Computing Systems, pp. 457–458. IEEE, Los Alamitos (2002)
10. Cano, C., Bellalta, B., Cisneros, A., Oliver, M.: Quantitative analysis of the hidden terminal problem in preamble sampling wsns. Ad Hoc Networks (2011) (in Press, Corrected Proof)
11. Ye, W., Silva, F., Heidemann, J.: Ultra-low duty cycle MAC with scheduled channel polling. In: Proceedings of the 4th International Conference on Embedded Networked Sensor Systems, p. 334 (2006)
12. El-Hoiydi, A., Decotignie, J.D., Hernandez, J.: Low power MAC protocols for infrastructure wireless sensor networks. In: Proceedings of the Fifth European Wireless Conference, pp. 563–569 (2004)
13. Hurni, P., Braun, T.: Increasing Throughput for WiseMAC. In: Proceedings of the Fifth Annual Conference on Wireless on Demand Network Systems and Services (2008)
14. Chen, G.: Component Oriented Simulation Toolkit (2004), http://www.cs.rpi.edu/~cheng3/
15. Chipcon. CC1000. Single Chip Very Low Power RF Transceiver, http://focus.ti.com/lit/ds/symlink/cc1000.pdf

QoS-Oriented Packet Scheduling for Efficient Video Support in OFDMA-Based Packet Radio Systems

Stanislav Nonchev and Mikko Valkama

Department of Communications Engineering, Tampere University
of Technology,Tampere, Finland
stanislav.nonchev@tut.fi, mikko.e.valkama@tut.fi

Abstract. Next-generation mobile networks will provide users with high data rates, increased mobility and various services. The initial step made in LTE and LTE-A is adopting the OFDMA air interface and utilization of dynamic resource allocation techniques maximizing the cell throughput and coverage as part of enhanced radio resource management (RRM) functionality. Moreover, the control of the network resource division among users is performed by packet scheduler and different scheduling strategies are applied according to traffic scenario. Typically, video traffic (real-time video streaming, mobile TV etc.) requires higher data rates and certain quality of service (QoS) constrains, i.e. packet size, arrival rate, head-of-line (HOL) packet delay, etc. In this article, we propose a flexible and fairness-oriented packet scheduling approach for real-time video delivery, built on advanced QoS-aware multiuser proportional fair (PF) scheduling principle. The performance of the overall scheduling process is investigated in details in terms of cellular system capacity, resource allocation fairness and video traffic QoS guarantees. Experimental results reveal the upper bounds of real-time video traffic support in downlink LTE multiuser network.

Keywords: Cellular system performance, radio resource management, packet scheduling, QoS; proportional-fair, fairness.

1 Introduction

The Third Generation Partnership Project (3GPP) organization developed the Long Term Evolution (LTE) standard with support to high-data-rates, increased mobility, low-latency and packet optimized radio access. LTE uses single-carrier frequency-division multiple access (SC –FDMA) for the uplink (UL) and orthogonal FDMA in downlink (DL). Scalable bandwidth operation, exploitation of diverse MIMO technologies and advanced convergence techniques are some of the key benefits in OFDMA-based developments. [1] – [3]. The available spectrum is divided into large number of orthogonal subcarriers forming the basic time-frequency transmission resource - physical resource block (PRB). This allows multi user access and efficient reduction of the effects of inter-symbol interference (ISI) and inter-carrier interference (ICI). Therefore, increased spectral efficiency and high data rates are achieved [5], [6].

C. Sacchi et al. (Eds.): MACOM 2011, LNCS 6886, pp. 168–180, 2011.
© Springer-Verlag Berlin Heidelberg 2011

The mobile traffic boost due to increased usage of video applications such as video streaming, mobile TV and multimedia online gaming requires increased system performance and user QoS guarantees. On the other hand, performance improvements are typically obtained through proper radio resource management functionalities and exploiting the available multi-user diversity in both time and frequency as well as spatial domains [6]–[12]. Another requirement for achieving such performance improvements is obtaining accurate channel feedback from each mobile station (MS) within the serving cell. Particularly, each MS can measure the effective signal-to-interference-plus noise-ratio (SINR), per active subcarrier or block of subcarriers, and send back the obtained channel state to the base station (BS) in terms of channel quality information (CQI) reports. Moreover, considering multiple-input multiple-output (MIMO) systems, the stream wise feedback is provided as a codeword containing both MIMO ranking information and CQI measurement. Most of the performance studies in OFDMA based mobile networks are based on simulations for best-effort traffic [9] and VoIP traffic [13] with advanced PS strategies but streaming video traffic has not been extensively studied with such scheduling techniques. Recently, Luo et al. in [14] propose quality-driven cross-layer optimized video delivery scheduling strategy, while Basukala et al. in [15] demonstrated the performance of packet scheduler schemes serving video streaming users. The initial potential of LTE video capacities is also demonstrated in [16] with simple frequency diversity scheme.

Clearly, the overall radio system performance in terms of throughput, coverage and fairness, depends heavily on PS functionality, being the key ingredient in the radio resource management process. Most of the literature studies on different multi-user packet scheduling techniques demonstrate that the well-known proportional fair (PF) scheduling principle is the right choice for OFDMA based systems [7], [8]. On the other hand, despite increased throughput and fairness the PF scheduler cannot guarantee the packet delay constraint for video services by default. Thus, higher system throughput does not guarantee higher video quality and therefore video performance metric should be taken into account in PS decision. Only a few scheduling strategies have considered user's QoS requirements together with practical system and application constrains [17]-[21]. Stemming now from our previous work in advanced PS scheduling developments reported in [7], [20], [21], we extend our studies here to incorporate QoS requirements into scheduling decisions by effectively controlling user fairness and BS's RRM process for increased video support.

Furthermore, we apply different simulation cases for video traffic applications investigating the limits of achieved gains from time-frequency-spatial domain packet scheduling with limited feedback and QoS constrains [22], [23]. The system model used for the performance evaluations of the proposed scheduling methods presented in this paper is according to the 3GPP evaluation criteria [2]. The overall outcome is measured in terms of capacity – the number of supported video streams of different users per cell.

The rest of the paper is organized as follows: Section 2 gives an overview of the packet scheduling process and describes the proposed QoS aware multi-stream PF (QoS-MSPF) scheduling scheme. Section 3, in turn, presents the overall system model and simulation assumptions. The simulation results and detailed analysis are presented in Section 4, while the conclusions are drawn in Section 5.

2 Packet Scheduling Process

Fig. 1 illustrates the overall RRM framework. The key entities in it are PS, LA and HARQ manager. Located in the BS, the PS functionality consists of selecting the users (UEs) to be scheduled on transmission time interval (TTI) basis and allocating the required frequency resources (PRBs). In more details, the scheduling decision is based on priority metric calculation for individual UEs depending on the selected scheduling strategy. Some of the advanced PF based scheduling techniques require users' CQIs per given TTI and per frequency domain PRB. MIMO functionality, in turn, requires both single-stream and dual-stream CQI feedback by each UE. In addition, PS is interacting with LA entity for choosing the modulation and coding schemes (MCS) for individual PRBs and obtaining information for new transmissions or retransmissions from HARQ manager. BS buffer information is required for verification of keeping with the set packet delay budget.

The proposed QoS-aware multi-stream PF (QoS-MSPF) scheduler is based on widely used two-stage PF approach (see e.g. [9], [21]) with additional QoS enabled guarantees for video traffic. In terms of the actual metric calculations, the proposed QoS-aware multi–stream PF (QoS-MSPF) scheduler uses the following metric.

$$\overline{\gamma}_{i,k,s} = arg\,max_i \left\{ \delta_i(n) \left(\frac{CQI_{i,k,s}(n)}{CQI_i^{avg}(n)} \right)^{\alpha_1} \times \left(\frac{T_i^{se}(n)}{T_{i,k,s}(n)} \frac{T_i(n)}{T_{tot}(n)} \right)^{-\alpha_2} \right\} \qquad (1)$$

which can be understood as an extension of the authors' earlier work in [20]. In the above metric, α_1 and α_2 are scheduler optimization parameters ranging basically from 0 to infinity. In expression (1), $T_i^{se}(n)$ is an estimate of the user throughput if user i is scheduled on sub-frame basis according to [18] and $T_{i,k,s}(n)$ is the estimated achievable throughput of user i at PRB k and stream s. $T_i(n)$ corresponds to average delivered throughput to the UE over the past and T_{tot} is the average delivered throughput (during the recent past) to all users ranked in TD stage served by the BS. $CQI_{i,k,s}$ is the CQI of user i at PRB k and stream s, and CQI^{avg}_i is the average CQI of user i calculated by traditional recursive method [24].

The $\delta_i(n)$ is, in turn QoS delay function factor defined as:

$$\delta_i(n) = \frac{max(d_i / B_i(n))}{d_{max}} \qquad (2)$$

where d_i is the delay of the packet of user i in the transmit buffer $B_i(n)$ at time instant n, and d_{max} is the maximum delay allowed.

The scheduling metric in (1) is essentially composed of three parts affecting the overall scheduling decisions. The first term takes into account the QoS requirements, i.e. packet delay budget. The second ratio is the relative instantaneous quality of the individual user's radio channels over their own average channel qualities. The third ratio is divided into two parts. The first one takes into account the estimated throughputs of individual UE's and the second one the achievable over total throughputs. The power coefficients α_1 and α_2 are additional adjustable parameters.

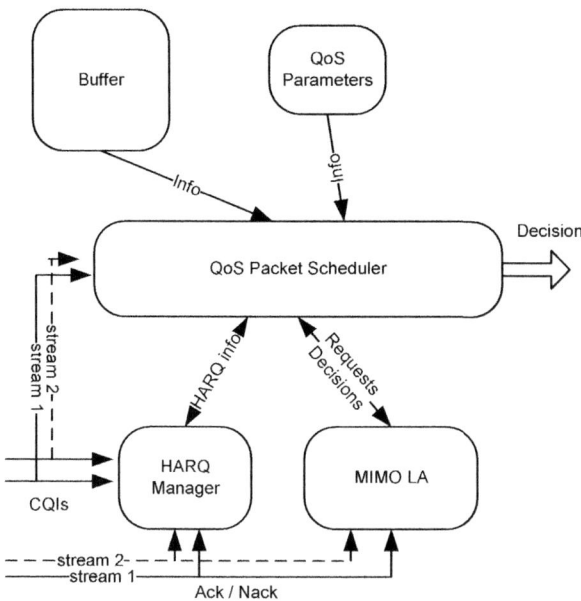

Fig. 1. RRM entities and packet scheduling process

In more details, in the first stage, which is the time-domain (TD) scheduling step executed within each TTI, UEs are ranked based on the full bandwidth channel state information, QoS parameters and the corresponding throughput calculations. These UEs form Group 1 of the whole Scheduling Candidates Set (SCS). Group 2 consists of users with pending retransmissions and Group 3 is formed by users having packet delay close to the delay budget. Furthermore, discard timer is used so that buffered packets that are already late will not be transmitted over the air interface. Thus, the accumulated delay for subsequent packet is also reduced.

In the second stage, the scheduling functionality is expanded in frequency-domain (FD) where the actual PRB allocation takes place.

Initially, the needed PRB's for pending re-transmissions (on one stream-basis only) signaled through HARQ channels are reserved – Group 2 UEs. The remaining PRBs are given to the delay sensitive users from Group 3 and the rest to the first transmission users from Group 1 determined through available buffer information. The actual priority metric in FD/SD stage is evaluated at PRB-level taking into account the available stream-wise channel state information, QoS parameters and the corresponding throughput calculations.

In general, dynamic resource allocation methods increase scheduling flexibility so that enough PRBs will be mapped to the UEs with good channel conditions and more resources will be available for the other SCS users. Consequently, prioritizing Group1 UEs will further decrease packet delays and reduce retransmissions. On the other hand, combined QoS- and channel-aware scheduling can offer performance enhancements at the expense of increased scheduling complexity, in terms of scheduling metric calculations and increased signaling overhead.

Keeping these at reasonable levels requires thus some constraints on the scheduling algorithm, so for simplicity we assume here that only one MIMO mode (SU or MU) and fixed modulation and coding scheme (MCS) is allowed per user within one scheduling element. Moreover, we limit the number of users for multiplexing in TD stage to further reduce the signaling overhead and complexity of FD/SD scheduling. Consequently, further decrease is examined by exploiting different reduce-feedback reporting schemes.

3   System Simulation Model

3.1   Video Traffic

Real –time video services are modeled as follows:

- Each frame of video data arrives at a regular interval determined by the number frames per second.
- Each frame is decomposed into a fixed number of slices, each transmitted as a single packet. The size of these packets/slices is modeled to have a truncated Pareto distribution.
- The video encoder introduces encoding delay intervals (modeled by a truncated Pareto distribution) between the packets of a frame.

In our studies, two different video streaming services with 128 kbps (Scenario 1) and 256 kbps (Scenario 2) constant bit rates (CBR) source video data are used in the simulations. The corresponding mean packet size with truncated Pareto distribution and mean inter-arrival packet time are 100 bytes - 6ms for Scenario 1, and 200 bytes - 4ms for Scenario 2 [23]. Packet delay budget, as well as discard timer threshold is set to 20 ms.

3.2   Video Capacity Estimation

The main target is to estimate the number of UEs that can be supported by the system based on deployed scenarios. Following 3GPP evaluation metrology, a user is considered to be in outage if 2% of the video packets for the user are erroneous or discarded due to exceeding delay limit when monitored over the whole video session duration. On the other hand, video capacity is defined as number of supported users per cell without exceeding the system saturation point. Here, the system saturation point is set to 5% of the cell outage level, i.e. to the point where 95% of the users in the cell are satisfied (having maximum of 2% packet loss rate as described above).

3.3   Simulation Environment

Quasistatic system level simulator is used to evaluate the proposed scheduling scheme in video traffic scenarios for LTE downlink. It includes detailed traffic modeling, multiuser packet scheduling and link adaptation including HARQ, following the 3GPP evaluation criteria [2].

The chosen Micro Case 1 deployment scenario consists of 10 MHz system bandwidth divided into 50 physical resource blocks (PRB) containing 600 data sub-carriers. In a single simulation run mobile stations are randomly distributed over standard hexagonal cellular layout with altogether 19 cells each having 3 sectors. Fast fading is updated per TTI according to Typical Urban (20 taps) radio channel, while shadow fading and distance dependent path loss remain constant during the whole simulation. Moreover, the UE velocity is fixed to 3 km/h. The main simulation parameters and assumptions are summarized in Table I.

The RRM functionalities are controlled by the packet scheduler together with link adaptation and HARQ entities. Moreover, link adaptation functionality consist of removing CQI imperfections, estimating supported data rates and MCS's, and stabilizing the 1st transmission Block Error Probability (BLEP) to the target range (typically 10-20%). HARQ is based on SAW protocol and a maximum of three retransmissions is allowed. MIMO functionality requires individual HARQ entry per stream which is also implemented. Link-to-system level mapping is based on the effective SINR mapping (EESM) principle [2].

The actual effective SINR calculations rely on estimated subcarrier-wise channel gains (obtained using reference symbols) and depend in general also on the assumed receiver topology. Here we assume per-antenna rate control (PARC) MIMO case, i.e. two transmits antennas at the BS and two receive antennas at each UE and the receivers are equipped with LMMSE detectors.

4 Simulation Results

In this section, we present the results obtained from the system simulations using the RRM algorithms described in the paper.

The system-level performance is generally measured and evaluated in terms of:

- Capacity
- Throughput
- CDF of the number of users scheduled per TTI
- CDF of the number of PRBs per UE
- CDF of packed delay
- Fairness distribution

In general, the video capacity depends on the video data rates, packet size and the choice of outage criteria. The user outage criteria is defined as 2% of the video packets are erroneous or discarded during the whole simulation. Capacity in turn corresponds to maximum number of supported users not exceeding 5 % cell outage level. The cell throughput is defined as the number of successfully delivered user bits per unit time. Fairness is measured using the Jain's fairness index [25].

The performance of the proposed QoS-MSPF scheduler is compared against reference PF scheduler with a delay dependent component for video traffic support [12] for the video traffic models as discussed in Section 3 A and evaluated using different power coefficients α_1 and α_2. Here α_2 is fixed here to 1 and the used values for α_1 coefficient are defined as $\alpha_1 = \{1,2\}$. Moreover, the power coefficient values are presented as index M, where M1 represents the first couple, i.e., $\alpha_1=1$, $\alpha_2=1$ and M2: $\alpha_1=2$, $\alpha_2=1$.

Table 1. Default Simulation Parameters

Parameter	Assumption
Carrier Frequency / Bandwidth	2000MHz / 10 MHz
Number of active sub-carriers	600
Sub-carrier spacing	15kHz
Sub-frame duration	0.5 ms
Channel estimation	Ideal
PDP	ITU Typical Urban 20 paths
Minimum distance between UE and cell	>= 35 meters – Macro
Max. number of frequency multiplexed UEs	10
UE receiver type	LMMSE
Shadowing standard deviation	8 dB
UE speed	3km/h
Total BS TX power (Ptotal)	46dBm
Fast Fading Model	Jakes Spectrum
CQI reporting schemes	Full CQI
CQI log-normal error std.	1 dB
CQI reporting time	5 TTI
CQI delay	2 TTIs
CQI quantization	1 dB
CQI std error	1 dB
MCS rates	QPSK (1/3, 1/2, 2/3),
	16QAM (1/2, 2/3, 4/5),
	64QAM (1/2, 2/3, 4/5)
ACK/NACK delay	2ms
Number of SAW channels	6
Maximum number of retransmissions	3
HARQ model	Ideal chase combining (CC)
1st transmission BLER target	20%
Scheduler forgetting factor	0.0025
Scheduling schemes used	RPF, QoS -MSPF (proposed)
Simulation duration (one drop)	120 seconds
Number of drops	10

Fig. 2 illustrates the number of supported video mobile users and average cell throughput for the different QoS-aware schedulers in Scenario 1 system simulation case. The obtained results with the proposed scheduler schemes are compared with the reference PF scheduler achieving video capacity of 94 users per sector and average sector throughput of 13,2 Mbps (subfigures (a) and (b)). By using the first term (M1) of the new metric calculation for QoS-MSPF we achieve video capacity gain in the order of 13% and additional 8% throughput increase. The achieved gain mainly comes from better utilization of the resources due to the scheduler priority metric calculation, as well as the increase in frequency-spatial domain multiplexed users.

For coefficient α_1 equal to 2 (M2) the new QoS-MSPF scheduler achieves video capacity gains in the order of 15% and throughput increase of 7% compared to reference PF scheduler.

The performance statistics obtained for Scenario 2 demonstrate similar trends, as in the previous case, as shown in Fig. 3. Starting from the reference scheduling case and full CQI reporting scheme the obtained video capacity is 52 users. The reduced number of supported users is due to increased video packet size reflecting on fulfilling the

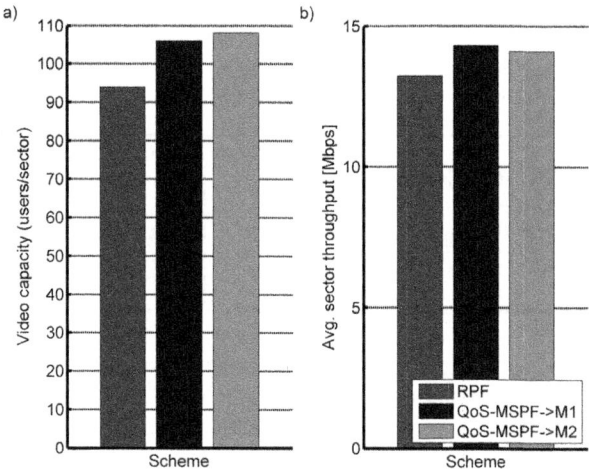

Fig. 2. Video capacity and average sector throughput for different scheduling schemes (a, b) in Scenario 1. M1-M2 refers to the proposed scheduler with different power coefficient values.

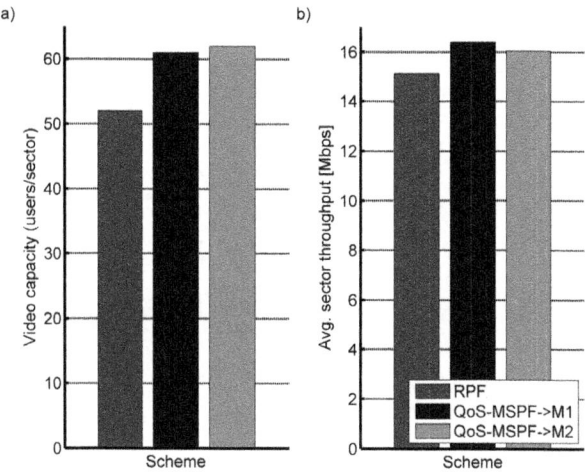

Fig. 3. Video capacity and average sector throughput for different scheduling schemes (a, b) in Scenario 2. M1-M2 refers to the proposed scheduler with different power coefficient values.

QoS requirements with more PRBs scheduled per user. In primary case M1, with full CQI, we obtain a 16% gain in video capacity correspond to 61 users and 9% throughput improvement. In the case of M2, additional 2% increase of the video capacity and throughput gains are achieved.

The performance results for both cases are summarized in Table 2.

Table 2. Obtained performance statistics compared to reference PF scheduler with different power coefficients (M1-M2) for the proposed scheduler

QoS -MSPF	Performance Statistics			
	Video Capacity Gain [%]		Throughput Gain [%]	
	Scenario 1 CBR 128 kbps	Scenario 2 CBR 256 kbps	Scenario 1 CBR 128 kbps	Scenario 2 CBR 256 kbps
M1	13	16	8	9
M2	15	18	7	6

Continuing on the evaluation of relative system performance using the proposed scheduler in different simulation cases are presented in Fig. 4 in terms of cumulative distribution function (CDF) of scheduled PRBs per TTI for individual scheduling scheme. Noticeably, the proposed scheduling scheme allocates more resources to the users shown on the Fig. 4. with right shift in CDF curve. Identical trends in PS functionality are seen in both simulation cases, which clearly correspond to increased system capacity.

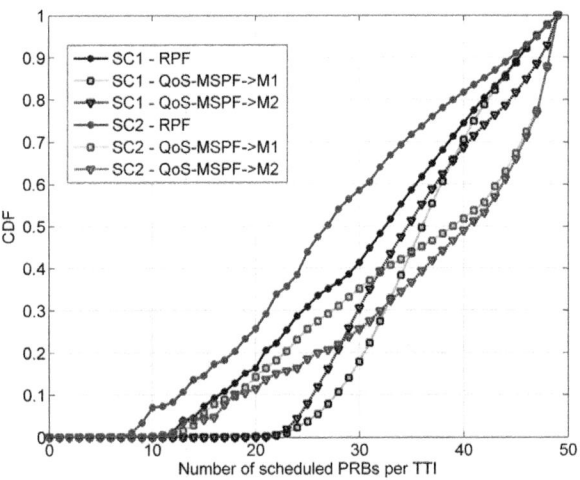

Fig. 4. CDF of scheduled PRB per TTI for simulated scenarios

Further illustrations on the obtainable system performance are illustrated on Fig. 5. with CDF of the number of scheduled users per TTI. We can clearly see from the figure that with the proposed scheduling scheme allows more users to be scheduled in each TTI and the achieved capacity gains are due to the increased usage of PRB resources as already concluded above. Similarity of the QoS-MSPF scheduler functionality in simulated scenarios is also seen here.

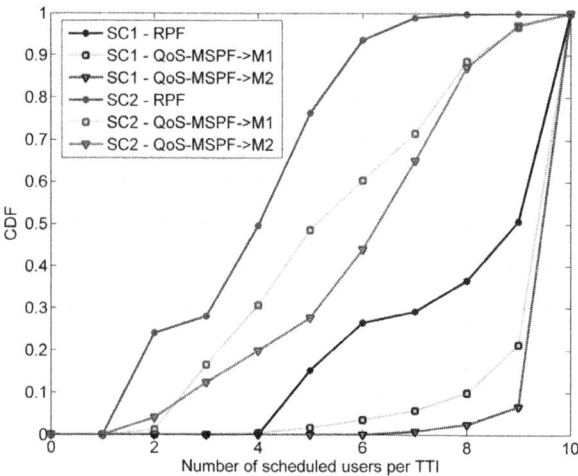

Fig. 5. CDF of scheduled users per TTI for simulated scenarios

Fig. 6 shows the CDF of packet delay for different schedulers. The CQI reporting process has a direct impact on the delay performance and therefore a combined approach of HOL and CQI criteria in priority metric calculation will benefit in such scenarios. The delay performance is strictly within the bounds of 20 ms for the simulated video traffic scenarios.

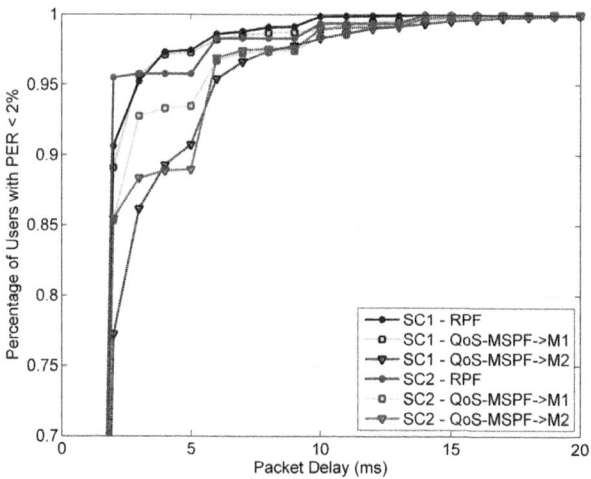

Fig. 6. CDF of packet delay for simulated scenarios

Fig. 7 illustrates the Jain's fairness indexes [24] for scheduling scheme based on the number of supported users.

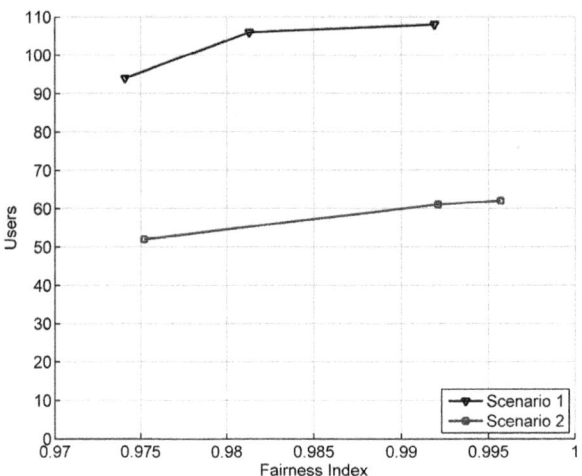

Fig. 7. Jian's fairness indexes of supported video users for simulated scenarios

The value of each curve corresponds to the used scheduler type (1st values refer to Reference PF scheduler, 2nd values refer to QoS-MSPF – M1 and 3rd values refer to QoS-MSPF – M2).We observe that the reference scheduling scheme has lower fairness indexes for all the simulated cases and the proposed QoS-MSPF scheduler clearly obtains better fairness. Having video traffic model with strict QoS requirements implies increased user fairness and thus fairness indexes above 0,90 (1 refers to complete fairness) are expected.

5   Conclusions

In this article, we have studied the potential of advanced QoS-aware multi-user packet scheduling algorithms for video traffic support in OFDMA type radio system context, using UTRAN long term evolution (LTE) downlink in Macro cell environment as practical example case. New video-optimized multi-stream proportional fair scheduler metric covering time-, frequency- and spatial domains was proposed that takes into account video traffic QoS requirements, instantaneous channel qualities (CQI's) as well as resource allocation fairness. Furthermore, detailed set of performance results for real-time video support are presented. As a practical example over 10 MHz bandwidth, more than 100 users can be supported for video traffic with source data rate of 128 kbps and more than 60 users can be supported in 256 kbps case.

Acknowledgements. This research has been financially supported by by the Finnish Funding Agency for Technology and Innovation (Tekes), under the project "Energy and Cost Efficiency for Wireless Access (ECEWA)".

References

1. 3GPP Technical Specification Group Radio Access Network Technical Specification 36.300 v8.0.0: Evolved Universal Terrestrial Radio Access (E-UTRA) and Evolved Universal Terrestrial Radio Access Network (EUTRAN); Overall description, (March 2007)
2. Physical Layer Aspects for Evolved UTRA, 3GPP Technical Report TR 25.814, ver. 7.1.0 (October 2006)
3. ITU global standard for international mobile telecommunications IMT-Advanced, IMT-ADV/1-E (March 2008)
4. WiMAX Forum™ (August 2006), http://www.wimaxforum.org
5. Dahlman, E., et al.: 3G Evolution: HSPA and LTE for Mobile Broadband. Academic Press, London (2007)
6. Tripathi, N.D., et al.: Radio Resource management in Cellular Systems. Springer, Heidelberg (2001)
7. Nonchev, S., Valkama, M.: Advanced radio resource management for multiantenna packet radio systems. International Journal of Wireless & Mobile Networks (IJWMN) 2(2), 1–14 (2010)
8. Sun, Y., et al.: Multi-user scheduling for OFDMA downlink with limited feedback for evolved UTRA. In: Proc. IEEE VTC 2006, Montreal, Canada (September 2006)
9. Pedersen, K.I., Monghal, G., Kovacs, I.Z., Kolding, T.E., Pokhariyal, A., Frederiksen, F., Mogensen, P.: Frequency domain scheduling for OFDMA with limited and noisy channel feedback. In: Proc. IEEE Vehicular Technology Conference (VTC 2007 Fall), Baltimore, MD, pp. 1792–1796 (September 2007)
10. Wei, N., et al.: Performance of MIMO with frequency domain packet scheduling. In: Proc. IEEE VTC 2007, Dublin, Ireland (May 2007)
11. Wengerter, C., Ohlhorst, J., Von Elbwert, A.G.E.: Fairness and throughput analysis for generalized proportional fair frequency scheduling in OFDMA. In: Proc. IEEE VTC 2005, Stockholm, Sweden (May 2005)
12. Elsayed, K., Khattab, A.: Channel-aware earliest deadline due fair scheduling for wireless multimedia networks. Wireless Personal Communications 38, 233–252 (2008)
13. Fan, Y., Kuusela, M., Lundén, P., Valkama, M.: Performance of VoIP on EUTRA Downlink with Limited Channel Feedback. In: Proc. IEEE ISWCS 2008, Reykjavik, Iceland (October 2008)
14. Haiyan, L., et al.: Quality-Driven Cross-Layer Optimazed Video Delivery over LTE. IEEE Communication magazine 48, 102–109: doi:10.1109/MCOM.2010.5402671
15. Basukala, R., et al.: Impact of CQI Feedback Rate/Delay on Scheduling Video Streaming Services in LTE Downlink. In: Proc. International Conference on Communication Technology ICCT 2010, Nanjing, China (November 2010)
16. Talukdar, A.K., Mondal, B., Cudak, M., Ghosh, A., Wang, F.: Streaming Video Capacity Comparisons of Multi-Antenna LTE Systems. In: Proc. VTC Spring, pp. 1–5 (2010)
17. Monghal, G., et al.: QoS Oriented Time and Frequency Domain Packet Schedulers for The UTRAN Long Term Evolution. In: Proc. VTC 2008 Spring, vol. 3, pp. 2532–2536 (May 2008)

18. Kolding, T.E.: QoS-Aware Proportional Fair Packet Scheduling with Required Activity Detection. In: VTC2006 Fall (September 2006)
19. Nguyen, T.-D., Han, Y.: A Proportional Fairness Algorithm with QoS Provision in Downlink OFDMA Systems. IEEE Communication Letters 10(11) (November 2006)
20. Nonchev, S., Valkama, M.: A new fairness-oriented packet scheduling scheme with reduced channel feedback for OFDMA packet radio systems. Int. Journal of Communications, Network and System Sciences (IJCNS) 7, 608–618 (2009)
21. Nonchev, S., Valkama, M.: Efficient packet scheduling schemes with built-in fairness control for multiantena packet radio systems. Int. Journal on Advances in Networks and Services, IJANS (2009)
22. Talukdar, A., Cudak, M., Ghosh, A.: Streaming Video Capacities of LTE Air-Interface. In: Proceedings of Conference (ICC)...
23. 3GPP, Feasibility Study for Orthogonal Frequency Division Multiplexing (OFDM) for UTRAN enhancement. 3GPP TR25.892 (2004)
24. Jalali, A., Padovani, R., Pankaj, R.: Data throughput of CDMA-HDR high efficiency-high data rate personal communication wireless system. In: Proc. IEEE VTC 2000 Spring, Tokyo (May 2000)
25. Chui, D., Jain, R.: Analysis of the increase and decrease algorithms for congestion avoidance in computer networks. Computer Networks and ISDN Systems (1989)

LTE Uplink Scheduling - Flow Level Analysis

D.C. Dimitrova[1*], J.L. van den Berg[1,2], G. Heijenk[1], and R. Litjens[2]

[1] University of Twente, Enschede, The Netherlands
d.c.dimitrova@ewi.utwente.nl
[2] TNO ICT, Delft, The Netherlands

Abstract. Long Term Evolution (LTE) is a cellular technology foreseen to extend the capacity and improve the performance of current 3G cellular networks. A key mechanism in the LTE traffic handling is the packet scheduler, which is in charge of allocating resources to active flows in both the frequency and time dimension. In this paper we present a performance comparison of three distinct scheduling schemes for LTE uplink with main focus on the impact of flow-level dynamics resulting from the random user behaviour. We apply a combined analytical/simulation approach which enables fast evaluation of flow-level performance measures. The results show that by considering flow-level dynamics we are able to observe performance trends that would otherwise stay hidden if only packet-level analysis is performed.

1 Introduction

Currently mobile operators are making a shift towards the UTRA Long Term Evolution (LTE) with Single Carrier - Frequency Division Multiple Access (SC-FDMA) as the core access technology for uplink. One of the key mechanisms for realising the potential efficiency of this technology is the packet scheduler, which coordinates the access to the shared channel resources. In LTE systems this coordination refers to both the time dimension (allocation of time frames) and the frequency dimension (allocation of subcarriers). These two grades of freedom, together with specific system constraints, make scheduling in LTE uplink a challenging optimization problem, see e.g. [7]. The complexity of this problem depends on many aspects among which the considered utility function (mostly aggregated throughput maximisation), fairness requirements and specific system characteristics, see [10,12,13]. As often the optimal solutions would be too complex for practical implementation, heuristics yielding reasonable system performance under practical circumstances are proposed, see e.g. [2,15].

In the present paper we take different approach towards the scheduling problem. Instead of searching for an optimal solution, we study how user behaviour affects performance at flow level. The initiations of finite sized flow transfers, occurring at random time instants and locations, is what we term *flow dynamics* and leads to a time - varying number of ongoing flow transfers. For two basic

---

[*] Corresponding author, P.O. Box 217, 7500 AE Enschede, The Netherlands.

C. Sacchi et al. (Eds.): MACOM 2011, LNCS 6886, pp. 181–192, 2011.
© Springer-Verlag Berlin Heidelberg 2011

types of schedulers - fair access and greedy access - we demonstrate the importance of flow dynamics for the final performance of both the overall system and the individual users. Such combined analysis of LTE uplink with user behaviour is not commonly found in the literature.

On the one hand, most research on LTE scheduling has been treating a downlink scenario, some examples being [11,14]. Considerable less work has been dedicated to the inherently different uplink scenario. On the other hand, studies that take into account flow dynamics are lacking. Most papers consider scenarios with a fixed number of active users in the system. For example, the authors of [8] define a theoretically optimal scheduling scheme and its suboptimal, practically feasible counterpart. Unfortunately, [8] fails to present the flow dynamics in a real system and does not consider the impact of a user's location on performance. This factor is accounted for by [15], which compares, for three channel-aware scheduling algorithms, the realised cell throughput for different number of users but does not specify whether the user population changes dynamically or is preset. Additionally, evaluating cell throughput does not give much insight on the performance of a single user.

In contrast to [8] and [15] we focus on the impact of flow behaviour on the performance of individual users considering also their location in the cell. Our investigations are done for two classes of schedulers - a resource fair class, where the active users are all assigned an equal number of subcarriers, and a greedy class, which aims to maximise system capacity (best performance reference). Intermediate results for the resource fair class were published in [6]. The current study extends [6] by introducing a greedy class of scheduler and deployment limitations on the performance; a more detailed discussion of the study can be found in [4].

Our modelling and analysis approach is based on a time-scale decomposition and resembles, at high level, the approach we used previously in the context of UMTS/EUL, see [5]. The approach combines a packet-level analysis, which captures details of the scheduler and the propagation environment, and simulation, which models flow dynamics. In particular, we use continuous-time Markov chains to represent the change in number of active users. Depending on the scheduler's complexity the steady-state distribution of the Markov chain can be found either analytically (yielding insightful closed-form expressions) or by simulation.

The rest of the paper is organised as follows. Section 2 introduces scheduling in LTE uplink in general and the studied schemes in particular. In Section 3 the network model is described. Subsequently, in Section 4 we present the performance evaluation approach and in Section 5 the numerical results at flow level. Finally, Section 6 concludes the presented work.

2   Scheduling

In this section we first give a general introduction to scheduling in the LTE uplink, necessary for understanding the proposed schemes. Subsequently, the proposed scheduling schemes are described.

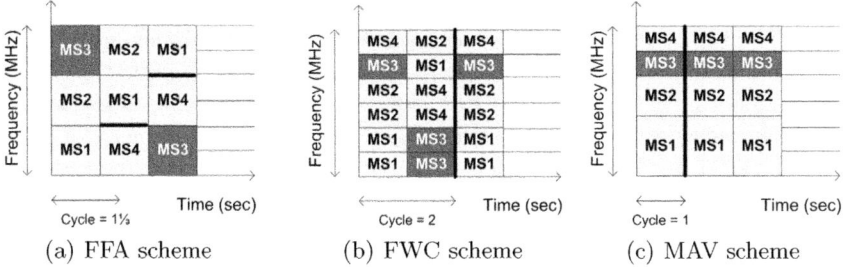

(a) FFA scheme   (b) FWC scheme   (c) MAV scheme

Fig. 1. Considered scheduling schemes for LTE uplink; examples with four users

2.1 LTE Uplink Scheduling

The radio access technology chosen for the LTE uplink is SC-FDMA (Single Carrier - Frequency Division Multiple Access), in which the radio spectrum is divided into nearly perfect mutually orthogonal sub-carriers. Hence, simultaneous transmissions from different mobile stations (MSs) do not cause intra-cell interference but they do compete for a share in the set of sub-carriers. The total bandwidth that can be allocated to a single MS depends on the resource availability, the radio link quality and the terminal's transmit power budget. Allocation of multiple sub-carries to the same user is possible as long as these sub-carriers are consecutive in the frequency domain. A key feature of packet scheduling in LTE networks is the possibility to schedule users in two dimensions, viz. in time and frequency. The aggregate bandwidth available for resource management is divided in sub-carriers of 15 kHz. Twelve consecutive sub-carriers are grouped to form what we term a 'sub-channel', with a bandwidth of 180 kHz; there are M sub-channels in the system bandwidth. In the time dimension, the access to the sub-channels is organised in time slots of 0.5 ms. Two slots of 0.5 ms form a TTI (Transmission Time Interval). The smallest scheduling unit in LTE is termed a *resource block* (RB) and has dimension of 180 kHz and 1 ms[1]).

The data rate that a user can realise is influenced by the number of RBs assigned to it by the scheduler, which determines the allocated bandwidth and the applied transmit power, and by its location, which determines the path loss and the *signal to interference plus noise ratio* (SINR). Some studies, e.g. [9], also argue that certain system characteristics such as the available bandwidth for signalling affect the performance. We investigate the issue in Section 5.2.

2.2 Scheduling Schemes

In our analysis we focus on two (types of) *resource fair* scheduling schemes, which assign equal resource shares to all active users, independently of their respective channel conditions. The first scheduler is termed *fair fixed assignment* because it assigns the same, a priori specified, number of resource blocks to each

---

[1] In fact, each scheduling entity of 180 kHz and 1 ms consists of two RBs, i.e. a RB has the duration of 0.5ms. In this study we use the term RB to refer to a 1 ms interval.

mobile station (see Figure 1(a)). The number of assigned resource blocks per MS, denoted m is hence the same for each mobile station, independently from its location, and is an operator-specified parameter. If the number n of active users is such that the total number of requested resource blocks is less than the available number of resource blocks per TTI, i.e. if $n \cdot m < M$, then a number of resource blocks are left idle. Naturally this reflects a certain degree of resource inefficiency in the scheme, especially for situations with low traffic load and hence few active users. When the number of active users is such that $n \cdot m > M$, more than a single TTI is needed to serve all users at least once. The total number of TTIs necessary form a *cycle* with length c expressed as $c = \max(1, n/M)$. According to this definition c is not necessarily integral (but at least one) and the start of a new cycle may fall within the same TTI as the end of the previous one.

The second scheme, the *fair work-conserving* scheme, aims to avoid the resource inefficiencies of the FFA scheme under low traffic loads, while still preserving the resource fairness property. The scheme's objective is to distribute the available resource blocks evenly over the active users within each individual TTI, see Figure 1(b). As a result the FWC scheduler is optimal in the class of resource-fair Round Robin schedulers. In principle, each of the n MSs is assigned M/n resource blocks in each TTI. Since M/n needs not be integral some users are assigned $\lfloor M/n \rfloor$ RBs (low allocation) and some - $\lceil M/n \rceil$ RBs (high allocation). In order to preserve fairness the RB allocation per user per TTI is alternated such that the total number of RBs per user over c TTIs is eventually the same. Hence the cycle length is equal to the smallest integer c such that $c \cdot M/n$ is integral, which is at most equal to n.

Furthermore, we consider a greedy scheduling scheme - *maximum added value* (MAV) - as a reference for a strategy that aims at maximising system throughput. The MAV scheme has as main objective to maximise the total data rate realised given the active users present in the system. The scheme assigns RBs to those users that can make best use of it. In particular, scheduling decisions are based on a metric termed *added value*, which, for a particular user, is the gain in data rate that a new resource block can deliver to that user. Of all active users the one with the highest added value is assigned the resource block, see Figure 1(c). This procedure continues until all resource blocks have been assigned thus resulting in cycle length $c = 1$. In the MAV scheduling it is possible that cell edge users are deprived from service if the system is under high load - since other users can make better use of the available resource blocks cell edge users get none.

3   Model

We consider a single cell divided in K circular zones of equal area in order to differentiate between users' distances to the base station. Each zone is characterized by a distance d_i to the base station, measured from the outer edge of the zone. Mobile users are uniformly distributed over the zones and flow arrivals follow a

Poisson process with rate λ. The arrival rate per zone $\lambda_i = \lambda/K$ is equal for all zones (due to equal area), where $i = 1, ..., K$. The distribution of the active users over the zones we term *state* $\underline{n} = (n_1, n_2, ..., n_K)$ where n_i defines the number of uses in zone i. Note that $n = \sum_{i=1}^{K} n_i$. All mobile stations are assumed to have the same maximum transmit power P_{max}^{tx}. This maximum power is equally distributed over the assigned RBs m_i, see [15], leading to transmit power per RB $P_i^{tx} = P_{max}^{tx}/m_i$. Note that for the FFA and FWC schemes m_i is the same for all zones but it differs in the case of the MAV scheduler. Each zone is characterized by a distinct path loss $L(d_i)$ defined by the Cost 231 Hata propagation model, according to which

$$L(d_i) = L_{fix} + 10a \log_{10}(d_i)[dB], \tag{1}$$

where L_{fix} is a parameter that depends on system characteristics such as antenna height and a is the path loss exponent. In the rest of the analysis linear scale is used for $L(d_i)$. Users belonging to the same zone i have the same distance d_i and hence experience the same path loss. At this stage of the research we consider only thermal noise N from the components at the base station. Note that intra-cell interference in LTE is not an issue due to the orthogonality of the sub-carriers in LTE. We assume that the RBs used within the cell are not reused in neighbour cells, i.e. inter-cell interference is of no concern. Given a known path loss, the received power (per zone) at the base station P_i^{rx} can be expressed as

$$P_i^{rx} = \frac{P_i^{tx}}{L(d_i)}, \tag{2}$$

Eventually, for the signal-to-interference-plus-noise ratio measured at eNodeB from user of zone i we can write:

$$SINR_i = \frac{P_i^{rx}}{N} = \frac{P_{max}^{tx}/m_i}{L(d_i)N}. \tag{3}$$

Note that the SINR is lower bound to a minimum target level $SINR_{min}$, required for successful reception, and is upper bound by the highest supported modulation and coding scheme (MCS). In our model we work with 16QAM since it should be supported by all terminal classes. All assumptions in the analysis, although simplifying the system model, do not weaken our conclusions since they have mainly qualitative impact.

4   Analysis

Our proposed evaluation approach consists basically of three steps. The first two steps take into account the details of the scheduler's behaviour, e.g. allocation of subcarriers, and the given state of the system, i.e. the number of active users and their distance to the base station. In the third step we create a continuous-time Markov chain, which describes the system behaviour at flow level. From the steady-state distribution of the Markov chain the performance measures, such as mean file transfer time T_i of a user in zone i, can be calculated.

4.1   Packet-Level Analysis

At the packet-level of the analysis approach we define the performance measure *instantaneous rate* r_i. It is the data rate realised by a user (from zone i) when it is scheduled and it is determined by the SINR as derived above, the possible modulation and coding schemes and the receiver characteristics related to that MCS. The instantaneous rate is calculated over all RBs that are allocated to a particular user. In our analysis we use the Shannon formula modified with a parameter σ to represent the limitations of implementation, see Annex A in [1]. Hence, for the instantaneous rate we can write:

$$r_i = (m_i \cdot 180\text{kHz})\sigma \log_2(1 + SINR_i), \qquad (4)$$

where $m_i \cdot 180$ kHz is the bandwidth allocated to a user in a zone i. Note that both $SINR_i$ and r_i are calculated over the same RB allocation.

In the FFA scheme (with a fixed number of RB allocation per user in a cycle) the instantaneous rate of a particular MS is always the same when the MSs is served. In the case of the FWC and MAV schemes however the instantaneous rate depends on the total number of users in the system. Furthermore, for the FWC r_i depends on whether low or high allocation occurs in the specific TTI, see Section 2.2, and hence for the FWC scheme we calculate two instantaneous rates $r_{i,L}$ and $r_{i,H}$ respectively.

4.2   Flow-Level Analysis

The flow-level behaviour can be modelled by a K-dimensional Markov chain with state space $\underline{n} = (n_1, n_2, ..., n_K)$, $n_i \geq 0$ and $i = 1, ..., K$. The jumps in the Markov chain represent the initiation and completion of flow transfers. The corresponding transition rates in a particular state are determined from the (a-priori) given arrival rates λ_i and the long-term flow throughputs $R_i(\underline{n})$ in that state. These throughputs can be derived from the instantaneous rates, see Equation (4), and from the cycle length. For the FFA scheduler the state-dependent throughput can be easily expressed as $R_i(\underline{n}) = r_i/c$. The MAV scheduler has by definition a cycle length of a single TTI and thus $R_i(\underline{n}) = r_i$. For the FWC scheme we need to consider the variation in low resource block allocation ($\lfloor M/n \rfloor$ blocks) and high resource block allocation ($\lceil M/n \rceil$ blocks). Each allocation applies for a fraction a_L and a_H, respectively, of the scheduling cycle as follow:

$$\text{Low allocation}: a_L = \left\lceil \frac{M}{n} \right\rceil - \frac{M}{n}, \qquad (5)$$

$$\text{High allocation}: a_H = \frac{M}{n} - \left\lfloor \frac{M}{n} \right\rfloor. \qquad (6)$$

Eventually for the state dependent throughput we can write for the FWC scheme:

$$R_i(\underline{n}) = a_L r_{i,L} + a_H r_{i,H}. \qquad (7)$$

The eventual transition rates in the Markov chain is given by $n_i R_i(\underline{n})/F$, where F is the mean flow size, and are scheduler specific.

The steady-state distribution of the Markov chain can be found either by simulating the (state transitions of) the Markov chain or, in special cases, by analytical approaches leading to explicit closed-form expressions. In particular, in our study the model of the FFA scheduler appeared to be similar to a M/M/1 processor sharing (PS) queuing model with multiple classes of customers and state dependent service rates. We will further discuss this below. The Markov chains for the FWC and the MAV scheduler are of more complex form and not trivial to solve, which is why we selected a simulation approach for these cases.

Explicit solution for the FFA scheme. We argue that the Markov chain of the FFA scheduler is similar to the Markov chain describing the behaviour of a M/M/1 PS queuing model with multiple classes of customers and state-dependent service rates. This queuing model is described and analysed in [3], Section 7. In [3] each 'task', given there are k active tasks, receives a service portion $f(k)$. The Markov chain of the FFA scheduler turns out to be the same as the Markov chain of the M/M/1 PS model. In particular, it is recognised that the cycle length of the FFA scheme, which depends on the number of active users n, actually determines the service portions $f(\cdot)$. Using the expression for c, given in Section 2.2, we have for the FFA scheme:

$$f(n) = \begin{cases} 1 & \text{for } n = 1, ..., L, \\ \frac{L}{n} & \text{for } n > L, \end{cases} \tag{8}$$

where $L = \lfloor M/m \rfloor$, i.e. the maximum number of MSs that can be served in a TTI. The two situations in Equation (8) occur due to the limited number of RBs per TTI.

Given the above relationship between the Markov chains, we can write for the mean flow transfer time T_i, see [3], of zone i:

$$T_i = \tau_i \frac{\sum_{j=0}^{\infty} \frac{\rho^j}{j!} \Phi(j+1)}{\sum_{j=0}^{\infty} \frac{\rho^j}{j!} \Phi(j)}, \tag{9}$$

where $\Phi(n) = \left(\prod_{j=1}^{n} f(j) \right)^{-1}$ and $\tau_i = F/r_i$ represents the average service requirement of mobile station in zone i; ρ is the system load defined as $\rho = \sum_{i=1}^{K} \lambda_i F/r_i$. Substituting $f(n)$ in (9) we get:

$$T_i = \frac{\tau_i * A}{\sum_{j=0}^{L} \frac{\rho^j}{j!} + \frac{L^L}{L!} (\rho/L)^{L+1} \frac{1}{1-\rho/L}}, i = 1, ..., K, \tag{10}$$

with

$$A = \sum_{j=0}^{L-1} \frac{\rho^j}{j!} + \frac{L^L}{L! \rho} \left((\frac{\rho}{L})^{L+1} \frac{L}{1-\rho/L} + (\frac{\rho}{L})^{L+1} \frac{1}{(1-\rho/L)^2} \right).$$

Note that the impact of the distance of each zone is taken in the specific flow size τ_i, expressed in time.

5   Numerical Results

In Sections 5.2 and 5.3 we present a quantitative evaluation of the three LTE uplink schedulers introduced in Section 2.2. Beforehand, in Section 5.1 we present the parameter settings.

5.1   Parameter settings

The cell with cell radius of 1km is divided in ten zones, i.e. $K = 10$. A system of 10 MHz bandwidth is studied, which, given that a RB has 180 kHz bandwidth (and including control overhead), results in 50 RBs available per TTI.

Mobile stations have maximum transmit power $P_{max}^{tx} = 0.2$ Watt. The lower bound on the SINR is -10dB while the upper bound on performance is determined by a 16QAM modulation that corresponds to SINR of 15dB. For the path loss we have used $PL_{fix} = 141.6$ and path loss exponent of $a = 3.53$, height of the mobile station 1.5m, height of the eNodeB antenna 30m and system frequency 2.6GHz. The thermal noise per subcarrier (180kHz) is -121.45dBm and with noise figure of 5dB the effective noise level per resource block is $N = -116.45dBm$. The attenuation of implementation σ is taken at 0.4, see [1] and Equation (4). The average file size F is 1Mbit and the rate λ at which users become active changes depending on the discussed scenario.

5.2   Fair Allocation Schedulers

This section compares the performance of the two fair allocation strategies FFA and FWC. The following issues are discussed: (i) impact of RB allocation on the Shannon rate, (ii) impact of the scheduling policy and (iii) impact of system limitations on performance.

Impact of RB Allocation. For five distances, namely, (100, 200, 250, 500 and 860) meters[2], we investigate how the Shannon data rate changes as the number of resource blocks increases. The results are shown in Figure 2. Interestingly, there is more to win from increasing RB allocation for closer distances, i.e., the curve slope for 100-250m is steeper and also its initial increase is quicker. For far distances, e.g., 500 and 860m, the data rate quickly saturates translating to little gain of adding more RBs.

Further, the intuitive expectation that the data rate decreases in the distance is confirmed by Figure 2. Note that the data rate is lower bound by the minimum SINR target level, i.e. for 860 meters the data rate becomes zero when the RB assignment will result in SINR below the target.

Moving towards flow-level evaluation, for an arrival rate of $\lambda = 0.5$ flows/sec, we compare the performance of the FFA scheme with a resource allocation of one, three and ten RBs[3]. Figure 3 confirms that performance generally decreases in

---

[2] Distances 250m and 860m correspond to 3GPP's macro 1 and macro 3 scenarios.

[3] These showed to be the most interesting assignments within the range one to ten RBs with a step of one.

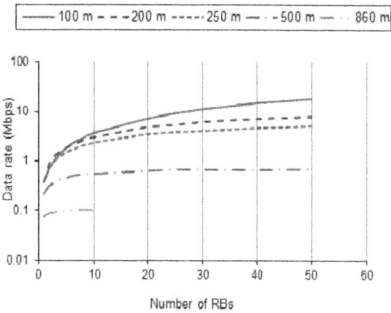

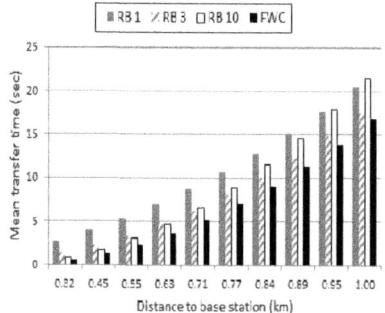

Fig. 2. Impact of RB allocation and distance on the achievable data rate

Fig. 3. Flow-level performance for an arrival rate of 0.5 flows/sec

the distance and improves in the number of RBs, e.g., $m = 1$ vs. $m = 3$. However, related to our previous observations, for $m = 10$ the mean flow transfer time gradually becomes worse than that for $m = 3$. As previously noted remote MSs do not have sufficient power capacity to reach $SINR_{min}$ for high number of RBs; they actually use fewer RBs in order to guarantee $SINR_{min}$ explaining the worsened performance.

Impact of Scheduling Policy. Next we investigate how scheduler specifics, namely, the user selection for service, affect the flow-level performance. Evaluation is performed for arrival rate of $\lambda = 0.5$ flows/sec. The impact of the scheduling policy is investigated by comparing the results for FFA with $m = 1$ and the FWC scheme, see Figure 3. Our choice is motivated by the similar system capacity of the two schemes. The FWC scheme visibly outperforms the FFA with $m = 1$ due to its more efficient distribution of RBs over the active users. Recall that the FWC schemes keeps on scheduling users in the same TTI even if all users have been served once. In the FFA scheme however once each user is assigned a resource block in the TTI the scheduling stops thus leaving RBs unused.

Impact of PDCCH Limitations. The potential performance gains that the freedom to schedule in the frequency dimension brings could be diminished by practical limitations. One such limitation, according to [9], is the radio resource set up for the Physical Downlink Control CHannel (PDCCH). PDCCH carries information from the base station towards a mobile (control packet) about its scheduled uplink transmission. The resource per TTI set aside for these control messages is limited and therefore, given a fixed size of the control package, only a limited number of uplink transmissions can be served within a TTI. The limit proposed by [9] is eight to ten users; in our evaluation we have chosen for ten users. In the rest of the discussion we will use the abbreviations FFA-lim and FWC-lim to refer to the PDCCH limited versions of the two resource fair schemes.

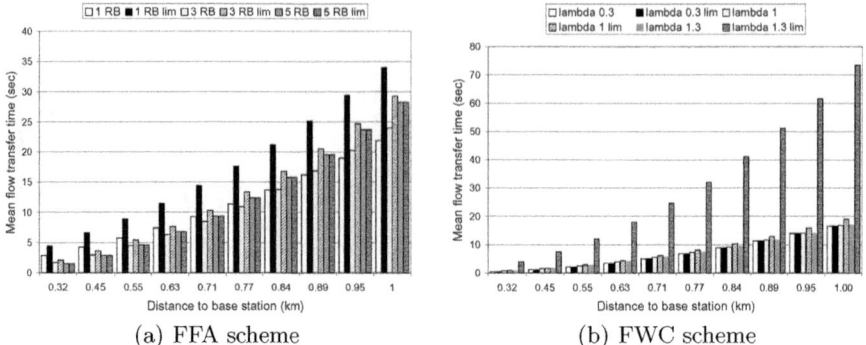

Fig. 4. Impact of PDCCH limitation on performance of (a) a FFA scheme and (b) a FWC scheme

Each of the access fair schemes we discuss, is affected differently by the PD-CCH limitation. The FFA scheme will simply serve at the most ten users in a TTI according to the chosen RB allocation policy. Any unused resource blocks will be therefore waisted, which suggests negative impact on performance. Figure 4(a) shows that, independently of the RB allocation policy, i.e. $m = 1, 3$ or 5, the FFA-lim scheme performs worse (or equal) than the original FFA scheme. The difference is biggest for $m = 1$ and non-existent for $m = 5$. The later observation can be explained by the fact that with $m = 5$ or more the maximum number of users that can be served in one TTI is ten or less. Hence the RB allocation policy self limits the number of simultaneous transmissions in one TTI to ten (or less).

For the FWC scheme the limitation of up to ten users implies that each user will get assigned at least five RBs. Although the mobile stations can fully utilise all allocated RBs remote users cannot reach the maximum possible data rate (highest modulation scheme). Hence, at high loads with FWC-lim MSs use the available RBs much less efficiently than in the original FWC scheme. At low load the two implementations behave practically the same. Based on the results for both FFA-lim and FWC-lim we can conclude that the effects of the limitation are scheduler specific but generally leads to increased mean flow transfer times.

5.3 MAV Greedy Scheduling

The performance of the two access fair (FFA with $m = 1$ and FWC) schemes and the greedy scheduler (MAV) for an arrival rate $\lambda =$ is presented in Figure 5(a). The MAV scheme outperforms the other two for close-by users but its performance is worse for remote users. The reason is the preference of MAV to schedule users that can make best use of the available RBs, i.e. close-by users with low path loss.

Figure 5(b) presents the average mean flow transfer time over all zones for various arrival rates. Surprisingly, the MAV scheme does not always have the

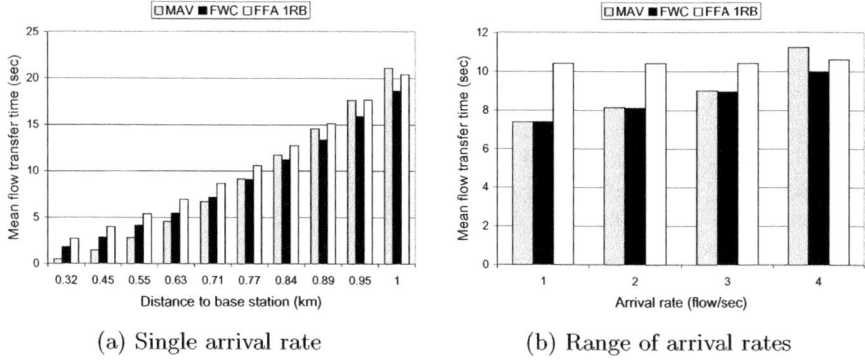

(a) Single arrival rate   (b) Range of arrival rates

Fig. 5. Mean flow transfer times for the three schedulers. (a) Impact of user's location for high load, i.e. $\lambda = 3$; and (b) impact of flow arrival rate on the overall flow transfer time.

best performance! This is explained as follows. Although MAV tries to maximise the total data rate in each state, such strategy is vulnerable to reaching states where the available resources cannot be efficiently used, i.e. states with mainly remote users. Situations as described above are more probable to occur for high load, which corresponds to the results presented in Figure 5(b). This hidden inefficiency of MAV also implies that for remote users it is more beneficial to schedule them frequently even if with few RBs per user.

The paradox is that the MAV scheme, which aims at optimising throughput on a per TTI basis, achieves a lower system capacity (overall throughout), when analysed at the flow level.

6   Conclusion

In this paper we presented an investigation on the impact that flow dynamics (changing number of users) has on performance given the complex scheduling environment of LTE uplink. Two low complexity access fair scheduling schemes are examined - both designed to provide equal channel access. Additionally, as a reference base for optimal system performance, a greedy resource allocation scheme is considered. All schemes are evaluated by a hybrid analysis approach, which accounts for packet-level details such as scheduler's specifics as well as for the dynamic behaviour of users at flow level, i.e. flow initiations and completions. Due to its hybrid nature the approach allows fast evaluation while considering sufficient details of the investigated model. The most valuable contribution of our research is that considering flow dynamics reveals trends that would be otherwise left unobserved. An excellent example is our finding that the greedy scheduler although designed to maximise system throughput for a given number of users seems to be, contrary to expectations, less efficient than the access fair schemes in the long term.

References

1. 3GPP TS 36.942. LTE; evolved universal terrestrial radio access (E-UTRA); radio frequency (RF) system scenarios
2. Al-Rawi, M., Jntti, R., Torsner, J., Sagfors, M.: On the performance of heuristic opportunistic scheduling in the uplink of 3G LTE networks. In: PIMRC (2008)
3. Cohen, J.W.: The multiple phase service network with generalized processor sharing, vol. 12, pp. 254–284. Springer, Heidelberg (1979)
4. Dimitrova, D.C.: Analysing uplink scheduling in mobile networks. A flow-level perspective (2010)
5. Dimitrova, D.C., van den Berg, J.L., Heijenk, G., Litjens, R.: Flow level performance comparison of packet scheduling schemes for UMTS EUL. In: Harju, J., Heijenk, G., Langendörfer, P., Siris, V.A. (eds.) WWIC 2008. LNCS, vol. 5031, pp. 27–40. Springer, Heidelberg (2008)
6. Dimitrova, D.C., van den Berg, J.L., Heijenk, G., Litjens, R.: Scheduling strategies for LTE uplink with flow behaviour analysis. In: Proceedings 4th ERCIM (2010)
7. Gao, L., Cui, S.: Efficient subcarrier, power and rate allocation with fairness considerations for OFDMA uplink. IEEE Transactions on Wireless Communications 7, 1507–1511 (2008)
8. El Hajj, A.M., Yaacoub, E., Dawy, Z.: On uplink OFDMA resource allocation with ergodic sum-rate maimization. In: PIMRC 2009 (2009)
9. Holma, H., Toskala, A.: LTE for UMTS, OFDMA and SC-FDMA Based Radio Access. John Wiley & Sons, Chichester (2009)
10. Huang, J., Subramanian, V.G., Agrawal, R., Berry, R.: Joint scheduling and resource allocation in uplink OFDM systems for broadband wireless access networks. IEEE Journal on Selected Areas in Communications 27, 226–234 (2009)
11. Kwan, R., Leung, C., Zhang, J.: Multiuser scheduling on the downlink of an LTE cellular system. Rec. Lett. Commun, 1–4 (2008)
12. Lee, S.B., Pefkianakis, I., Meyerson, A., Xu, S., Lu, S.: Proportional fair frequency-domain packet scheduling for 3GPP LTE uplink. In: IEEE INFOCOM 2009 minisymposium (2009)
13. Maestro Ruiz de Temino, L.A., Berardinelli, G., Frattasi, S., Mogensen, P.: Channel-aware scheduling algorithms for SC-FDMA in LTE uplink. In: Proceedings PIMRC (2008)
14. Wengerter, C., Ohlhorst, J., von Elbwart, A.G.E.: Fairness and throughput analysis for generalized proportional fair frequency scheduling in OFDMA. In: Vehicular Technology Conference, VTC 2005 Spring (2005)
15. Yaacoub, E., Al-Asadi, H., Dawy, Z.: Low complexity scheduling algorithms for the lte uplink. In: IEEE Symposium on Computers and Communications, ISCC 2009, pp. 266–270 (2009)

An Integrated Wireless Communication Architecture for Maritime Sector

Liping Mu, Ram Kumar, and Andreas Prinz

Faculty of Engineering and Science, University of Agder
Jon Lilletuns vei 9, 4879 Grimstad, Norway
{liping.mu,ram.kumar,andreas.prinz}@uia.no

Abstract. The rapid evolution of terrestrial wireless systems has brought mobile users more and more desired communication services. Maritime customers are asking for the same, such as the concepts of "Broadband at Sea" and "Maritime Internet". Quite a lot of research work has focused on the development of new and better maritime communication technologies, but less attention has been paid on interworking of multiple maritime wireless networks or on satisfying service provisioning. To address this, an integrated wireless Communication Architecture for Maritime Sector (CAMS) has been introduced in this article. CAMS is aimed at 1) granting maritime customers uninterrupted connectivity through the best available network and 2) providing them with the best-provisioned communication services in terms of mobility, security and Quality of Experience (QoE). To address mobility challenge, the IEEE 802.21 standard is recommended to be used in CAMS in order to achieve seamless handover. CAMS provides application-level QoE support attending to the limited communication resources (e.g. bandwidth) at sea. Certain security considerations have also been proposed to supplement this architecture.

Keywords: Communication Architecture, Network Integration, Maritime.

1 Introduction

Due to the development of new applications and the fast evolution of wireless communication technologies, maritime customers are demanding better communication solutions to satisfy the increasing user requirements. In this context, concepts like "Broadband at Sea" and "Maritime Internet" have become popular [1].

Newer security and transport related applications such as video surveillance for piracy prevention and real-time updates of navigational data are increasingly being used. Besides, the usage of personal and business purpose applications like telephony and email are also considered while implementing communication systems for ship's management.

Some of these newly envisaged applications demand a strict network Quality of Service (QoS) such as guaranteed bandwidth and lower delays, and some require uninterrupted Internet connectivity. On the other hand, the fast evolution

C. Sacchi et al. (Eds.): MACOM 2011, LNCS 6886, pp. 193–205, 2011.

of wireless communication technologies provides maritime customers opportunity to achieve better and faster ship-to-ship and ship-to-shore communications. For example, maritime mesh networks based on long range wireless technology (WiMAX) [2] is a promising solution, and satellite broadband such as VSAT (Very Small Aperture Terminals) service is changing maritime communications dramatically. At the same time, last-mile wireless access technologies, such as IEEE 802.11, IEEE 802.16, 3GPP standards for cellular access networks, keep contributing to the near-shore communications. In order to efficiently use these wireless communication systems and take advantage of the various available features, procedures to integrate these networks and to automatically select the best underlying network are desired. To satisfy the different maritime communication requirements, network resources have to be utilized reasonably and communication services have to be provisioned and tailored to user requirements. Furthermore, mobility handling mechanisms are necessary so as to achieve a seamless mobility experience when switching between different underlying networks.

In this article, an integrated wireless Communication Architecture for Maritime Sector (CAMS) is introduced to address both application requirements and rapid technology evolution. CAMS is aimed at satisfying always-best-connected requirement and better services-provisioning in terms of mobility, security and QoE.

The rest of the article is organized as follows. In Section 2, maritime customer communication requirements are identified. Section 3 extracts the key system requirements for maritime communication. Then, in Section 4, the integrated maritime communication architecture is presented. Finally, Section 5 concludes this paper and points out future work.

2   Maritime Customer Communication Requirements

Maritime communication is becoming more important in both commercial and research fields, especially in countries like Norway, which has economic dependency on an ocean area about six times the size of its mainland. After having contacted many maritime customers [1], we have acquired a detailed list of user requirements for maritime communication as given below.

2.1   Make Use of Available Bandwidths as Much as Possible

Customers on ship are willing to keep in touch with shore centers and to use Internet anytime, anywhere on any device, and they prefer to have the possibility of being best connected to the available network in terms of bandwidth, quality and cost. For example, when the ship is moving to an area covered by terrestrial communication networks, services provided by these systems are mostly desirable.

2.2   Classify Data Traffic to Optimize the Usage of Bandwidth

Bandwidth is a limited resource especially in the maritime scenario that drastically changes with geography. For example, in harbors WiFi is available to support high bandwidth with very low price, whereas far out into the sea (far northern area for Norway), only satellites can provide low bandwidth connectivity characterized with high cost and long propagation delays. Therefore, maritime communication resources have to be utilized reasonably and intelligently by classifying and prioritizing the communication traffic.

2.3   Service Continuity at Different Locations and via Different Devices

Continuous land-based assistance and navigation are always in high demand. Service continuity becomes an important topic especially during the switching between different maritime wireless networks. For instance, a customer on-board who fills out an important on-line report to the shore center while the ship moves from communicating via satellite to WiMAX in a port, would want to keep the session uninterrupted during the transition.

2.4   More Secured Information Exchange and Internet Connectivity

It has become a security problem for shipping companies that the crew, while surfing the Internet and often unintentionally, exposes the on-board systems to viruses and hacking attacks. Security is a critical factor in the "Maritime Internet" context. Authentication and authorization mechanisms are needed for preventing attacks to the system. Also, traffic control to some extent is necessary for preventing less important data traffic from clogging the channels so as to enable the critical data to get through.

3   System Requirements for Maritime Communication

If we translate these maritime user communication requirements into system requirements, the target communication system is expected to have the following capabilities: provide optimum connectivity, mobility handling, QoE support and security.

3.1   Connectivity

With respect to maritime communications, almost all of them are based on wireless communication technologies. Compared to terrestrial wireless communication, it is challenging to deploy cellular systems at sea to achieve high data-rate transmission because of the geographic restrictions. So far, Frequency Modulation (FM) radio technology like narrowband Ultra High Frequency (UHF) and Very High Frequency (VHF) are widely used for ship-to-shore communication, with cellular systems used for near port waters. Satellites such as International Maritime Satellite (INMARSAT) are often used for long-range ship-to-ship and ship-to-shore communications. However, due to the fact that FM radio transmission has a low data-rate characteristic and satellite communication is quite expensive, considerable effort has been devoted to the development of new maritime wireless communication technologies and cheaper satellite services. Maritime mobile WiMAX networks have drawn much attention [2]. Furthermore, advances in antenna technology and satellite coverage have combined to make VSAT Ku Band satellite services very attractive, as they can provide higher data-rate transmission, good Quality of Service, compatibility with IP networks and flat-rate charging.

All in all, the target maritime communication system needs to use these existing or future maritime wireless networks to provide customers basic connectivity services.

3.2   Mobility

There are four types of mobility defined in [3] mainly from the user's point of view: *terminal, personal, session* and *service mobility*. In [4], four levels of network interworking for mobility handling are distinguished from an operator's perspective:

- *Level A would allow a user to get access to a set of services available in a visited network while relying on his/her home network credentials;*
- *Level B would allow users to be able to get access to specific services located in their home network when connected through a visited network;*
- *Level C does not require users to re-establish active session(s) when moving between networks;*
- *Level D provides seamless service continuity to satisfy service requirements also during mobility.*

An intrinsic characteristic in maritime wireless communication scenarios is heterogeneity, which refers to the coexistence of multiple and diverse wireless networks with their corresponding radio access technologies [4] and network protocols. Therefore, integrating heterogeneous wireless networks in the maritime communication scenario is required in order to take advantage of the different features of each one of them, and all four levels of interworking are desired in the target maritime communication system for mobility handling.

3.3   QoE

Bandwidth at sea is a very limited resource due to the geographical restrictions, which frequently exhibits great variations with the high mobility of maritime communication entities and the switching between different underlying wireless networks. The QoS for an application session is determined by a number of factors, such as the maximum bandwidth that can be allocated to it and the current state of the network. It mainly focuses on the network perspective and attempts to objectively measure the service delivered by the operator: bit rate, delay, jitter, bit error rate and so on. Whereas in the maritime communication scenario, customers have the possibility of choosing from multiple underlying networks; applications on board often have different capacity, integrity and se-curity requirements related to different traffic types (e.g. distress calls, alert messages transmission, remote navigation assisting, confidential business data transmission and multimedia entertainment applications). Therefore, subjective factors regarding quality of service should be also considered in the target com-munication system. ITU-T has defined the QoE concept as *"overall acceptability of an application or service, as perceived subjectively by the end-user"* [5]. By considering both QoS and QoE when delivering communication services to mar-itime customers, application context and user expectations will be fairly treated besides objective QoS provided by the network operator.

3.4   Security

End-to-end security for ship-to-shore communication is vital, as ship-to-shore communications are mainly related to remote operation, navigation and safe shipping in which the integrity of exchanged information is vital. Additionally, business information traveling among maritime partners has to be kept as confi-dential; individual information for crew use is often sensitive. These confidential or sensitive information cannot be exposed or subjected to malicious intent. Hence, security mechanisms are highly desirable in the target maritime commu-nication system.

4   An Integrated Wireless Communication Architecture for Maritime Sector

Existing maritime wireless networks are often independent systems without in-terworking between them. Maritime communication service provisioning there-fore has to be supported by means of specialized service platforms that could deal with quality, security and mobility simultaneously. In order to accomplish that, the first key step is to design an efficient maritime communication platform architecture.

The Internet architecture was designed to push the intelligence to the end systems with dumb networks to provide fast service provision, but it only works very well when the network qualities are stable. Telecom network architectures are designed to have complex networks to benefit simple terminals and relevantly guaranteed service provisioning, but the services they satisfy are often simple and flat. Nevertheless, it is not difficult to identify the key technologies and marketing strategies within the Internet and Telecom network architectures that have made them so successful. For example, IP technology - a common interconnection ele-ment to address heterogeneity - in the Internet paradigm has brought incredible success and rapid growth. Similarly, the combination of mobility handling and QoS provisioning in the Telecom world has attracted ubiquitous users.

Although none of these two architectures apply directly to maritime scenar-ios, a tailored communication architecture - CAMS - that optimally leverages these two paradigms can best satisfy the maritime communication requirements

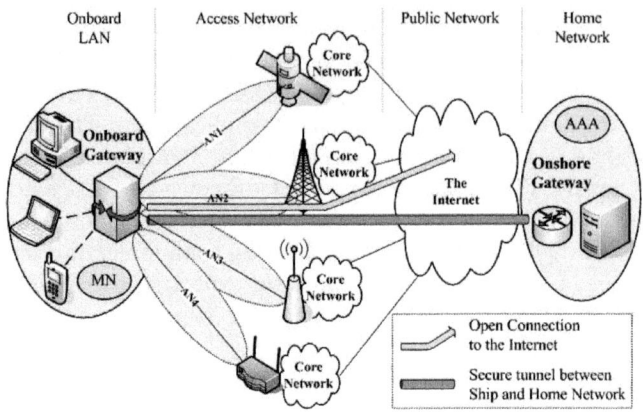

Fig. 1. An Integrated Communication Architecture for Maritime Sector

based on relevantly harsh conditions. The architecture is shown in Fig.1. In this architecture, IP is used as 1) the unifying technology to integrate different access networks 2) to follow the all-IP principle direction in communication evolution. The on-board gateway as a mobile node is equipped with multiple interfaces corresponding to different access technologies (e.g., AN1: satellite networks, AN2: WiMAX networks, AN3: cellular networks, AN4: WiFi networks). It cooperates with the onshore network which behaves like its home network in order to fulfill the mobility handling, QoE support and security enhancement tasks, which will be explained in detail in the following sections.

It is worth mentioning that the selection of this architecture model is not only based on performance criteria, but on its cost and feasibility as well. Any candidate architecture has to be able to backwardly integrate existing infrastructures while at the same time be easily evolved. Hence, two characteristics of our maritime communication architecture in terms of integration ability and scalability are central:

(1): In CAMS, the onshore network behaves like a home network for maritime customers. Therefore, separate subscriptions between customers and any network operator are not required. Customers have direct agreements with our home network, and our home network has separate service level agreements with each network operator.

(2): In CAMS, direct links between different networks are not necessary. Networks are connected with each other via the Internet, which is considered as loose-coupling architecture [6] for network integration. Compared with the tight-coupling model, it allows the independent deployment of each wireless network system.

4.1   Mobility Handling and Security Enhancement

Before finalizing any mobility handling solution, future trends for mobility handling must be considered. Given the mobility management tendencies described in [7], we feel three of them are most important in a maritime scenario:

(1): Different network operators will clearly provide coverage areas for the maritime customers. Hence, it is important for the communication architecture to be independent of administrative concerns.

(2): Existing mobility studies focus on solving issues between two specific technologies and many mobility mechanisms are within specific network architectures, e.g., mobility handling in IP Multimedia Subsystem (IMS) and Ambient Networks. Therefore, it is desirable to have a more general or intelligent mobility handling mechanism that could be used in all heterogeneous maritime wireless networks.

(3): Mobility management is tending towards a cross-layer approach and favoring both user and network requirements. In other words, it will become common to gather an assortment of information from several sources: link to application layer taking into account QoE factors.

These mobility handling tendencies need to be taken care of in our maritime communication architecture. Since handover is the key enabling function for seamless mobility and service continuity, it is necessary to explain handover concept first. *Handover* indicates the process by which the mobile node obtains facilities and preserves traffic flows upon the change from one point of the network attachment to another, and according to [8], there are three primary characteristics of the networks that can serve to categorize handover: subnets, administrative domains, and access technologies. Therefore, six types of handover have been defined: *intradomain, interdomain, intrasubnet, intersubnet, intratechnology* and *intertechnology handover*. We will discuss mobility handling for *interdomain, intersubnet, intertechnology handover* based on interworking-level concept which has been introduced in Section 3. Inter-entity handovers are relevantly more common in the maritime environment and considered more difficult than intra-entity ones.

Interdomain Service Access - Level A and Level B. An interdomain handover involves the switching between different administrative domains, and requires authorization for acquisition or modification of resources assigned to the mobile. In CAMS, the onshore network behaves like a "home network" for maritime customers so as to let them be independent of administrative concerns. Therefore, Level A interworking is required to allow them to get access to services available in all "visited networks". Authentication, authorization, and accounting (AAA) functions need to be implemented in target system (see AAA Server Service and AAA Client Service in Fig.1). AAA functions allow customers to perform authentication and authorization processes in a visited network based on subscription profiles and security credentials. AAA services are known to cause significant overall handover delay. To address this, media-independent pre-authentication interdomain handover optimization [8] can be applied in CAMS for mitigating the total delay.

In order to get access to specific services provided by networks other than the serving one - Level B interworking - requires a data transfer mechanism. Virtual Private Networking (VPN) technology uses data encapsulation to achieve secure data transfer between two or more networked devices which are not on the same private network and to keep the transferred data private from other devices or other intervening networks. There are different VPN approaches when it comes to wireless VPN. Columbitech has proposed a session-layer solution: using Wireless Transport Layer Security (WTLS) standard [9]. The WTLS solution enables secure and convenient remote access to the corporate network in an environment with multiple wireless access networks. Wireless VPN technology over WTLS standard is desired to be used in CAMS in order to achieve three aims:

- *Enable the transfer of user data between networks in order to give access to specific services provided in a network other than the serving one.*
- *Allow initialized incoming connections when using access networks with Network Address Translation (NAT) function.*
- *Enhance security for ship-to-shore communications based on tunneling technology (e.g., remote assistant and remote maintenance applications which demand high security).*

On-board LAN, onshore home network and onshore head office can constitute a virtual private network, in which AAA mechanism and tunneling technology are both applied. Therefore, security could be enhanced in two aspects. Primarily, only authorized users are allowed to access the ongoing information. Then, encryption can help achieve data integrity by protecting message contents from being modified under transit along the communication path.

Intersubnet Service Continuity - Level C. Service continuity during intersubnet handover often relies on the maintenance of a permanent mobile terminal IP address which can be addressed by Mobile IP or its variants. In Mobile IPv4, a foreign agent which works together with the home agent is needed on the visited network, while in Mobile IPv6, there is no need to deploy special routers as "foreign agents". Also, IEEE 802.21 standard which we will introduce later defines a set of handover enabling functions (for MobileIP) with required functionality to perform enhanced handovers. Therefore, MIPv6 is preferable in CAMS. However, considering that 1) MIPv4 works with IPv4 and MIPv6 was designed for IPv6 2) the slow adoption and migration from IPv4 to IPv6 3) the handover performance comparison between Host Identity Protocol (HIP) and MIPv6 in [10] and 4) HIP supports mobility between different IP address realms and easier NAT traversal [11], it is difficult to say which mobility management policy is better in the maritime context: stick to the current MIPv4 solution and move to MIPv6 when IPv6 is available or embrace HIP-based mobility handling directly. From the literature [10, 11, 12], we could expect that HIP is better than Mobile IP solutions in CAMS, while future testing and evaluation is needed.

Seamless Intertechnology Handover - Level D. Intertechnology handover is also referred to as vertical handover which can be further classified into two types [13]: *downward vertical handover* and *upward vertical handover*. Downward vertical handover is to switch between two networks that are both available. Hence, it often happens for convenience reasons (e.g., user's preference, higher bandwidth, lower delay, etc.), and the communication is still alive if the handover does not happen. Upward vertical handover to another available network is mandatory in order to keep the communication active, because the mobile customer is moving out of the coverage of the current serving network. In this sense, decision making for downward vertical handover will be much more complex and deserves more effort than the upward one. It is more important because of customers' desire, e.g., when the ship approaches the shore, customers are willing to use WiFi connection. It is more complex because it needs more information for feeding handover decision maker from all involved parts - networks, terminal and user - which is often difficult to get.

In [13], vertical handover process has been divided into three phases: network discovery, handover decision and handover implementation. Handover implementation phase usually involves link establishment, higher layer mobility management and AAA functions. Higher layer mobility performing and AAA functions introduce significant delays during handover because of the difficulty of information collection and the lack of smooth cooperation between link and higher layer functions.

In order to address these deficiencies and help with handover decision making, IEEE 802.21 standard [14] has been introduced. IEEE 802.21 defines an abstraction layer between link and network layer which can be exploited by the IP stack (or any other upper layer) to better interact with the heterogeneous underlying technologies by mapping technology-specific primitives. A new link layer entity called Media-Independent Handover Function (MIHF) is specified in the standard. This MIHF entity mainly aims at exchanging of information and commands between upper and lower layers. The main function of MIHF is to coordinate the exchange of information and commands between the different devices involved in making handover decisions and executing handovers [15]. To upper layers, it provides a media-independent interface in order to collect information from link layer and to control link behavior. Regarding the different link layer technologies, it supports mapping between the common interface and a set of media-specific primitives. MIHF is designed both for terminals and networks; therefore, remote interfaces such as terminal-network and network-network interfaces will work together with local interfaces to aid the interactions among all devices involved in the handover. These interactions are provided by a set of services: event, command and information services [15].

Since the MIHF entities within terminals and networks can talk to each other, handover could be initiated from both sides. In the maritime communication scenario, the initiation is preferred to be done by the terminal (e.g. the on-board gateway equipped with multiple interfaces) for flexibility and prioritizing user's preference. While served by a given access network, the MIHF entity of the mobile terminal can interact with the MIHF entity in the serving network in order to get the information from other available networks, making it possible to initiate an intertechnology handover with desired pre-configuration for the target network [16] to reduce the handover delay. However, it is often necessary to have a list of candidate access networks in the mobile node, and the MIHF entities need to be added within all devices involved in the handover, together with the

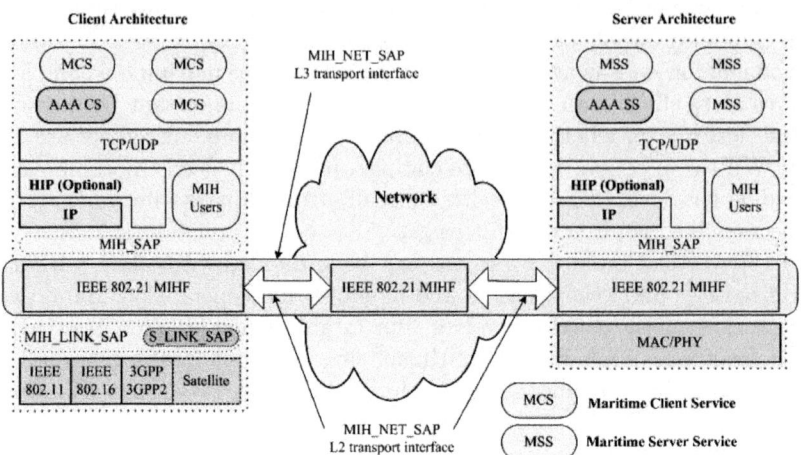

Fig. 2. Maritime Communication Architecture Protocols Stack

relevant protocols. Fig.2 below shows the protocols stack in the client side on board and the server side on shore of our maritime communication architecture.

IEEE 802.21 framework does not standardize the actual handover execution mechanism: handover decision-making or mobility management procedure. It recommends applying the Signal-to-Noise Ratio (SNR) metric for the handover decision-making. However, in the maritime scenario, using only SNR for handover decision-making is not enough since 1) there are different communication applications with different QoE requirements and 2) there are heterogeneous wireless access networks with different QoS characteristics. Therefore, several metrics could be combined together intelligently and dynamically so as to achieve more reasonable handover decision-making: SNR (or received signal strength (RSS)), QoS (e.g., bandwidth, data rate, access delay, losses), QoE (e.g., context information, price, user preferences, power consumption). Furthermore, a back-and-forth (ping-pong) effect should be avoided either by a more robust handover decision-making algorithm or by post-handover mechanisms.

IEEE 802.21 is designed to enable interoperability mainly among IEEE 802, 3GPP, and 3GPP2 networks. Similarly, ETSI has defined a broadband satellite multimedia (BSM) architecture [17] to provide a mechanism to carry IP-based protocols over different satellite networks by adding a satellite independent service access point (SI-SAP) interface layer, aiming to achieve interoperability among these satellite networks with different link layer technologies. BSM does not specify mobility management mechanisms. However, the methodologies of heterogeneity handling between BSM architecture and IEEE 802.21 framework are similar, hiding the differences by adding a common abstraction layer. Therefore, we could integrate SI-SAP within the IEEE 802.21 MIH framework to enable the handover between satellite networks and non-satellite networks in the maritime communication scenario, which is also recommended in [18].

4.2   QoE Support and Security Enhancement

Maritime communications are mainly based on wireless networks which often provide limited bandwidth with different QoS provisioning. Furthermore, maritime customers expect to have applications on board with differentiated parameters in terms of capacity, integrity and security. To address this requirement based on the restricted resources, application-level QoE support could be a good alternative. Application-level QoE support can be done by 1) differentiating applications with different priorities and 2) queuing their connections based on network conditions. The priorities are assigned according to customers preferences and the connection control takes place at the egress of the on-board gateway.

In CAMS, at first, different servers with different IP addresses can be used to separate applications. For example, there are basically two categories of applications: one for administrative system and the other for welfare. Under each category, there are several sub-categories. Within administrative system, there are emergency messaging sending, safety and monitoring data transmission, reporting information exchanging and so on. They could be assigned with secondary priorities. Different traffic types (data, voice, video) can be separated as well, according to different port numbers and protocols, such as real-time and non real-time traffic. They could be assigned with third-level priorities. Therefore, the priority map is chaining different queuing "disciplines" together nicely where ongoing packets are sorted by filtering them on their protocols, ports, sources and destinations. The application-level QoE support mechanism is shown in Fig.3.

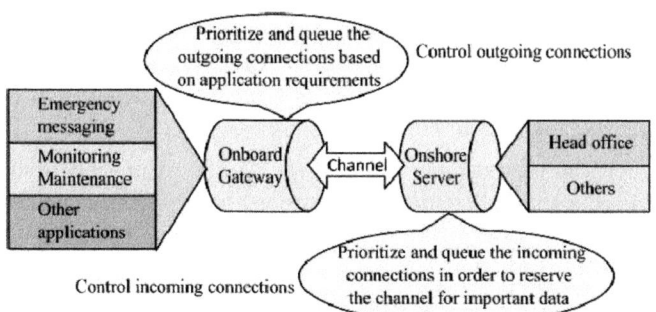

Fig. 3. Application-level QoE Support Mechanism

By adding graphical user interface to the Linux QoS configuration technique, the on-board gateway is able to intelligently allocate limited resources in accordance with prioritized egress connection demands based on customers preferences. However, it has to be carefully implemented to be available only for authorized users. The application-level QoE support is mainly for shaping outgoing traffic. It is difficult to shape incoming traffic from user side, because QoS policy decisions for ingress traffic are controlled outside the on-board network infrastructure. However, the onshore gateway can be used as an ingress connection "controller" by queuing the incoming connections in order to reserve the channel for important data.

QoE support mechanism allows the customer to configure the system in order to make sure that more important data gets sent first, and various connections are given more fair treatment than usual. Together with our proposed VPN solution including a secure tunnel between the on-board gateway and the home network to carry sensitive information related to, e.g. ship's navigation and management, the on-board gateway has the capability to route certain packets through the encrypted tunnel, while separately forwarding unencrypted packets to the open Internet (see Fig.1). The unencrypted packets belong to value-added services provided to on-board customers who require such connectivity like browsing or multimedia. This two-prong approach helps the architecture to have a fine grained control over the data whilst avoiding home network with unnecessary data and routing information. The secure VPN tunnel connects the two trusted networks (on-board and home) through untrusted networks (access core and the Internet). By combining separation of traffic and VPN technology, security can be further enhanced. However, more detailed security mechanisms will be left for future work.

5   Conclusion and Future work

In this work we have introduced an integrated wireless communication architecture that tries to provide maritime customers ubiquitous services by integrating heterogeneous underlying wireless networks. Solutions for addressing key issues such as quality, security and mobility are covered in this architecture with more detailed discussion of seamless handover. We believe that future maritime communication will benefit much from integration of existing networks, and quality, security and mobility have to be carefully addressed simultaneously considering user preferences. However, future work is required to demonstrate the performance of our proposed architecture:

- A new maritime handover decision-making algorithm will be designed and tested in order to intelligently switch among heterogeneous maritime wireless networks and handover between satellite networks and non-satellite networks will be further studied.
- Application-level QoE support on both on-board and onshore gateways will be tested to prove the efficiency of reasonable utilization of limited resources according to different application requirements.
- Wireless VPN technology and AAA functions will be applied to the maritime scenario for measuring the security improvement.

References

1. MARCOM: Broadband at Sea, Internet for coast, polar regions, offshore and sea farming, http://www.marcom.no/
2. Pathmasuntharam, J.S., Jurianto, J., Kong, P.Y., Ge, Y., Zhou, M., Miura, R.: High Speed Maritime Ship-to-Ship/Shore Mesh Networks. In: 7th International Conference on ITS Telecommunications, pp. 1–6 (2007)

3. Schulzrinne, H., Wedlund, E.: Application-layer mobility using SIP. IEEE Service Portability and Virtual Customer Environments, 29–36 (2000)
4. Ferrus, R., Sallent, O., Agusti, R.: Interworking in heterogeneous wireless networks: Comprehensive framework and future trends. IEEE Wireless Communications 17, 22–31 (2010)
5. TU-T Recommendation Std : Vocabulary and effects of transmission parameters on customer opinion of transmission quality. ITU-T, P.10/G.100 (2008)
6. Buddhikot, M., Chandranmenon, G., Han, S., Lee, Y.W., Miller, S., Salgarelli, L.: Integration of 802.11 and third-generation wireless data networks. In: IEEE 22nd Annual Joint Conference of Computer and Communications, vol. 1, pp. 503–512 (2003)
7. Fernandes, S., Karmouch, A.: Vertical Mobility Management Architectures in Wireless Networks: A Comprehensive Survey and Future Directions. IEEE Communications Surveys & Tutorials, 1–19 (2010)
8. Dutta, A., Famolari, D., Das, S., Ohba, Y., Fajardo, V., Taniuchi, K., Lopez, R., Schulzrinne, H.: Media-independent pre-authentication supporting secure interdomain handover optimization. IEEE Wireless Communications 15, 55–64 (2008)
9. Columbitech: Columbitech Wireless VPN - Technical Description (2007)
10. Jokela, P., Rinta-aho, T., Jokikyyny, T., Wall, J., Kuparinen, M., Mahkonen, H., Melén, J., Kauppinen, T., Korhonen, J.: Handover performance with HIP and MIPv6. In: 1st International Symposium of Wireless Communication Systems, pp. 324–328 (2005)
11. Nikander, P., Gurtov, A., Henderson, T.R.: Host Identity Protocol HIP: Connectivity, Mobility, Multi-Homing, Security, and Privacy over IPv4 and IPv6 Networks. IEEE Communications Surveys & Tutorials 12, 186–204 (2010)
12. Ratola, M.: Which Layer for Mobility? - Comparing Mobile IPv5, HIP and SCTP. In: Seminar on Internetworking in the Spring 2004, Espoo, Finland, T-110.551 (2004)
13. Chen, W.T., Liu, J.C., Huang, H.K.: An adaptive scheme for vertical handoff in wireless overlay networks. In: 10th International Conference on Parallel and Distributed Systems, pp. 541–548 (2004)
14. IEEE Draft Std: IEEE Draft Standard for Local and Metropolitan Area Networks: Media Independent Handover Services. P802.21/D14 (2008)
15. De La Oliva, A., Banchs, A., Soto, I., Melia, T., Vidal, A.: An overview of IEEE 802.21: media-independent handover services. IEEE Wireless Communications 15, 96–103 (2008)
16. Dutta, A., Chakravarty, S., Taniuchi, K., Fajardo, V., Ohba, Y., Famolari, D., Schulzrinne, H.: An Experimental Study of Location Assisted Proactive Handover. In: Global Telecommunications Conference, pp. 2037–2042 (2007)
17. ETSI Std: Satellite Earth Stations and Systems (SES); Broadband Satellite Multimedia (BSM); Services and architectures. European Telecommunications Standards Institute, TR 101 984 (2007)
18. Hu, Y.F., Berioli, M., Pillai, P., Cruickshank, H., Giambene, G., Kotsopoulos, K., Guo, W., Chan, P.M.L.: Broadband satellite multimedia. Communications 4, 1519–1531 (2010)

Delay Analysis of Wireless Broadband Networks with Non Real-Time Traffic

Sergey Andreev[1], Zsolt Saffer[2], and Andrey Turlikov[3]

[1] Tampere University of Technology (TUT), Finland
sergey.andreev@tut.fi
[2] Budapest University of Technology and Economics (BUTE), Hungary
safferzs@hit.bme.hu
[3] State University of Aerospace Instrumentation (SUAI), Russia
turlikov@vu.spb.ru

Abstract. In this paper, we present the analysis of the mean overall packet delay of non real-time traffic in IEEE 802.16-based wireless broadband networks. We consider the case of contention-based bandwidth reservation. The system model accounts for both bandwidth reservation and packet transmission delay components of the overall delay. The queueing analysis is based on the description of the joint content of the outgoing subscriber station buffer and the base station grant buffer. This is achieved by means of a properly chosen bivariate embedded Markov chain. The mean overall packet delay is computed from its equilibrium solution. The analytical approach is verified by means of simulation. The corresponding analytical and simulation results show excellent agreement with each other.

Keywords: IEEE 802.16, queueing system, Markov chain, contention-based bandwidth reservation.

1 Introduction and Background

In wireless broadband networks, the users are distributed across a large geographic area and communicate via a base station (BS). As such, the BS is the coordinator of the network activity, which controls user communication in its vicinity. Recently, the proliferation of IEEE 802.16-based [1] broadband networks is observed. This is due to their relatively low cost, wide coverage and MAC mechanisms supporting a variety of quality of service (QoS) requirements.

The performance evaluation of IEEE 802.16 QoS features with bandwidth reservation is addressed by numerous research papers (see e.g. [2], [3], and [4]). The overall operation of the considered wireless broadband network is shown in Figure 1, in which both downlink (DL) and uplink (UL) transmissions are demonstrated. In the DL and the UL data packets are sent from the BS to its subscriber stations (SSs) and in the opposite direction, respectively. Initially, a SS issues a bandwidth request (BW-Req) in the UL (1UL), which is received by the BS (2UL). After processing these requests, the BS forms a transmission

C. Sacchi et al. (Eds.): MACOM 2011, LNCS 6886, pp. 206–217, 2011.
© Springer-Verlag Berlin Heidelberg 2011

schedule and then forwards it to the SSs in the DL (1DL). Each SS receives the schedule (2DL) and transmits own data packets accordingly in the dedicated time-frequency slots (3UL, 4UL). If necessary, the BS may also transmit data packets to SSs in the DL (3DL, 4DL). As such, the overall system operation consists of bandwidth reservation and packet transmission functionalities, therefore the overall system model should account for both bandwidth reservation and packet transmission stages.

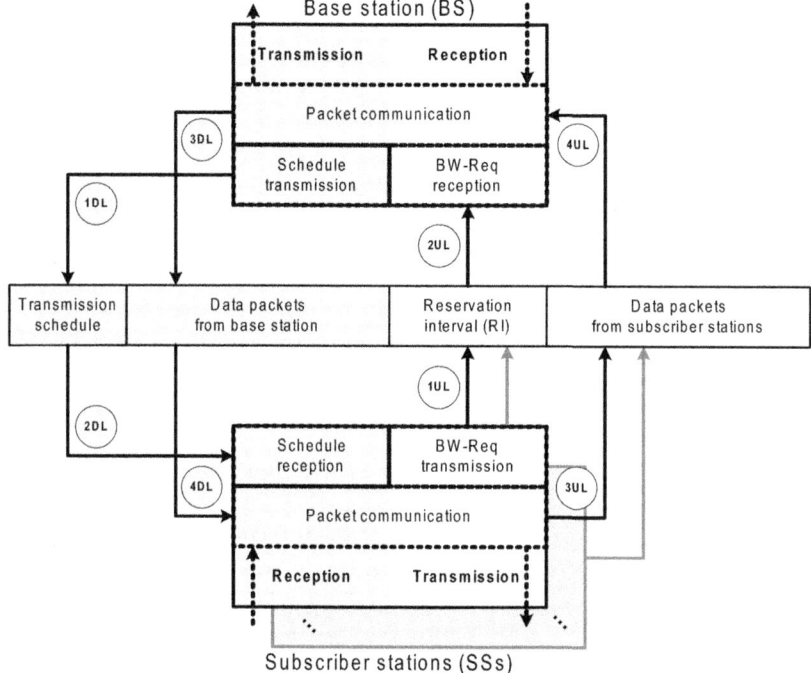

Fig. 1. System overall description

There has been little effort taken to address both aforementioned stages of the wireless broadband network functionality. This is due to the complexity of the overall system operation. The performance of IEEE 802.16 network was studied either by simulation [5], [6] or particular special cases were addressed analytically [7]. Moreover, in the majority of existing research papers the reservation and the transmission are considered separately. However, the operation of the real-world network (see Figure 1) includes both functionalities, which should be taken into account. In our previous work [8], we have studied the overall delay by addressing its both components and constructed a simple analytical upper bound on its mean value. In this paper, we continue our work and calculate the exact value of the mean overall delay.

2 System Model

In this section, we briefly outline the model of IEEE 802.16-based network, which is used to evaluate the delay at both reservation and scheduling stages. For more details, see our previous paper [8].

We consider the system that comprises a BS and N SSs, in which we focus only on the uplink transmissions. The delay analysis is conducted for non real-time (nrtPS) QoS profile. Only contention-based polling schemes are considered. Particularly, we concentrate on the broadcast polling.

The system operation time is divided into frames and T_f denotes the frame duration. The duration of a packet transmission is τ. At each SS, the packet arrival process is Poisson. The arrival rate is λ_i at SS i. Thus the overall arrival rate is $\lambda = \lambda_i N$. The duration of each contention-based transmission opportunity is ν. Moreover, the reservation interval (RI) of each frame comprises exactly K contention-based transmission opportunities.

A BW-Req is issued by the i-th SS whenever at least one new data packet arrives, of which the BS should be notified. The request contains the information about all the newly arrived packets since the last request sending. If a packet arrives to an empty outgoing buffer of SS i during the RI the SS must wait with sending the BW-Req for this packet until the next RI. We define $p_i^{(b)}$ as the probability of the successful BW-Req transmission at SS i, given that this SS takes part in the contention process (i.e. there is at least one new i-packet belonging to SS i in its outgoing buffer).

Additionally, below we introduce a set of assumptions to shape the system model.

Assumption 1. The probability of the successful BW-Req transmission at each SS in the RI of a frame, $p_i^{(b)}$, is assumed to be constant (see [8]).

Assumption 2. The BS maintains an individual grant buffer of infinite capacity for each SS.

Assumption 3. The grants in the individual BS grant buffer of each SS are processed in first-come-first-served order.

Assumption 4. Each SS can transmit exactly one packet in each UL sub-frame.

Assumption 5. For each SS, the feedback on the success/failure of its own BW-Req transmission, which is necessary for the collision resolution algorithm operation, is available.

The system is stable when for every SS on average the number of arriving packets does not exceed the number of departing packets, i.e.

$$\lambda_i < \frac{1}{T_f}, \quad i = 1, \dots, N. \tag{1}$$

In general, our approach enables asymmetric traffic arrival patterns and different $p_i^{(b)}$ for the individual SSs. However, determining this probability for asymmetric system is more complicated. For the sake of simplicity, we consider only the symmetric model, i.e. at each SS the arrival rate of the uplink traffic is the same, λ_i. Similarly, $p_i^{(b)}$ is also the same for every SS.

3   Queueing Analysis

In this section, we detail a queueing model for the reservation and scheduling parts of the system. The statistical behavior of a SS is independent of that one for the other SSs, since each SS has an individual BS buffer and a separate data packet transmission period in the uplink sub-frame. Consequently, it is enough to model the behavior of the tagged SS separately from the rest of the system. Accordingly, we consider the system from the point of view of the tagged SS i.

We study the behavior of the tagged SS i at the embedded epochs, which are the end epochs of the first contention-based transmission opportunities in the RIs of the frames. In the queueing model, we assume that the BW-Req transmissions happen at the embedded epochs, i.e. in several cases somewhat earlier than in the real system, in which they happen at the end of the contention-based transmission opportunities. From the point of view of the queueing model, the "service start" of an i-packet is associated with an embedded epoch, in the frame preceding the one, in which that i-packet is transmitted. Such a "service start" of an i-packet is modeled by the event that the corresponding i-grant leaves the i-grant buffer of the BS, i.e. that i-grant is scheduled. The interval between the end epochs of the first contention-based transmission opportunities in the RIs in two consecutive frames is called a *cycle*.

By definition, the time instant of the successful BW-Req transmission from SS i is the *i-reservation event*. Similarly, by definition the instants of scheduling the BS grants in the BS grant buffer of SS i are the *i-scheduling events*. The positioning of the embedded epochs relatively to the corresponding *i-reservation* and *i-scheduling events* are shown in Figure 2.

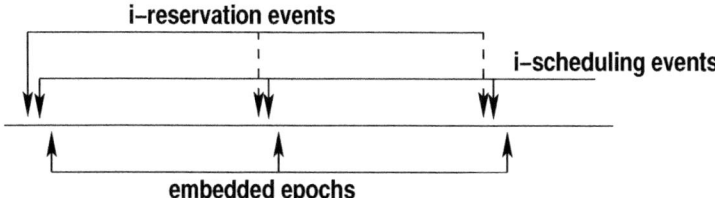

Fig. 2. Positions of the embedded epochs

The main assumption of the queueing analysis (see Assumption 1) is that the probability of the successful BW-Req transmission at SS i, given that this SS takes part in the contention process, $p_i^{(b)}$, is constant.

3.1   The Joint Content of the Outgoing and BS Grant Buffers of SS i at the Embedded Epochs

Let $q_i^{(r)}(\ell)$ be the number of i-packets in the outgoing buffer of SS i at the end of the first contention-based transmission opportunity in the RI in the ℓ-th frame for $\ell > 0$. Similarly, let $q_i^{(s)}(\ell)$ be the number of i-grants in the BS grant buffer of SS i at the end of the first contention-based transmission opportunity in the RI in the ℓ-th frame for $\ell > 0$. The sequence $\{(q_i^{(r)}(\ell), q_i^{(s)}(\ell)), \ell > 0\}$ is a bivariate homogeneous embedded Markov chain on the state space $(\{0, 1, \ldots\}, \{0, 1, \ldots\})$. We say that the chain is in state (j, k) when $q_i^{(r)}(\ell) = j$ and $q_i^{(s)}(\ell) = k$. Let $p_i(j, k, n, m)$ denote the probability of transition from state j, k to state n, m in this Markov chain, i.e.

$$p_i(j, k, n, m) = P\{q_i^{(r)}(\ell+1) = n, q_i^{(s)}(\ell+1) = m \mid q_i^{(r)}(\ell) = j, q_i^{(s)}(\ell) = k\},$$
$$\ell \geq 1, \quad j, k, n, m \geq 0. \tag{2}$$

Let us consider the transitions from state (j, k) to state (n, m) in the above defined Markov chain. The transition from state $(0, 0)$ to state $(0, 0)$ happens either if there are no i-packet arrivals during the actual cycle or there is exactly one i-packet arrival during a cycle and the BW-Req transmission at the end of that cycle is successful, i.e. the newly generated i-grant is immediately scheduled to be sent. Thus the probability of this transition is given as

$$p_i(0, 0, 0, 0) = e^{-\lambda_i T_f} + p_i^{(b)} \lambda_i T_f e^{-\lambda_i T_f}. \tag{3}$$

The transition from state $(0, 0)$ to $(n, 0)$ for $n \geq 1$ happens if there are n i-packet arrivals during a cycle and the BW-Req transmission at the end of that cycle is not successful. This leads to

$$p_i(0, 0, n, 0) = (1 - p_i^{(b)}) \frac{(\lambda_i T_f)^n}{n!} e^{-\lambda_i T_f}, \quad n \geq 1. \tag{4}$$

The transition from state $(0, k)$ to $(0, k-1)$ for $k \geq 1$ happens if there are no i-packet arrivals during the actual cycle. Thus we have

$$p_i(0, k, 0, k-1) = e^{-\lambda_i T_f}, \quad k \geq 1. \tag{5}$$

The transition from state $(0, k)$ to $(0, k)$ for $k \geq 1$ happens if there is exactly one i-packet arrival during a cycle and the BW-Req transmission at the end of that cycle is successful, i.e. the newly generated i-grant is immediately scheduled to be sent. This results in

$$p_i(0, k, 0, k) = p_i^{(b)} \lambda_i T_f e^{-\lambda_i T_f}, \quad k \geq 1. \tag{6}$$

The transition from state $(0, k)$ to $(0, m)$ for $k \geq 0$ and $m > k$ happens if there are exactly $m - k + 1$ i-packet arrivals during a cycle and the BW-Req transmission at the end of that cycle is successful. The corresponding transition probability is given as

$$p_i(0, k, 0, m) = p_i^{(b)} \frac{(\lambda_i T_f)^{m-k+1}}{(m - k + 1)!} e^{-\lambda_i T_f}, \quad k \geq 0, \ m > k. \tag{7}$$

The transition from state $(0, k)$ to $(n, k-1)$ for $n \geq 1$ and $k \geq 1$ happens if there are exactly n i-packet arrivals during a cycle and the BW-Req transmission at the end of that cycle is not successful. This leads to

$$p_i(0, k, n, k-1) = (1 - p_i^{(b)}) \frac{(\lambda_i T_f)^n}{n!} e^{-\lambda_i T_f}, \quad n, k \geq 1. \tag{8}$$

The transition from state $(1, 0)$ to $(0, 0)$ happens if there are no i-packet arrivals during the actual cycle and the BW-Req transmission at the end of that cycle is successful. Thus it results in

$$p_i(1, 0, 0, 0) = p_i^{(b)} e^{-\lambda_i T_f}. \tag{9}$$

The transition from state $(j, 0)$ to $(n, 0)$ for $j \geq 1$ and $n \geq j$ happens if there are exactly $n - j$ i-packet arrivals during a cycle and the BW-Req transmission at the end of that cycle is not successful. The corresponding transition probability is given as

$$p_i(j, 0, n, 0) = (1 - p_i^{(b)}) \frac{(\lambda_i T_f)^{n-j}}{(n - j)!} e^{-\lambda_i T_f}, \quad j \geq 1, \ n \geq j. \tag{10}$$

The transition from state $(1, k)$ to $(0, m)$ for $k = 0$, $m \geq 1$ or $k \geq 1$, $m \geq k$ happens if there are exactly $m - k$ i-packet arrivals during a cycle and the BW-Req transmission at the end of that cycle is successful. This yields

$$p_i(1, k, 0, m) = p_i^{(b)} \frac{(\lambda_i T_f)^{m-k}}{(m - k)!} e^{-\lambda_i T_f}, \quad k = 0, \ m \geq 1, \ \text{or} \ k \geq 1, \ m \geq k. \tag{11}$$

The transition from state (j, k) to $(0, m)$ for $j \geq 2$, $k \geq 0$ and $m \geq k + j - 1$ happens if there are exactly $m - k - j + 1$ i-packet arrivals during a cycle and the BW-Req transmission at the end of that cycle is successful. This leads to

$$p_i(j, k, 0, m) = p_i^{(b)} \frac{(\lambda_i T_f)^{m-k-j+1}}{(m - k - j + 1)!} e^{-\lambda_i T_f}, \quad j \geq 2, \ k \geq 0, \ m \geq k + j - 1. \tag{12}$$

Finally the transition from state (j, k) to $(n, k - 1)$ for $j \geq 1$, $k \geq 1$ and $n \geq j$ happens if there are exactly $n - j$ i-packet arrivals during a cycle and the BW-Req transmission at the end of that cycle is not successful. The corresponding transition probability is given as

$$p_i(j, k, n, k-1) = (1 - p_i^{(b)}) \frac{(\lambda_i T_f)^{n-j}}{(n - j)!} e^{-\lambda_i T_f}, \quad j \geq 1, \ k \geq 1, \ n \geq j. \tag{13}$$

Let $p_i^{(e)}(j, k)$ denote the equilibrium joint probability that the above Markov chain is in state j, k. To keep the computation of the joint probabilities tractable we apply an upper limit X_i both on the number of i-packets in the outgoing buffer of SS i and on the number of i-grants in the BS grant buffer of SS i, i.e. $j, k \leq X_i$. This results in finite number of equilibrium joint probabilities and transition probabilities and hence finite number of equilibrium equations. The proper value of X_i depends on the required precision and can be determined on iterative manner until the difference of consecutive values of probabilities $p_i^{(e)}(j, k)$, for every $j, k \leq X_i$, becomes less than the specified error. In the computation, the probabilities $p_i^{(e)}(j, k)$ for $j > X_i$ or $k > X_i$ are set 0, since they can be neglected.

Let $\mathbf{e}_j^{X_i+1} = (0, \ldots, 0, 1, 0, \ldots, 0)$ denote the $1 \times (X_i + 1)$ vector with 1 at the j-th position. Additionally, let $\otimes$ stand for the Kronecker product. We define the $1 \times (X_i + 1)^2$ vector $\boldsymbol{\theta}_i$ representing the equilibrium joint probabilities of the above Markov chain as

$$\boldsymbol{\theta}_i = \sum_{j=0}^{X_i} \sum_{k=0}^{X_i} p_i^{(e)}(j, k) \; \mathbf{e}_j^{X_i+1} \otimes \mathbf{e}_k^{X_i+1}. \tag{14}$$

We also define the $(X_i + 1)^2 \times (X_i + 1)^2$ matrix $\boldsymbol{\Pi}_i$ representing the transition probabilities of the embedded Markov chain as

$$\boldsymbol{\Pi}_i = \sum_{j=0}^{X_i} \sum_{k=0}^{X_i} \sum_{n=0}^{X_i} \sum_{m=0}^{X_i} p_i(j, k, n, m) \left(\mathbf{e}_j^{X_i+1} \otimes \mathbf{e}_k^{X_i+1} \right)^T \left(\mathbf{e}_n^{X_i+1} \otimes \mathbf{e}_m^{X_i+1} \right) \tag{15}$$

In the matrix $\boldsymbol{\Pi}_i$ the values of j, k and the values of n, m specify the row and the column indices of the corresponding transition probability $p_i(j, k, n, m)$.

The equilibrium joint probabilities of the embedded Markov chain can be uniquely determined from the following system of linear equations

$$\boldsymbol{\theta}_i \boldsymbol{\Pi}_i = \boldsymbol{\theta}_i, \quad \boldsymbol{\theta}_i \mathbf{e}^{(X_i+1)^2} = \sum_{j=0}^{X_i} \sum_{k=0}^{X_i} p_i^{(e)}(j, k) = 1, \tag{16}$$

where $\mathbf{e}^{(X_i+1)^2}$ denotes the $(X_i+1)^2 \times 1$ column vector having all elements equal to one.

The mean number of packets in the outgoing buffer of SS i at the end of the first contention-based transmission opportunity in the RI, $E[q_i^{(r)}]$, can be computed from the equilibrium joint distribution as

$$E[q_i^{(r)}] = \sum_{j=0}^{X_i} \sum_{k=0}^{X_i} j \; p_i^{(e)}(j, k). \tag{17}$$

Similarly, the mean number of i-grants in the BS grant buffer of SS i at the end of the first contention-based transmission opportunity in the RI, $E[q_i^{(s)}]$, can be computed also from the equilibrium joint distribution as

$$E[q_i^{(s)}] = \sum_{j=0}^{X_i} \sum_{k=0}^{X_i} k \; p_i^{(e)}(j, k). \tag{18}$$

3.2 The Mean of the Joint Content of the Outgoing and BS Grant Buffers of SS i At an Arbitrary Moment

Let q_i stand for the joint content of the outgoing and BS grant buffers of SS i at an arbitrary moment, i.e. the sum of the number of i-packets in the outgoing buffer of SS i and the number of i-grants in the BS grant buffer of SS i at an arbitrary moment.

The number of i-grants can change only just before the embedded observation epochs. This implies that the number of i-grants in the BS grant buffer of SS i at an arbitrary moment is the same as the one at the last embedded epoch.

The number of i-packets in the outgoing buffer of SS i at an arbitrary moment is the sum of the i-packets at the last embedded observation epoch and those, which arrive in the interval from the last embedded observation epoch to the arbitrary moment. This interval is the backward recurrence cycle time, whose mean length is $\frac{T_f}{2}$. Thus using (17) and (18), the mean number of i-packets in the outgoing buffer of SS i at an arbitrary moment can be expressed as

$$E[q_i] = \sum_{j=0}^{X_i}\sum_{k=0}^{X_i} j\, p_i^{(e)}(j,k) + \sum_{j=0}^{X_i}\sum_{k=0}^{X_i} k\, p_i^{(e)}(j,k) + \frac{\lambda_i T_f}{2}. \qquad (19)$$

4 Overall Delay Analysis

4.1 The Components of the Overall Delay

We define the *overall delay* (W_i) of the tagged i-packet as the time interval spent from its arrival into the outgoing buffer of SS i up to the end of its successful transmission in the UL. We define also the *grant time of the tagged i-packet* as the time of the i-scheduling event of its i-grant, i.e. the end epoch of the first contention-based transmission opportunity in the RI in the frame preceding the one, in which the tagged i-packet is transmitted. The *overall delay* is composed of several parts:

$$W_i = W_i^r + \nu + W_i^s + W_i^t + \tau. \qquad (20)$$

where the individual parts are defined as follows.

- W_i^r – reservation delay from the moment the i-packet arrives into the outgoing buffer of SS i to the start of the successful transmission of the corresponding BW-Req in the RI.
- ν – time of the successful BW-Req transmission, which equals the duration of the transmission opportunity.
- W_i^s – scheduling delay from the end of the successful BW-Req transmission of the tagged i-packet to its grant time.
- W_i^t – transmission delay from the grant time of the tagged i-packet to the start of its successful transmission in the next UL sub-frame
- τ – data packet transmission time.

4.2   Reservation and Scheduling Delays

The definition of the reservation delay implies that the reservation delay of the tagged i-packet is exactly the sojourn time of the tagged i-packet in the outgoing buffer of SS i. Similarly, it follows from the definition of the scheduling delay that it equals to the sojourn time of the i-grant assigned to the tagged i-packet in the BS grant buffer of SS i.

Consequently, the mean of the sum of the reservation and scheduling delays can be determined by applying Little's law on the mean number of joint content of the outgoing and BS grant buffers of SS i at an arbitrary moment. Using (19), this leads to

$$E\left[W_i^r + W_i^s\right] = \frac{1}{\lambda_i} \left(\sum_{j=0}^{X_i} \sum_{k=0}^{X_i} j \; p_i^{(e)}(j,k) + \sum_{j=0}^{X_i} \sum_{k=0}^{X_i} k \; p_i^{(e)}(j,k) \right) + \frac{T_f}{2}. \quad (21)$$

4.3   Transmission Delay

The transmission delay is a sum of the fixed time from the grant time of the tagged i-packet to the start of transmission of the i-packets in the next frame. Hence the mean transmission delay can be expressed as

$$E[W_i^t] = T_f + (K-1)\nu + (i-1)\tau. \quad (22)$$

4.4   Mean Overall Delay

Taking the mean of (20) and substituting the expressions (21) and (22), we obtain the expression of the mean overall delay as

$$E\left[W_i\right] = \frac{1}{\lambda_i} \left(\sum_{j=0}^{X_i} \sum_{k=0}^{X_i} j \; p_i^{(e)}(j,k) + \sum_{j=0}^{X_i} \sum_{k=0}^{X_i} k \; p_i^{(e)}(j,k) \right) + \frac{3T_f}{2} + i\tau + K\nu. \quad (23)$$

5   Numerical Results and Conclusion

In this section, we apply the derived analytical model to the performance evaluation of the uplink nrtPS packet service in the IEEE 802.16-2009 network [1] with contention-based reservation mechanism. We provide numerical examples to assess the performance of the IEEE 802.16 uplink nrtPS service flow evaluated with the considered analytical model. In order to generate performance data, a simulation program for IEEE 802.16-2009 MAC was developed. The program is an event-driven simulator that accounts for the discussed assumptions of the considered system model.

In our simulations, we set the default values recommended by WiMAX Forum [9] system evaluation methodology, which are also common values used in

Table 1. Basic evaluation parameters

Parameter	Value
PHY layer	OFDMA
Frame duration (T_f)	5 ms
Sub-channelization mode	PUSC
DL/UL ratio	2 : 1
Channel bandwidth	10 MHz
MCS	16 QAM $^3/_4$
Packet length	160 bytes
Number of SSs (N)	15
Total capacity per frame for all SSs 15 packets	

practice [10] (see Table 1). We assume a 10 MHz TDD system with 5 ms frame duration, PUSC sub-channelization mode and a DL : UL ratio of 2 : 1. In the numerical examples we use normalized arrival flow rate, in which the critical arrival rate that saturates the system is 1.

According to [11], the UL sub-frame comprises 175 slots. Assuming MCS of 16 QAM $^3/_4$, the IEEE 802.16-2009 system transmits 16 bytes per UL slot. We consider fixed packet length of 1600 bytes (10 slots) for all service flows, which results in capacity for sending 15 packets per UL sub-frame. The remaining 25 UL slots represent the necessary control overhead including exactly 1 contention-based transmission opportunity per RI to minimize the overhead (i.e. $K = 1$).

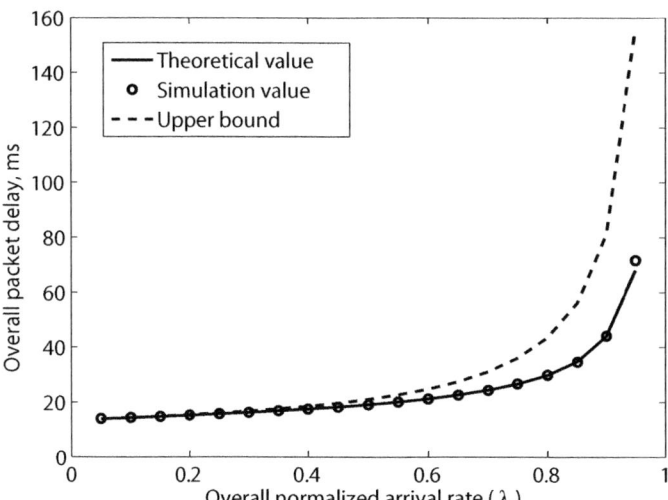

Fig. 3. Numerical results: overall delay vs. arrival rate

The determination of the probability of the successful BW-Req transmission $p_i^{(b)}$ for symmetric system can be found in our previous work [8].

In Figure 3 and Figure 4, we compare analytical and simulation results for the mean overall packet delay. In particular, in Figure 3 and in Figure 4 the dependency of the mean delay on the overall normalized arrival rate at fixed

$p_i^{(b)} = 0.5$ and on $p_i^{(b)}$ at fixed normalized $\lambda = 0.5$ can be seen, respectively. The presented analytical approach to the overall mean packet delay computation demonstrates excellent agreement with simulation data. Moreover, we also plot the closed-form analytical upper bound from [8] to conclude that the currently proposed analysis is much more precise in predicting the mean delay values.

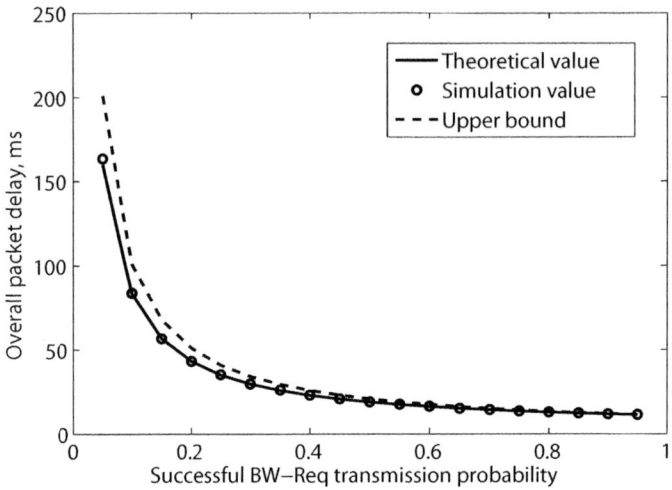

Fig. 4. Numerical results: overall delay vs. contention success probability

6   Final Remarks

It is our future work to use a public simulator to further verify the presented analytical approach also under real-world settings.

Furthermore, we notice that a potential perspective to continue this work is to investigate the determination of the probability of the successful BW-Req transmission $p_i^{(b)}$ also for the asymmetric system. It would enable the relaxation of the assumption on symmetric uplink traffic used in the numerical evaluation.

Acknowledgments. This work is supported by the Russian Foundation for Basic Research (projects #10-08-01071-a and #11-08-01016-a) as well as by the Branch of Nano- and Information Technologies of Russian Academy of Sciences (project 2.3).

References

1. IEEE 802.16-2009, Part 16: Air Interface for Broadband Wireless Access Systems, Standard for Local and Metropolitan Area Networks (May 2009)
2. Vinel, A., Zhang, Y., Ni, Q., Lyakhov, A.: Efficient request mechanism usage in IEEE 802.16. In: IEEE Global Telecomm. Conf., GLOBECOM (2006)
3. Vinel, A., Ni, Q., Staehle, D., Turlikov, A.: Capacity analysis of reservation-based random access for broadband wireless access networks. IEEE Journal on Selected Areas in Communications 27(2), 172–181 (2009)

4. Saffer, Z., Andreev, S., Koucheryavy, Y.: Performance evaluation of uplink delay-tolerant packet service in IEEE 802.16-based networks. EURASIP Journal on Wireless Communications and Networking 1, 1–12 (2011)
5. Redana, S., Lott, M.: Performance analysis of IEEE 802.16a in mesh operation mode. In: Proc. of the 13th IST SUMMIT, Lyon, France (June 2004)
6. Klein, A., Pries, R., Staehle, D.: Performance study of the WiMAX FDD mode. In: Proc. of the OPNETWORK 2006, Washington D.C. (August 2006)
7. Doha, A., Hassanein, H., Takahara, G.: Performance evaluation of reservation medium access control in IEEE 802.16 networks. In: IEEE International Conference on Computer Systems and Applications, pp. 369–374 (March 2006)
8. Andreev, S., Saffer, Z., Turlikov, A., Vinel, A.: Upper bound on overall delay in wireless broadband networks with non real-time traffic. In: Al-Begain, K., Fiems, D., Knottenbelt, W.J. (eds.) ASMTA 2010. LNCS, vol. 6148, pp. 262–276. Springer, Heidelberg (2010)
9. WiMAX Forum, home page, http://www.wimaxforum.org/
10. Sivchenko, D., Bayer, N., Xu, B., Rakocevic, V., Habermann, J.: Internet traffic performance in IEEE 802.16 networks. In: European Wireless Conf. (2006)
11. So-In, C., Jain, R., Tamimi, A.K.: Capacity evaluation for IEEE 802.16e mobile WiMAX. Journal of Computer Systems, Networks, and Communications 1, 1–12 (2010)

Non-saturated Analysis of the Contention-Based Access in WiMAX

Giovanni Giambene and Snezana Hadzic-Puzovic

University of Siena, Via Roma, 56, I-53100 Siena, Italy
giambene@unisi.it

Abstract. Broadband wireless communications are an important need. WiMAX is a technology that provides wireless connectivity. Even if this standard envisages several mechanisms for quality of service support, best effort traffic class is analyzed here since it still represents an important percentage of the traffic load. This is the reason why this paper provides an analytical study of the contention-based access scheme. In particular, an embedded Markov chain model is proposed to describe the system in non-saturated conditions. This approach permits to take into account the behavior of subscriber stations queues as well as the queues of transmission requests received at the BS. We also integrated in the model the round robin policy for the service of stations. The analytical model results have been compared with simulation results in terms of several quantities of the model. We expect that this approach can be used for the optimized selection of access parameters.

Keywords: WiMAX, MAC, non-Saturated Analysis.

1 Introduction

Today, the use of wireless systems is constantly growing. *Worldwide interoperability for wireless Microwave Access* (WiMAX) is a technology able to provide a broadband wireless access on the basis of the IEEE 802.16 standard. This paper focuses only on the point-to-multipoint mode, where the *Base Station* (BS) is responsible for bandwidth allocation in both downlink (BS to *Subscriber Stations*, SS's) and uplink (SS's to BS) directions. As for the *physical* (PHY) layer, we refer here to the WirelessMAN *Orthogonal Frequency Division Multiplexing* (OFDM) PHY air interface, which is defined in the IEEE 802.16d standard; in particular, we consider the *Time Division Duplexing* (TDD) case. This system is based on OFDM and uses a frequency band in the range from 2 to 11 GHz or from 10 to 66 GHz. The current standard version is IEEE 802.16-2009 [1].

The following combinations of modulation and coding are available: QPSK 1/2, QPSK 3/4, 16QAM 1/2, 16QAM 3/4, 64QAM 2/3, and 64QAM 3/4. The IEEE 802.16 standard envisages four service classes: *Unsolicited Grant Service* (UGS), *real-time Polling Service* (rtPS), *non-real-time Polling Service* (nrtPS), and *Best Effort* (BE) [2]. This paper deals with uplink traffic management for the *Best Effort* (BE) traffic class with contention-based access for SS's. In particular, our aim is to propose an analytical approach that is suitable to understand the impact of MAC parameters on protocol performance.

C. Sacchi et al. (Eds.): MACOM 2011, LNCS 6886, pp. 218–229, 2011.

The MAC protocol for WiMAX BE traffic class is based on the WiFi back-off algorithm. Hence, an analytical approach could be adopted that is similar to the Bianchi's work in [3] that refers to a *saturated* condition. This is actually the case in recent literature [4],[5],[6]. Saturated analysis [3] permits to capture the behavior of the protocol and to design the access parameters (window size, number of access resources, etc.) in the most critical situation. However, the saturated analysis could not be applied for the delay analysis since by definition it would entail an unstable queue (saturation means that the queue never becomes idle). This limit could be overcame by the study in non-saturated conditions, as done in [7] and [8]. This is the reason why we propose here a non-saturated analysis for the BE contention-based traffic of WiMAX with the aim to investigate the impact on the access protocol performance due to several MAC parameters. The non-saturated study has been carried out here by means of a more accurate model of the access scheme and considering the presence of both SS transmission queues and the queues of *Bandwidth REQuests* (BW-REQ's) at the BS.

2   Contention-Based Access in WiMAX

The BE traffic class has no specific quality of service requirements and is based on a contention-based access scheme for uplink. In particular, BW-REQ's are sent by SS's on a separated channel; then, the BS allocates resources to the correctly-received BW-REQ's by means of grants sent to SS's (UL-MAP signalling). The detailed description of the contention-based access is provided below.

The uplink sub-frame resources are divided among ranging, contention, and data. The contention phase is organized in *Transmission OPportunities* (TxOP's): there are K TxOP's per frame. On the basis of the settings of the NIST WiMAX simulator adopted in this paper [9], a BW-REQ burst is formed of a short preamble (1 OFDM symbol) plus a 6-byte *Generic MAC Header* (GMH) plus a trailer. This is slightly different with respect to the standard, where a BW-REQ is totally formed of 2 OFDM symbols.

The initial back-off window ($W_s = 2^s$) and the following values are selected by the BS and are communicated to the SS's via the UCD message. The window sizes are specified as a power of two; for example, the value $s = 4$ indicates an initial back-off window from 0 to 15.

As soon as an SS needs to send a BW-REQ (i.e., as soon as another packet needs to be serviced in the SS queue), it enters the contention phase. The access algorithm operates as follows: the SS will select a random number in the interval $[0, W_s - 1]$ that will be used to indicate the number of TxOP's that will be skipped in the contention phase. Then, the SS transmits the BW-REQ on a suitable transmission opportunity and waits for a given number of subsequent UL-MAP messages (on the basis of timer T_{16}) to receive a data transmission grant from the BS (if the BW-REQ has been received without collisions and has been satisfied). If timer T_{16} expires without an allocation, the SS doubles the back-off window (as long as it is less than the maximum value, $W_f = 2^f$) and repeats the contention procedure. This process continues until the maximum number of retries has been reached (request retries limit = 16). If this happens, the SS discards the packet.

The BW-REQ sent by the SS is cumulative for the whole contents of the SS transmission queue. BW-REQ queues are serviced by the BS according to a *Round Robin* (RR) service discipline, where the maximum resource that can be allocated to an SS (grant) corresponds to the uplink frame capacity. The scheduler tries first to allocate the whole uplink capacity of a frame for the service of an SS queue (the corresponding resource is here called a 'block', i.e., the allocation of a fragment for the whole uplink data traffic capacity); if the information data to be allocated to an SS is lower than a block, more than one SS can be scheduled in a frame (each of them receives the allocation of less than a 'block').

The bigger the K value, the lower the risk of collisions, but the lower the resources for data traffic, thus increasing the transmission delay. This is an interesting trade-off to be investigated. A too high T_{16} value could cause too delay to react to collisions. On the other hand, if T_{16} is too small (the minimum T_{16} value is 10 ms), useless reattempts would be triggered for requests successfully-received at the BS, but not yet served due to the congestion of uplink resources (service delay).

3   Literature Survey

In this Section, we survey the most relevant analytical approaches to study the contention-based access of WiMAX, considering both saturated and non-saturated studies in order to highlight the original contribution of this paper.

The authors of [4] developed an analytical model based on the Markov chain proposed for IEEE 802.11 [3], and adapted it for the IEEE 802.16 case. The model contains two types of states: back-off states and waiting states. The first set of states represents the contention, while the second models the SS waiting for a bandwidth allocation after a successful/unsuccessful BW-REQ transmission. The probability that the BS will provide a grant to a successfully-transmitted BW-REQ in each waiting state has a constant value, q, depending on *Call Admission Control* (CAC) decisions. Moreover, the impact of timer T_{16} is investigated. This model is practically applied to the saturated case. The average access delay is derived. Finally, capacity maximization is studied proposing to adjust dynamically the contention parameters.

In [5], the authors defined an analytic approach for fixed WiMAX, based on the classical Markov model used for IEEE 802.11 [3]. The effect of timer T_{16} is approximated by a set of idle states. It is assumed that successfully-received BW-REQ's are allocated in the following frame, while unsuccessful BW-REQ's entail to wait for T_{16} expiration. The authors propose an optimization method to determine the number of TxOP's depending on the number of SS's. This analytical approach is interesting even if it is over-simplified since not all the successful BW-REQ's can be allocated in the next frame; everything depends on the congestion of transmission resources.

In [6], the authors developed a fixed-point model for the analysis of BW-REQ failure probability for the contention-based access of WiMAX. It is considered that failure could be due to either collision or resource congestion and an accurate analytical model is proposed for evaluating throughput and packet access delay in saturated conditions. It is also shown that the initial contention window value could be selected to maximize the throughput.

The authors of paper [7] propose a Markov model considering various traffic and channel conditions. BW-REQ failure is here due to either collision or error caused by channel noise, but resource congestion (i.e., T_{16} expiration) is not taken into account. In order to model non-saturated conditions, a set of additional waiting states is added to account for the wait of a new arrival and the right synchronism of next TxOP's. A certain probability is used to model the transition to leave the waiting states and to enter the back-off phase; this is the probability of at least one Poisson arrival (of BW-REQ) in the mean access delay to service a BW-REQ. A grouping scheme is here investigated to reduce the number of SS's that contend each time. Performance analysis is carried out in terms of mean access delay and throughput showing a significant impact of channel errors. However, the behavior of SS queues and T_{16} are not modeled.

In [8], the authors adopt an analytical approach for two types of bandwidth allocation mechanisms (i.e., contention-based and unicast polling) in non-saturated conditions. The authors propose two scheduling algorithms for the BS: the first one aims to maximize the bandwidth utilization (i.e., using the minimum number of resources for both types of bandwidth request mechanisms) under a maximum delay constraint; the second one aims to minimize the delay for a given bandwidth utilization.

The original contribution of this paper for the study of the contention-based access in WiMAX is as follows: (*i*) novel non-saturated analysis; (*ii*) account for the behavior of both SS queues and the BW-REQ queues at the BS; (*iii*) impact of T_{16} on access behavior. At the best of our knowledge, these major characteristics are not covered together in current literature.

4   Analysis

Let us consider that the network model used for studying the contention-based access is only composed of one BS and N SS's. We adopt the following study assumptions:

– Each SS has just one best-effort data connection.
– No piggy-backing is used: an SS during a contention (or transmission) phase cannot generate another BW-REQ.
– A BW-REQ is unsuccessful due to either a collision event or resource congestion (i.e., there is no allocation within T_{16}).
– In the analysis, we consider that infinite BW-REQ transmission attempts can be made for the transmission of a packet.
– For the BW-REQ contention phase study, we consider two types of queues in the system at MAC layer: there are the SS's queues, where packets arrive according to a Poisson process with mean rate λ/N per SS, while on the BS side there are queues that contain all successfully-received BW-REQ's for each SS (at most one BW-REQ per SS). We use the following idle queue probabilities: P_0^* for the SS queues and P_0 for the BW-REQ queues on the BS side.
– Packet collision probability p is constant and independent of the state. This is an approximation for the non-saturated case [10].
– In our simulator, BW-REQ's are aggregated and made for all the packets in the SS queue (this is mandatory according to the IEEE 802.16 standard); in the theory, a BW-REQ is sent for each packet fragment.
– All the SS's belong to the same modulation and coding class.

- For each new arrival we consider here that a single block is generated (a further study is needed to generalize such assumption to a generic message length).
- In the theory we do not consider that when T_{16} expires for a given BW-REQ the request still remains in the BW-REQ queue at the BS and is serviced according to the RR cycle.

A generic SS is modeled by a Markov chain embedded to the end of TxOP intervals as shown in Figure 1, where m denotes a generic stage starting from that with index $i = f - s + 1$. Note that the n_f states ($T_{16} = n_f \times T_{frame}$) of squared shape in the shaded box (as well as the corresponding ones on the other rows of the state diagram) model the time spent (in TxOP units) waiting for a grant assignment. Note that the following constraints is valid for n_f: $1 \leq n_f \leq N$ (in the service of BW-REQ queues, if we have N users it does not provide any advantage to have $n_f > N$). Each state of square shape corresponds to K states, where K denoted the number of TxOP's per frame; one TxOP can convey one BW-REQ.

After a successful packet transmission, an SS re-enters the back-off phase only if its queue is not empty with probability $1 - P_0^*$ (note that in the saturated study, an SS always has a new packet ready to be sent), otherwise the SS will wait for a new packet to arrive in the idle states (denoted as $(-1, j)$, $j \in [0, K-1]$ and encircled by an ellipse in Figure 1). An SS leaves the idle states and enters the first row of the back-off phase with the probability of at leat one Poisson arrival in the SS queue in T_{frame}:

$$P_r = 1 - e^{-\frac{\lambda}{N} T_{frame}}. \tag{1}$$

A BW-REQ could be unsuccessful due to collision or lack of allocated resources in time; this occurs with probability p_f, as follows:

$$p_f = p + (1 - p) \left(1 - \sum_{i=1}^{n_f} q_i\right), \tag{2}$$

where each probability q_i is defined as:

$$q_i = Prob. \{grant\ received\ in\ (i - 1)T_{frame}\ to\ iT_{frame}\}. \tag{3}$$

Probabilities q_i are related to the service of BW-REQ queues at the BS. These queues are complex to be investigated since they are serviced according to an RR scheme, thus entailing a certain degree of correlation among them [11]. q_i values are computed considering as a first approximation that the BW-REQ queues are idle with probability P_0 independently of each other, so that when an SS BW-REQ is received it is in the generic position of the RR cycle (all the positions have the same probability to occur equal to $1/N$) and that the BW-REQ's of the other SS's in front of it could be present or not depending on probability P_0 (binomial-type distribution). q_i values do not depend on the 'row' of the Markov chain modeling the access since they are not related to the back-off phase level, but rather to the service of BW-REQ's at the BS. Note that if $n_f \geq N$, T_{16} never expires for a successful BW-REQ and $\sum_{i=1}^{n_f} q_i = 1$ (otherwise this sum of q_i is lower than 1 and timer T_{16} could expire especially for higher-traffic load conditions).

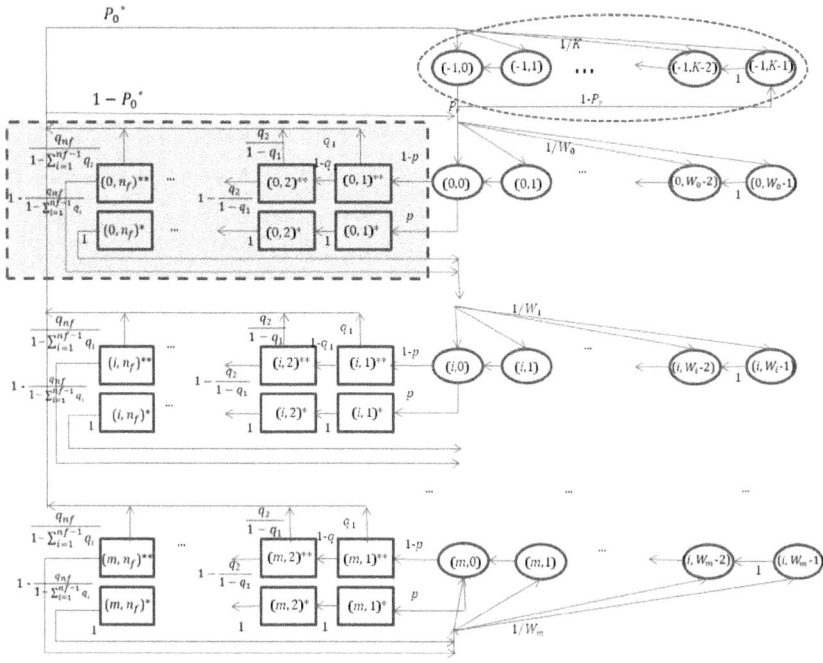

Fig. 1. Markov chain model for an SS with contention-based access (BE class)

After the BW-REQ transmission, the SS will wait for a fixed number of subsequent (frames) to receive a grant from the BS. This waiting period is specified by timer T_{16}, also know as *contention-based reservation timeout*. There are two cases in which the SS does not receive the response from the BS: either BW-REQ collided with another request by an SS, or the BS is unable to provide a grant in time (i.e., congestion of resources). Hence, the waiting phase is divided in two parts: the collision sub-chain – denoted with $(i,j)^*$ states in Figure 1, and the non-collision sub-chain – denoted with $(i,j)^{**}$ states; here j denotes the number of frames measured as number of corresponding TxOP's spent waiting for an allocation. When T_{16} expires, the SS will either move to the idle phase (with probability P_0^*) or will re-enter the back-off phase to transmit another packet in its queue (with probability $1 - P_0^*$) selecting a uniform random number within the minimum back-off window. Figure 2 below describes the study input, the parameters, and the approximations made; we also show important relations between input conditions and study assumptions and approximations. In particular, the adoption of the RR service discipline has impact on the derivation of P_0 and q_i. Moreover, the transmission mode has impact on the packet length and in turn this influences the RR service and then P_0 and q_i.

Our model takes into account the sharing of resources among SS's in both the contention phase and the sub-sequent transmission phase with two queuing levels: there are queues on the SS side for the transmission of data on the basis of grants and there are queues on the BS side for the BW-REQ's that are received by the SS's and need to be serviced with resource allocations. It is important to remark that the originality of the analytical approach proposed in this paper stands in the non-saturated study that requires the use of probabilities P_0^*, P_0, P_r, and the consideration of the impact of timer T_{16} on the service of BW-REQ's and the related use of probabilities q_i.

From Figure 1 we can write probability equilibrium conditions for each state. Then, we sum equilibrium equations along rows. We obtain:

$$(1 - p_f)P_0^* \sum_{i=0}^{m} b(i,0) + (1 - P_r)b(-1,0) = b(-1,0) \rightarrow b(0,0)P_0^* = P_r b(-1,0)$$
$$b(i,0) = b(i-1,0)p_f \rightarrow b(i,0) = b(0,0)p_f^i, \ 0 < i < m$$
$$[b(m,0) + b(m-1,0)] \, p_f = b(m,0) \rightarrow \frac{p_f^m}{1-p_f} b(0,0) = b(m,0).$$

$$(4)$$

To define all back-off states, the following equations are used:

$$b(i,j) = \frac{W_i - j}{W_i} \begin{cases} (1 - p_f) \sum_{k=0}^{m} b(k,0), \ i = 0 \\ p_f b(i-1,0), \ i \in (0,m) \\ [b(m,0) + b(m-1,0)]p_f, \ i = m. \end{cases}$$

$$(5)$$

By imposing the normalization of the sum of state probabilities we obtain the following formula for $b(0,0)$:

$$b(0,0) = \frac{1}{\left[\frac{1}{2(1-p_f)} + W_s \frac{1-(2p_f)^{f-s+1}}{2-4p_f} + W_s 2^{f-s} \frac{p_f^{f-s+1}}{2(1-p_f)} + M \right]},$$

$$(6)$$

where

$$M = \frac{(1-K)P_0^*}{2} + \frac{KP_0^*}{P_r} + \frac{pn_f K}{1-p_f} + \frac{(1-p)K \left[n_f \left(1 - \sum_{j=1}^{n_f-1} q_j \right) + \sum_{j=1}^{n_f-1} jq_j \right]}{1-p_f}.$$

$$(7)$$

The probability that an SS transmits a BW-REQ in a randomly-chosen TxOP is:

$$\tau = \sum_{i=0}^{m} b(i,0) = \frac{b(0,0)}{1-p_f}.$$

$$(8)$$

A collision will occur with the probability p that at least two SS's are transmitting a BW-REQ in the same TxOP; p can be derived as:

$$p = 1 - (1 - \tau)^{N-1}.$$

$$(9)$$

The mean packet transmission delay (access delay), T_{pkt}, can be expressed as:

$$T_{pkt} = \left[T_1 + T_2 + \frac{n_f p_f}{1-p_f} + \frac{\sum_{i=1}^{n_f} iq_i}{\sum_{i=1}^{n_f} q_i} \right] T_{frame},$$

$$(10)$$

where

$$T_1 = \sum_{i=1}^{f-s+1} p_f^{i-1}(1-p_f) \left[\sum_{j=1}^{i} \frac{2^{j-1}W_s - 1}{2K} \right]$$

$$(11)$$

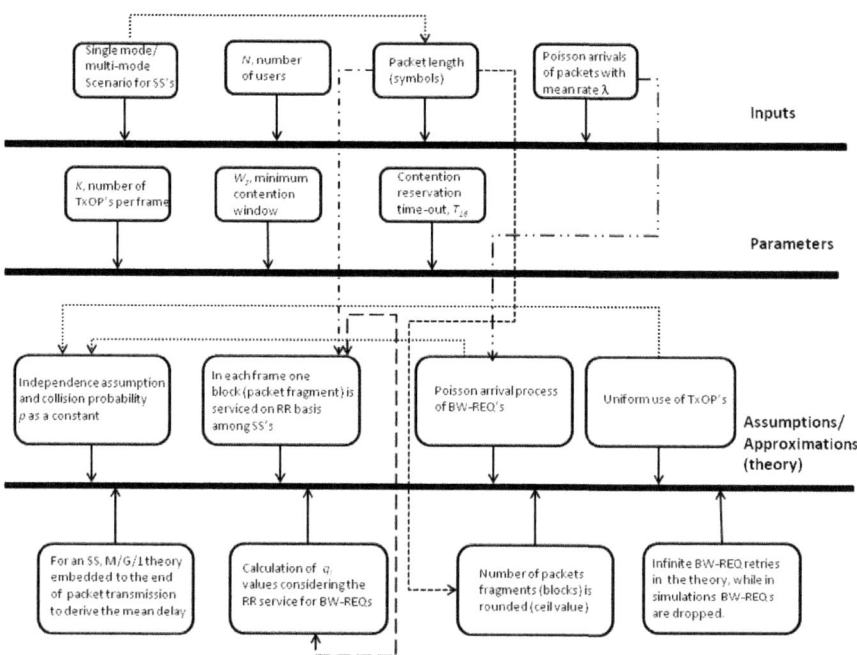

Fig. 2. Block diagram and interactions of our theoretical study considering, inputs, parameters, and assumptions/approximations

$$T_2 = \sum_{i=f-s+2}^{\infty} p_f^{i-1}(1-p_f) \left[\sum_{j=1}^{f-s+1} \frac{2^{j-1}W_s - 1}{2K} + (i - f + s - 1) \times \frac{2^{f-s}W_s - 1}{2K} \right]. \tag{12}$$

Note that the term T_1 in T_{pkt} accounts for the time spent with the contention attempts from 1 to $f - s + 1$; the term T_2 models the time spent with the contention attempts from $f - s$ up to infinity (with a fixed back-off window size equal to the maximum); the term depending on the q_i values accounts for the mean service delay for a BW-REQ that is serviced within the deadline T_{16}.

The idle probability for the SS transmission queue, P_0^*, can be determined by means of the idle condition for a generic single-server queue:

$$P_0^* = 1 - \frac{\lambda}{N} T_{pkt}, \tag{13}$$

where T_{pkt} is given by (10) and where λ/N denotes the mean packet arrival rate to the queue of an SS.

Finally, probability P_0 (empty queue probability of the BW-REQ queues at the BS) can be expressed in terms of the state probabilities of the Markov chain in Figure 1: P_0 is given by the sum of all the state probabilities of the chain excepts those related to the q_i branches where we have a BW-REQ in the queue at the BS. Hence, P_0 can be obtained considering that BW-REQ queues are not empty only in waiting states $(i, j)^{**}$:

$$P_0 = 1 - b(0,0) \frac{(1-p)K \left[n_f \left(1 - \sum_{j=1}^{n_f-1} q_j \right) + \sum_{j=1}^{n_f-1} j q_j \right]}{1 - p_f}. \qquad (14)$$

Note that $P_0^* < P_0$ because an idle SS queue entails an idle idle BW-REQ queue, but an SS can be non-empty with an idle BW-REQ queue due to collisions that delay the arrival of the BW-REQ at the BS.

We have thus obtained a non-linear system with four equations (8), (9), (13), and (14) in the unknown terms p, τ, P_0^*, and P_0 that can be solved by means of an iterative method supported by Matlab with starting point $p = 0$, $\tau = 1$, $P_0^* = 0.8$, and $P_0 = 0.8$. We can see that this model characterizes both the SS queues (by means of P_0^* and T_{pkt}) and the BW-REQ queues (by means of parameters P_0 and q_i). We have adopted a graphical approach (not described in this paper) to verify that the iterative method allows a single solution.

The stability condition for the generic SS queue is $\frac{\lambda}{N} T_{pkt} < 1$ Erl. The complexity here is that $T_{pkt} = T_{pkt}(\lambda)$. Of course, the global system admits an M/G/1-like model with stability limit $\lambda T_{frame} < 1$ Erl (we consider the total arrival process with mean rate λ and the block service time of T_{frame}); the global system has, however, server vacations.

These considerations permit to understand that an M/G/1-type queuing model could be adopted to characterize the delay performance of an SS. Here, the mean service time (i.e., T_{pkt}) of a packet includes the mean access delay (to send successfully a BW-REQ) and the mean service time according to the RR cycle and the related BW-REQ queues at the BS. Further details on these aspects are beyond the scope of this paper and will be the subject of further work.

5   Results

A WiMAX simulator has been used based on the WiMAX NIST model [9] for ns-2 [12]. The simulator settings are described in Table 1. In the simulator no piggybacking is used and BW-REQ's are of the aggregated type.

Table 1. Simulation parameter values (3.5T1 WiMAX profile @ 3.5 GHz)

Parameter	value
DL/UL ratio of the TDD frame	0.3/0.7
Frame duration, T_{frame}	5 ms
Channel bandwidth, BW	7 MHz
Receive/Transmit gap	20 physical slots
Cyclic prefix, $G = T_g/T_u$	0.25
Queue length of each SS	1500 packets
DCD/UCD interval	10 s
Sampling factor for 7 MHz BW, s_f	8/7

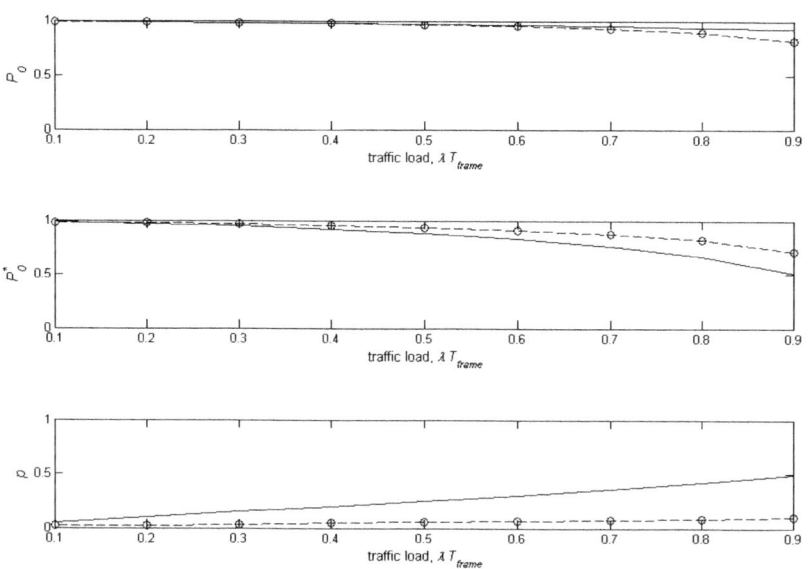

Fig. 3. Comparisons between theory (*solid lines*) and simulations (*dashed lines with circle marker*) as a function of λT_{frame}

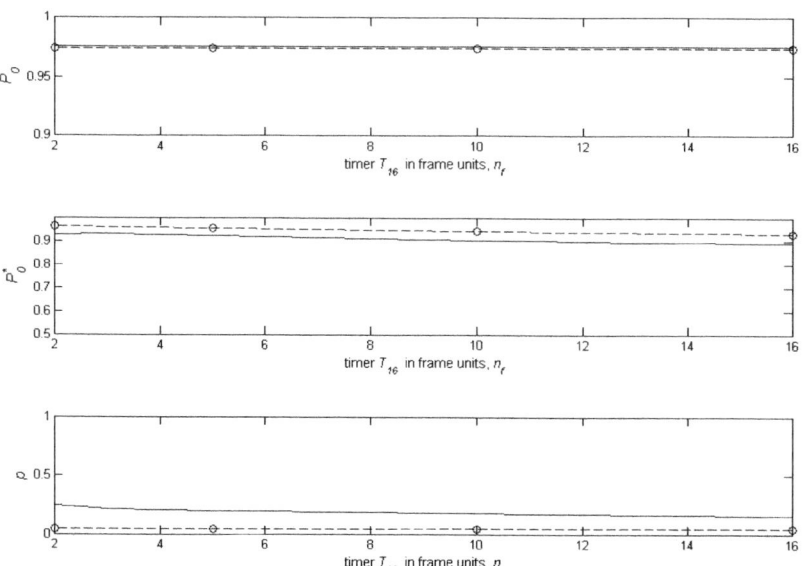

Fig. 4. Comparisons between theory (*solid lines*) and simulations (*dashed lines with circle marker*) as a function of T_{16}

With our settings, $K = 3$ TxOP's need 5 OFDM symbols for the contention phase, while 67 OFDM symbols are available for data traffic in uplink. The following Figure 3 describes the comparison between theoretical results and simulations for the following configuration of typical parameters: $N = 20$ SS's, $s = 2$ exponent of the initial window, $K = 3$ TxOP's, and $T_{16} = 25$ ms ($n_f = 5$). We note that p increases with the traffic load since collisions increase; correspondingly, P_0 decreases (there are more BW-REQ's to be serviced at the BS). Moreover, P_0^* decreases with the traffic load because SS queues are more congested, as we can deduce from equation (13). We can see that even if there is a certain degree of approximation, theoretical results follow simulations ones, especially for P_0 and P_0^*. The approximation increases with the input traffic load due to the following reasons: (*i*) queues are more correlated each other due to the RR discipline (in the theory, BW-REQ queues are considered to be independent each other); (*ii*) the arrival process of BW-REQ's is not exactly Poisson as the traffic load increases. Probability p is more sensitive to these approximations.

Finally, Figure 4 shows theoretical and simulations results as a function of T_{16} for $N = 20$ SS's, $s = 2$, $K = 3$ TxOP's, and $\lambda T_{frame} = 0.4$. Also this graph highlights a good agreement between theory and simulations.

6   Conclusions

Focusing on the point-to-multipoint mode of WiMAX, where the BS decides about resource allocations in both uplink and downlink, this paper proposes an analytical approach for contention-based access (BE class) that is more refined than current literature combining non-saturated approach, the consideration of timer T_{16}, and the model of MAC queues at both SS's and BS sides. Preliminary results have been shown that permit to appreciate the proposed analytical model as compared to simulation results.

A further study is needed to include the analysis of the SS queues according to an M/G/1 model, where the service statistics depends on the contention-based scheme analyzed in this paper. Moreover, work will be needed to extend this study to a multi-mode case. Finally, an optimization could be carried out for the parameters of this model and also applied in a scenario with more realistic traffic conditions (e.g., TCP-based elephant connections).

References

1. IEEE. IEEE Standard for Local and metropolitan area networks Part 16: Air Interface for Broadband Wireless Access Systems. (IEEE Std 802.16^{TM}-2009), New York, USA (May 29, 2009)
2. Nuaymi, L.: WiMAX: Technology for Broadband Wireless Access. John Wiley and Sons, Chichester (2007)
3. Bianchi, G.: Performance Analysis of the IEEE 802.11 Distributed Coordination Function. IEEE Journal Sel. Areas. in Comms. 18(3), 535–547 (2000)
4. Pourmohammadi, Y., Agharebparast, F., Minhas, M.R., Alnuweiri, H.M., Leung, V.C.M.: Analytical Modeling of Contention-Based Bandwidth Request Mechanism in IEEE 802.16 Wireless Networks. IEEE Transactions on Vehicular Technology 57(5), 3094–3107 (2008)

5. Perera, S., Sirisena, H.: Analysis of Contention Based Access for Best Effort Traffic on Fixed WiMAX. In: Proc. of the Fourth International Conference on Broadband Communications, Networks and Systems (IEEE BROADNETS 2007), Raleigh, NC, USA, September 10-14, pp. 552–558 (2007)
6. Vu, H.L., Chan, S., Andrew, L.: Performance Analysis of Best-Effort Service in Saturated IEEE 802.16 Networks. IEEE Transactions on Vehicular Technology 59(1), 460–472 (2010)
7. Ni, Q., Hu, L., Vinel, A., Xiao, Y., Hadjinicolaou, M.: Performance Analysis of Contention Based Bandwidth Request Mechanism in WiMAX Networks. IEEE Systems Journal 4(4), 477–486 (2010)
8. Chuck, D., Chen, K., Chang, J.M.: A Comprehensive Analysis of Bandwidth Request Mechanisms in IEEE 802.16 Networks. IEEE Trans. Veh. Technol. 59(4), 2046–2056 (2010)
9. NIST Web site with, http://www.antd.nist.gov/seamlessandsecure.shtml
10. Huang, K.D., Duffy, K.R., Malone, D.: On the Validity of IEEE 802.11 MAC Modeling Hypotheses. IEEE/ACM Transactions on Networking 18(6), 1935–1948 (2010)
11. Kleinrock, L.: Queuing Systems, vol. II. Wiley, New York (1976)
12. NS-2 Network Simulator (Vers. 2.29),
http://www.isi.edu/nsnam/ns/ns-build.html

A Two-Priority Queueing System with Trunk Reservation, Infinite Capacity Buffers for Customers of Both Priorities, and Different Service Intensities for High-Priority and Non-priority Customers

Carmine De Nicola[1], Rosanna Manzo[1],
Alexander Pechinkin[2], and Sergey Shorgin[2]

[1] Dipartimento di Ingegneria Elettronica e Ingegneria
Informatica, University of Salerno,
Via Ponte don Melillo, 84084 Fisciano (SA), Italy
denicola@diima.unisa.it, rmanzo@unisa.it
[2] Institute of Informatics Problems, Russian Academy of Sciences,
Vavilova str. 44, building 2, 119333 Moscow, Russia
{apechinkin,sshorgin}@ipiran.ru
http://www.ipiran.ru

Abstract. A two-priority queueing system with trunk reservation, Poisson input flows of both priorities customers, infinite buffers and different exponential distributions of both priorities customers service times is considered. Trunk reservation means that there are some channels which can be used only by customers of high priority. Analytic relations to calculate the main stationary distributions of both priorities customers quantities are obtained.

Keywords: Queueing system, relative priority, trunk reservation.

1 Introduction

In modern information and communication systems with large number and volume of information flows, it often happens that customers of different priorities are serviced by channels of the same group (trunk). In the case, as a rule, high priority customers should be serviced with higher quality (depending on the system type, quality can be measured by customer loss probability, or average delay time, or other similar characteristic), and interruption of service even for less priority customers is not permitted. It is obvious that, in this case, full accessibility of channels (even in the case when customers are serviced from the queue taking into account the customer priority) may unfairly increase quality of service for low-priority customers.

To avoid this situation the simple method called System with Trunk Reservation (STR) can be used. According to this method, a threshold n_i is

C. Sacchi et al. (Eds.): MACOM 2011, LNCS 6886, pp. 230–240, 2011.

assigned to the customers of i-th priority, and these customers are accepted for service only if the number of busy channels is less than n_i.

Probably, the first to describe STR was P. J. Burke (Bell Company, USA) in 1961 for service of a two-priority trunk. Afterwards it has been used in a number of communication systems, in particular in RITA system (France) [1, 2]. In its original form (without queues) this system had been applied in the development of flows dynamic control methods with loading restriction in networks with circuit switching. For example, it was proposed in [3, 4] to reserve certain channels in such way that the transmission of the low-priority messages via the reserved channels will not be permitted. In [5] a refined dynamic strategy had been presented: instead of specific channels reservation, for each direction of transmission some quantity of channels is reserved. This modification of STR is considered in the present article.

Researches of STR have been accomplished along with its practical implementation (see [1, 6–11]). In particular, in [10] a method of STR evaluation with an arbitrary number of priorities, Poisson input flows and identical exponential service of all priorities customers had been proposed. On the base of this technique, in [11] easily implementable algorithms which allow to calculate the main stationary characteristics of a two-priority STR with a Markov input flow and identical exponential service of all priorities customers were developed. At last, in [12] a two priority STR with a Markov input flow, phase distributions of different priorities customers service times (with different parameters of these distributions), and finite buffers for high-priority and low-priority customers had been investigated. In the present paper, analytical relations are obtained allowing to calculate stationary distributions of both priorities customers numbers in a two-priority system with trunk reservation, Poisson input flows of both priorities customers, infinite buffers and exponential distributions of service times of both priorities customers with different parameters.

2   The System Description

We consider a queueing system with two independent input Poisson flows of two type customers. The flows have intensities λ_u, $u = 1, 2$. Service times of each type customers are exponentially distributed with parameters μ_u, $u = 1, 2$. We introduce the notation $\lambda = \lambda_1 + \lambda_2$.

There are n^* servers in the system. However the second type customers (low-priority) are admitted for service only in the case when the number of busy servers is less than $n_0 < n^*$; they are allocated in the queue of low-priority customers which has an infinite capacity. Customers of the first type (high-priority) are serviced if at least one free server is available, otherwise they join the customers in the infinite queue of high-priority customers. Interruption of service of any type customers is not permitted.

Let us assume that the stationary mode of this system functioning exists. The necessary condition of stationary distribution existence is $\lambda_1/(n^* \mu_1) < 1$, a simple sufficient condition is $\lambda_1/\mu_1 + \lambda_2/\mu_2 < n_0$. We do not cite here the necessary and sufficient condition which may be derived in the following way. A new system should be considered, similar to the initial one, but with an infinite number of low-priority customers in the low-priority queue. The stationary mode of the initial system exists iff the mean quantity of low-priority customers passing for a time unit in the new system from low-priority queue to servers is greater than input flow intensity λ_2 in the initial system.

Further in the paper the relations allowing to calculate stationary distributions of high-priority and low-priority customers quantities in the system will be obtained.

3 Auxiliary Matrices

We say that the customers arrival/service process is in the layer n if the total quantity of customers at the servers and in high-priority queue is equal to n, $n \geq 0$.

Let us select in the n-th layer $n + 1$ states (phases) of the arrival/service process as $n = \overline{0, n_0}$, and $n_0 + 1$ phases as $n > n_0$. Numbers of phases change from 0 to n or from 0 to n_0. The phase number is equal to the quantity of low-priority customers at servers.

Introduce the matrices $\Lambda_n^{(u)}$, $n \geq 0$, $u = 1, 2$, M_n, $n \geq 1$, N_n, $n \geq 0$, and Ω which determine customers arrival and service process.

The matrices $\Lambda_n^{(1)}$ and $\Lambda_n^{(2)}$ have sizes equal to $(n+1) \times (n+2)$ for $n = \overline{0, n_0 - 1}$ and $(n_0 + 1) \times (n_0 + 1)$ for $n \geq n_0$:

$$\Lambda_n^{(1)} = \begin{pmatrix} \lambda_1 & 0 & 0 & \cdots & 0 & 0 & 0 \\ 0 & \lambda_1 & 0 & \cdots & 0 & 0 & 0 \\ 0 & 0 & \lambda_1 & \cdots & 0 & 0 & 0 \\ \vdots & \vdots & \vdots & \ddots & \vdots & \vdots & \vdots \\ 0 & 0 & 0 & \cdots & \lambda_1 & 0 & 0 \\ 0 & 0 & 0 & \cdots & 0 & \lambda_1 & 0 \end{pmatrix}, \quad n = \overline{0, n_0 - 1};$$

$$\Lambda_n^{(1)} = \Lambda^{(1)} = \lambda_1 E, \quad n \geq n_0;$$

$$\Lambda_n^{(2)} = \begin{pmatrix} 0 & \lambda_2 & 0 & 0 & \cdots & 0 & 0 \\ 0 & 0 & \lambda_2 & 0 & \cdots & 0 & 0 \\ 0 & 0 & 0 & \lambda_2 & \cdots & 0 & 0 \\ \vdots & \vdots & \vdots & \vdots & \ddots & \vdots & \vdots \\ 0 & 0 & 0 & 0 & \cdots & \lambda_2 & 0 \\ 0 & 0 & 0 & 0 & \cdots & 0 & \lambda_2 \end{pmatrix}, \quad n = \overline{0, n_0 - 1};$$

$$\Lambda_n^{(2)} = \Lambda^{(2)} = \lambda_2 E, \quad n \geq n_0.$$

The sizes of the matrices M_n are equal to $(n+1) \times n$ for $n = \overline{1, n_0}$ and $(n_0 + 1) \times (n_0 + 1)$ for $n > n_0$:

$$
M_n = \begin{pmatrix}
n\mu_1 & 0 & 0 & \cdots & 0 & 0 \\
\mu_2 & (n-1)\mu_1 & 0 & \cdots & 0 & 0 \\
0 & 2\mu_2 & (n-2)\mu_1 & \cdots & 0 & 0 \\
0 & 0 & 3\mu_2 & \cdots & 0 & 0 \\
\vdots & \vdots & \vdots & \ddots & \vdots & \vdots \\
0 & 0 & 0 & \cdots & (n-1)\mu_2 & \mu_1 \\
0 & 0 & 0 & \cdots & 0 & n\mu_2
\end{pmatrix}, \quad n = \overline{1, n_0};
$$

$$
M_n = \begin{pmatrix}
n\mu_1 & 0 & \cdots & 0 & 0 & 0 \\
\mu_2 & (n-1)\mu_1 & \cdots & 0 & 0 & 0 \\
0 & 2\mu_2 & \cdots & 0 & 0 & 0 \\
\vdots & \vdots & \ddots & \vdots & \vdots & \vdots \\
0 & 0 & \cdots & (n_0-1)\mu_2 & (n-n_0+1)\mu_1 & 0 \\
0 & 0 & \cdots & 0 & n_0\mu_2 & (n-n_0)\mu_1
\end{pmatrix}, \quad n = \overline{n_0+1, n^*-1};
$$

$$
M_n = M = \begin{pmatrix}
n^*\mu_1 & 0 & \cdots & 0 & 0 & 0 \\
\mu_2 & (n^*-1)\mu_1 & \cdots & 0 & 0 & 0 \\
0 & 2\mu_2 & \cdots & 0 & 0 & 0 \\
\vdots & \vdots & \ddots & \vdots & \vdots & \vdots \\
0 & 0 & \cdots & (n_0-1)\mu_2 & (n^*-n_0+1)\mu_1 & 0 \\
0 & 0 & \cdots & 0 & n_0\mu_2 & (n^*-n_0)\mu_1
\end{pmatrix}, \quad n \geq n^*.
$$

The sizes of the matrices N_n are equal to $(n+1) \times (n+1)$ at $n = \overline{0, n_0}$ and $(n_0+1) \times (n_0+1)$ at $n > n_0$:

$$
N_n = \begin{pmatrix}
-n\mu_1-\lambda & 0 & \cdots & 0 & 0 \\
0 & -(n-1)\mu_1-\mu_2-\lambda & \cdots & 0 & 0 \\
\vdots & \vdots & \ddots & \vdots & \vdots \\
0 & 0 & \cdots & -\mu_1-(n-1)\mu_2-\lambda & 0 \\
0 & 0 & \cdots & 0 & -n\mu_2-\lambda
\end{pmatrix}, \quad n = \overline{1, n_0-1};
$$

$$
N_n = \begin{pmatrix}
-n\mu_1-\lambda & 0 & \cdots & 0 \\
0 & -(n-1)\mu_1-\mu_2-\lambda & \cdots & 0 \\
\vdots & \vdots & \ddots & \vdots \\
0 & 0 & \cdots & -(n-n_0)\mu_1-n_0\mu_2-\lambda
\end{pmatrix}, \quad n = \overline{n_0, n^*-1};
$$

$$
N_n = N = \begin{pmatrix}
-n^*\mu_1-\lambda & 0 & \cdots & 0 \\
0 & -(n^*-1)\mu_1-\mu_2-\lambda & \cdots & 0 \\
\vdots & \vdots & \ddots & \vdots \\
0 & 0 & \cdots & -(n^*-n_0)\mu_1-n_0\mu_2-\lambda
\end{pmatrix}, \quad n \geq n^*.
$$

When the summation is possible, we suppose

$$
N_n^{(1)} = N_n + \Lambda_n^{(2)}.
$$

The size of the matrix Ω is equal to $n_0 \times (n_0 + 1)$:

$$\Omega = \begin{pmatrix} 0 & 1 & 0 & \cdots & 0 & 0 \\ 0 & 0 & 1 & \cdots & 0 & 0 \\ \vdots & \vdots & \vdots & \ddots & \vdots & \vdots \\ 0 & 0 & 0 & \cdots & 1 & 0 \\ 0 & 0 & 0 & \cdots & 0 & 1 \end{pmatrix}.$$

In other words, the matrix Ω converts the vector $\boldsymbol{p} = (p_1, \ldots, p_{n_0})$ into the vector $\boldsymbol{p}' = (0, p_1, \ldots, p_{n_0})$.

Let us assume that at the initial moment the customers arrival/service process $\nu(t)$ was in the state n, $n = \overline{n_0, n^*}$, the low-priority queue was empty, and the phase number was equal to i. Let us introduce the matrices $F_k(n)$, $k \geq 0$. The element $(F_k(n))_{ij}$ of the matrix $F_k(n)$ represents the probability of the event that immediately after the moment when for the first time the process $\nu(t)$ is in the state $n - 1$ (note that in the case $n = n_0$ this instant can be also the time when a low-priority customer arrives for the first time from the low-priority queue to a server but this low-priority customer is not yet considered as arrived to the server), the phase number is j and there are exactly k customers in the low-priority queue. The following relations allow to calculate matrices $F_k(n)$ recursively on n beginning from $n = n^*$ and on k from $k = 0$:

$$F_0(n^*) = -N^{-1}[M + \Lambda^{(1)} F_0^2(n^*)]; \tag{1}$$

$$F_k(n^*) = -N^{-1}\left[\Lambda^{(1)} \left(F_0(n^*)F_k(n^*) + \sum_{i=1}^{k-1} F_i(n^*)F_{k-i}(n^*) + \right. \right.$$

$$\left. \left. + F_k(n^*)F_0(n^*) \right) + \Lambda^{(2)} F_{k-1}(n^*) \right], \quad k \geq 1; \tag{2}$$

$$F_0(n) = -N_n^{-1}[M_n + \Lambda^{(1)} F_0(n+1)F_0(n)], \quad n = \overline{n_0, n^* - 1};$$

$$F_k(n) = -N_n^{-1}\left[\Lambda^{(1)} \left(F_0(n+1)F_k(n) + \sum_{i=1}^{k} F_i(n+1)F_{k-i}(n) \right) + \right.$$

$$\left. + \Lambda^{(2)} F_{k-1}(n) \right], \quad k \geq 1, \quad n = \overline{n_0, n^* - 1}.$$

Note that it is convenient to solve the equations (1) and (2) by an iterative method, taking zero matrices as initial ones.

Let us suppose $F_k = F_k(n_0)$, $k \geq 0$.

Assuming again that at the initial moment the customers arrival/service process $\nu(t)$ was in the state n, $n = \overline{n_0, n^*}$, the low-priority queue was empty, and the phase number was equal to i, introduce matrices $G(n)$. The element $G_{ij}(n)$ represents the probability of the event that immediately after the moment when for the first time the process $\nu(t)$ is in the state $n-1$ (note that, as earlier, in the case $n = n_0$ this moment can be also the time when a low-priority customer for the first time arrives from the low-priority queue to a server but this low-priority customer is not considered as arrived to the server), the phase number is j. Draw the relations allowing to calculate matrices $G(n)$ recursively on n beginning from $n = n^*$:

$$G(n^*) = (-N^{(1)}_{n^*})^{-1}[M + \Lambda^{(1)}G^2(n^*)]; \qquad (3)$$

$$G(n) = (-N^{(1)}_n)^{-1}[M_n + \Lambda^{(1)}G(n+1)G(n)], \quad n = \overline{n_0, n^* - 1}.$$

It is convenient to solve the equation (3), as well as the equation (1), using an iterative method.

Further some characteristics connected with average times of the system stay in certain states will be necessary, too.

Returning to the assumption that at the initial moment the process $\nu(t)$ was in the state n, $n = \overline{n_0, n^*}$, and the phase number was equal to i, introduce the matrices $S_k(n)$, $k \geq n$ whose element $(S_k(n))_{ij}$ is the average time of the system stay in the states, when the process $\nu(t)$ was equal to k and the phase number was equal to j, before the moment when for the first time the process $\nu(t)$ was in the state $n - 1$ (we remind that in the case $n = n_0$ it may be also the moment when a low-priority customer for the first time arrives from low-priority queue to a server). Matrices $S_k(n)$ satisfy the relations:

$$S_{n^*}(n^*) = (-N^{(1)}_{n^*})^{-1}[E + \Lambda^{(1)}G(n^*)S_{n^*}(n^*)]; \qquad (4)$$

$$S_k(n^*) = (-N^{(1)}_{n^*})^{-1}\Lambda^{(1)}[S_{k-1}(n^*) + G(n^*)S_k(n^*)], \quad k > n^*; \qquad (5)$$

$$S_n(n) = (-N^{(1)}_n)^{-1}[E + \Lambda^{(1)}G(n+1)S_n(n)], \quad n = \overline{n_0, n^* - 1}; \qquad (6)$$

$$S_k(n) = (-N^{(1)}_n)^{-1}\Lambda^{(1)}[S_k(n+1) + G(n+1)S_k(n)], \quad n = \overline{n_0, n^* - 1}, \; k > n. \qquad (7)$$

Relations (4)–(7) give the possibility to use a recursive procedure on n and k for calculating matrices $S_k(n)$.

Let us introduce the notation $S_k = S_k(n_0)$, $k \geq n_0$.

For the last time we now use the assumption that in the initial moment the process $\nu(t)$ was equal to n, $n = \overline{n_0, n^*}$, and the phase number was equal to i. Introduce the matrix $T_k(n)$, $k \geq 0$. The element $(T_k(n))_{ij}$ is the average time of the system stay in the states when there were exactly k customers in the low-priority queue and the phase number was equal to j. Let $t(n)$ be a column vector whose coordinates $t_i(n)$ are the average times of the system stay in the states, when there were exactly k customers in the low-priority queue (without account of a phase) before the moment when for the first time the process $\nu(t)$ was in the state $n - 1$ (with mentioned above remark about the case $n = n_0$). The matrices $T_k(n)$ and vectors $t(n)$ are determined by the recursive formulae:

$$T_0(n^*) = -N^{-1}[E + \Lambda^{(1)}T_0(n^*) + \Lambda^{(1)}F_0(n^*)T_0(n^*)];$$

$$T_k(n^*) = -N^{-1}\left[\Lambda^{(1)}\left(T_k(n^*) + F_0(n^*)T_k(n^*) + \right.\right.$$

$$+ \sum_{i=1}^{k} F_i(n^*) T_{k-i}(n^*) \Bigg) + \Lambda^{(2)} T_{k-1}(n^*) \Bigg], \quad k \geq 1;$$

$$T_0(n) = -N_n^{-1} \big[E + \Lambda^{(1)} T_0(n+1) + \Lambda^{(1)} F_0(n+1) T_0(n) \big], \quad n = \overline{n_0, n^* - 1};$$

$$T_k(n) = -N_n^{-1} \Bigg[\Lambda^{(1)} \Bigg(T_k(n+1) + F_0(n+1) T_k(n) + \sum_{i=1}^{k} F_i(n+1) T_{k-i}(n) \Bigg) +$$

$$+ \Lambda^{(2)} T_{k-1}(n) \Bigg], \quad k \geq 1, \quad n = \overline{n_0, n^* - 1};$$

$$\boldsymbol{t}(n^*) = (-N_{n^*}^{(1)})^{-1} \big[\mathbf{1} + \Lambda^{(1)} \boldsymbol{t}(n^*) + \Lambda^{(1)} G(n^*) \boldsymbol{t}(n^*) \big];$$

$$\boldsymbol{t}(n) = (-N_n^{(1)})^{-1} \big[\mathbf{1} + \Lambda^{(1)} \boldsymbol{t}(n+1) + \Lambda^{(1)} G(n+1) \boldsymbol{t}(n) \big], \quad n = \overline{n_0, n^* - 1}.$$

Here $\mathbf{1}$ is the column vector $(1, \ldots, 1)^T$, whose size is determined by the size of the matrix multiplied by the vector from the left.

Introduce the notations $T_k = T_k(n_0), \quad k \geq 0$, and $\boldsymbol{t} = \boldsymbol{t}(n_0)$.

4   The Embedded Markov Chain

The embedded Markov chain for the given system can be constructed by various methods. We determine it in the following way.

Consider the following moments:

the moments of any servers release or customers arrivals to the system in the case when there were less then n_0 busy servers before these moments;

the moments of any servers release in the case when there were exactly n_0 busy servers before these moments.

We denote the sequence of such moments as $\{\tau_l, \ l \geq 1\}$.

Remark that immediately after the moment of the second type there are exactly $n_0 - 1$ customers in the systems (all of them are serviced at servers) or a low-priority customer arrives to a server from the queue.

The set of states of the embedded Markov chain is given by the pair (i, m), $m \geq 0$. Here i is the phase (of arrival/service process) in the corresponding layer. The second component m is defined in a more sophisticated way. Namely, if $m = \overline{0, n_0 - 1}$, then, as usual, m is the number of customers in the system (i.e. the layer number, or the number of busy servers). However, if $m \geq n_0$ then the number of busy servers is equal to n_0, and $m - n_0$ is the number of low priority customers in the queue. The Markov chain itself is composed of a phase and the number of busy servers (layer number), or the number of busy servers (layer number) plus the number of low-priority customers in queue immediately after the moments τ_l.

Denote with $P = (P_{m_1 m_2})$, $m_1, m_2 \geq 0$, the matrix of the transition probabilities of the embedded Markov chain. Remark that elements $P_{m_1 m_2}$ are themselves matrices with sizes given by the numbers of phases of corresponding layers.

Let us introduce $F_k^* = F_k \Omega$.

Matrices $P_{m_1 m_2}$ are determined by the following formulae:

$$P_{m,m-1} = -N_m^{-1} M_m, \quad m = \overline{1, n_0 - 1};$$

$$P_{m,m+1} = -N_m^{-1}(\Lambda_m^{(1)} + \Lambda_m^{(2)}), \quad m = \overline{0, n_0 - 1};$$

$$P_{m_1 m_2} = F_{m_2 - m_1 + 1}\Omega = F_{m_2 - m_1 + 1}^*, \quad m_1 \geq n_0, \ m_2 \geq m_1 - 1, \ m_2 \neq n_0 - 1;$$

$$P_{n_0, n_0 - 1} = F_0.$$

Remaining matrices $P_{m_1 m_2}$ are zero ones.

Thus, the matrix P is the following:

$$P = \begin{pmatrix}
0 & P_{01} & 0 & 0 & \cdots & 0 & 0 & 0 & 0 & \cdots \\
P_{10} & 0 & P_{12} & 0 & \cdots & 0 & 0 & 0 & 0 & \cdots \\
0 & P_{21} & 0 & P_{23} & \cdots & 0 & 0 & 0 & 0 & \cdots \\
0 & 0 & P_{32} & 0 & \cdots & 0 & 0 & 0 & 0 & \cdots \\
0 & 0 & 0 & P_{43} & \cdots & 0 & 0 & 0 & 0 & \cdots \\
\vdots & \vdots & \vdots & \vdots & \ddots & \vdots & \vdots & \vdots & \vdots & \cdots \\
0 & 0 & 0 & 0 & \cdots & P_{n_0-1,n_0-2} & 0 & P_{n_0-1,n_0} & 0 & \cdots \\
0 & 0 & 0 & 0 & \cdots & 0 & F_0 & F_1^* & F_2^* & \cdots \\
0 & 0 & 0 & 0 & \cdots & 0 & 0 & F_0^* & F_1^* & \cdots \\
0 & 0 & 0 & 0 & \cdots & 0 & 0 & 0 & F_0^* & \cdots \\
\vdots & \vdots & \vdots & \vdots & \vdots & \vdots & \vdots & \vdots & \vdots & \ddots
\end{pmatrix}.$$

Denote by $\boldsymbol{p}^*$ a row vector of the stationary probabilities of the embedded Markov chain. It is natural that coordinates $\boldsymbol{p}_m^*$, $m \geq 0$, of the vector $\boldsymbol{p}^*$ are themselves row vectors with coordinates $(\boldsymbol{p}_m^*)_i$ where the index i means a phase.

The vector $\boldsymbol{p}^*$ satisfies the simultaneous equilibrium equations (SEE)

$$\boldsymbol{p}^* = \boldsymbol{p}^* P \tag{8}$$

with the normalization condition

$$\sum_{m=0}^{\infty} \boldsymbol{p}_m^* \mathbf{1} = 1. \tag{9}$$

In order to solve the SEE (8) it is convenient to apply an algorithm based on the consecutive simplification of the Markov chain by means of states elimination method (see [13], p. 22). Let us outline a short description of this algorithm.

Let the embedded Markov chain be in the state $(i, n_0 + 1)$ at the initial moment. Designate with R a matrix whose element R_{ij} is the probability of the event that at the moment when this chain is for the first time in the layer n_0, the phase number will be equal to j. Then

$$R = \sum_{k=0}^{\infty} F_k^* R^k. \tag{10}$$

The equation (10) could be easily solved by an iterative method.
Introduce

$$\tilde{R} = \sum_{k=1}^{\infty} F_k^* R^{k-1}.$$

Consider the (stochastic) matrix

$$\tilde{P} = \begin{pmatrix} 0 & P_{01} & 0 & 0 & \dots & 0 & 0 & 0 \\ P_{10} & 0 & P_{12} & 0 & \dots & 0 & 0 & 0 \\ 0 & P_{21} & 0 & P_{23} & \dots & 0 & 0 & 0 \\ 0 & 0 & P_{32} & 0 & \dots & 0 & 0 & 0 \\ 0 & 0 & 0 & P_{43} & \dots & 0 & 0 & 0 \\ \vdots & \vdots & \vdots & \vdots & \ddots & \vdots & \vdots & \vdots \\ 0 & 0 & 0 & 0 & \dots & P_{n_0-1,n_0-2} & 0 & P_{n_0-1,n_0} \\ 0 & 0 & 0 & 0 & \dots & 0 & F_0 & \tilde{R} \end{pmatrix},$$

which is derived from the matrix P by means of the states elimination beginning
from the $(n_0 + 1)$-th one.
Then SEE

$$p^* = p^* \tilde{P} \tag{11}$$

has a solution p_m^*, $m = \overline{0, n_0}$, coinciding (up to a constant) with the solution
of the initial SEE (8). It is convenient to use states elimination algorithm for
solving SEE (11), too.
Remaining coordinates p_m^*, $m > n_0$, could be easily calculated by the formula

$$p_{n_0+m}^* = \sum_{k=0}^{m-1} p_{n_0+k}^* F_{m+1-k}^* (E - \tilde{R})^{-1}, \quad m \geq 1.$$

It is sufficient to use the normalization condition (9) to determine the
unknown constant.

5   Stationary Characteristics of the System

In this section we present formulae for the main marginal stationary states probabilities of the considered queueing system functioning.
Assume that at the initial time moment the embedded Markov chain has
been in the state (i, n), $n \geq 0$. Designate with m_n the column vector whose
coordinates $(m_n)_i$ are the averages times till a next moment of the embedded
Markov chain state change. Then

$$m_n = -N_n^{-1} \mathbf{1}, \quad n = \overline{0, n_0 - 1};$$

$$m_n = T, \quad n \geq n_0.$$

The stationary average time $\overline{m}$ between adjacent moments of the embedded Markov chain state changes is equal to

$$\overline{m} = \sum_{n=0}^{\infty} \boldsymbol{p}_n^* \boldsymbol{m}_n.$$

Introduce the following notations:

$\boldsymbol{p}_n$, $n \geq 0$, is a row vector whose coordinates $(\boldsymbol{p}_n)_i$ are the stationary probabilities of the event that the process $\nu(t)$ is in the state n and the phase (number of low-priority customers at servers) is equal to i;

$\boldsymbol{\pi}_n$, $n \geq 0$, is a row vector whose coordinates $(\boldsymbol{\pi}_n)_i$ are the stationary probabilities of the event that there are n customers in the low-priority queue and the phase is equal to i.

Then

$$\boldsymbol{p}_n = -\frac{1}{\overline{m}} \boldsymbol{p}_n^* N_n^{-1}, \quad n = \overline{0, n_0 - 1};$$

$$\boldsymbol{p}_n = \frac{1}{\overline{m}} \sum_{k=n_0}^{\infty} \boldsymbol{p}_k^* S_n, \quad n \geq n_0;$$

$$\boldsymbol{\pi}_0 = \frac{1}{\overline{m}} \left(-\sum_{k=0}^{n_0-1} \boldsymbol{p}_k^* N_k^{-1} + \boldsymbol{p}_{n_0}^* T_0 \right);$$

$$\boldsymbol{\pi}_n = \frac{1}{\overline{m}} \sum_{k=0}^{n} \boldsymbol{p}_{n_0+k}^* T_{n-k}, \quad n \geq 1.$$

As we know distributions $\boldsymbol{p}_n$, $n \geq 0$, and $\boldsymbol{\pi}_n$, $n \geq 0$, it is possible to easily calculate other marginal stationary distributions. For example, stationary distributions p_n, $n \geq 0$, and π_n, $n \geq 0$, of the high-priority and low-priority customers numbers in the system (without account of phases) are determined by the following formulae:

$$p_n = \sum_{m=n}^{n_0+n} (\boldsymbol{p}_m)_{m-n}, \quad n \geq 0;$$

$$\pi_n = \sum_{m=0}^{n} (\boldsymbol{p}_{n-m})_m, \quad n = \overline{0, n_0 - 1}; \qquad \pi_n = \sum_{m=0}^{n_0} (\boldsymbol{p}_{n-m})_m, \quad n \geq n_0.$$

6   Inference

On the base of the above analytical relations, one can easily develop a software for calculating marginal stationary distributions of high-priority and low-priority customers quantities in the system functioning, including the case of a great number of servers.

The obtained results could be spread for some generalizations of the considered system, in particular, for determining joint stationary distribution of high-priority and low-priority customers quantities in the system, stationary distributions of high-priority and low-priority customers quantities in the system, stationary distributions of high-priority and low-priority customers sojourn times in the system and even for three or more priorities systems investigation. Moreover, it is possible on the base of the approach described in [12] to analyze systems with Markov input flow and phase type distributions of high-priority and low-priority customers. But in the case the task requires a high computational effort.

Acknowledgments. The work has been accomplished with financial support from the Russian Foundation for Fundamental Research (project No. 11-07-00112).

References

1. Grandjean, C.H.: Traffic Calculations in Suturation Routing with Priorities. Electr. Commun. 49(1), 72–79 (1974)
2. Ludwig, H., Roy, R.: Saturation routing network limits. Proceedings of the IEEE 65(9), 1353–1362 (1977)
3. Weber, J.H.: Some Traffic Characteristics of Communications Networks with Automatic Alternate Routing. Bell System Techn. J., 1201–1247 (March 1962)
4. Weber, J.H.: Simulation Study of Routing and Control in Communications Networks. Bell System Techn. J., 2639–2676 (November 1964)
5. Grandjean, C.H.: Call Routing Strategies in Telecommunications Networks. Electr. Commun. 42(3), 380–391 (1967)
6. Jaiswal, N.K.: Priority Queues. Academic Press, N.-Y (1968)
7. Esoqbue, A.O., Singh, A.J.: A Stochastic Model for an Optimal Priority Bed Distribution in a Hospital. Oper. Res. 24, 884–889 (1976)
8. Otterman, J.: Grande of Service Direct Traffic mixed with Store-and-Forward Traffic. Bell System Techn. J., 1415–1437 (April 1962)
9. Liu, F.K.: A Combined Delay and Loss System with Priority. In: ICC, vol. 39(7), pp. 39-7–39-13 (1973)
10. Pechinkin, A.V., Fedorov, V.M.: Evaluation method for multi-channel system with priority service and channels reservation. Sistemnoe modelirovanie, vol. (15). Computing Center of the Siberian Branch of the Academy of Sciences of the USSR, Novosibirsk (1990)
11. Burygin, S.V., Glazunov, A.S., Pechinkin, A.V.: System of priority service with channels reservation and Markov input flow. Series Applied Mathematics and Infofrmatics, vol. 1, pp. 80–89. Bulletin of Russian Peoples Friendship University (2001) (in Russian)
12. Pechinkin, A.V.: Two-priority system with reservation of channels and Markov input flow. Informatics and Applications 5(1), 2–11 (2011) (in Russian)
13. Bocharov, P.P., D'Apice, C., Pechinkin, A.V., Salerno, S.: Queueing Theory. In: VSP, Utrecht–Boston (2004)

Buffer Sizing in TxSDMA Systems

Boris Bellalta[1], Vanesa Daza[1], Jaume Barcelo[2], and Miquel Oliver[1]

[1] Department of Information and Communication Technologies,
Universitat Pompeu Fabra, Barcelona
{boris.bellalta,vanesa.daza,miquel.oliver}@upf.edu
[2] Department of Telematics Engineering,
Universidad Carlos III, Madrid
jaume.barcelo@uc3m.edu

Abstract. Multi-packet transmission from a single node to multiple destinations by exploiting the spatial dimension of the channel is a promising technique to increase the capacity of wireless networks. From the link layer point of view, this feature is known as Transmit Spatial Division Multiple Access (TxSDMA) and is supported by the use of multiple smart antennas at the transmitter. In this paper we analyze the impact of the buffer size on the performance of TxSDMA systems under QoS constraints. Results provide further insights in the cross-relations between the number of antennas, number of active users and the buffer size. The analysis done is based on a novel TxSDMA queueing model that, despite its simplicity, provides very accurate results for the range of situations in which TxSDMA systems work.

Keywords: MIMO, Multi-user, SDMA, Queueing model.

1 Introduction

Space Division Multiple Access (SDMA) [1] is a channel access technique that exploits the spatial dimension of the channel to transmit multiple data packets simultaneously from a single transmitter (equipped with multiple antennas) to multiple receivers (equiped at least with a single antenna), known as TxSDMA, or from multiple transmitters (equipped at least with a single antenna) to a single receiver (equipped with multiple antennas), known as RxSDMA. The specific case in which a transmitter equipped with multiple antennas sends multiple packets to a single receiver also equipped with multiple antennas is called Spatial Division Multiplexing (SDM) as there are no transmissions from/to different users. Both SDMA and SDM can rely on MIMO (Multiple-Input Multiple-Output) signal processing techniques to create the required spatial streams.

Nowadays, the benefits of spatial multiplexing are taken into consideration in the specifications of, among others, 3GPP LTE [2], IEEE 802.16 [2], IEEE 802.11 [3] and IEEE 802.3.15-based 60 GHz Ultra Wide Band (UWB) [4] technologies, as it allows to significantly increase the wireless transmission resources, and therefore, the capacity that such systems can achieve.

C. Sacchi et al. (Eds.): MACOM 2011, LNCS 6886, pp. 241–253, 2011.

Research on TxSDMA has mainly focused on the design of efficient joint beamforming and user selection strategies as a trade-off between computational complexity and their ability to near-attain the upper-bound system sum-rate [5]. An usual assumption in such works is to consider that the transmitter has multiple saturated queues, one for each active user, thus avoiding the impact that the queueing dynamics have on the system performance. Moreover, important performance metrics such as the delay or packet losses due to buffer overflows are not addressed.

Nevertheless, some works already include the queueing state together with physical layer and channel information in the so-called cross-layer scheduling schemes [6]. These works include the presence of non-saturated queues with random arrivals in the scheduling formulation, showing that it has a big impact on the scheduling strategy as well as in the performance achieved [7,8,9,10]. However, there is still a lack of detailed frame/packet-level queuing models to capture in detail the interactions between the physical (PHY) and link layers parameters at a packet level, as well as addressing the link layer requirements of such systems, such as the frame overheads or the resources required to manage the CSI (Channel State Information) feed-back. To the best of our knowledge, only in [11] a detailed queueing system for a V-BLAST multi-user downlink scenario is developed.

This paper is intended to provide further insights on the impact of queueing on the performance of TxSDMA systems, as well as on the relation of the queueing process with the number of antennas at the Access Point (AP) and the number of active users in the cell. In detail, the specific contributions of this paper are:

1. The formulation and discussion of the impact that queueing has on the capacity of TxSDMA systems.
2. Further developments to the queueing model presented in [12]. New presented results show the range of situations in which the model is accurate and which cover the usual working conditions of TxSDMA systems.
3. Further insights on the relationship between the queue size, the number of active Mobile Nodes (MNs) and the number of antennas, as well as how they impact on the system performance.
4. Guidelines to set the buffer size in TxSDMA systems given the number of antennas and active MNs.

The paper is structured as follows. The scenario, together with the assumptions considered, is introduced in Section 2. Section 3 discusses the impact that the queueing process has on the system capacity and presents the TxSDMA queuing model. Section 4 presents the results, including the validation of the TxSDMA queueing model. Finally, the main conclusions of this work are summarized and the future research lines are stated.

2   System Model and Assumptions

A single access point (AP) equipped with M antennas, M radio-frequency (RF) chains and a finite-buffer of size K packets is considered. Packets of length L_d

bits (constant) and destined to the N single-antenna MNs nodes arrive to the AP following a Poisson process with aggregate rate λ, equally distributed among all active destinations. MNs report the estimated CSI (Channel State Information) to the AP, that uses it to create the required beams. This scenario is depicted in Figure 1 and a simplified model of the AP is shown in Figure 2.

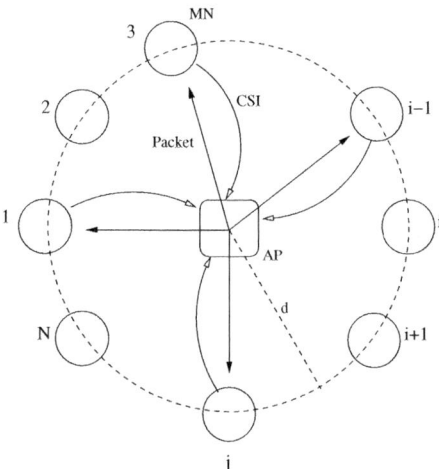

Fig. 1. Specific scenario with $M = 4$ antennas serving frames to N MNs

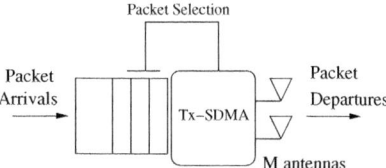

Fig. 2. Schematic model of an AP equipped with M antennas

A FIFO-based scheduling (packet selection) algorithm is considered. It selects $s \in [1, min(q, M)]$ packets from those $q \in [1, K]$ packets stored in the queue when a new transmission is scheduled, which happens just after the previous one has finished or, if the queue has become empty, immediately after the arrival of a new packet. Specifically, the AP always schedules the first packet waiting for transmission and then, it selects sequentially up to $min(q, M) - 1$ packets, directed to not yet selected destinations. Through the paper, the frame that results from assembling s packets at each transmission is called a space-batch. In Figure 3 the general structure of a space-batch is shown. It consist of four parts:

- *Preamble and space-batch information (of length L_{sb} bits)*: Initial preamble used to synchronise all receivers and headers required to inform those MNs that have been selected to receive a packet in next space-batch.
- *Training Sequences (of length L_{tr} bits each sequence)*: Required to estimate the channel state between each transmitting antenna at the AP and the receiving antenna at the selected MNs.
- *CSI feed-back (of length L_{CSI} bits each slot)*: MNs report to the AP the estimated CSI. Note that in each space-batch there are M slots for CSI feed-back regardless the value of s.
- *Stream Header and Packet ($L_h + L_d$ bits)*: A header is added to each transmitted packet. The Stream Header includes information related only to its packet and its recipient.

A quasi-static fading channel that changes from space-batch to space-batch is considered. Operation at the high SNR (Signal-to-Noise Ratio) region is addressed and, regardless the size of each space-batch and the specific selected destinations, it is assumed that the probability of a space-batch suffering transmission errors is negligible. Additionally, all space-batches are transmitted at a single transmission rate equal to R bps.

The duration of a space-batch is constant (only depends on the number of antennas) and is equal to:

$$T(M) = \frac{L_{sb} + M \cdot L_{tr} + M \cdot L_{CSI} + L_h + L_d}{R} \tag{1}$$

Therefore, we define the efficiency of a space-batch transmission as

$$\eta(s, M) = \frac{s \cdot L_d}{L_{sb} + M \cdot L_{tr} + M \cdot L_{CSI} + L_h + L_d} \tag{2}$$

that depends on s and M. Note that the dependence with s relates the efficiency to the queue occupation.

In Figure 4, a specific example of the system operation is shown for $M = 2$ antennas and a queue of $K = 4$ packets. The $(i - 1)$-th space-batch comprises a single packet as the transmission is scheduled as soon as a new packet arrives

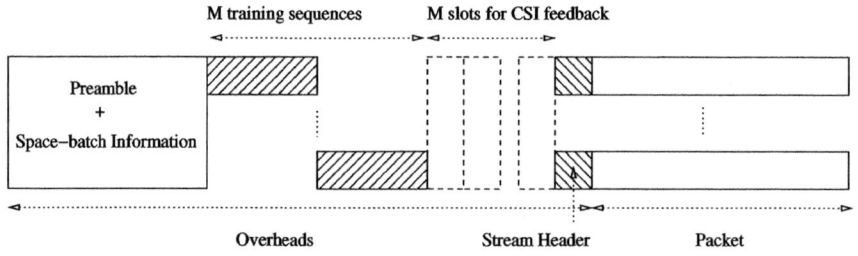

Fig. 3. Frame structure of an Space-batch for a TxSDMA system where the AP has M antennas

to the AP. During the $(i-1)$-th space-batch transmission, two packets directed to the 2-th and 4-th MNs are buffered and assembled together in the i-th space-batch after the end of the the $(i-1)$-th space-batch transmission. Similarly, during the i-th space-batch transmission two packets directed to the 4-th MN arrive to the queue, as well as one directed to the 5-th MN, which is blocked because there is no free space in the buffer[1]. Observe that, when the $(i+1)$-th space-batch is scheduled, there are only two packets in the transmission buffer and both are directed to the 4-th MN. In such situation, only one packet will be transmitted.

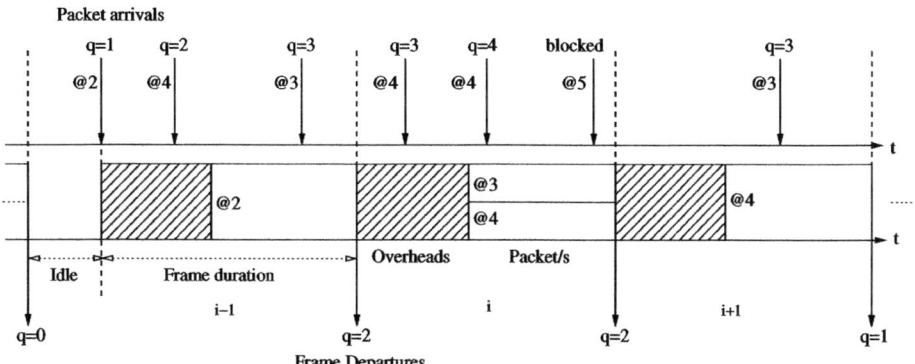

Fig. 4. Temporal evolution of the AP's queue with $M = 2$ antennas. The q values are the queue state (number of frames in the queue) just after a frame arrival or a space-batch departure. The @x refer to the packet destination.

3 Queueing in TxSDMA Systems

3.1 Throughput-Delay Tradeoff

In the considered scenario the maximum achievable throughput is:

$$S_{max} = \eta(\min(N, M), M)R \tag{3}$$

where $\eta(\min(N, M), M)$ is the system efficiency (Equation 2). Note that it is assumed that the transmitter has always at least one packet directed to $\min(N, M)$ different destinations and that the buffer is of infinite size, i.e., there are no packet losses caused by queue overflows.

Equation 3 can be extended to account for the presence of a finite transmission buffer fed with random arrivals (Poisson):

$$S_{buffer} = \rho \cdot \eta(E[s], M)R \tag{4}$$

---

[1] It could be argued that is better to drop one of the stored packets directed to the 4-th MN than to block the new arrived packet as it would increase the number of destinations present in the queue.

where $\rho \sim \lambda \cdot (1 - P_b) \cdot \frac{T(M)}{E[s]}$ is the fraction of time that the system is active, P_b is the probability to discard a packet at its arrival to the queue and $E[s] \leq min(N, M)$ is the average number of packets assembled together in a space-batch. Therefore, S_{buffer} clearly depends on both the buffer size and the number of active MNs.

Increasing the buffer size K, given that the arrival traffic load is high enough, can allow to S_{buffer} to become closer to S_{max} as the number of packets stored in the queue will increase, causing that both $\rho \rightarrow 1$ and $E[s] \rightarrow min(N, M)$. However, the downside is that the system delay is proportional to $(1 - \rho)^{-1}$, thus tending to infinite as K increases. Nevertheless, for a certain range of values, increasing K can result in a lower delay as the efficiency achieved by scheduling large space-batches will compensate the larger queue occupation.

3.2 Model

The TxSDMA queueing model used in this paper was presented in [12] where a Multi-rate TxSDMA system was considered. Here, the model has been simplified to account for a single rate, thus obtaining more compact and simpler expressions. Due to lack of space, only the final expressions are included. for further details on the model refer to [12].

The TxSDMA model is solved in three steps: i) first, for all s and q values, the probability to schedule s packets from q packets stored in the queue is computed; ii) the departure distribution, π^d, is computed by using the discrete-time embedded Markov chain method and iii) the PASTA (Poisson Arrivals See Time Averages) property of the Poisson arrivals is applied to find the probability distribution at arbitrary times, π^s, as a function of π^d.

Step 1: Let $A_{q,s,N}$ be the event s packets are scheduled from q frames stored in the queue given that there are N active MNs. Then, the probability of this event is

$$p(A_{q,s,N}) = \frac{\binom{N}{s}}{N^q} \cdot \sum_{(\mu_1,\ldots,\mu_s) \in \Psi_{q,s}} PR^q_{\mu_1,\ldots,\mu_s} \tag{5}$$

where $PR^q_{\mu_1,\ldots,\mu_s}$ denotes the permutation with repetition of q elements in sets of $\mu_1,\ldots,\mu_s$ elements and $\Psi_{q,s} = \{(\mu_1,\ldots,\mu_s) \in \mathbb{Z}^s_+ \mid \mu_1 + \ldots + \mu_s = q\}$.

Step 2: The probability distribution at departure epochs, π^d, is computed solving the linear system $\pi^d = \pi^d P$, together with the normalization condition $\pi^d 1^T = 1$. P is the probability transition matrix, where each $i, j \in [0, K]$ position is represented by the probability $\bar{p}_{i,j}$. Each $\bar{p}_{i,j}$ is computed averaging all the different space-batch sizes that make that transition possible, that is

$$\bar{p}_{i,j} = \sum_{s=1}^{max(1,min(i,M))} p^\bullet(A_{i,s,N}) p_{i,j}(s) \tag{6}$$

where

$$p^\bullet(A_{i,s,N}) = \begin{cases} p(A_{1,s,N}), & i = 0 \\ p(A_{i,s,N}), & i \geq 1 \end{cases} \tag{7}$$

takes into accounts the specific case in which the system is empty and $p_{i,j}(s)$ is the transition probability from any state i to any state j, computed from:

$$p_{i,j}(s) = \begin{cases} p_{1,j}(s) & i = 0, \ j \in [0, K] \\ \frac{(\lambda T(M))^v}{v!} e^{-\lambda T(M)}, & i \geq 1, \ j \in [i - s, K - s - 1] \\ 1 - \sum_{j=i-s}^{K-s-1} p_{i,j}(s) & i \geq 1, \ j = K - s \end{cases} \quad (8)$$

where $v = (j - i) + \varsigma$ is the number of arrivals during the service time of the on-going space-batch.

Finally, from the empty queue state, $i = 0$, to any state j, the transition probability $p_{0,j}(s)$ is given simply by the same probability of being in state $q = 1$, $p_{1,j}(s)$, as the system remains inactive while the system is empty, then $p_{0,j}(s) = p_{1,j}(s)$.

Step 3: The probability distribution at arbitrary times is computed as the percentage of time that a node spends in the target state between two consecutive space-batches departures, this is:

$$\pi_u^s = \begin{cases} \frac{\frac{1}{\lambda}}{E[T_{dep}]} \pi_0^d & u = 0 \\ \frac{\frac{1}{\lambda}}{E[T_{dep}]} \sum_{i=0}^u \pi_i^d \left(\sum_{s=1}^{\max(1,min(i,M))} p^\bullet(A_{i,s,N}) \sum_{j=u+1-s}^{K-s} p_{i,j}(s) \right) & u \in [1, K - 1] \\ 1 - \sum_{k=0}^{K-1} \pi_k^s & u = K \end{cases} \quad (9)$$

where $E[T_{dep}] = \frac{1}{\lambda} \pi_0^d + T(M)$.

3.3   Performance Metrics

Once the $\boldsymbol{\pi}^d$ and $\boldsymbol{\pi}^s$ distributions are obtained, several performance metrics can be derived from them:

- Blocking Probability: $P_b = \pi_K^s$
- Queue utilization: $\rho = 1 - \pi_0^s$
- System throughput: $S = \lambda(1 - P_b)L_d$
- System Delay (Applying the Little's Law): $E[D] = \frac{E[Q]}{\lambda(1-P_b)}$, where $E[Q] = \sum_{i=1}^K i\pi_i^s$.
- Average number of packets per space-batch:

$$E[s] = \sum_{i=0}^K \sum_{s=1}^{\max(1,min(i,M))} p^\bullet(A_{i,s,N})\pi_i^d$$

4   Results

The scenario presented in Section 2 is considered here. The value of the parameters used are shown in Table 1. The traffic aggregate arrival rate has been chosen to be equal to the 90 % of the maximum system throughput, this is $\lambda = 0.9 \cdot \eta(min(N, M), M) \cdot R/L_d$ packets/second.

A simulator of the described scenario has been built from scratch using the C++ language and based on the COST (Component Oriented Simulation Toolkit) libraries [13]. The results provided by the TxSDMA queueing model are compared with the ones obtained by simulation, showing the accuracy of the presented model.

The goal of this section is twofold. First, the impact of the number of antennas, the number of active MNs and the buffer size on the performance of a TxSDMA system is evaluated. Second, the buffer size of a TxSDMA system is fixed given a required maximum blocking probability.

Table 1. Parameters

Parameter	Value
L_{sb}	320 bits
L_{tr}	64 bits
L_{CSI}	64 bits
L_h	128 bits
L_d	8000 bits
R	120 Mbits/second

4.1   Cross-Relations between M, N and K

In Figures 5(a) and 5(b) the blocking probability and delay are respectively shown. As it can be observed, a large buffer results in a lower blocking probability and a higher average delay. When the number of antennas increases, a higher number of users results in large space-batches (Figure 5(c)), thus providing a lower blocking probability and a lower delay. Note that for a small buffer size, the observed blocking probability is not only related to the buffer size itself as also, the probability to assemble large space-batches is reduced.

As it can be observed, the performance achieved by a TxSDMA system equipped with M antennas is closely related to the values of K and N. In general, from previous results it can be deduced that the size of the buffer can be more relevant than the number of MNs in the performance that a TxSDMA system can achieve.

The presented TxSDMA queueing model provides very accurate results for a wide range of values of M, N and K. As expected, the conditions in which it is accurate are those where the assumption used to build the model holds. Otherwise, the model is optimistic as it predicts larger space-batches than the ones scheduled in the simulated TxSDMA system.

4.2   Buffer Size vs. Number of Antennas

The TxSDMA queueing model is now used to set the buffer size of an AP equipped with M antennas given that the blocking probability has to be lower than 10^{-2}. For each value of M, the buffer size is chosen as the lower K value that satisfies the constraint on the maximum packet losses. To consider the impact

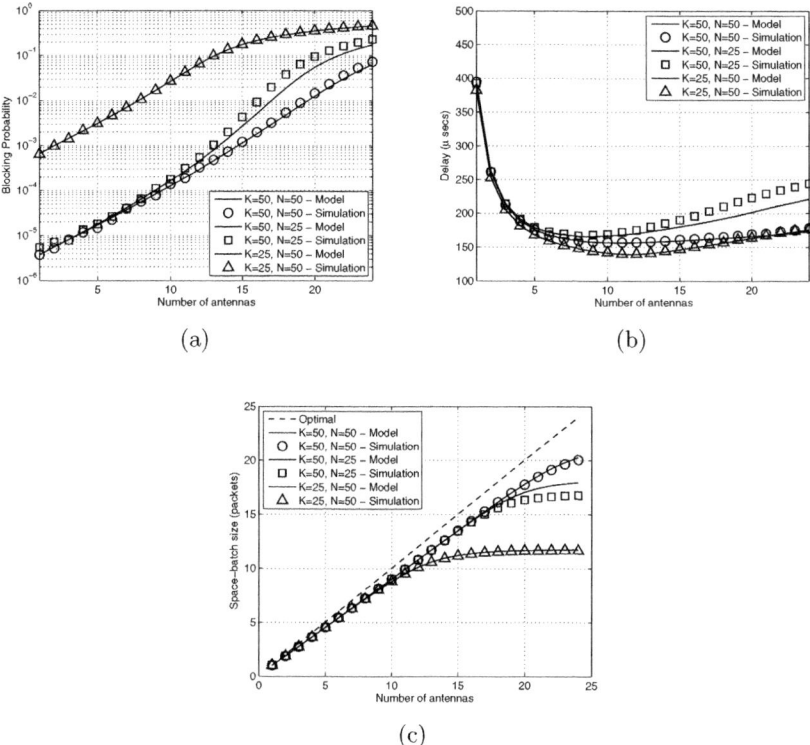

(a)   (b)

(c)

Fig. 5. Blocking probability, Delay and space-batch size

of different number of active MNs, different values of N are considered: $N = 8$, $N = 16$, $N = 25$ and $N = 50$.

In Figure 6 the buffer size that satisfies a blocking probability lower than 10^{-2} is plotted. It can be observed that the required buffer size increases with the number of antennas. Note that there is a linear increase until the number of antennas is similar to the number of active MNs, point at which the required buffer starts to increase faster.

Using the computed values of K from Figure 6, the average system delay is shown in Figure 7(a). Until a certain value, increasing the number of antennas reduce the system delay despite the larger buffer sizes. This is justified by the higher packet departure rate that compensates the larger queue occupation (Figure 7(b)). This tendency changes when previous situation is no further satisfied. Moreover, note that the model starts to lose accuracy at the same point that the delay starts to increase (Figure 7(a)).

It is worth to note that given M antennas, the average space-batch size required to satisfy the blocking probability constraint is independent of the number of active MNs (Figure 7(c)). This result confirms the importance of the buffer size to allow the transmission of large enough space-batches.

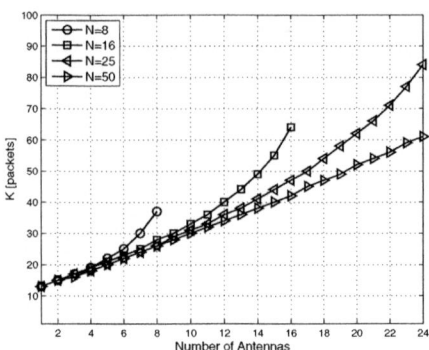

Fig. 6. Blocking Probability with Multiple Antennas

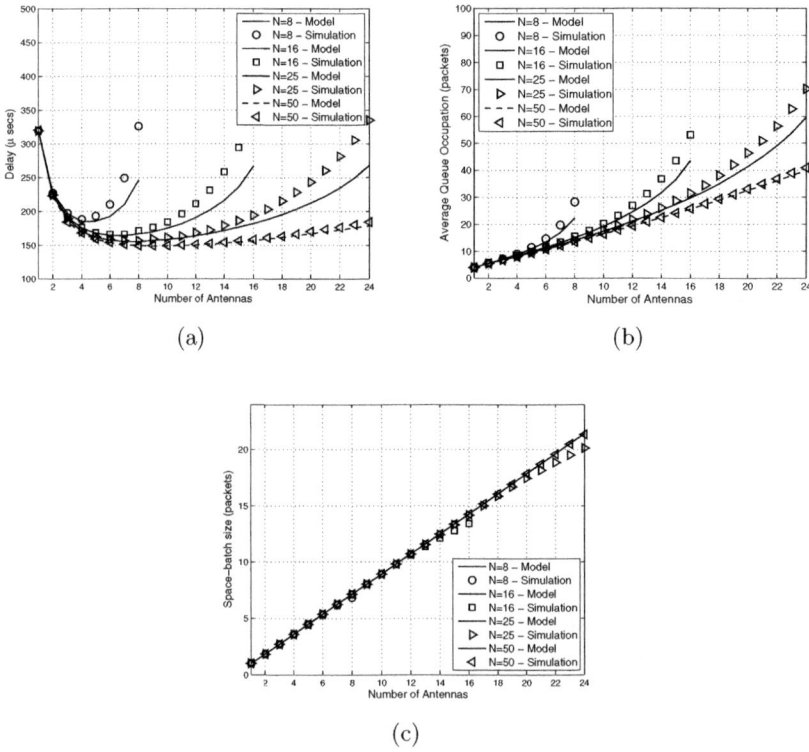

(a)   (b)

(c)

Fig. 7. Blocking Probability with Multiple Antennas

Finally, to conclude this section, observe that the TxSDMA queueing model is always optimistic, specially if the number of antennas is higher than a certain value. Previous to that number of antennas, the TxSDMA queueing model provides very accurate results for all performance metrics. Therefore, to determine the range of values in which the presented model is accurate is of crucial importance. In Table 2, the blocking probability obtained from both the TxS-DMA queueing model and the TxSDMA simulator are shown. Given that an error higher than $\epsilon = 0.001$ is not accepted, the model remains accurate until the number of antennas is equal to 4, 7, 10 and 18 for a number of active MNs equal to 8, 16, 25 and 50 respectively.

Based on this previous observation, a simple 'rule of thumb' can be defined as the TxSDMA queueing model is accurate always that the number of active MNs is approximately 3 times greater than the number of antennas, this is $N > 3 \cdot M$, regardless the buffer size. Note that this value seems very reasonable in typical scenarios for TxSDMA systems. For instance, two suitable scenarios where the model can be applied are: 1) a WLAN (Wireless Local Area Network) where the AP has $M = 4$ antennas and there are $N = 12$ MNs and 2) a cellular network where each BS is equipped with $M = 8$ antennas and there are at least $N = 24$ MNs.

Table 2. Blocking probabilities for different number of antennas and MNs

-	N=8		N=16		N=25		N=50	
M	Model	Sim	Model	Sim	Model	Sim	Model	Sim
1	0.00835	0.00844	0.00835	0.00846	0.00835	0.00838	0.00835	0.00832
2	0.00855	0.00852	0.00839	0.00849	0.00834	0.00834	0.00830	0.00840
3	0.00869	0.00873	0.00816	0.00823	0.00800	0.00803	0.00987	0.00983
4	0.00930	0.00977	0.00804	0.00814	0.00969	0.00972	0.00942	0.00931
5	0.00870	0.01023	0.00812	0.00818	0.00950	0.00957	0.00901	0.00902
6	0.00938	0.01493	0.00845	0.00881	0.00945	0.00955	0.00875	0.00876
7	0.00832	0.02394	0.00908	0.00969	0.00958	0.00975	0.00856	0.00853
8	0.00874	0.05183	0.00808	0.00912	0.00987	0.01022	0.00842	0.00837
9			0.00940	0.01161	0.00829	0.00877	0.00837	0.00845
10			0.00930	0.01319	0.00887	0.00961	0.00837	0.00839
11			0.00973	0.01674	0.00966	0.01089	0.00846	0.00863
12			0.00899	0.02001	0.00869	0.01027	0.00856	0.00878
13			0.00923	0.02766	0.00993	0.01250	0.00877	0.00908
14			0.00910	0.03788	0.00937	0.01269	0.00901	0.00936
15			0.00946	0.05267	0.00917	0.01409	0.00934	0.00980
16			0.00906	0.06777	0.00923	0.01611	0.00974	0.01040
17					0.00976	0.01933	0.00826	0.00899
18					0.00878	0.02104	0.00876	0.00975
19					0.00841	0.02491	0.00938	0.01059
20					0.00863	0.03110	0.00825	0.00961
21					0.00948	0.03976	0.00889	0.01070
22					0.00962	0.04892	0.00972	0.01211
23					0.00954	0.05816	0.00877	0.01136
24					0.00974	0.06882	0.00974	0.01310

5   Conclusions

The importance of properly setting the buffer size for TxSDMA systems has been pointed. Moreover, further insights on the relationship between the buffer size, number of antennas and number of active MNs in TxSDMA have been presented.

These cross-relations are captured by the presented TxSDMA queueing model. The model has been validated and the conditions in which it provides very accurate results have been discussed.

The results presented here will be used as a benchmark for future works to understand the impact on the system performance of more realistic channel models, pre-coding/beamforming techniques, the overheads required for channel estimation and CSI feed-back, as well as of different traffic patterns.

Acknowledgements. This work has been partially supported by the Spanish Government under projects TEC2008-0655 (Plan Nacional I+D), TEC2009-13000 (Plan Nacional I+D+i), CSD2008-00010 (Consolider-Ingenio Program) and by the Catalan Government (SGR2009#00617).

References

1. Tse, D., Viswanath, P.: Fundamentals of Wireless Communication. Cambridge University Press, Cambridge (2005)
2. Li, Q., Li, G., Lee, W., Lee, M.-i., Mazzarese, D., Clerckx, B., Li, Z.: MIMO techniques in WiMAX and LTE: a feature overview. IEEE Communications Magazine 48(5), 86–92 (2010)
3. Kuzminskiy, A.M., Karimi, H.R., Morgan, D.R., Papadias, C.B., Avidor, D., Ling, J.: Downlink SDMA for IEEE 802.11A/G: A Means for Improving Legacy Mobile Throughput Using a Multi-Antenna Access Point. In: IEEE PIMRC 2005 (September 2005)
4. Xia, P., Yong, S.-K., Oh, J., Ngo, C.: A practical SDMA protocol for 60 GHz millimeter wave communications. In: 42nd Asilomar Conference on Signals, Systems and Computers (October 2008)
5. Kountouris, M., de Francisco, R., Gesbert, D., Slock, D.T.M., Salzer, T.: Low Complexity Scheduling and Beamforming for Multiuser MIMO systems. In: Signal Processing Advances in Wireless Communications, SPAWC 2006 (2006)
6. Anton-Haro, C., Svedman, P., Bengtsson, M., Alexiou, A., Gameiro, A.: Cross-Layer Scheduling for Multi-User MIMO Systems. IEEE Communications Magazine, 39–45 (2006)
7. Swannack, C., Uysal-Biyikoglu, E., Wornell, G.W.: Low Complexity Multiuser Scheduling for Maximizing Throughput in the MIMO Broadcast Channel. In: Proc. Allerton Conf. Commun., Contr., and Computing (October 2004)
8. Wang, C., Murch, R.D.: Optimal Downlink Multi-user MIMO Cross-layer Scheduling Using HOL Packet Waiting Time. IEEE Transactions on Wireless Communications 5(10) (October 2006)
9. She, F., Luo, H., Chen, W., Wang, X.: Joint Queue Control and User Scheduling in MIMO Broadcast Channel under Zero-Forcing Multiplexing. In: IEEE International Conference on Communications, ICC (May 2008)

10. Torabzadeh, M., Ajib, W.: Packet Level Scheduling schemes for Multi-User MIMO Systems with beamforming. In: Proc. ACM Int. Wireless Communications and Mobile Computing Conf (ACM IWCMC 2010), Caen, France (July 2010)
11. Hassibi, B., Hossain, E.: Cross-Layer Analysis of Downlink V-BLAST MIMO Transmission Exploiting Multiuser Diversity. IEEE Transactions on Wireless Communications 8(9) (November 2009)
12. Bellalta, B., Daza, V., Oliver, M.: An Approximate Queueing Model for Multi-rate Multi-user MIMO systems. IEEE Communication Letters (2011) (in press)
13. Chen, G.: Component Oriented Simulation Toolkit (2004), http://www.cs.rpi.edu/~cheng3/

Author Index